A Tribute

If Paul Laurence Dunbar were alive today, perhaps he would appreciate most to know that students of all ages, rich and poor, would have access to the literary legacy he left to the American people.

During the first half of the twentieth century, Paul Laurence Dunbar was one of America's most celebrated poets. His works were recited in most homes, churches, and schools in African American communities throughout the United States.

African American teachers never failed to include in their teachings his immortal "In the Morning." The audience would be quiet and still when the stern mother came on stage and called, "'Lias! 'Lias! Bless de Lawd!" and from that moment on giggles and laughter were heard throughout the auditorium.

Mr. Dunbar is noted not so much by what he says as how he says it—in the spirit and language of the people of his day. He was educated but always humble enough to appreciate the people of lowly life.

Paul Laurence Dunbar could move from one literary mood to another and still retain his inherent eloquence. Hardly any chagrin can be found in his lines of "lowly language"; his words were never intended to demoralize, simply to give color and spice to his characters.

As we approach the twenty-first century, the name *Paul Laurence Dunbar* has become as obscure as his works. Integrated classrooms have taken their toll on many great writers of color. While many African American teachers don't devote as much time to black authors as in the past, many European American teachers are not familiar with many black authors. So persons who wish to study the lives and works of famous African American writers must often do so at their own leisure, and it is for this reason that this collection is being reprinted.

Winston-Derek Publishers, Inc.
1992

JAMES W. PEEBLES, PH.D.
Publisher

Paul Laurence Dunbar.

AT THE AGE OF TWENTY-FOUR.

The Life and Works of Paul Laurence Dunbar

CONTAINING
HIS COMPLETE POETICAL
WORKS, HIS BEST SHORT
STORIES, NUMEROUS
ANECDOTES AND A
COMPLETE BIO~
GRAPHY OF THE
FAMOUS POET.

By

Lida Keck Wiggins

And an Introdiuction by

WILLIAM DEAN HOWELLS

From "Lyrics of Lowly Life"

PROFUSELY ILLUSTRATED WITH
OVER HALF A HUNDRED
FULL PAGE PHOTO
AND HALF~TONE
ENGRAVINGS.

Published by

WINSTON-DEREK PUBLISHERS, INCORPORATED

NASHVILLE, TENNESSEE

TO SOW THE FALLOW SOIL

Copyright © 1992 by Winston-Derek Publishers

Published by Winston-Derek Publishers, Inc.
Nashville, Tennessee 37209

ISBN: 1-55523-473-9
Printed in the United States of America

Contents

PART I

PART II

5

CONTENTS

CONTENTS

8 CONTENTS

CONTENTS

PART III

Illustrations

Introduction

I THINK I should scarcely trouble the reader with a special appeal in behalf of this book, if it had not specially appealed to me for reasons apart from the author's race, origin, and condition. The world is too old now, and I find myself too much of its mood, to care for the work of a poet because he is black, because his father and mother were slaves, because he was, before and after he began to write poems, an elevator-boy. These facts would certainly attract me to him as a man, if I knew him to have a literary ambition, but when it came to his literary art, I must judge it irrespective of these facts, and enjoy or endure it for what it was in itself.

It seems to me that this was my experience with the poetry of Paul Laurence Dunbar when I found it in another form, and in justice to him I cannot wish that it should be otherwise with his readers here. Still, it will legitimately interest those who like to know the causes, or, if these may not be known, the sources, of things, to learn that the father and mother of the first poet of his race in our language were negroes without admixture of white blood. The father escaped from slavery in Kentucky to freedom in Canada, while there was still no hope of freedom otherwise ; but the mother was freed by the events of the civil war, and came North to Ohio, where their son was born at Dayton, and grew up with such chances and mischances for mental training as everywhere befall the children of the poor. He has told me that his father picked up the trade of a plasterer, and when he had taught himself to read, loved chiefly to read history. The boy's mother shared his passion for literature, with a special love of poetry, and after the father died she struggled on in more than the poverty she had shared with him. She could value the faculty which her son showed first in prose sketches and attempts at fiction, and she was proud of the praise and kindness they won him among the people of the town, where he has never been without the warmest and kindest friends.

In fact, from every part of Ohio and from several cities of the adjoining States, there came letters in cordial appreciation of the critical recognition which it was my pleasure no less than my duty to offer Paul Dunbar's work in another place. It seemed to me a happy omen for him that so many people who had known him, or known of him, were glad of a stranger's good word ; and it was gratifying to see that at home he was esteemed-for the things he had done rather than because as the son of negro slaves he had done them. If a prophet is often without honor in his own country, it surely is nothing against him when he has it. In this case it deprived me of the glory of a discoverer ; but that is sometimes a barren joy, and I am always willing to forego it.

What struck me in reading Mr. Dunbar's poetry was what had already struck his friends in Ohio and Indiana, in Kentucky and Illinois. They had felt, as I felt, that however gifted his race had proven itself in music, in oratory, in several of the other arts, here was the first instance of an American negro who had evinced innate distinction in literature. In my criticism of his book I had alleged Dumas in France, and I had forgetfully failed to allege the far greater Pushkin in Russia ; but these were both mulattoes, who might have been supposed to derive their qualities from white blood vastly more artistic than ours, and who were the creatures of an environment more favorable to their literary development. So far as I could remember, Paul Dunbar was the only man of pure African blood and of American civilization to feel the negro life æsthetically and express it lyrically. It seemed to me that this had come to its most modern consciousness in him, and that his brilliant and unique achievement was to have studied the American negro objectively, and to have represented him as he found him to be, with humor, with sympathy, and yet with what the reader must instinctively feel to be entire truthfulness. I said that a race which had come to this effect in any member of it, had attained civilization in him, and I permitted myself the imaginative prophecy that the hostilities and the prejudices which had so long constrained his race were destined to vanish in the arts ; that these were to be the final proof that God had made of one blood all nations of men. I thought his merits positive and not comparative ; and I held that if his black poems had been written by a white man, I should not have found them less admirable. I accepted them as an evidence of the essential unity of the human race, which does not think or feel black in one and white in another, but humanly in all.

Yet it appeared to me then, and it appears to me now, that there is a precious difference of temperament between the races which it would be a great pity ever to lose, and that this is best preserved and most charmingly suggested by Mr. Dunbar in those pieces of his where he

studies the moods and traits of his race in its own accent
of our English. We call such pieces dialect pieces for
want of some closer phrase, but they are really not dia-
lect so much as delightful personal attempts and failures
for the written and spoken language. In nothing is his
essentially refined and delicate art so well shown as in
these pieces, which, as I ventured to say, describe the
range between appetite and emotion, with certain lifts far
beyond and above it, which is the range of the race. He
reveals in these a finely ironical perception of the negro's
limitations, with a tenderness for them which I think so
very rare as to be almost quite new. I should say, per-
haps, that it was this humorous quality which Mr. Dun-
bar had added to our literature, and it would be this
which would most distinguish him, now and hereafter.
It is something that one feels in nearly all the dialect
pieces ; and I hope that in the present collection he has
kept all of these in his earlier volume, and added others
to them. But the contents of this book are wholly of his
own choosing, and I do not know how much or little he
may have preferred the poems in literary English. Some
of these I thought very good, and even more than very
good, but not distinctively his contribution to the body of
American poetry. What I mean is that several people
might have written them ; but I do not know any one
else at present who could quite have written the dialect
pieces. These are divinations and reports of what passes
in the hearts and minds of a lowly people whose poetry
had hitherto been inarticulately expressed in music, but
now finds, for the first time in our tongue, literary inter-
pretation of a very artistic completeness.

I say the event is interesting, but how important it

shall be can be determined only by Mr. Dunbar's future performance. I cannot undertake to prophesy concerning this; but if he should do nothing more than he has done, I should feel that he had made the strongest claim for the negro in English literature that the negro has yet made. He has at least produced something that, however we may critically disagree about it, we cannot well refuse to enjoy; in more than one piece he has produced a work of art.

W. D. HOWELLS.

Foreword

IN preparing this biography of Paul Laurence Dunbar for his publishers, his biographer was greatly helped and encouraged by many persons who knew and loved him. Among those to whom special thanks are due are the poet's mother, Mrs. Matilda Dunbar of Dayton, and his friends, Dr. H. A. Tobey, Mr. Charles Thatcher, Mayor Brand Whitlock, and Mr. Charles Cottrill of Toledo.

Many letters of inquiry were written, and in almost every case prompt and helpful replies received. The other facts given or anecdotes told were found in letters written in the poet's own hand to intimate friends.

It has been the steadfast purpose of his biographer to give to the world only such data as could be established in fact, and if she has failed in any instance the error was of the head and not the heart.

It would have been a pleasant thing to have reproduced all the appreciative letters that came in connection with the writing of this biography, but as that would have been impossible, it has seemed well to quote from two of the many.

Having been told that upon one occasion, President Roosevelt had said, in speaking of Mr. Dunbar :

"I like that young man, though I do not agree with his philosophy," a letter was addressed by Mr. Dunbar's biographer to the President. In response to this inquiry Mr. Roosevelt wrote as follows :

Oyster Bay, L. I., August 2, 1906.

MY DEAR MRS. WIGGINS:

I have your letter of the 27th. While I only had the pleasure of meeting Mr. Dunbar once or twice, I was a great admirer of his poetry and his prose.

I do not believe I ever spoke such a sentence as that you quote in reference to him. I had been struck by the artistic merit of his work, and had not thought of what you speak of as its " philosophy " save in the sense that all really artistic work has a philosophy of application to the entire human race.

Sincerely yours,

THEODORE ROOSEVELT.

Having observed by newspaper reports that Mr. James Lane Allen was a friend of the black poet's, though a man of southern birth, a letter was sent him by Mr. Dunbar's biographer. His reply is beautifully characteristic, and the paragraph which he generously sends for use in the Life is quoted verbatim here —

" I think that Paul Laurence Dunbar reached, in some of his poems, the highest level that his race has yet attained in lyric form, and feeling : and if it can be of service to you to make use of this opinion, it is gladly at your service."—JAMES LANE ALLEN.

By all races and under all skies the poems of Paul Laurence Dunbar are being read, and a decade later the world will have learned to know, better than it does now, the loss it sustained when the greatest poet of his race, and one of the greatest of any race, passed into the silence and dropped the veil.

To his biographer, who visited him many times, during the last two years of his life, the friendship of such a man

PRESIDENT THEODORE ROOSEVELT

Who was a great admirer of Mr. Dunbar's literary productions,
and who was a personal friend of the poet.

HON. JOHN HAY

Who being the American Ambassador to England at the time of Mr. Dunbar's visit to London, paid him marked attention, and arranged an entertainment at which Mr. Dunbar recited his poems before a highly intellectual and cultured audience.

meant more than mere prose may tell. After a visit to
the poet, when he was particularly cheerful and full of
hope, these lines " wrote themselves down " as a slight
appreciation of the privilege of calling on Paul Laurence
Dunbar.

I come from the home of a poet,
　　Who wove me, with exquisite art,
A cloak of the threads of his fancy —
　　Rich 'broidered with flowers of the heart.

Oh, wonderful cloak that he wove me,
　　For, under its magical spell,
I heard in the lilt of a linnet
　　An anthem of infinite swell.

I sat 'mid the fragrance of roses,
　　Tho' never a rose blossomed there,
And perfume of jasmine flowers mingled
　　With violet scents in the air.

Life's lowly were laureled with verses,
　　And sceptred were honor and worth,
While cabins became, through the poet,
　　Fair homes of the lords of the earth.

The plane, where life's humble ones labor
　　In sorrow and sadness untold,
Shone forth in my eyes' quickened vision,
　　A field of the fabric of gold.

With sorrow, blest cloak, I relinquished
　　Thy influence, sweet and ideal,
For a world where the Real is called "fancy,"
　　And fancied things only are " real."

　　　　　　　　　　　　　　— *Lida Keck Wiggins.*

PART I

Life of Paul Laurence Dunbar

CHAPTER I

BIRTH AND PARENTAGE

AT Dayton, Ohio, in the year 1871, Mrs. Matilda
Murphy, an ex-slave, was married to Joshua Dunbar,
who, having escaped to Canada before the war, had later
enlisted in the Fifty-fifth Massachusetts Infantry, and was,
at the time of his marriage, an old man. Neither Joshua
Dunbar nor his wife could read or write, but both had ardent
ambitions to know more of the world and of the achieve-
ments of their fellow men. Matilda Dunbar's master was
a cultured gentleman of Lexington, Kentucky, and as a
little girl, she was allowed to sit at his feet and listen as
he read aloud to his wife from the great writers. Espe-
cially was she delighted when he read poetry—the music
of it, the rhythm and the imagery fired her imagination
and left an unfading impression upon her mind. It was
always with regret and sometimes with a hidden tear that
little Matilda left her seat on the floor at her master's knee
and retired to bed. She dared not express a wish to re-
main—she was only a slave child and was not expected

to have opinions of her own.   During her girlhood and
even after she went to Dayton, Ohio, and married her
first husband, Mr. Murphy, she still loved to hear verses
read and was a very capable judge of the merits of a
metrical composition.   After her marriage with Joshua
Dunbar, she learned from school-children, whom she coaxed
into her humble home, the coveted letters of the alpha-
bet.   One by one she mastered them, and then began
spelling out words, and finally sentences.   Her husband,
although well advanced in years, taught himself reading,
and after long hours spent at his trade, which was that of
a plasterer, he read universal history and biography.

In 1872 this pair became the parents of a boy baby.
When the momentous question of " naming the baby "
came to be discussed, Mr. Dunbar insisted that the child
be called Paul.   His young wife thought the name too
" old-fashioned " for a baby.   Mr. Dunbar had a quaint
and formal manner of addressing his wife, and upon this
occasion said :

" Matilda Madam, don't you know that the Bible says
Paul was a great man ?   This child will be great some
day and do you honor."

Thus the question was settled, and the child was chris-
tened Paul Laurence, the Laurence being in compliment
to a Dayton friend.   The father of Paul Dunbar proved
a prophet.   The boy was a genius.   At as early an age
as seven years he wrote his first bit of verse.   It was a
child's poem and naturally expressed childish sentiment,
but even then the flickerings of a great talent were ap-
parent.   There had to be a beginning, and to those who
view this short life from first to last it would almost seem
that the young poet knew his work must be done quickly,

MRS. MATILDA DUNBAR

The poet's mother, who as a child was held in slavery.

PRESIDENT WILLIAM McKINLEY

Who conferred on Mr. Dunbar the honor of a commission to act as aide with rank of Colonel in his inaugural parade. Mr. Dunbar accepted the invitation and rode in the procession.

as the time was short.   His soul was old when his body came into the world.

At school, Paul Dunbar was a diligent pupil, his favorite studies being spelling, grammar and literature.   It is to the everlasting credit of his teachers that they encouraged him in his writing, and praised the little poems which he carried to them in a bashful way.   Perchance if they had been indifferent to these early attempts, the shrinking lad would never have had courage to go forward. Timidity and modesty marked his bearing through life.

When in high school he edited *The High School Times*, a monthly publication issued by the pupils of the Steele High School.   This work was done with so much tact and evinced such extraordinary talent that many an older head predicted the boy's future renown.

In 1891 he graduated from the high school with honors, and the class song composed by him was sung at the commencement exercises.

Commencement meant to Paul Dunbar the beginning of his hard struggle for existence.   His father having died in 1884, it devolved upon the boy to support his mother. It is doubtful if in all history a child were ever more faithful and loyal to a mother than this young poet.   While yet in school he had assisted her in her humble tasks as a washerwoman, and carried home the clothes to her patrons.   He did odd jobs about hotels and other places, and was always willing and eager to lend a helpful hand. His graduation over, Dunbar sought regular work.   Having obtained an education, he quite naturally hoped for better things than mere menial employment.   He was destined to meet with disappointment.   On every hand his color told against him, and at last in sheer despair,

he was compelled to accept a position as elevator boy in
the Callahan Building at Dayton.   Here he earned four
dollars a week, upon which to support his mother and
himself.   Many a young man, possessing such a sensi-
tive soul, would have recoiled from so humble an occu-
pation.   Not so with this budding genius.   With brave
heart he set about his task, determined to gain recogni-
tion later.   There were few flowers in his path and many
cruel thorns.   He gathered the roses, inhaled their fra-
grance, and immortalized their beauty in verse, and the
thorns he bore bravely as a part of human life.   Thus
he learned early to be a philosopher, and in consequence
a great poet.   Every moment that could be snatched
from his busy hours was utilized in improving his brilliant
mind.   His soul, attuned to the infinite music which is ever
to be heard even among most unfavorable surroundings,
detected a melody in the grating of the elevator cables
and the thud of the car as it stopped for passengers.
The people he served were of lively interest to the lad,
and into very ordinary faces his artistic mind painted un-
guessed nobility and beauty.   His humble home, his dear
mother and his beloved black people formed the all-
sufficient inspiration for his earlier dialect poems.   Many
of these were stories told by his mother, as the family
sat before the fire on winter nights, but he always added
a touch of quaint philosophy, or a breath of pathos,
which lifted them above the level of folk-lore and gave
them a dignity and depth which were all his own.   The
best things he wrote in those early days were the poems
which were couched in classic English, and the produc-
tion of such verses proved far more than his dialect the
remarkable scope of his mentality.

In 1892, when the Western Association of Writers met at Dayton, Mrs. Truesdale, one of Dunbar's former teachers, brought about an invitation for him to deliver the address of welcome. The printed program did not contain the name of the person who was to give the address, but at the appointed hour, having secured a limited leave of absence from his elevator, young Dunbar went to the hall. He entered as a shadow, walked gracefully down the aisle, and mounted the rostrum. He was introduced to the audience by Dr. John Clark Ridpath and delivered the " welcome " in metrical form, written in the best of English and full of haunting melody. His manner of reading was almost as wonderful as his composition, and the cultured audience was delighted and amazed. As quickly as he came he disappeared, and hurried back to his work. The members of the association were convinced that they had been listening to a genius; and many inquiries were made concerning the lad. He was later made a member of the Association.

The following day Dr. James Newton Matthews, Mr. Will Pfrimmer and Dr. Ridpath went to the Callahan Building and sought him out. They found him at his post of duty and by his side in the elevator were a late copy of the *Century Magazine*, a lexicon, a scratch tablet and a pencil. Dunbar, writing to a friend of this meeting said:

" My embarrassment was terrible. In the midst of a sentence, perhaps, a ring would come from the top of the building for the elevator, and I would have to excuse myself and run up after passengers."

Dr. Matthews questioned Dunbar concerning his life, and secured copies of a number of his poems. A few

weeks later he wrote a press-letter about the young poet
and quoted these poems. This letter was published in
many of the leading newspapers in America and England.
A copy of it fell into the hands of James Whitcomb
Riley, who after reading the verses, wrote the young poet
a letter in which he called him " his chirping friend," and
praised his work, particularly the one entitled "Drowsy
Day." This letter was one of Dunbar's treasures and
he kept it all his life.

CHAPTER II

"OAK AND IVY"

things begin to look up. for Dunbar

THE years 1892 and 1893 were memorable in the life of Paul Laurence Dunbar. Encouraged by a number of men, who promised to supply financial support, the young man began to have ambitions to publish a book of his poems. One evening, after a hard day on the elevator, he went to his home, and said to his mother :

"Ma, where are those papers I asked you to save for me?" The "papers" to which he referred were manuscript and newspaper copies of his poems. His mother, having but little room in their tiny home, utilized the kitchen for dining-room as well, and on the table in the middle room, Paul had piled his papers during the years of high school. His mother allowed the pile to grow, though she did not know that it contained his manuscripts, and thought that the papers to which he referred were his botany sheets and things of that kind. Finally, being criticised by her neighbors for allowing such a stack of papers to lie on her table, she gathered them all together, and put them in a large box under the old fashioned "safe," in her kitchen. So, when her son came home that particular evening and asked anxiously for his "papers," she said :

"They're out there under the safe."

Dunbar selected from the pile a little bundle, which he carried away with him next morning, saying, "Ma, I'm going to publish a book."

33

He went to the office of the United Brethren Publishing House and unfolded his plans to the agent of that institution. His "friends" who had promised financial backing, had laughed at him when he asked them to make their word good, so he had to approach the publisher empty-handed. Here again he met with disappointment. They would not "take the risk," and unless he could secure $125.00 to pay for the books they would not undertake their publication. One hundred and twenty-five dollars! They might as well have asked for a thousand. Poor Dunbar, unable to conceal his disappointment, was leaving the house with a sad countenance, wholly discouraged. At this juncture, Mr. William Blacher, the business manager of the concern, noticing his disheartened appearance, called him to his desk and said :

"What's the matter, Paul?"

"Oh, I wanted to have a volume of poems printed, but the house can't trust me, and I can never get $125.00 to pay for it in advance."

Mr. Blacher's heart was touched. He knew the boy, and appreciated him. He had read his verses, and knew that they were "real poems," truly inspired. He told young Dunbar that he would stand between him and the house for the amount required, and that the book would be published for the Christmas holidays.

The boy's bright face was aglow with happiness when he reached his mother's home that night, and there were tears of joy in his eyes when he said :

"Oh, ma, they're going to print my book."

Several weeks later, one snowy morning, there came a rap at the door of the Dunbar home. Mrs. Dunbar, wiping her hands free of suds on her apron, opened the door. A man stood outside with a large package of books for " Mr. Paul Dunbar."

" These are a few of Mr. Dunbar's books," he said. " And, by the way, what is this Dunbar? Is he a doctor, a lawyer, a preacher, or what ? "

His mother modestly replied—" Who? Paul? Why Paul is just an elevator boy, and a—poet."

In less than two weeks after the appearance of the little volume which was entitled " Oak and Ivy Poems," Paul Dunbar again approached the desk of Mr. Blacher. This time he walked with a confident tread, and reaching into his pocket, produced the exact amount of his indebtedness, one hundred and twenty-five dollars ! The boy had sold enough books while going up and down in his elevator to pay for the whole edition !

Soon after this Judge Dustin, of the Common Pleas Court, became interested in the lad, and gave him a position as page at the Dayton Court House. He also gave Dunbar a chance to read law.

About this time, a review of his book, " Oak and Ivy," appeared in the *Toledo Blade*, and several of his poems were reproduced. Among these was his " Drowsy Day." This article and the poems attracted the attention of Mr. Charles Thatcher, a rising attorney of Toledo, who wrote to Dunbar, asking him to send a copy of " Oak and Ivy," and to tell him something of his life. Mr. Dunbar answered this letter from Richmond, Indiana, where he had been invited by one of the most prominent ladies of that city, to come and read a poem at a church social. He said that there was very little to tell of his early life, as it had been uneventful, and that he had been running an elevator in Dayton at $4.00 per week, and out of his earnings attempting to support himself and his widowed mother, and to pay for the little home which he had bought through the building and loan association, but that the bulk of his payments went for interest. He also said that he expected to go to Detroit in the near future, as a friend was trying to arrange a reading for him there. Mr. Thatcher answered the letter immediately, and asked him to stop off at Toledo on his way to Detroit, as he wished to meet him personally.

April 15, 1893, Dunbar went to Toledo, on his way to Detroit, and called at the office of the attorney, who was immediately impressed with his gentlemanly bearing and with his desire to secure an education.

Mr. Thatcher was impressed by the earnest expression of the young man's face, and with his evident honesty of purpose. After considerable conversation, he suggested to Dunbar that he might secure several gentlemen to join him and arrange to loan him an amount each year, necessary to meet his expenses while in college: and that if this were done, he could give his note to each person who advanced money, with a view to paying the sum when he was able. He placed the matter before Dunbar as a business proposition, and not in the light of charity. The poet did not hesitate a moment. He promptly declined the offer, saying with admirable pride, although with due appreciation of his friend's kindness:

"I feel that I can accomplish it alone, and very much prefer to do so, if I am able."

He went to Detroit, and gave readings, which added to his reputation as a reader and a poet. While there he received a telegram from Mr. Thatcher to come back by way of Toledo, and to be prepared to recite for the West End Club the following Wednesday evening. Dunbar wrote his new patron, thanking him, and saying: "I am studying hard for Wednesday night, and hope I shall please the members of the West End Club." This club had been recently organized and once a week some person delivered a lecture or a paper. That night it so happened that Dr. W. C. Chapman, of Toledo, who had lately returned from a trip South, was on the program for a paper. Its title was "The Negro in the South." The doctor did not know that Dunbar was to appear later, nor did he know that he was in the audience. He indulged in severe criticisms of the negro, accusing him of laziness, but added that there were noted exceptions to the rule, and referred to Paul Laurence Dunbar. When, a little later, it was announced that "Paul Laurence Dunbar" would "favor the club with several original selections," the doctor was covered with embarrassment. The young black man rose with dignity and said:

"I will give you one number which I had not intended reciting when I came: it is entitled, 'An Ode to Ethiopia.'"

One would have thought that he was a lawyer defending a man for his life. He seemed to feel that an attack had been made upon his race and that he was its sole defender. The zeal and ardor with which he recited showed that his soul was in the theme. His eyes flashed, his white teeth gleamed, and his whole person was a-tremble with emotion. After the recital he said to Mr. Thatcher:

"I do not know but that I showed too much spirit in

3

rendering 'An Ode to Ethiopia,' but I could not
help it."

All who heard him that night were impressed with his
genius, and touched by the fact that a boy of twenty had
taken up the fight to defend a race numbering more than
six millions.   Of himself he might well have been speak-
ing when, in the last stanza of the Ode, he cried :

> "Go on and up !   Our souls and eyes
> Shall follow thy continuous rise :
>   Our ears shall list thy story
> From bards who from thy root shall spring
> And proudly tune their lyres to sing
>   Of Ethiopia's glory."

CHAPTER III

THE WORLD'S FAIR—"A 'SPECIAL PROVIDENCE'"

AT the opening of the World's Columbian Exposition an opportunity came for young Dunbar to go to Chicago. At first he hesitated, not wishing to leave his mother alone. Mrs. Dunbar, feeling that the fair would be an education in itself for her boy, insisted upon his going. When all was in readiness, and the hour had come to say good-bye, he leaned on the mantelpiece and sobbed like a child, saying :

" Oh, ma, I don't want to go—it is such a wicked city : I know I shall learn a great deal but I'm afraid to venture. I don't want to go."

His mother, choking down her own tears, talked to her son, and finally overcame his mood. He went to Chicago, and after several unsuccessful attempts to obtain suitable employment, he was given a position by Hon. Fred Douglass, then in charge of the exhibit from Hayti. For this work Mr. Douglass paid Paul Dunbar $5.00 a week, out of his own pocket. After a while Dunbar sent for his mother, who, always willing to follow her son, went to him. She was not too proud to work, and so did light housekeeping for a family there, thus making a bit of a home for her beloved child.

On " Colored Folks' Day " at the fair, Paul Laurence Dunbar was called upon to render several "selections," before thousands of his own people. The verses were greatly appreciated, but when it was announced, by an

Episcopal clergyman from Washington, D. C., that the
compositions were original, the applause was deafening.
Fred Douglass, in speaking to an acquaintance about
the young poet, during the time he was employed at the
Haytian building, said :

"I regard Paul Dunbar as the most promising young
colored man in America."

How much the young poet appreciated the friendship
of the elder man may be learned by his beautiful tribute
to him at the time of his death.   The last stanza, which
reads as follows, is characteristic :

> "Oh, Douglass, thou hast passed beyond the shore,
>   But still thy voice is ringing o'er the gale !
> Thou'st taught thy race how high her hopes may soar,
>   And bade her seek the heights, nor fail.
> She will not fail, she heeds thy stirring cry,
> She knows thy guardian spirit will be nigh,
> And, rising from beneath the chast'ning rod,
> She stretches out her bleeding hands to God ! "

After the fair, Mr. Dunbar and his mother returned to
Dayton.   Finding that it would be impossible to earn
sufficient funds for a college course, the young man re-
luctantly wrote his Toledo friend, Mr. Thatcher, saying
that he would reconsider his original decision, and accept
the loan which had been offered him.   The young at-
torney was quite willing to fulfil his part of the promise,
but the other men, who had given their word, now had
excuses to offer, and the project failed to materialize.
This was a heart-breaking blow to poor Paul Dunbar,
but he bore it bravely with indomitable will and more
than human courage.

Very soon after this, he was approached by a man who claimed to be organizing a " Black Jenny Lind Concert Company," and who made the poet an offer to go with him as his reader. Heart and soul the young man went to work, writing new poems, committing others to memory, and preparing himself thoroughly in every way. But, just ten days before he was to have started on the road, he received word that the " company " had disbanded, and that his services would not be needed. Poor Dunbar was almost frantic: winter was approaching: he had no funds with which to buy food and fuel: his clothing and that of his mother was insufficient, and he had given up everything in the way of work to go with the " Jenny Lind " organization. A call came to go to Detroit to give a reading, and this he did, but the affair proved to be one given for " charity," and Dunbar, poorer than any for whom the recital was given, was expected to give his services gratis. Thus impoverished he was compelled to write again to Toledo. This time; doubtless with a breaking heart, he wrote to Mr. Thatcher : " Could some of the money which was offered for my college course be sent me to relieve present embarrassments ? I have no funds and no work, and a foreclosure is threatened on the little home I have been paying for through the Building & Loan Association."

The appeal was not in vain : the money was sent, and the home saved. The relief, however, being only temporary, the boy poet soon grew desperate and wrote to a friend under date of November 7th, 1894 :

" There is only one thing left to be done, and I am too big a coward to do that." Small wonder that thoughts of suicide should come to this sensitive soul when every avenue of honest pursuit was closed against him. Truly —

> " Every door is barred with gold,
> And opens but to golden keys,"

and poor Paul Dunbar didn't have the keys—and in addition to that he was a negro ! Twice burdened indeed is he who carries upon his shoulders the load of poverty and the stigma of race prejudice.

In the fall or winter of 1893, Miss Mary Reeve of Dayton,—a woman of rare intellectuality, who reviewed books for magazines, went to Toledo to be the guest of Dr. and Mrs. H. A. Tobey at the Toledo State Hospital. Dr. Tobey was at that time superintendent of the institution, and is one of America's greatest experts on insanity. He is a man of broad mind, universal sympathies and decidedly democratic ideals. Miss Reeve and he discussed many of the vital problems of the day, and upon one occasion the doctor said that the only question he ever asked about any person was: "What is there in the individual, regardless of creed, nationality or race." His companion replied :

"I suspect then that you would be interested in a negro boy we have down in Dayton. I don't know much of him myself, but my sister, Mrs. Conover (this is the Mrs. Frank Conover to whom Mr. Dunbar afterwards dedicated his collection of poems entitled "Lyrics of Sunshine and Shadow") says he has written some very wonderful things."

"I would not be interested in him," replied the doctor,

"because he is a negro : I would only be interested in him for what he is."

A little later Miss Reeve sent the doctor a copy of Dunbar's first book, "Oak and Ivy." He read the little poems casually, not giving them much thought, and was not especially impressed. He went to Dayton a few months later, however, and while there inquired about Paul Laurence Dunbar. He heard of his obscure origin, his hardships and his hopeless condition. He also learned that the boy had been faithfully helping his mother in her humble tasks as a laundress : that he had graduated from high school: had held a position as elevator boy, and that he had ambitions to study law. All this appealed to Dr. Tobey. His sympathies were enlisted for the boy because he was making such a noble struggle. When he returned home he sought again the little volume, "Oak and Ivy," and this time, being in closer touch with its author, he saw new beauty in the lines. Several of the poems he read over and over, each time finding greater depths and truths almost sublime. Finally, one Sunday evening, after going over the book once more, he wrote a letter to the author, enclosing a sum of money, and asking that the number of books for which the amount would pay be sent him, as he wished to distribute them among his friends. He also spoke many encouraging words to the young poet, and expressed a desire to be of service to him if that were possible. He did not receive a reply from Mr. Dunbar for three or four days, and then came the answer. This letter is so remarkable in many ways, and is such a revelation of the character of the young man at that time, that it is given verbatim below :

Dayton, Ohio, July 13th, 1895.

MY DEAR DR. TOBEY :—

If it is a rule that tardiness in the acknowledgment of favors argues lack of appreciation of them, you may set it down that the rule has gone wrong in this case. Your letter and its enclosure was a sunburst out of a very dark and unpromising cloud. Let me tell you the circumstances and see if you do not think that you came to me somewhat in the rôle of a " special providence."

The time for the meeting of the Western Association of Writers was at hand. I am a member and thought that certain advantages might come to me by attending. All day Saturday and all day Sunday I tried every means to secure funds to go. I tried every known place, and at last gave up and went to bed Sunday night in despair. But strangely I could not sleep, so about half-past eleven I arose and between then and 2 A. M., wrote the paper which I was booked to read at the Association. Then, still with no suggestion of any possibility of attending the meeting, I returned to bed and went to sleep about four o'clock. Three hours later came your letter with the check that took me to the desired place. I do not think that I spent the money unwisely, for besides the pleasure of intercourse with kindred spirits which should have been sufficient motive, I believe that there were several practical advantages which I derived from the trip, whence I have just returned.

I wish I could thank you for the kindness that prompted your action ; I care not in whose name it was done, whether in Christ's, Mahomet's or Buddha's. The thing that concerned me, the fact that made the act a good and noble one was that it *was* done.

Yes, I am tied down and have been by menial labor, and any escape from it so far has only been a brief respite that made a return to the drudgery doubly hard. But I am glad to say that for the past two or three years I have been able to keep my mother from the hard toil by

DR. HENRY A. TOBEY

To whom Mr. Dunbar dedicated his "Folks from Dixie," and
who had possibly the greatest influence of any
person upon the poet's life and work.

WILLIAM DEAN HOWELLS

Whose article in *Harper's Weekly* gave Mr. Dunbar his first
introduction into the great world of letters.

which she raised and educated me.   But it has been and is a struggle.

Your informant was mistaken as to my aspirations.   I did once want to be a lawyer, but that ambition has long since died out before the all-absorbing desire to be a worthy singer of the songs of God and nature.   To be able to interpret my own people through song and story, and to prove to the many that after all we are more human than African.   And to this end I have hoped year after year to be able to go to Washington, New York, Boston and Philadelphia where I might see our northern negro at his best, before seeing his brother in the South : but it has been denied me.

I hope, if possible, to spend the coming year in college, chiefly to learn how and what to study in order to cultivate my vein.   But I have my home responsibilities and unless I am able to make sufficient to meet them I shall be unable to accomplish my purpose.   To do this I have for some time been giving readings from my verses to audiences mostly of my own people.   But as my work has been confined to the smaller towns generally the result has not been satisfactory.

Perhaps I have laid my case too plainly and openly before you, but you seem to display a disposition to aid me, and I am so grateful that I cannot but be confidential. Then beside, a physician does not want to take a case when there is reticence in regard to the real phases of it. And so I have been plain.   Sincerely,

PAUL L. DUNBAR.

140 Ziegler Street,
Dayton, Ohio.

CHAPTER IV

MAJORS AND MINORS

In August, 1895, Dr. Tobey wrote the young poet, inviting him to come to the Institution at Toledo and read for the patients. Having, in the meantime, learned that Mr. Charles Cottrill, a brilliant young colored man of Toledo, was a family friend of the Dunbars, Dr. Tobey insisted on having him at the hospital to formally introduce the poet. A carriage was sent to meet Mr. Dunbar at the railway station, and Dr. Tobey and Mr. Cottrill stood at a window, awaiting its return. When it came back and young Dunbar alighted, the doctor exclaimed :

" Thank God, he's black ! "

His companion, being of a much lighter color than Dunbar, was momentarily offended, but the doctor redeemed himself by adding :

" Whatever genius he may have cannot be attributed to the white blood he may have in him."

In the autumn of the same year, Dr. Tobey sent a second invitation to Paul Dunbar to come to Toledo and give a reading at the Asylum. The doctor having learned of Mr. Charles Thatcher's great interest in and friendship for the Dayton boy, asked the attorney to be his guest at this recital. Thus Dunbar's two great friends joined hands for his future welfare.

At this second recital Mr. Dunbar read poems which were new to his Toledo friends, and which had not been published in "Oak and Ivy."

They talked with him at the close of the program, and found that he cherished hopes of getting a second book published at Dayton on the same terms as the first. Under his arrangement with the Dayton house he did not own the plates of his book, but when he secured orders for a number of volumes, the firm would bind them for him, from the loose sheets kept on hand.

His two friends told him that they would assume the financial part of the new publication, and that when the books were printed they would belong to the author. Dunbar was very happy over this arrangement and set about immediately to find a Toledo publisher. He finally arranged in a very businesslike way, with the Hadley & Hadley Printing Company to publish an edition of 1,000 copies of a second book. This little volume was called "Majors and Minors," and contains many of the finest things he ever wrote. His mind was not mature, then, as it was in later efforts, but his thoughts were honest, pure and fearless, and there was not the slightest trace of over-polish or artificiality. Mr. Dunbar was so conscientious that very few of the poems which had appeared in his first book, were reprinted. He said, concerning the matter:

"Some poets get out 'new' books that are largely composed of poems that have been published before. I do not believe that such a practice is right."

The poet hoped to have this book ready for the Christmas holidays of 1895, but to his great disappointment, it did not appear until early the following year.

During the days which preceded the publication of "Majors and Minors," and before the binders began work, Dr. Tobey was so anxious to possess the poems in printed form that he went to the office of Hadley & Hadley, secured an unbound volume, and eagerly cut the leaves with his pocket knife.

So many of the vital questions of Paul Laurence Dunbar's life were settled seemingly by mere accident, or at least remarkably strange coincidences! The very day that Dr. Tobey came into possession of this first copy of "Majors and Minors," he was called into professional consultation in the city, which made it necessary for him to remain at a hotel over night. At this hotel he met a friend who was fond of poetry, and with him Dr. Tobey sat in the office reading Dunbar's verses until almost midnight. As they stepped to the desk to get their keys, the actor, James O'Neal and his wife and Mr. Nixon, who was O'Neal's leading man in "Monte Christo," then being played in Toledo, came in. Dr. Tobey's friend introduced the actors to him. Mr. O'Neal being very weary, excused himself, and retired. Mr. Nixon lingered.

"I know," said Dr. Tobey, "that you actor folks are always being bored by people wanting you to read and give opinions of poems, but I have something here that I wish you would read, if you will."

Mr. Nixon politely took the crude little copy of "Majors and Minors," and began reading—"When Sleep Comes Down to Soothe the Weary Eyes." At first he read the poem quietly, leaning over the counter. Then he read it aloud—then he gave it a dramatic rendition, his face showing his delight and surprise at the beauty and depth of the lines. He read other poems, and until three o'clock the following morning, remained on his feet, poring over the poems of a poor and almost unknown negro boy. He then said :

" Dr. Tobey, I thank you for giving me this opportunity : in my opinion no poet has written such verses since Poe."

" Majors and Minors " was soon published, and Dunbar went to Toledo to try to sell his books. Naturally shrinking and unnaturally timid, he met with poor success. To the great, unfeeling, uncaring public he was simply a shabby negro " book agent " for whom they had no time nor interest. His friends sent him to their friends, but almost always he met with discouragement. The average person thought :   " What do I want with a ' nigger's ' book ? "

He said when speaking of the book-agent experiences to his friends : " As a rule, if I can get through the front office, and meet the men to whom you send me, they are courteous and kind."

With a soul as sensitive as a delicate flower the young bard was ill-fitted for so hard a rôle as that of a book-agent. It seemed that fate chose for this black singer the hardest lot she could devise. He had borne burdens all his life, but this was too heavy for him, and one night, after an unusually discouraging day, poor Dunbar went to see his friend, Dr. Tobey.

" Well, my boy, how goes the battle ? "

" Oh, doctor," replied Dunbar, with unbidden tears streaming down his cheeks, " I never can offer to sell another book to any man."

" Paul, why don't you make up a speech ? "

" Oh," he replied, " I have tried to do that, but my

tongue cleaves to the roof of my mouth, and I cannot say a word."

The doctor, though full of sympathy, replied :

" You're no good book agent.   I was down town to-day for a few hours and I sold three of your books to as many of the most prominent men of Toledo on condition that you deliver them in person and make the acquaintance of each of the purchasers."

That same evening Dunbar, in his childlike way said, as though confessing a misdemeanor to a parent :

" I ought not to have done it, I suppose, but I spent fifty cents to see ' Shore Acres ' last night."   That sum took him to the upper gallery in a back row of seats.   " I saw it once before, and I could not resist the temptation. It is a poem from beginning to end.   Have you seen it, doctor ? "

" No, but my wife and I are going to-morrow night."

Dunbar answered :   " Don't fail."

The doctor, as though suddenly inspired, said :

" Paul, I'm glad you spoke of that play.   From what I have heard of the author, Mr. Herne, I believe he would be interested in what you have done and are doing.   I want you to take one of your books with your compliments, down to the Boody House, and leave it with the night clerk for Mr. Herne."   The clerk, a Mr. Childs, had learned of Dunbar through Mr. Nixon's readings upon the night previously described in these pages. When this matter had been agreed upon between Mr. Dunbar and the doctor, the latter left him for a few moments and went down to the public office of the Institution.   A representative of one of the greater New York dailies was at the time a guest of Dr. Tobey and his family. Addressing him, Dr. Tobey said:

" Mr. T——, with your permission, I'm going to bring down here and introduce to you the most wonderful man you ever met."

The newspaper man looked somewhat incredulous, but knowing Dr. Tobey's word could be relied upon, replied that he should be delighted to meet the wonderful individual to whom he referred.

His host then went in search of Paul Dunbar, and not telling him what he had said to the New York man, brought him in and introduced them.   If the scribe had been incredulous before he was even more so now when he saw a slender, bashful and shabbily dressed negro walk in with Dr. Tobey.   Introductions over, Dr. Tobey said:

" Paul, I have been telling this gentleman something about you and I want you to recite for us a few of your poems."

Dunbar rose and in rising seemed to shake off the self-consciousness and restraint that had been upon him.   His face grew radiant with the beautiful thoughts to which he gave utterance, and he read a number of his very finest verses with inimitable skill.

When he had finished, the New York man complimented him, and thanked him profusely for the entertainment he had afforded.   Then as soon as he could, he called Dr. Tobey aside and said:

" Dr. Tobey, *you have* introduced me to the most wonderful man I ever met.   His poems are sublime and his interpretation faultless.   I can never thank you enough for having given me a chance to meet him."

The next evening, in obedience to Dr. Tobey's request, Mr. Dunbar carried his little book to the hotel, and having inscribed it to Mr. Herne, would have left it there. It so chanced, however, that Mr. Herne had sought another hotel, where he could have greater quiet, and the Boody House clerk suggested to Dunbar that he take the book and give it to Mr. Herne, personally. This Dunbar said he would do, and the next morning went to Mr. Herne's hotel. In describing this incident in later years, Mr. Dunbar said :

" I approached the hotel with fear and trembling and must confess that I was greatly relieved to find that Mr. Herne was out."

He took the book back to the clerk at the Boody House, who kindly volunteered to see that it reached Mr. Herne. This he did, taking it himself to the clerk of the other hotel, and leaving it for the actor.

That was on Friday, and the following Sunday afternoon the poet went out to the hospital, all aglow with joy over a letter which he had received from Mr. Herne. It read as follows :

Detroit, Mich.

MY DEAR MR. DUNBAR :

While at Toledo, a copy of your poems was left at my hotel by a Mr. Childs. I tried very hard to find Mr. Childs to learn more of you. Your poems are wonderful. I shall acquaint William Dean Howells and other literary people with them. They are new to me and they may be to them.

I send you by this same mail some things done by my daughter, Julia A. Herne. She is at school in Boston.

Her scribblings may interest you. I would like your opinion. . . .

A am an actor and a dramatist. My latest work—"Shore Acres" you may have heard of. If it comes your way, I want you to see it, whether I am with it or not. How I wish I knew you personally! I wish you all the good fortune that you can wish for yourself.

Yours very truly,

JAMES A. HERNE.

Later in that same good year of 1896 Paul Dunbar met a friend who was destined to be one of the stars of hope in his literary sky. Dr. Tobey, ever alert to the interests of his young friend, wrote to Colonel Robert G. Ingersoll—in New York, and sent him a copy of "Majors and Minors," saying:

"I know you are too busy a man to read all the poems in this book, so I take the liberty of marking a number which I consider the stronger ones. I do not profess to be literary, but think I probably have ordinary human feeling and common sense, and I would like you to read over the poems I have marked, and which I think unusual. If after reading them you feel the same way, it would be a great consolation to Mr. Dunbar in his poverty and obscurity if you would write a letter of commendation."

Ten days later the doctor received the following reply:

No. 220 Madison Avenue,
April, 1896, New York City.

MY DEAR DR. TOBEY:

At last I got the time to read the poems of Dunbar. Some of them are really wonderful—full of poetry

4

and philosophy. I am astonished at their depth and subtlety. Dunbar is a thinker. "The Mystery" is a poem worthy of the greatest. It is absolutely true, and proves that its author is a profound and thoughtful man. So the "Dirge" is very tender, dainty, intense and beautiful. "Ere Sleep Comes Down to Soothe the Weary Eyes" is a wonderful poem : the fifth verse is perfect. So "He Had His Dream" is very fine and many others.

I have only time to say that Dunbar is a genius. Now, I ask what can be done for him ? I would like to help.

Thanking you for the book, I remain

Yours always,

R. G. INGERSOLL.

When one considers the youthfulness of the heart and hand that penned the poems to which Mr. Ingersoll referred, one is filled with wonder and amaze. It will not be out of place to quote here that "perfect" fifth verse of "When Sleep Comes Down to Soothe the Weary Eyes." It is as profound as "Thanatopsis" and as musical as "Hiawatha" or any of the "standard" poems of the world :

"Ere sleep comes down to soothe the weary eyes
　　How questioneth the soul that other soul,—
The inner sense that neither cheats nor lies,
　　But self exposes unto self, a scroll
Full writ with all life's acts, unwise or wise,
　　In characters indelible and known :
So trembling with the shock of sad surprise
　　The soul doth view its awful self alone,
Ere sleep comes down to soothe the weary eyes."

CHAPTER V

A REMARKABLE BIRTHDAY PRESENT

TRUE to his promise, Mr. Herne sent a copy of " Majors and Minors " to William Dean Howells, who was soon impressed (to quote part of a recent letter to the author of this biography) " by the little countrified volume, which inwardly was full of a new world."

Modesty is a hall mark of genius. Dunbar had it in a superlative degree, and that Mr. Howells possesses the same beautiful trait is evident when one reads the next sentence of the letter written his biographer under date of June 1, 1906 :

" I want to say that many western friends fully felt the quality of Dunbar's work before I had the good luck of drawing notice to it in a prominent place, and so far as any credit is concerned, it is they who deserve it."

The " prominent place " to which Mr. Howells refers was *Harper's Weekly*. In the same issue which gave an account of William McKinley's first nomination at Minneapolis, which issue had an enormous circulation, appeared a full-page review of Paul Laurence Dunbar's little book—" Majors and Minors," and an unprecedented appreciation of the young man's work by Mr. Howells. He could not have found a more opportune time for introducing the young poet to the reading world. No longer could the sweet singer of Ethiopia be spoken of as obscure or unknown. Like the sun which suddenly slips

from behind a sombre cloud and floods the world with
glory, so the name of Paul Laurence Dunbar, swept into
sight and passed majestically before the reviewing stand
of the entire reading world. He literally retired one
night unknown, and woke at the dawn of his twenty-
fourth birthday to find himself a famous man.   Advert-
ently or inadvertently Mr. Howells had chosen June 27,
1896, for the appearance of his article, thus presenting the
young man with the most magnificent birthday present
he could ever hope to receive.

Having concluded his critique of " Majors and Minors,"
Mr. Howells remembering that the boy was possibly in
need of something more substantial than appreciative
phrases, dear as they would be, added :

" I am sorry that I cannot give the publisher, as well as
the author of this significant little book ; but I may say
that it is printed by Hadley & Hadley of Toledo, Ohio."

Immediately letters began pouring into the office of the
printers, many were addressed to Dunbar, asking for his
photograph and every imaginable kind of query.   Others
ordered the book.   Among the orders was one from the
American Consul at Athens, Greece.   In fact demands
came from all parts of the world.

When Mr. Dunbar, having been told, by a friend, of
the *Harper's* article, bought a copy at a Dayton news-
stand he was almost overwhelmed with emotion, and, as
he described it : " Didn't know whether to laugh or cry,
but guessed he did a little of each."

Mr. James Lane Allen became interested in Paul Dun-
bar and his poems about this time, and called the atten-
tion of several New York magazine editors and reviewers
to the verses of the negro bard.   These men gave the

young poet flattering notices and helped to make permanent his new-made fame.

He and his mother had occasion to be absent from home for a few days about this time, and while they were away the postman slipped the mail through the slats of a front window shutter.   When Mrs. Dunbar attempted to open this shutter, two hundred letters snowed down upon the floor.   Many of these contained money for copies of "Majors and Minors."   All exhibited a complimentary interest in the youthful poet and his wonderful verses.

On the following Fourth of July, Dr. Tobey, realizing that to insane persons, holidays are the most unhappy occasions of all, arranged, as was his custom, to hold an elaborate celebration.

He invited Paul Laurence Dunbar and his mother to come to Toledo, as he wished him to give a number of readings.   Unknown to the poet, he also invited fifty or sixty prominent persons from Toledo and elsewhere. Among these guests was the late Governor Foster.   When Mr. Dunbar and his mother arrived at the Institution they were given an affectionate greeting by Dr. Tobey and his family, and then the doctor told them of the distinguished guests who had already arrived and were awaiting them.

"It has all come at once, Paul.   Mr. Howells has made you famous," said the doctor, with an arm about the younger man's shoulders.   "They all want to meet you now.   Those who 'made fun' of you because of your color and your poverty are now eager to clasp your hand : those who were indifferent are now enthusiastic.   This is going to be the testing day of your life.   I hope you will bear good fortune and popularity as well and as bravely as you have met your disappointments and your humiliations. If so, that will indeed be a proof of greatness."

It was with much difficulty that Dr. and Mrs. Tobey were able to prevail upon Mrs. Dunbar to go down to the recital. She could not understand why people wanted to meet her! So little do many of the meek souls who are really worth while, realize their importance in the world. It is a question whether Dunbar would ever have been a poet, had it not been for his mother's passion for poetry, and the prenatal influence of this love upon her child. Many times she said to her son:

"Oh, Paul, if I could have had an education I might have written poetry too." And loyal Paul would reply with love and reverence beaming from his eyes, "Well, ma, you gave me the talent, and I am writing the songs for you." Some such conversation may have been the inspiration of his lovely poem "When Malindy Sings" which he dedicated to her.

By many eloquent persuasions, that memorable Fourth of July morning, Matilda Dunbar was led to overcome her timidity and go down to the drawing-room. Had she cherished a remaining doubt as to her probable welcome there, it was instantly set at rest. Every one wanted to meet the "little black mammy" of the poet, and all gave her a hearty handshake and kindly word, and Paul's honors were divided that day with his beloved mother.

Dunbar recited many poems that morning—among them his "Ships that Pass in the Night" and of his rendition of that poem Governor Foster afterwards remarked:

"Of all things I ever heard, I never listened to anything so impressive as his rendition of the 'Ships that Pass in the Night.' "

That night, after the long, triumphant day was done, the poet sitting alone with his thoughts and his fame, poured out his soul to God in verse.   The entire poem he called " The Crisis."   The last stanza shows, as in a mirror, the honest soul of the young author—and his ardent desire to be true to his better self, and thus a saviour to his race —

" Mere human strength may stand ill-fortune's frown,
    So I prevailed, for human strength was mine :
But from the killing strength of great renown
    Naught may protect me save a strength divine.
        Help me, O Lord, in this my trembling cause,
        I scorn men's curses, but I dread applause ! "

CHAPTER VI

DUNBAR'S " MANAGER "

SOON after the appearance of Mr. Howells' article in *Harper's Weekly* (June 27, 1896), Mr. Dunbar called at the office of a friend in Toledo, who volunteered to write Mr. Howells concerning a suitable manager for the poet-reader. Mr. Dunbar accepted this offer, and a three or four page letter was written Mr. Howells. The novelist soon responded, giving the name of a gentleman who he thought would be satisfactory to Mr. Dunbar and his friends. This gentleman also received a note from Mr. Howells, and at once began correspondence with the Toledo man in regard to Dunbar. He was anxious to have the poet come to New York, and his Toledo friend wrote the prospective manager that if he would take care of the young man after his arrival in New York, his fare to that city would be forthcoming, but that the boy had no money.

Scarcely a year had elapsed since Dunbar, obscure and unread, had written his then unknown friend, Dr. Tobey, that he had " hoped year after year to be able to go to Washington, New York, Boston and Philadelphia—but that it had been denied him." He had now given a successful evening of his readings at the national capital and was about to start for New York.

The prospective " manager " wrote that he would pay his board while at the metropolis, and his Toledo friend, as good as his word, sent Dunbar a generous check for his passage and suitable clothing.

It seemed to the young man that all his good things came from Toledo, and he christened that city his "adopted home." With high hope he started eastward, and in a few days made the acquaintance of his manager.

Feeling that duty, as well as desire, demanded that he call on William Dean Howells and thank him for the great kindness he had done him, the young poet went to Far Rockaway Beach, where the novelist was spending the summer at his cottage.

With fluttering heart, Paul Dunbar approached the door and rang the bell. The maid who answered it, seeing only a very much embarrassed negro youth, was not particularly effusive, but left him standing while she carried his card to Mr. Howells. One may imagine her surprise when the novelist, hurrying to the door, caught Dunbar's hand with one of his, and throwing an arm about the young man's shoulders said:

"Come in : come in : I am so happy to see you and to meet you personally."

Mr. Dunbar arrived at Far Rockaway soon after luncheon, but Mr. Howells kept him for tea and until midnight. Of that visit he has written to the author of this biography saying : "I am glad you are writing his life, and I shall look for it with true interest. Perhaps you may like to set down that Dunbar came to see me in my cottage at Far Rockaway, and took tea with us there. I thought him one of the most refined and modest men I had ever met, and truly a gentleman.

"Yours sincerely,

"WILLIAM DEAN HOWELLS."

Mr. Howells, being a genius and consequently an artist is "color-blind" so far as intellect and good breeding are concerned, and he could not have shown a royal guest more honor or deference than he gave the negro poet.

When Dunbar was about to go, it was remarked that the night had grown chill. He had no overcoat, and Mr. Howells insisted upon putting his own coat upon his guest. The next morning, Dunbar returned the coat with a note in which he said: "In wearing your coat, I felt very much like the long-eared animal in the fable of the ass clad in the lion's skin."

Early in August, 1896, while Mr. Dunbar was still in New York, his friend, Mr. Charles Thatcher, of Toledo, met him in the metropolis. He also met Major Pond, who was about to become Mr. Dunbar's manager, and asked him what he thought of the poet. The Major replied:

"I had him come over to my house a few evenings ago, and there give a reading to about thirty invited guests. The 'white' readers are not in it with him when it comes to delighting an audience. I want to make a contract to place him on the road for a period of two years, etc."

Mr. Thatcher then learned from Mr. Dunbar that Major Pond had introduced him to several New York publishing houses, and that the manuscript for a third book of poems, which he had entitled "Lyrics of Lowly Life" had been left with Messrs. Dodd, Mead & Company.

Mr. Thatcher went to Narragansett Pier in a few days after this, telling Mr. Dunbar to be ready to go there if he received word to that effect. He carried with him to the pier a copy of "Majors and Minors." He read a number of the verses to friends who were spending the summer at the New Matthewson Hotel there, and all expressed a desire to meet the author, and to hear him recite. There were several southern people among those who made this request. A telegram was sent to Mr. Dunbar to come at once prepared to give a recital. The proprietor of the hotel donated the ballroom and the services of an orchestra for the occasion.

Dunbar never appeared to better advantage than upon that particular evening. Among other things selected for the program was his dialect poem—"The Cornstalk Fiddle." The orchestra accompanied him while he chanted the lilting lines, and when he came to the sixth stanza —

> "Salute your partners," comes the call,
> "All join hands and circle round,"
> "Grand train back," and "Balance all,"
>   Footsteps lightly spurn the ground.
> "Take your lady and balance down the middle,"
>   To the merry strains of the corn-stalk fiddle,

he acted out the various figures of the country dance described.

His lithe form, graceful as a gazelle's, glided about the stage, with a rhythm of movement which showed that his whole being responded to the music of the orchestra and to the beauty of his own conception. Every emotion depicted in the lines came out upon his face and found expression in his wonderful eyes. The audience went wild with excitement and the wine of their applause only served to stimulate his efforts. The recital was a great success, and the southern people who had been carried back to "old plantation days" by the vivid poem-pictures and skilful acting of the wonderful negro boy, were the most enthusiastic of the audience.

Before leaving Narragansett Pier, Mr. Dunbar was presented to the widow of Jefferson Davis, at her request. After a brief conversation with the young man, Mrs. Davis, who had been unable to attend the recital, asked him to give her a few readings, as a " special favor ! " So delighted was this stately daughter of the " Old Dominion " that she gave her unstinted praise and applause when he finished.   This scene is one worthy to go down in history as a signal triumph for the African race. A full-blooded negro reciting his own poems to the widow of Jeff Davis !   Great things had indeed come out of Nazareth !

Delightful events followed one another in rapid succession in those days for Paul Dunbar.   Before he went back to New York, Major Pond wrote him that Dodd, Mead & Company had accepted his manuscript, at a good price, and that if he desired they would advance him $400.00 on prospective royalties !

Resisting all temptations to spend this first large sum of money, according to his tastes, Mr. Dunbar paid it all out on debts which he felt that he owed to his friends who had " advanced " it to him.

His arrangement with the new " manager " was not so satisfactory as it had promised to be, but Mr. Dunbar feeling that he needed such discipline, decided to go ahead with it, if possible.

He and his mother, having taken up their residence in Chicago previous to his New York visit, Mr. Dunbar went there and resumed his readings.   He also wrote many newspaper and magazine articles and numerous poems while in that city.

CHAPTER VII

ENGLAND

In January of 1897, Mr. Dunbar had an offer to go to England as a public entertainer with a daughter of his former New York manager, and feeling that this might be the only opportunity he would ever have of crossing the sea, he accepted the proposition, though the terms were hard and his manager extremely mercenary. Philosophically he said: "They are going to make it hard for me, but I need the training, and I shall try to keep my upper lip well starched."

On February 8th, Mr. Dunbar sailed for England, and in a letter written his mother on shipboard, he confided:

"You will be surprised to hear that Alice Ruth Moore ran away from Boston, and came to bid me good-bye. She took everybody by storm. She was very much ashamed of having run away, but said she could not bear to have me go so far without bidding me good-bye. She is the brightest and sweetest little girl I have ever met, and I hope you will not think it is silly, but Alice and I are engaged. You know this is what I have wanted for two years."

Thus, childlike and trustful, he wrote to his mother of the happy culmination of his first and only love affair. While in England he wrote again to his mother, saying he hoped to get "Alice to set the day," as soon as he returned to America.

Although his "manager" soon deserted him, Mr. Dunbar found a warm and influential friend in the American embassador, Hon. John Hay, who arranged an entertainment at which Dunbar read several of his best poems before a number of the brightest men and women of London. Other poems, having been set to music by prominent English musicians, were sung by them at this recital.

He was a guest at a banquet given by the great Savage Club of London, where he was asked to recite, and after the first number, was lifted bodily to the table, and enthusiastically encored.

Writing of this occasion to a friend in America, Dunbar said:

"I have attended a banquet given by the great Savage Club of London. I was the guest of the secretary of the Royal Geological Society, and my host was more than gratified at the reception which I had when I was called upon to take part in the post-prandial program, as I received two requests to come back. The audience was very critical, and if they did not like a speaker would hiss him down.

"I have also been entertained at tea by Mr. and Mrs. Henry M. Stanley. I there met some very decent people, but the men, poor fellows, did not have eye-glasses enough to go around, and so each had one stuck in the corner of his eye!"

Concerning an evening's entertainment which Mr. Dunbar gave at the Southplace Institute, a London paper carried the following notice:

"A large audience at the Southplace Institute, listened yesterday to Mr. Paul Laurence Dunbar's recitations of some of his own poems, which have excited so much interest among literary men in the United States. Mr. Dunbar is thought to be the first of his race who has thorougnly interpreted the dialect, spirit and humor of the American negro, and his performance was indeed unique. The pieces selected were from his ' Lyrics of Lowly Life,' one of these, ' When Malindy Sings,' being an artistic blending of drollery and of pathos.   Another, ' Accountability,' represents the necessitarian philosophy of a stricken rogue : and a third was a pretty love-ballad. The poet made a very fine impression on all present."

Paul Dunbar was never an idler, and although he would certainly have been justified in putting in his leisure hours, tramping about the interesting streets of old London, and adding to his store of new-world knowledge a veneer of old-world mould and tradition, he conscientiously remained at his poor lodgings, and wrote his first novel.   By this act, he exhibited that desire to be provident which is so frequently lacking in members of his race. The book, written in London, was his first serious prose effort, and was entitled " The Uncalled."   It was really a history of his own life.   So few were the avenues open to an educated colored man, that it was thought only " natural" that Dunbar should turn to the ministry.   His knowledge of negro ministers gave him to know that he was thoroughly capable in an intellectual way to cope with the best.   Situated as he was, with the wolf of poverty ever growling and threatening at his door—it is greatly to the credit of the young man that he did not yield to the temptation of entering the ministry as a " means of support."   But, if Paul Dunbar was anything in those early days, he was honest.   He did not believe in eternal punishment, and he would not preach it. Realizing that he had not received the divine " call," he would not go.   His novel reflects the struggle he had—

and his final triumph. The book was dedicated to his fiancée, "Alice," who is the heroine of the story.

It is painful to chronicle that at the very moment when Dunbar's recitals were about to bring him a few of the dollars of which he stood so sorely in need, his erstwhile "manager" returned and showing a contract of which she had never consented to give the poet a copy—claimed all the proceeds!

Thus he was left penniless in a strange land. In this condition he was compelled to send home to America for funds for his return voyage. Money was cabled him, and he returned to America, poorer in purse, but considerably richer in sad and happy experiences. As he said in a letter from London:

"It amuses me to hear of the things the American papers are saying, when I am so halting over here between doubt and fear! But let come what may, I have been to England!"

As soon as Mr. Dunbar reached New York, he sold his novel to *Lippincott's Magazine*. True to his innate honesty, he pressed upon his friend who had cabled him funds, the amount he owed, though by so doing, he literally took the "bread out of his own mouth."

"The Uncalled" received favorable comment, but not being in a popular vein did not prove especially successful when issued later in book form.

Viewing his English venture as a whole, one may not describe it better than did the poet himself, upon his return to America:

"Do you know, disastrous as it was financially, I do not regret my trip. The last few weeks were a great compensation for all I suffered!"

DR. WILLIAM BURNS

The young physician who was in constant attendance upon the poet during the last three years of his life, and whose sudden death was a terrible blow to Mr. Dunbar. They had been warm friends from childhood.

COLONEL ROBERT G. INGERSOLL

Who, attracted by the merit of Mr. Dunbar's poems, expressed
a desire to "help," and who secured for him a situation
in the Congressional Library at Washington, D. C.

CHAPTER VIII

THE CONGRESSIONAL LIBRARY

THE time had now arrived for Colonel Robert G. Ingersoll to make good his promise to "help." While Mr. Dunbar was in London, he received an encouraging letter from the Colonel, advising him that he thought it likely he could secure a position for Mr. Dunbar in the Congressional Library. How well this promise was fulfilled is shown by a paragraph in the records of the Library at Washington, which reads:

" Paul Laurence Dunbar, appointed from New York to position assistant in Reading Room, Library of Congress, October 1, 1897, at a salary of $720.00 per annum: resigned December 31, 1898, to give full time to his literary work."

Mr. Daniel Murry, under whom Mr. Dunbar worked at the Library, wrote his biographer concerning the appointment as follows:

" In 1897, Mr. Dunbar was made an assistant to me that he might learn library methods and have, at the same time, one who would take an interest in his advancement. The late Colonel Robert Ingersoll was largely responsible for his taking the position, believing that it would afford him an opportunity to acquire information that could be turned to account in his literary career. . . ."

Under a dating of October 11, 1897, Dunbar said, in a letter to a friend:

"I have landed the position at Washington. It is a small one, but it means a regular income, the which I have always so much wanted. . . .

"I am home for the purpose of getting my mother ready for the Washington trip. Her health is very far from good, and I want her settled with me, as soon as possible. Must leave here Saturday night at the latest."

While Mr. Dunbar was happy to have obtained regular employment, and went to his work with his native enthusiasm, it was with real regret that he said farewell to his childhood home at Dayton. Of this leave-taking he wrote while packing —

"I am at last at home getting things ready for our removal to the east. There are a good many dear memories clustering around this rickety old house that awake to life on the thought of leaving it permanently."

In going to Washington and becoming identified with the brilliant life of the national capital, Paul Dunbar did not forget his Toledo friend, through whose influence all this happiness and good fortune reached him, and at the very beginning of his career at the Library he wrote that friend thanking him and saying:

"My dear Dr. Tobey—I shall show little of human gratitude if I fail to deserve the kindness you have shown."

It was this ever-manifest spirit of loving gratitude exhibited towards his benefactors that made them so eager and willing to do what they could to aid him. His heart, toward this particular friend, was always that of a trusting child.

Having established his mother in a pretty home, Mr. Dunbar set conscientiously to work at the Library. The exacting duties were hard for one of his temperament, but he made a brave struggle to master the detail cheerfully.

In December, 1897, he wrote an Ohio friend —

" I am working very hard these days, so if it is only for the idle that the devil runs his employment bureau, I have no need of his services."

He has spoken of this year as " his pouring time " as so many offers of positions and so many requests for poems and stories " poured in " upon him. One of the flattering offers that came to him was the tender of a professorship in Literature and Rhetoric at Claflin University, South Carolina. He did not accept this, but was pleased to know that it had been offered him. The colored people of the country were anxious that he be given work which they thought would be consistent with his brilliant attainments, and they did not think that the Library position was of any special credit to Paul Laurence Dunbar. But the poet, having " come up through great tribulation " wisely chose to stand by this post which insured him a " regular income," and afforded him such splendid opportunities for extending the scope of his knowledge.

From the first Mr. Dunbar's articles were in demand by the Washington dailies, but these contributions were, for the most part, in prose and Paul Dunbar was essentially a poet. Of the newspaper efforts he said : " The age is materialistic. Verse isn't. I must be with the age. So, I am writing prose."

This mood was not of long duration. As well try to compel the lark to ape the cackle of a chicken, as to guide Paul Dunbar's pen for long in the paths of prose. His work was very creditable, because whatever he did was

done well, but to write thus was to "plod," and he pre-
ferred, as he so gracefully said in one of his poems:

"To fling his poetical wings to the breeze, and soar in
a song, etc."

One of the notable song-poems written while he was in
the capital city was the college song composed for
Booker T. Washington's school at Tuskegee, Alabama.

Almost a decade later, this was sung by a choir of fif-
teen hundred student voices upon the occasion of the
twenty-fifth anniversary of the founding of Tuskegee In-
stitute.

The verses called "Tuskegee Song," and set to the
music of "Fair Harvard," follow:

> Tuskegee, thou pride of the swift-growing South,
>   We pay thee our homage to-day,
> For the worth of thy teaching, the joy of thy care,
>   And the good we have known 'neath thy sway.
>
> Oh, long-striving mother of diligent sons,
>   And of daughters whose strength is their pride,
> We will love thee forever, and ever shall walk
>   Thro' the oncoming years at thy side.
>
> Thy hand we have held up the difficult steeps,
>   When painful and slow was the pace,
> And onward and upward we've labored with thee
>   For the glory of God and our race.
>
> The fields smile to greet us, the forests are glad,
>   The ring of the anvil and hoe
> Have a music as thrilling and sweet as a harp
>   Which thou taught us to hear and know.
>
> Oh, Mother Tuskegee, thou shinest to-day
>   As a gem in the fairest of lands,
> Thou gavest the heaven-blessed power to see
>   The worth of our minds and our hands.

We thank thee, we bless thee, we pray for thee years
  Imploring, with grateful accord
Full fruit for thy striving, time longer to strive,
  Sweet love and true labor's reward.

The last line of the fifth stanza—"The worth of our minds and our hands" voices in a phrase the dominant note in Paul Dunbar's philosophy. First—educate the mind, then the hand. Many of his contemporaries in both races teach otherwise, believing that the negro's "hand" should first be given cunning, then his brain cultivated. Dunbar very shrewdly exclaimed upon one occasion :

"How could his hand be educated without his head to direct it ? " And again, in speaking to a young woman who had come to interview him, he said, in quick response to her exclamation :

"The head and hand must work together."

"Why do you say that ? So many people will not agree with me when I tell them that."

Thus, even in the Tuskegee song, Mr. Dunbar inculcates his theory. He fully appreciated Tuskegee, however, and its famous founder, and once wrote a very excellent tribute to Mr. Washington.

The days at the Library were the most strenuous in the life of Paul Laurence Dunbar. After his office hours were over, he would work far into the night at his writing. Before he had been in Washington six months he had written all the stories found in his prose book "Folks from Dixie," which appeared, singly, in the *Cosmopolitan* and then were collected into book form. No one can read these beautiful southern stories without realizing the sense of justice to each race which Mr. Dunbar inculcates. There are no bitter tirades against the masters : no exaggerated pen pictures of down-trodden negroes : he simply tells the truth !

This book was dedicated to Dr. H. A. Tobey, to whom in sending a first copy of the volume the poet wrote :

"I am afraid that the wish to express my gratitude to you and something of the pleasure and pride I take in our friendship has led me to take some liberties with your name. But I can only hope that you will take the dedication in the spirit in which it is offered—that of gratitude, friendship and respect for the man who has brought light to so many of my dark hours."

Having reached a place where he felt justified in such a step, he was married on March 6, 1898, to his boyhood sweetheart, Miss Alice Ruth Moore of New Orleans. Miss Moore was a young woman of great talents and beauty, and had gained no enviable position in the world of letters. Perhaps the poet's own words, quoted from a letter sent to Dr. Tobey at the time, will describe the affair better than any others could do : as it shows his childlike love and trust for his old friend, and his desire that the " doctor " be pleased.

Washington, D. C. ——, '98.

DEAR DOCTOR :

I am almost afraid to write you, but out it must come. I am married !

I would have consulted you, but the matter was very quickly done.

People, my wife's parents and others—were doing everything to separate us. She was worried and harassed until she was ill. So she telegraphed me and I went to

New York. We were married Sunday night by the
bishop (Bishop Potter of the Episcopal Church—a great
friend of the poet's) but hope to keep it secret for a while,
as she does not wish to give up her school.

Everything is clean and honorable and save for the fear
of separation there was no compulsion to the step.

I hope you will not think I have been too rash.

Sincerely yours,
PAUL L. DUNBAR.

Dr. Tobey answered this letter in a few days, and Dun-
bar again wrote him —

Washington, D. C., April 6, 1898.

MY DEAR DR. TOBEY:

I was very glad to get your letter and find that you
did not think ill of my step. I must confess I was very
anxious as to how you would take it. As to mother—I
told her before it took place—she was in the secret, though
not at first willing. All has come around all right now
and my wife will be with me on the 18th. My announce-
ment cards will then go out. Mother is quite enthusiastic
and my new mother-in-law has yielded and gracefully ac-
cepted the situation.

Aren't you saying I had better have got out of debt be-
fore taking a wife? Honest, aren't you? Well, see her
and know her and I won't need to make any plea for my-
self. Her own personality will do that.

To his biographer to whom was given the privilege of
reading letters covering a long period of years, it was
very evident that those bearing dates of his first married
years contained the only mention of real happiness that
came into his shadowed life.

The confining and exacting work at the Library, to-
gether with the dust from the books made distressing in-
roads upon the never abundant health of the poet. The

consuming thirst for knowledge and the irrepressible de-
sire to create new beauties for the art galleries of literature,
were out of proportion to his physical resources, and in
the autumn of 1898 he resigned his library position to de-
vote what strength he could spare to literary and orator-
ical effort.

While still employed at the Library, Mr. Dunbar was
called to New York to attend a meeting at which the
higher education of the negro was discussed. He was
invited to recite and did so. A gentleman from Boston,
who had gone to the meeting, intending to discourage the
higher education of the negro, immediately subscribed
one thousand dollars for a fund towards that end. Dun-
bar afterwards smilingly said to an acquaintance, when re-
lating this incident:

"Little did he know that I had never been beyond the
high schools of Dayton."

In the audience was a gentleman from Albany, who on
his return told Mrs. Merrill—a prominent society woman
of Albany, New York, that when she desired to give
another public function she could not do better than to
secure Dunbar, and before the poet left New York, a tele-
gram was sent to his Washington address by Mrs. Mer-
rill, asking terms for a recital. Up to that time $50.00
had been the amount received. His wife, appreciating
that he must be wanted badly, answered:

"One hundred dollars." The offer was accepted, and
the time fixed for the recital.

When Mr. Dunbar alighted at the Albany station, upon
the occasion of this second visit to that city, he handed
the check for his trunk to a negro porter. The man
looked at him in poorly concealed surprise and said:

"Wha' do yo' want dat trunk to go?"

Dunbar answered, "To the Kenmore Hotel."

"Yo' gwine to wuk dah?"

"No," said the poet, and started on.

Again he was addressed by the porter: "Wha' yo' want dat trunk to go?"

"To the Kenmore," said Dunbar with dignity.

The man stared at him incredulously and for the third time ventured a question: "What yo' gwine to do dah?"

Dunbar answered, "Stop."

The porter's amazement had now reached the superlative degree—but he regained his speech long enough to say:

"Well, go on!"

So did the shadow of prejudice ever fall across the path of poor Paul Dunbar. The negro porter is only a type. Having been held so long in the bonds of slavery, and having been taught from the cradle that the black man is his white brother's intellectual inferior, it is impossible for some of the race to realize the fact that there are exceptions to the rule. This truth was ever present in Dunbar's mind, and once he exclaimed bitterly:

"My position is most unfortunate. I am a black white man," and so he was.

Upon reaching the Kenmore Hotel, Mr. Dunbar was shown to a suite of rooms, consisting of sitting-room, bedroom and bath. Soon a negro waiter came to take his order for dinner, and looked at him in surprise. Then he said:

"How did you get dese rooms? Dese is de rooms dat Helen Gould occupied las' week. Guess Mis' Merrill done seed de pr'ietah." He would not have dared say

such words to a white patron, regardless of his mental
calibre, but here was one of the greatest geniuses that the
world has known, insulted because of his color, by one of
his own race! Blind, narrow, prejudiced humanity!
How small all this will look in the light of eternity!

This recital at Albany was one of the most successful
that Mr. Dunbar had ever given, and brought him in
touch with the best of Albany society, and with many of
the leading men of the state.

That Paul Dunbar made good use of the opportunities
afforded at the Library for broadening the horizon of his
mind was ever after evident. It was seldom, indeed, that
a conversation on any important theme was inaugurated
in his presence, that he was not able to join it intelligently.
He made a thorough and unbiased study of race prob-
lems, and although he was always loyal to and hopeful
for the man of pure African blood, and while he realized
the wholesome results of centuries of refinement, educa-
tion and culture in the Caucasian, he was far too loyal and
too honest not to realize that each race and every race
has its own peculiar gifts and graces. Among his papers,
found after he passed away, was a scrap on which he had
written :
"It is one of the peculiar phases of Anglo-Saxon con-
ceit to refuse to believe that every black man does not
want to be white."
When Horace J. Rollin, the pioneer exponent of the
ultimate wholesome and beneficent result of race-blending,
embodied the evolutionary theory in his notable novel,
"Yetta Ségal," Paul Dunbar, to whom the author sent a

copy of the book, wrote a most remarkable letter. It is such a revelation of the depths of research which his plummet had sounded, and is couched in such characteristically courteous, though cautious phrase, that it is given in full herewith :

Library of Congress,
Washington, D. C., July 28, '98.

MY DEAR MR. ROLLIN :

The delay which I have allowed in answering your letter so long ago received, does not denote me truly ! It is all false in indicating that I am not greatly interested in your inquiry into the psychic phenomena of race blending.

While so far I have found the observable result of race blending less strong than either of the parent races, yet, I can see how the cosmopolite of the future might be the combination of the best in all the divisions of the human family—each race supplying what all the others lacked.

Your letter has made me think, and I am glad to see such a work as yours coming from Ohio which has done too little in the scientific and literary world.

I hope your work will have the success which I really believe its importance deserves.

Thanking you for your good letter and asking your forgiveness for an unavoidable delay in answering, I am
Sincerely yours,
PAUL LAURENCE DUNBAR.

CHAPTER IX

TUSKEGEE, THE SOUTH,—BREAKING HEALTH

IN February, 1899, Mr. Dunbar went to the Tuskegee School of Booker T. Washington, and while there gave a reading in the chapel to the students and teachers. He also gave a number of lectures on English composition before the two advanced classes of the school.

The annual conference of negro farmers convened during Mr. Dunbar's visit to Tuskegee, and he reported this for the Philadelphia *Press*. A story is told of a little incident which occurred in connection with this convention. Mr. Washington is said to have gone to Mr. Dunbar's room the evening before the convention, and is quoted as having said, more in a spirit of mischief than earnest:

" Paul, I want you to write me a poem of welcome to be read to-morrow."

Dunbar, with a serious face and just the twinkle of a smile in his eyes, replied:

"All right, sir, you shall have it."

That night, Paul Dunbar burned the midnight oil, but next day when it came his turn to say a word of welcome to the members of the conference, he rose with alacrity, and stepping to the front of the stage, read a poem of such beauty and appropriateness that his audience was charmed. No congratulations were more extravagant than those of Booker T. Washington, for he alone knew that the poem was the product of the past twenty-four hours !

Mr. Dunbar made a rather extensive tour of the south before going back to Washington.

It will be remembered by the observant reader of this biography that in an early letter of Mr. Dunbar's he said that he wished to make a thorough study of his black brother in the North before seeing him in the South. It is interesting and pleasing to reflect that Mr. Dunbar was one of the rare few, who, planning their life-work from the beginning, are able to carry these plans through as originally designed.

Mr. Dunbar had certainly had ample opportunity for the study of the negro in the North before he made his itinerary of the southern states. His stories called " The Strength of Gideon," written south of Mason and Dixon's line, and published in northern magazines, and a second book, published four years later, under title of " In Old Plantation Days," shows that he did not exhaust his fund of Dixie-folk lore in the " Strength of Gideon."

Soon after Mr. Dunbar's return to Washington, in March, 1899, he received a very flattering call to come to Boston and read at the Hollis Street Theatre (at a meeting held in the interests of Tuskegee Institute). He accepted, but that his strength was unequal to the effort is shown by a letter, written to an Ohio friend from West Medford, Mass., dated March 20th, 1899:

"I am lying in bed ill and Mrs. Dunbar is kind enough to take down my letters for me.

"My readings here have been very successful, the one at the Hollis Street Theatre, Boston, having quite a triumph. But they have been a little too much for me, and I am now suffering from a cold, fatigue and a bad throat.

" I thank you for writing Mr. T.   I hope I am not too poetical to take an interest in the realities of life of which he speaks.   He may be sure I am doing what I can in my humble way for the betterment of my brother in the South."

Mr. Dunbar's fourth book of verse—" Lyrics of the Hearthside "—came out in 1899, and was very appropriately dedicated to " Alice," his wife, who was also his amanuensis, his secretary and his wise counselor.

In April of 1899, Mr. Dunbar read his poems at Lexington, Kentucky, with great success.   He then made preparations to go to Albany, where he was to have given a recital before a distinguished audience and to have been introduced by the Governor, Theodore Roosevelt.

With his doting mother and devoted wife he began the eastern journey, but when he reached New York, he was taken ill with pneumonia, and obliged to go to the home of an old friend of his own race, who lived in humble rooms on an upper floor of a shabby apartment building.

As soon as Dunbar's friends learned of his serious illness, they began sending him messages, flowers and luxuries.   They sought him out too, and called in person. Not wishing to disturb him, but being extremely anxious to know about his health, William Dean Howells went to his humble lodgings, and toiling up the stairs, inquired about him at the back door !

When he was able to hold a pen he wrote to his friends. In one of these letters he said :

" I am going to trust myself to write, though I am pretty weak yet.   .   .   .   After leaving the hospital, my doctor insists that I must go to the Adirondacks, and stay there through October, then to Colorado. They think I am a millionaire ! But there are pleasant things ! Yesterday Bishop Potter sent me two basket-loads of luxuries. To-day I received notice from the board of trustees (white) of Atlanta University (colored) that they had conferred on me the honorary degree of Master of Arts in recognition of my literary work. Of course it is an empty honor, but very pleasant."

Three weeks later Mr. and Mrs. Dunbar went to Brodhead's Bridge, New York, where they might have the mountain air and the benefit of beautiful surroundings.

Mr. Dunbar's mother spent that summer in Hampton, Virginia. Concerning this outing of his mother's the poet wrote a friend :

"Mother, I may have told you, is at Hampton, and thereby hangs a tale, which I think you can appreciate. When she first went down, the woman with whom she stopped charged her a very reasonable price. Then there was an influx of visitors, and inquiries poured in as to my health. When the landlady found out that she was the mother of the author she had read of, *she raised the board*. Sic Fama !"

Although the poet went to the Catskills for recreation and quiet, his feverish desire to work gave him no rest, and according to his own account, he wrote and had accepted in the first month he was there, one three-thousand word article, two stories and three poems, and many other things not catalogued.

E. C. Stedman wrote Mr. Dunbar asking permission to use some of his work in a new American Anthology, and this was readily given by the poet.

Many persons suffering from pulmonary troubles have found relief in the balmy air of the Catskills, but poor Paul Dunbar was so little benefited that he was compelled to take the much-dreaded journey to Colorado. Mrs. Matilda Dunbar returned from Virginia and accompanied her son and his wife on their western journey. Their first stop was at Denver, and Mr. Dunbar sent a note to Dr. Tobey, which is important in that it shows how Dunbar's fame had gone before him.

Denver, Colorado, September 12, '99.

MY DEAR DOCTOR :

Here we are, the whole " kit and bilin' " in Denver, and already I feel considerably reconciled to my fate.   I am well impressed with the town, though I have been here but a few hours.

Only one thing—or really, several things in one—have bothered me—the reporters.   They have taken the house and I have not yet had time to rest from my journey.

.   .   .   The *Denver Post* wishes to pay my expenses if I will travel slowly over the state and give occasionally my impressions of it.   They wired me at Chicago, and have sent two men to interview me since I have been there.   They claim the trips would be healthful, that my wife could go along with the best accommodations, and that I only need do what I want in the way of writing. These people are the New York *Journal* of the west !

In the early days of October, 1899, the Dunbars found a suitable home at Harmon, a small town near Denver. Mr. Dunbar described this temporary domicile as a " dainty little house, very pleasant and sunny."

From Harmon he wrote, soon after going there, to an Ohio friend, " I have an old cob of a horse, and some kind of a buggy for me to jog in as the doctor forbids much walking and entirely prohibits bicycling."

This "old cob of a horse" became so dear to the poet that he immortalized her in his dialect poem "That ol' mare of mine," for which he received a sum equal to half the price he paid for the mare.

That Mr. Dunbar realized his cure could not be permanent, but that he was determined to be patient and cheerful is manifested by a few paragraphs in a Denver letter of his:

"Well, it is something to sit down under the shadow of the Rocky Mountains even if one only goes there to die."

"Have you been reading Stevenson's letters as they run in the *Scribner's Magazine?* There was a brave fellow for you, and I always feel stronger for reading his manly lines."

He speaks in this same characteristic epistle of his health and of the doctors having examined his sputum, and says, "I too have looked upon the 'little red hair-like devils' who are eating up my lungs. So many of us are cowards when we look into the cold, white eyes of death, and I suppose I am no better or braver than the rest of humanity."

The life of Paul Laurence Dunbar while in Colorado was a long, losing fight for health. Hope and fear were alternate guests in his heart, but while his naturally optimistic spirit drank deep of the sunshine, his lungs constantly weakened by the ravages of the "little red devils" of disease—could not assimilate the beneficent qualties of the light and air.

As often as his strength would permit he recited, many of the wealthiest homes of Denver being opened to

6

him, and he also made a number of short trips to various other towns and cities.

One of the stars in Dunbar's social firmament was the friendship for him of Major William Cooke Daniels, a young merchant of Denver. The young man was passionately fond of Paul Dunbar and of his poetry. Almost every day he rode out to see Dunbar, or sent his carriage and coachman for him to come to the palatial home in the city. But, Dunbar was proud and sensitive, and although he fairly worshiped young Daniels, we find him writing an Ohio friend —

"I must tell you more about this friend of mine some time. He is just two years my senior, but was Major in Lawton's Division, and commended for bravery and efficiency. He is a fine fellow, but I am going to terminate my friendship with him. You will wonder why. Well he is immensely wealthy for his age, possessing something like two millions of dollars, and all the favors come from his side. I spend an afternoon each week with him. He has the finest private library in Denver, and he presses upon me the loan of expensive books. He wants to take me duck-shooting and provide everything. We smoke together and read and chat for hours, but the books and cigars are always his. When I was doing my new story, he actually took time from his business (the management of the finest department store here) to help me on a stampede scene. He is an enthusiast and I like him, but somehow I always feel a bit cheaper by his kindness, though I know I should not, for he is very genuine."

The friend to whom Dunbar wrote this letter wisely pointed out to him that Mr. Daniels was no doubt receiving as much as he gave, and that he doubtless prized the poet's charming society more than silver or gold.   It is therefore with satisfaction that we note the " new **novel**" —called " The Love of Landry," dedicated to " my friend Major William Cooke Daniels."   It is a Colorado novel, and shows how quickly and naturally Mr. Dunbar learned to write of the western plains and ranches.   He was a veritable mental chameleon, taking on the exact color of his surroundings, but better still, he was able to transmit his impressions to paper so vividly that the characters and scenes stand out before the reader's vision as though painted on canvas.

CHAPTER X

BACK TO WASHINGTON

IN the spring of 1900, the Dunbars went back to Washington. The Colorado trip did not accomplish for Mr. Dunbar's health what they had all hoped it might, but he returned to Washington, trusting that he should now be able to live there and make it his headquarters. Early in the summer, however, it was found necessary for him to "move on" again, and he and his wife went again to the Catskills. A rather pleasant summer was spent there, but the ravages of consumption had only been checked, and it was with a sinking heart that the gifted man returned once more to Washington.

It has seemed right to quote just here a paragraph or two from an article which appeared in the March, 1906, issue of *Talent Magazine*. This quotation will explain at last an incident of which many of Mr. Dunbar's friends read with much surprise and regret at the time of its occurrence.

While one must acknowledge, with the poet, that he made a grievous mistake, still this admission is tinged with a feeling of shame that American newspapers must needs have heralded the unfortunate affair all over the country.

The incident to which Mr. Pearson of *Talent* refers happened late in the autumn of 1900.

"It has been frequently reported in the public prints that Dunbar was a drunkard. Though it was founded on truth, it was not the whole truth. With a friend I had engaged Dunbar to give an evening of readings at Evanston, Illinois. We had thoroughly advertised the event, and a large audience from the University and the city were present to hear him. At eight o'clock, a messenger brought me word that he had broken a dinner engagement at the Woman's College, and that no word had been received from him. After an anxious delay he arrived a half hour late and with him were a nurse, a physician and his half-brother, Mr. Murphy. The first number or two could not be heard, but not until he had read one poem the second time did we suspect the true cause of his difficulty in speaking. His condition grew steadily worse, so that most of the people left in disgust. The report was passed about that he was intoxicated. The Chicago papers printed full accounts of the incident, and it was copied throughout the country.

"The following letter which has never been published, explains the situation.

"*321 Spruce St., Washington, D. C.*
"PROFESSOR P. M. PEARSON:
"DEAR SIR: Now that I am at home and settled, I feel that an explanation is due you from me. I could not see you as you asked, because I was ashamed to. My brother went, but you were gone.

"The clipping you sent is too nearly true to be answered. I had been drinking. This had partially intoxicated me. The only injustice lies in the writer's not knowing that there was a cause behind it all, beyond mere inclination. On Friday afternoon I had a severe hemorrhage. This I was fool enough to try to conceal from my family, for, as I had had one the week before, I knew they would not want me to read. Well, I was nervously anx-

ious not to disappoint you, and so I tried to bolster myself
up on stimulants.   It was the only way that I could have
stood up at all.   But I feel now that I had rather have dis-
appointed you wholly than to have disgraced myself and
made you ashamed.

"As to the program, I had utterly forgotten that there
was a printed one.   I am very sorry and ashamed, be-
cause I do not think that the cause excuses the act.

"I have cancelled all my engagements and given up
reading entirely.   They are trying to force me back to
Denver, but I am ill and discouraged, and don't care much
what happens.

"Don't think that this is an attempt at vindication.   It
is not.   Try to forgive me as far as forgiveness is possible.
"Sincerely yours,
"PAUL L. DUNBAR.

"P. S.   I have not told you that I was under the doctor's
care and in bed up until the very day I left here for Chi-
cago.   There had been a similar flow, and I came against
advice, and now I see the result.

"Such an explanation silences criticism.   But the re-
port has been widely circulated, and afterwards it was often
revived, without cause."

The winter of 1900–01 was spent with Washington as
his permanent address, but even though his health would
ill permit of it, he made a number of trips to various parts
of the country to recite.

On March 1st, 1901, Mr. Dunbar received a parchment
appointing him as aid with rank of colonel in the Inau-
gural Parade of President McKinley.   Concerning this
appointment, Mr. Dunbar said, several years later to his
biographer,—

"When the document was brought to me, I refused

positively to appear in the parade, as I did not consider myself a sufficiently good horseman.   So I sent the gentleman away with that answer, but as soon as he was out of the house, my wife and mother made siege upon me, and compelled me to run after him.   I remember the occasion well, how I ran down my front steps in house-jacket and slippers and calling to my late visitor, told him that I had changed my mind, perforce."   Mr. Dunbar appeared in the inaugural parade, three days afterwards.

A month later finds him writing from Jacksonville, Florida, to a friend in the North :

"Down here one finds my poems recited everywhere. Young men help themselves through school by speaking them, and the schools help their own funds by sending readers out with them to the winter hotels.   Very largely I am out of it.   Both my lungs and my throat are bad, and, from now on, it seems like merely a fighting race with Death.   If this is to be so, I feel like pulling my horse, and letting the white rider go in without a contest."

Fooled by the false courage that alternates with despair in the lives of tuberculosis sufferers, Dunbar spent a hopeful summer, in spite of this spring-time discouragement. He even went so far as to buy a house and establish a beautiful home in Washington.   But Fate did not intend that this darling child of Genius should enjoy for long any of the good things of life, and less than a year later, the most terrible tragedy of his life occurred.   His home was broken up, and he left Washington forever.   In such very personal and heart-touching matters it has always seemed to his biographer that the world should have no interest.   This brilliant pair, having walked for several

years together, at last came to a parting of the ways.
Neither has spoken to say why they parted there, each
going ever after alone—and, an attempt at explanation
would be unkind to the living and unjust to the dead.
One of his friends has given his biographer a letter writ-
ten under date of July 27th, 1902, which being as much
as the poet cared to reveal to a lifelong and trusted friend,
should suffice even the most curious of those interested in
the story of his life.   He writes as follows :

" You will be seriously shocked to hear that Mrs. Dun-
bar and I are now living apart, and the beautiful home I
had at Washington is a thing of the past. . . . I am
greatly discouraged and if I could do anything else, I
should give up writing.   Something within me seems to
be dead.   There is no spirit or energy left in me.   My
upper lip has taken on a droop."

This letter is written from Chicago, where Mr. Dunbar
went, accompanied by his faithful little mother, when the
crash came.

Mr. Dunbar wrote his old friend, Mr. Charles Thatcher
at Toledo, in December of 1902 —

" My plans are few but definite.   There is a mid-
winter's book of poems forthcoming— ' Lyrics of Love
and Laughter,' and an illustrated one for next fall.   An
Ohio novel is promised to *Lippincott's*, and dialect.
stories and verses to various periodicals.   Besides this I
shall possibly read in the southwest during the latter part
of January.   My appearance is robust, but my cough is
about as bad as it can be."

Thus the unquenchable ambition of Paul Laurence
Dunbar whipped the frail flesh to its labor and accom-
plished an almost unbelievable amount of work in those

two years—when his heart was broken and his spirit crushed.

His days were not all cloudy, however, the sun shone sometimes and he was almost his old self again.

A little story told his biographer by his mother, while the silent tears coursed down her cheeks, will serve to show how his hard lot was softened in at least one instance.

"I was sitting one morning," said Mrs. Dunbar, "on our front steps, when I saw a lady and a little boy approaching. Something told me that they were coming to our house. The boy carried a book, and when they came nearer I recognized it as one of my son's. Sure enough, they turned in at our steps and the lady said :

" ' Is Mr. Dunbar living here ? '

" I replied, ' Yes.'

" ' Could we get to see him ? '

"I asked them to come in, and I went to my son's room and summoned him. Paul was ill that morning, but he went down-stairs when he heard that a little boy wanted to see him. My son was very fond of children you know.

"The lady introduced herself to my son as Mrs. Ada Barton Bogg and her son, Master Harry Barton Bogg. The boy told Paul that he had come to ask him to autograph the book of poems he had just bought. Of course Paul did it, and he and the boy held a very lively conversation. As they were leaving we overheard Harry say to his mother :

" ' Why, mamma, he wasn't a bit like I thought he would be. I thought he would just sit up straight like he had a stick down his back, and never laugh at all.'

"Possibly an hour later, our door bell rang, and a box of flowers was handed in.   The box was addressed to my son and contained a great bunch of gorgeous peonies with 'the boy's' card.   My son was so delighted that he put on his hat and went down town for a vase to put the flowers in, and wrote the child a letter beside."

Out of this incident a correspondence sprang between the poet and the child, and a friendship was begun which lasted as long as Mr. Dunbar lived.   So proud was the boy's mother of these letters that at the time of the poet's death, she reproduced several of them in *Quill*, the organ of the Illinois Woman's Press Association, of which she is president.   They give one such a delightful glimpse into the child-heart of Paul Laurence Dunbar that with Mrs. Bogg's permission we have copied verbatim into this biography, the article, quoting from them.

PAUL LAURENCE DUNBAR

In the passing of Paul Laurence Dunbar we have lost a friend who was dear to us because the friendship came through his love of " the boy," and because, too, of his own sweet personality.   We shall always have with us the memory of his gentle presence, his courteous manner, his soft, musical voice, and as we turn the pages of a correspondence mostly to " the boy " our eyes are dimmed as we read.   Here is one written during his last convalescence from pneumonia, while here in Chicago : " My Dear little Friend : My peonies came with your card and I have sworn eternal friendship for you.   My passion is for flowers—and you, what have you done to me ?   Sent me off spending my hard-earned dollars to get an antique vase to put them in.   Thank you, my dear boy."

HON. FREDERICK DOUGLASS

Who gave Paul Dunbar a position in the Hayti building
at the World's Columbian Exposition, paying him out
of his own pocket, and who spoke of Dunbar as the
"most promising young colored man in America."

MASTER HARRY BARTON BOGG, Jr.

(Mr. Dunbar's favorite boy friend, with whom he corresponded
to the day of his death.)

After he went to his home, in Dayton, he often wrote "the boy," always cheerfully.   In one letter he says: " My Dear Boy: It was a little earlier than this last year when you came and brought sunshine into my sick room, and I want to celebrate that day.   From Ohio to Illinois let us say 'good luck,' and I want to hope that your cheeks are glowing to-day as brightly as the flowers you brought."

Again he writes:

My Dear Boy: I call you " dear boy " because I love the name. This will be a great secret between us.   .   .   . I wrote yesterday to your mother, but, of course, you understand that it is awfully different writing to grown-ups, and that they never see through the things that we see through—their vision has gone beyond the sight of our dearer youth.   .   .   .   I thank you exceedingly for your picture, which has cheered me unspeakably, and which I keep over on my dresser, where I can see it now and then among the medicine bottles.   Lovingly, your boy friend.

It was not long after this that Mr. Dunbar grew too weak to write, and the last letters were dictated.   In one he speaks of " the boy's " strength and vigor, adding: "He looks, oh, so healthy !   I wish I were half so well. My love to him and tell him that I should love to run my fingers through those curls on his head."

In one of his last letters he says :   " The winter has kept me continuously in bed—one may as well be in Patagonia as here.

" To-day I struggled out and got a glimpse of the sun. I see only the four walls of my room, and I welcome any change—am thankful for the rain on the window pane."

At the last a mutual friend in Dayton carried some blossoms to Mr. Dunbar for us, and afterwards wrote us : "Mrs. Dunbar (his mother) met me at the door and insisted on my seeing him.   When he was told I brought him flowers, he said at once : 'They can't be from the boy, can they?'   I told him he had guessed right, and I cannot express to you his pleasure.   I left him a very weak but happy man."

On the fly leaf of one of his books he wrote for us :

> An angel robed in spotless white
> Bent down and kissed the sleeping night ;
> Night woke to blush, the sprite was gone —
> Men saw the blush and called it Dawn.
>
> —A. B. B.

LAST DAYS OF PAUL LAURENCE DUNBAR
(Being a Series of Personal Reminiscences of the Poet)

One summer day in 1904, I was invited by the talented reader, Miss Anna Loy May, to accompany her to the home of Paul Laurence Dunbar, where she made frequent pilgrimages to recite for him the poems and sketches he loved to hear. Together we traversed the pretty street, which leads to the Dunbar home. The house is a commodious brick structure, shaded by magnificent elms, and on the lawn, at a point where the sick man's eyes could rest upon it, when he sat by a southern window, was a luxuriant bed of pansies.

As we stepped upon the piazza, Mr. Dunbar's collie dog inaugurated a rather too-friendly greeting, and in another moment, the door was opened by the poet himself, who immediately apologized for his dog by saying:

"My dog never barks at any one but poets: he is jealous for his master's reputation!" He asked me several jocular questions, and then, looking at me in a quizzical sort of way, exclaimed :

"Did you expect to find me a long-faced, sanctimonious individual of whom you would be afraid?"

"Y-es, Mr. Dunbar, I will confess it—I had formed some such opinion."

"And now you are disappointed, aren't you?" he asked laughing more like a mischievous schoolboy than a world-famous man and an invalid.

"A trifle," I replied, "but very delightfully so."

This pleased him greatly, and we began to talk of common acquaintances in both races, of art and literature and kindred themes. The "surprise" I sustained in finding Mr. Dunbar such a cheerful and optimistic person continued during our entire call.

A characteristic that appealed particularly to me was his impulsive way of showing delight when I chanced to mention the name of some one who proved to be a common friend.

After we had conversed for possibly an hour Mr. Dunbar reminded Miss May that she had not yet "read" for him. As her cultured voice gave utterance to the lines of several of his favorite selections it was interesting to study the changing expressions upon the poet's face. At one point he laughed almost boisterously, at another he was moved to tears. In every line of his fine face one could see the evidences of culture and the shining of the poetic mind.

His eyes were especially expressive, and were truly "windows of the soul." Mr. Dunbar's wit was so spontaneous, and so much a part of him that one could not be long in his society without observing the glint of a golden mirth in his glance or conversation. After Miss May had finished reading that afternoon, the poet left the room for a few moments. When he came back a half-grown black chicken perched contentedly upon his shoulder. He made no remark, but sitting down quietly, began talking again. My knowledge of the chicken as a domestic pet was limited, and my amazement at the evident fearlessness of this specimen caused me to exclaim :

"Why, Mr. Dunbar, is that a chicken ? "

"No, madame, it is a pig," replied the poet with never the ghost of a smile.

Our laughter at this rejoinder brought to the door Paul Dunbar's mother who feared the unusual excitement might bring on one of the distressing attacks of coughing which so wracked and weakened his delicate frame.

Paul Dunbar's mother! How shall I describe her? There is such a world to say about that " little black mammy" whom he so dearly loved! But the story of Paul Dunbar's last days, or any of his days, would have been impossible without frequent mention of his devoted mother. No "good angel" in human guise ever more faithfully fulfilled a heavenly mission than did she through all the weary years of her son's long illness.

Framed by the oaken panels of the doorway, Matilda Dunbar presented a wholesome and attractive picture. She is small of stature, with the same beautiful eyes which were so noticeable in her son's face, the same bright smile and cordial way, and a gentility of manner and modulation of voice which show what possibilities there are for the negro woman if she will but take advantage of them.

I shall never forget the looks of love upon his face and of pride upon hers as he introduced " my mother." Then in a tender and gentle tone she said :

" Paul, dear, I fear you are over-doing. Aren't you talking too much ? "

"No, no, ma, I'm having a most delightful time," he replied and bade her take a seat near him.

A young colored man called to take the poet to drive. His embarrassment was apparent when he found Mr. Dunbar entertaining two " white " women friends, but Dunbar greeted him most affectionately, and presented him to us as his " talented friend Mr. H., who writes beautiful verses." What a graceful and generous thing it was for the greatest poet of his race to thus bring to our knowledge immediately the fact that the new arrival possessed a talent for making verse. Too ill to go driving, he was compelled to decline his friend's hospitality, but his beautiful words of gratitude sent the young man away with a beaming face and a happy heart. It never seemed to matter to Paul Dunbar whether a man was rich or poor, black or white or yellow, if he offered him a kindness or expressed a good wish, the poet took pains to show his appreciation in as public a way as he could. He was almost wholly free from the blight of ingratitude.

Mr. Dunbar would have had us remain indefinitely, but knowing that we had already drawn over-deep upon his slender store of vitality, we literally "tore ourselves away" promising a speedy return.

A Chinese Tea Party

Our second visit to Paul Laurence Dunbar was on a gray day in October. There was a chill in the air, and a drizzle from the clouds. A cold wind, like an advance agent for winter, was feeling the pulse of the people as though to discern how they felt towards the coming show. If the world could have been judged that day, by our wishes, winter would have felt far from complimented. Knowing the tendency of the artistic temperament to be depressed when the sun is not shining, I expected to find the sick man indulging in an attack of the blues. On the contrary, as soon as he entered the room, we felt that it was flooded with sunshine. He was simply bubbling over with good cheer and fun, and we were soon oblivious to the weather.

"Now, ladies, we are going to have a Chinese tea party this afternoon, and I am to be chef," said our host.

We expressed our delight and told him how complimented we felt to have a famous man for a "chef," but he laughed heartily at this, and asked us to follow him up-stairs to "Loafingholt." This is the name he gave his den or library, and it was well chosen, for there was every inducement to laziness and rest. The entire house was artistic in its appointments, and reflected everywhere the spirit of its master, but this room—his own particular sanctum sanctorum was the most charmingly characteristic apartment of them all. The walls were lined with book-shelves, above which were hung illuminated mottoes from the works of Riley, Stevenson and others of his favorites. A framed certificate gave evidence of the fact that Mr. Dunbar was a member of the famous Pen and Pencil Club of Washington, with an office in that organization. Another frame held an autograph copy of "My Country 'tis of Thee." On the top shelf of each book case were photographs of eminent men and women of both races, among them Black Patti, who called on Mr. Dunbar when giving a concert in Dayton, and presented him with her portrait. The pictures were almost all autographed. Dainty bits of bric-à-brac showed the poet to be a connoisseur in other fields than that of literature. The books were almost all presented to him by the authors. An arts-and-crafts bookcase contained copies of his own productions, and the collection was not one of which he needed to be ashamed.

His desk showed that he had been at work, recently, and there were bits of unfinished poems strewn upon it.

A couch piled high with gay sofa pillows, afforded a

7

cozy place for the poet to rest when tired of writing or of
guests, and an Indian blanket rug in bright crimson gave
the dignified room its needed bit of vivacious coloring.
There were sleepy-hollow chairs and other "loafing"
places in the room, and altogether it was very appropri-
ately named.

In a corner near the door, was a handsome tabourette
upon which was disposed the tea service.   Such a pretty
service it was with its foreign-looking sugar bowl and
cream pitcher and its squatty little tea-pot, with the Jap-
anese cups so delicate and thin that one could almost
"see through them."

While we admired his books and his pictures or en-
gaged in merry conversation, Mr. Dunbar made the tea
over his alcohol lamp—and presently approached me with
a cup of the fragrant brew.

"This is genuine Chinese tea, ladies," he remarked.
"It was brought to me by a friend direct from the Celes-
tial Kingdom."

He then offered us sugar and cream.   I added sugar to
my tea, and immediately regretted it, for he said in mock
horror :

"There, now! you've spoiled it—the idea of Chinese tea
with sugar in it."

I acknowledged my ignorance, and asked him why he
offered me sugar for "Chinese tea."

"Just to see if you knew," laughed Mr. Dunbar with a
wickedly mischievous smile.

Over the tea-cups there was interesting talk, interesting
because one could not converse many moments with Paul
Laurence Dunbar without hearing something entertaining
or profitable.   He liked to say things to make one

"think," as he once expressed it, and he usually suc-
ceeded.   He seemed to be alive to all the vital problems
of the age, and to have decided opinions upon each and
every one.   He was exceedingly witty and often said
brilliantly funny things at most unexpected moments.

He was greatly gratified to learn that I had committed
several of his language poems to memory and that I pre-
ferred these to his dialect verses.   The fact that the world
at large, passing over his great productions in classic
English, blindly "turned to praise a jingle in a broken
tongue," was one of the real griefs that sapped his life and
energy.   "I am tired, so tired of dialect," he said.   "I
send out graceful little poems, suited for any of the maga-
zines, but they are returned to me by editors who say,
'We would be very glad to have a dialect poem, Mr.
Dunbar, but we do not care for the language composi-
tions.'   I have about decided to write under a nom de
plume, and I have chosen a beautiful name."   We asked
him to satisfy feminine curiosity by telling us the name,
but he refused to do so, saying he was determined to
"fool the editors."   He then told us laughingly of a
"bright young lady" who wrote to him criticising him
for using various kinds of negro dialect in one volume.
"Just think of it! a literary critic and yet doesn't know
that there are as many variations of the negro dialect as
there are states in the Union!   For instance an Alabama
negro does not speak any more like a Virginia colored
man than a Yankee talks like a man from Colorado."
Thus again and again he proved how thoroughly he had
studied his race, north and south, east and west, and how
well equipped he was when he went to his task of writing
dialect poems.   He gave the world the first idealized

negro verse, and he gave the white race and all races to know that there is more real sentiment and artistic feeling in the negro brain than was ever dreamed of in the philosophy of the average Caucasian Horatio. He remarked early in life that he hoped to prove that his race was human as well as African, and he did much more—he proved that they were artistic as well as humbly useful.

After we had finished our tea, Mr. Dunbar was disposed to continue our talk indefinitely, but his strength was scarcely sufficient for such a long strain, and soon his mother called one of us outside for a moment and said :

"I beg your pardon, ladies, but I expect you had better leave my son now as he may have a severe attack of coughing. Don't tell him I told you, for he will fear that it may offend you."

We soon therefore begged another engagement, and left him, though he urged us to stay. Our conduct after we left him was not consistent with our protestations that we could not stay another moment, for we lingered below stairs to talk with his mother. We were startled to hear Mr. Dunbar call :

"Miss May, oh, Miss May, come to the stairs a moment." She obeyed, and in a stage whisper he said : "You ladies had better not talk to mother, she may get to coughing." He had evidently overheard her warning to us, and was retaliating.

Thus his love of fun and his inexhaustible wit, served to send us away with a smile and a hope that perhaps after all his life would be spared for many years to come. It was always difficult, when talking with him, to realize that his days were numbered and that the seal of Death was set upon him.

AN IMPROMPTU MUSICALE

Among the things that were dear to the heart of Paul Laurence Dunbar was music—vocal or instrumental—he loved it, and he was, in his prime, no mean performer on the violin.

One afternoon I went to see him on a matter of business, but ere I had been there long, he told me that I was "in luck," for there was to be a musicale in half an hour. Soon his guests began to arrive. Among them were prominent persons of both races. Mr. Dunbar sat on a couch smiling and chatting with every one,—the gayest of the throng. One of the colored women began the program by singing several of Mr. Dunbar's favorite songs. One of these was "Lead Kindly Light." This was a great favorite of the poet's, and he once wrote a companion-piece to it which by many is thought to be as beautiful as the original poem. His poem is called a Hymn, and is really his own prayer to God for help in his illness. The last stanza is especially beautiful:

> "Lead gently, Lord, and slow,
> For fear that I may fall:
> I know not where to go
> Unless I hear thy call.
> My fainting soul doth yearn
> For thy green hills afar —
> So let thy mercy burn —
> My greater, guiding star!"

The young woman who sang for us that afternoon was wholly African, and her voice was typical of the race. Well may the negro be proud of his musical ability. Seldom indeed have I heard a soloist of any race whose tones could equal those that delighted us that day. The

poet's very soul came into his expressive eyes as he lis-
tened.   No applause was more earnest and no encore
more sincere than his, as he asked for more and more.

After the music a young woman of the party read sev-
eral of her poems at Mr. Dunbar's request.   His praise
was very delicate and intelligent, and showed the poet's
desire to accentuate the gifts of others.

After the program Mr. Dunbar fell to talking of Theo-
dore Roosevelt, of whom he spoke as one of his dearest
friends.   He asked his mother to bring him his " Christ-
mas present, and when Mrs. Dunbar returned she brought
with her two volumes, and Mr. Dunbar handed them
around saying, " See ! I'm all 'puffed up' over these."
The books were two of the works of the President, in-
scribed as follows :

" To Paul Laurence Dunbar from Theodore Roosevelt,
Christmas, 1903."

He then told of the poem he had sent Mr. Roosevelt at
the time of his second campaign, and of the President's
complimentary letter concerning it.   All were enthusiastic
and wanted to hear the poem.   So, after much persuasion,
Mr. Dunbar read for us the lines :

" There's a mighty sound a comin',
  From the East and there's a hummin'
    And a bummin' from the bosom of the West,
  While the North has given tongue,
  And the South will be among
    Those who holler that our Roosevelt is best.

" We have heard of him in battle
  And amid the roar and rattle
    When the foemen fled like cattle to their stalls :
  We have seen him staunch and grim
  When the only battle hymn
    Was the shrieking of the Spanish Mauser balls.

" Product of a worthy sireing,
  Fearless, honest, brave, untiring —
    In the forefront of the firing, there he stands:
  And we're not afraid to show
  That we all revere him so,
    To dissentients of our own and other lands.

"Now, the fight is on in earnest,
  And we care not if the sternest
    Of encounters try our valor or the quality of him,
  For they're few who stoop to fear
  As the glorious day draws near,
    For you'll find him hell to handle when he gets in fightin' trim."

Ill as he then was and weakened by the ravages of the disease that was killing him, one's imagination could readily picture what he must have been in his prime. His eyes flashed, and there was a sparkle in them that told how much he enjoyed giving a proper interpretation to his own poems.

Before I left him that afternoon, he took occasion to tell me that he was to have his " class " that night, and that he must rest a bit before the pupils came. I asked in amazement what class he meant, and he said, with an enthusiasm which left no doubt as to his heart-interest in the work:

" Why my class in spelling and reading. Some people think our people should be nurses and boot-blacks, but I am determined that they shall not make menials out of all of us." This class he taught for weeks, giving literally of his very life for the betterment of his race.

AN " INTERVIEW "

The fourth time I went to the Dunbar home, I had a

commission from a magazine to interview him. As the lower rooms were filled with callers, he took me up to "Loafingholt." He bade me take an easy chair, assuring me that my "job" would be very difficult, and then sat down opposite with the air of a martyr about to be tied to the stake. This was somewhat disconcerting, and I must have looked my embarrassment for he soon began talking naturally of his health and the pretty view from his window, etc., until I was quite at my ease and able to "ask questions."

Presently I said, "Mr. Dunbar, tell me what is your real reason for writing? Do you write for fame, for money or just for the pleasure of creating art?"

"I? why do I write?" he asked as though surprised at the query . "Why, I write just because I love it."

Knowing that the majority of his race are noted for their superstitions, and having a curiosity to learn whether education and refinement would eradicate the racial trait, I asked him a leading question.

"Well, I don't know," he ejaculated, with a far away look in his eyes. "Some people would laugh, I suppose, but things really do 'happen' sometimes which are strange to say the least."

"Yes?" I encouraged.

"Well, once when I was a small boy, just at the age when I thought I knew more than my mother—a queer thing occurred. The flowers in our front yard all came out in bloom in the dead of winter. Our neighbors' plants did not bloom and ——"

"Did anything come of it?" I found myself breathlessly asking.

"Wait a moment," he said, "something else happened

too—a pair of horses hitched to a hearse ran off and stopped before our gate."

" Were you frightened ? " I asked.

" Not I—I was too ' wise ' you know, but my mother was terribly worried. We had an old gentleman with us then, and, if you will believe me—he took ill and died in two weeks. Even since then I have believed in the truth of the old nursery rhyme —

> " ' Flowers out of season,
> Trouble without reason ! ' "

He recounted other instances which had come under his observation of the couplet's having " come true," speaking in a saddened tone of his having found a violet blossoming under his library window on All Saints' Day. This incident inspired three of his best known poems. The first he called " To a Violet Found on All-Saints' Day." The others are " Weltschmertz," and " The Monk's Walk," published in " Lyrics of Love and Laughter." " That was indeed a flower ' blooming out of season,' and I never had much real happiness after that," he said. I knew that he was thinking of his unhappy married life for the incident occurred in Washington.

Since then I have had more respect for so-called " superstitions " and if the wholly practical must call these things mere coincidences, to some of us they can but seem a trifle more.

Mr. Dunbar patiently answered my other questions, and I left him, feeling how kind he was and how considerate, how lavish of his needed strength, and how generous of himself.

Poems "While You Wait"

Doubtless there are hundreds of instances, memory-cherished by his friends, of Mr. Dunbar's having produced impromptu verses of remarkable cleverness and beauty. One or two of these I will recount, merely as examples of his ability to work under high pressure—a gift as rare as it is unusual.

Having business in Dayton, I had not intended going out to see Mr. Dunbar, but as was my custom, I called him by telephone. As soon as he recognized my voice, he said :

" I am feeling fine to-day, and you must come out before leaving town. I shall have something for you when you get here ! "

He did not give me the slightest hint as to what the " something " would be, but I went out to see him.

When I reached the house his mother admitted me, and Mr. Dunbar called from the parlor, where he sat curled up on a couch, for all the world like a small boy.

" Just wait a moment, I'm hunting for a rhyme."

Mrs. Dunbar and I had conversed but a few minutes when we heard him say exultantly :

" Ah, that's it—good ! " and the next instant he was with us, smiling and bowing to me, and holding towards me a scrap of paper on which he had written in his own delicate hand (a feat by no means common on those latter days) the following :

To a Poet and a Lady

You sing, and the gift of a State's applause
Is yours for the rune that is ringing,
But tell me truly is that the cause ?
Don't you sing for the love of singing ?

You think you are working for wealth and for fame,
But ah, you are not and you know it,
For Wife is the sweetest and loveliest name,
And every good wife is a poet !

These lines, written to please me, and not meant for a public reading, nevertheless contain, as did everything he wrote, a grain of helpful truth, and a delicate suggestion of the poet's love for the home and its mistress. He did not prostitute his talent, but even when the occasion was of a trivial character, he conscientiously gave his story a new dignity in the telling.

Mr. Dunbar was ever grateful for kindnesses shown him and took occasion to remark that day :

" My stenographer is not here to-day, or she would type the verses for you."

" Why, have you a secretary Mr. Dunbar ? "

" Yes, the loveliest young woman in the world comes almost every day and does my writing for me, and she does it gratis—will not think of accepting compensation." His face fairly beamed as he said it, and one could not help seeing how he appreciated this service from a young woman of his sister race. Could he but have heard what she said to me after he died, he would have understood why she came day after day to write for him—" I never knew the beauty and breadth of life until I knew Paul Laurence Dunbar," said the young woman with moist eyes, " and I can never tell you what those days spent in his society meant to me." She then told me of his having composed aloud his last poem—" Sling Along " while she wrote it down in shorthand. It was with great difficulty that he talked that day, because of the frequent spells of coughing that attacked him, but one can see that even then he was possessed with a spirit of fun and happy humor.   The lines which have not yet appeared in print are as follows :

Sling Along.

Sling along, sling along, sling along,
     De moon done riz,
     Dem eyes o' his
     Done sighted you
     Where you stopped to woo.
Sling along, sling along,
     It ain't no use fu' to try to hide,
     De moonbeam allus at yo' side,
     He hang f'om de fence, he drap f'om de limb,
     Dey ain't no use bein' skeered o' him,
Sling along, sling along.

Sling along, sling along, sling along,
     De brook hit flow,
     Fu' to let you know,
     Dat he saw dat kiss,
     An' he know yo' bliss.
Sling along, sling along.
     He run by yo' side,
     An' he say howdydo,
     He ain't gine to tell but his eye is on you,
     You can lay all yo' troubles on de highest shelf
     Fu' de little ol' brook's jes talkin' to his se'f,
Sling along, sling along.

Sling along, sling along, sling along,
     De' possum grin,
     But he run lak sin,
     He know love's sweet,
     But he prize his meat,
Sling along, sling along.
     He know you'd stop fu' to hunt his hide,
     If you los' a kiss and a hug beside,
     But de feas' will come and de folks will eat,
     When she tek yo' han' at de altah sea,
Sling along, sling along.

The Dunbar house, at 219 North Summit Street, Dayton, Ohio, where Mr. Dunbar's last days were spent, and where he died. His mother still resides in this house, which he bequeathed to her.

Mr. Dunbar's desk and his arts and crafts bookcase, which contained copies of his own books, and autograph copies of the works of many of his contemporaries.

Another instance of his wonderful skill in writing from inspiration, is the story of his " Rain Songs."

The day was dark and the rain fell drearily outside his window.   Only a poet's mind could have conceived anything beautiful in such a prospect.   A young man friend was with him.   Suddenly Mr. Dunbar, gazing intently out at the vision in the rain, said to his companion :

" Did you ever think of the rain's looking like harp-strings ? "

" No "—said the young man, " I cannot say that I ever did."

" Well—how does this sound ? " and the poet is described as having repeated the words slowly, as though saying them after some one whose voice, audible to him, could not be heard by his companion —

> " The rain streams down like harp-strings from the sky,
> The wind, that world-old harper sitteth by,
> And ever, as he sings his low refrain,
> He plays upon the harp-strings of the rain."

DUNBAR'S LAST BIRTHDAY

Feeling that the poet's days on earth were swiftly passing by, and that perchance this (June 27th, 1905) would be (as it proved) his last birthday, a number of his friends in Dayton, planned a surprise for him.

It being a beautiful afternoon, Mr. Dunbar's physician gave him permission to go driving with a friend who, quite innocently, of course, called with a carriage.

In the poet's absence his friends took possession of his home and made it ready for the " party."   His chair, at the head of the table, was festooned in royal purple, and his favorite flowers were everywhere in evidence.   A great birthday cake and dainty viands made an ideal supper table.

Upon his return from the drive, Mr. Dunbar came slowly up the steps and across the veranda. When he opened the door, he was met by a perfect avalanche of congratulations! Taken wholly unaware, he was for a moment unable to speak, but, with something of his old spirit, he entered into the affair, and was soon the gayest of them all.

At supper there were clever speeches and happy repartee. One of the toasts was given by Dr. William Burns, Mr. Dunbar's dearest friend among his own people.

This brilliant young physician was Mr. Dunbar's constant attendant for the last three years of his life, going with him whenever he ventured from home to recite, and caring for him always as tenderly as a brother. He was a man of sterling worth and beautiful personality, and it is small wonder that the poet loved him almost to idolatry. Special mention is thus made because in the following November the young physician was struck down in the very height of his professional successes and passed into the Mystery four months before his famous friend and patient. The passing of Dr. Burns has been thought by many to have hastened the end of Paul Laurence Dunbar, and, ill as he was, at the time his physician died, he insisted on being taken in a carriage to his lodgings. Witnesses say that Mr. Dunbar took the hand of Dr. Burns, and talked to him just as though he were still there in spirit as well as flesh. He was driven back to his home, but always refused to admit that " Bud," as he called the doctor, was dead. His mind weakened by disease and sorrow, could not grasp this last dreadful tragedy.

No gloomy forebodings, however, dimmed the happiness of the birthday supper, and the picture presented by that festal board is one worthy the brush of a master, because it was a revelation and a prophecy.   Sitting side by side at the poet's table were young people of both the black and white races.   Each face was of an exceptionally fine intellectual mould—each individual was an artist in his line.   An Episcopal clergyman of the Negro race, touched elbows with a beautiful young business woman, a representative of Dayton's " Four Hundred " met on an equal intellectual footing the cultured young physician, whose skin alone was black.

The sight must have been gratifying to the mind of Paul Laurence Dunbar, for he could but have seen in this happy mingling of intellectual negroes and broad-minded whites an omen for the future of his race.   His own personality had much to do with the matter, but if the race has produced one genius like Paul Dunbar, it can produce others, and therein lies its hope of final recognition.

A short time after his birthday party, Mr. Dunbar was visited by a delegation from the Ohio Federation of Colored Woman's Clubs, meeting in Dayton, and enjoyed exceedingly making the acquaintance of women of his own race who were interested in the higher education.

During this convention, Mrs Mary Church Terrell, a Washington friend of Mr. Dunbar's, and a woman who has gained an enviable reputation in the world of letters was a house-guest at the Dunbar home.   Writing of this visit in the April, 1906, issue of the *Voice of the Negro*, Mrs. Terrell pays so beautiful a tribute to Mr. Dunbar that a portion of it is given herewith.   It shows that Mr. Dunbar was appreciated by the more intellectual members of his own race as well as by those of the sister races.

Mrs. Terrell says:

"During the few days spent with Mr. Dunbar last summer I discovered there were depths in his character that I had never sounded and qualities of heart of which I had never dreamed, although I saw him frequently when he lived in Washington.

"Owen Meredith says that

"'The heart of a man is like that delicate weed
Which requires to be trampled on, boldly indeed
Ere it gives forth the fragrance you wish to extract.
'Tis a simile, trust me, if not new, exact.'

"Whether affliction and sorrow always bring out the best there is in a man, I cannot say. I do know, however, that the physical and mental pain which Paul Laurence Dunbar endured for a year before he passed away, developed the highest and noblest qualities in him. When I saw Paul Dunbar last summer, he was shut in, wasted and worn by disease, coughing his young and precious life away, yet full of cheer, when not actually racked with pain, and perfectly resigned to fate. I shall always think of his patience under his severe affliction as a veritable miracle of modern times. In the flush of early manhood, full of promise of still greater literary achievement in the future than he had been able to attain in the past, fond of life as the young should be and usually are, there he sat, rapidly losing his physical strength every hour, and yet, miracle of miracles, no bitter complaint of his cruel fate did I hear escape his lips a single time. The weakness and inertia of his worn and wasted body contrasted sadly and strangely with the strength and activity of his vigorous mind.   As I looked at him, pity for the afflicted man himself and pity for the race to which he belonged and which I knew would soon sustain such an irreparable loss in his death almost overcame me more than once.   As incredible as it may appear, his moods were often sunny and then it was delightful to hear the flood of merriment roll cheerily from his lips.   .   .   .

"It was gratifying to see the homage paid Mr. Dunbar by some of the most cultured and some of the wealthiest people of the dominant race in Dayton.   .   .   .

"On one occasion after some beautiful girls who had called to pay their respects to Mr. Dunbar, had gone, in a nervous effort to relieve the tension of my own feelings, I turned to him and said :

"'Sometimes I am tempted to believe you are not half so ill as you pretend to be.   I believe you are just playing the role of interesting invalid, so as to receive the sympathy and homage of these beautiful girls.'

"'Sometimes I think I am just loafing myself,' he laughingly replied.   How well he remembered this was shown a short while after I returned home.   He sent me a copy of his 'Lyrics of Sunshine and Shadow,' which at that time was his latest book.   On the fly leaf he had written with his own hand, a feat which during the first year of his illness he was often unable to perform, the following lines :

> "Look hyeah, Molly,
>   Ain't it jolly,
> Jes' a loafin' 'oun' ?
>   Tell the Jedge
>   Not to hedge
> For I am still in town.

8

"Whether Paul Dunbar will be rated a great poet or not, no human being can tell. It is impossible for his contemporaries either to get a proper perspective of his achievement or to actually guage his genius. Personally I believe he will occupy as high a place in American literature as Burns does in the British, if not higher.

"But whether Paul Dunbar will be rated great or not, it is certain that he has rendered an invaluable service to his race. Because he has lived and wrought, the race to which he belonged has been lifted to a higher plane. Each and every person in the United States remotely identified with his race is held in higher esteem because of the ability which Paul Dunbar possessed and the success he undoubtedly attained.

"Indeed the whole civilized world has greater respect for that race which some have the ignorance to underestimate and others the hardihood to despise, because this black man, through whose veins not a drop of Caucasian blood was known to flow, has given such a splendid and striking proof of its capacity for high intellectual achievement."

MY LAST VISIT TO PAUL LAURENCE DUNBAR

The austere face of a winter sun was hidden behind a veil of forbidding gray, and the earth and sky were monk-garbed and sombre-eyed that last day that I saw Dunbar.

His bed had been brought down-stairs, so that his mother could be near him as she performed her household duties, and as he lay there among the pillows one could see how weak he was, how wasted and how frail. But, as I entered the room, approached his bed and took his hand, his smile was just as bright and his words were just as brave as they had been in the earlier days of our acquaintance. There was the customary badinage, the never-failing inquiry as to why I had not been to see him for so long, and the pathetic enthusiasm over the world-interests which for him were so soon to be as naught.

By and by he was permitted to sit in his chair by the window, and to me it seemed as a throne, where all the lovers of art should fall down and worship. But ah what a weak king he was, how like a little child! Yet his great eyes were still bright, and his heart aglow with the flame that warmed it to the last.

Presently as he sat there he said to his mother who was passing through the room —

"Ma, I never did get to see my flowers that came this morning."

"Well, Paul, I have them in the parlor, where it is cold, so that they will keep till Sunday!"

"Oh, I forgot," he said with a sigh, "that the flowers cannot live in a room that is warm enough for me!"

In a few moments Mrs. Dunbar brought in a vase, filled with gorgeous American Beauty roses, and I placed them on a little stool at his feet, where he could look at them for a while.

Oh, how he gazed at those flowers! so wistfully, as though he envied them their glorious beauty and perfect development—so tenderly, as though each rose had a human heart and an ache in it—so reverently, as though the vase were a shrine and he an ardent devotee!

Then with moist eyes and a heart-breaking smile he said, turning to his mother —

"Take them away, ma, so they may 'keep for Sunday.'"

He then fell to talking of Wilberforce—the African missionary of whom the papers were saying such dreadful things at the time, claiming that he had gone back to savagery and cannibalism.

"It is an outrage! Oh, how I wish I were able to do something to correct those stories. They are absolutely false, and it is such an awful blow to the race!"

He spoke feelingly of the missionary who had been educated by the United Brethren church,—and one could see how he chafed under the weakness that chained him down when he longed so to go forth and do battle for his race.

That same day we chanced to speak of Alice and Phœbe Cary. I told him of several visits I had made their brother at the old home near College Hill, Ohio, and of my having found in a history of the family a mention of the coat of arms, won by a remote Cary on English battle-fields. When I quoted the Latin legend, and gave him my version of the translation he thought I had it wrong, and was not satisfied till I went up to his library and found his Latin grammar. I shall never forget how eagerly he scanned the well-worn text-book, though his hand trembled so he could scarcely hold the volume. It was pitiful indeed to see him thus employed, when one knew how soon he must lay forever aside his precious books and leave them all behind.

That was the last time I saw him alive. Two months later, a message came over my telephone: "Paul Dunbar is dead."

It was with a strange mixture of feelings that I started

HON. BRAND WHITLOCK, Mayor of Toledo

Who counted Dunbar as one of his dear friends, and who when
asked for a word for this biography said: "Say that his picture
hangs on my library wall with that of Walt Whitman, Thoreau
and others of my favorites."

A corner in "Loafingholt," Mr. Dunbar's library, where he was fond of entertaining his friends and serving tea.

once more for Dayton—on the day of Mr. Dunbar's funeral.

Down town I bought a few flowers and was about to go in search of a messenger to take them out to the Dunbar home, when I noticed a colored man with another florist's box, addressed in large letters: "For Paul Laurence Dunbar." The man was waiting for a car, and approaching him I said: "Will you take my flowers too?"

"Yes, ma'am," he replied, and I could not but see that his eyes were full of tears.

Handing him a bit of silver I said, "Here is your fee." I have never had any one look at me so reproachfully as did that poor colored man that day —

"Money? No, indeed. It is all I can do for poor Paul now."

Later I called at the Summit Street home, and saw him, for the first time, wholly at rest and free from pain.

His Death and Burial

On February 9th, 1906, it became apparent, early in the afternoon, that Mr. Dunbar's end was fast approaching. A physician and then a minister came. Thrice the poet asked the time, and whether it was day or night. Then the minister read the Twenty-third Psalm, which had always been Mr. Dunbar's favorite portion of Scripture. The dying man lay quietly listening. When the reader ceased, Dunbar, in a fast-failing voice, began to repeat the psalm for himself, and when he came to the words —

"When I walk through the valley of the shadow —"

God must indeed have been "with him," for it was then that he fell asleep.

After all his shortcomings, his weaknesses and his mistakes, he found at the last the peace that his life had never known.

On the afternoon of February 12th at the Eaker Street A. M. E. Church in Dayton, the funeral services were held. On the church records of this little sanctuary, the name of Paul Laurence Dunbar had been written in his own hand in childhood days, and it had never been erased. His mother, therefore, thought it appropriate and right to have his burial service there. So many were the flowers sent that they not only banked the little pulpit and clustered about the casket, but beautiful bouquets were distributed about the house. Eloquent tributes were paid the dead poet by the pastor of the church, Professor Scarborough of Wilberforce University, and other clergymen of both races, but it seemed to me that the most touching of them all was the address of his loyal friend, Dr. H. A. Tobey, of Toledo. Among other things Dr. Tobey said: "I never loved a man so much. 'Golden Rule Jones, Brand Whitlock and myself were three great cronies, because we were three ' cranks,' I suppose, but we took Paul in and made him one of us."

He spoke of Mr. Dunbar's distinguished friends, referring particularly to Mr. William Dean Howells and Colonel Robert G. Ingersoll, paying Mr. Ingersoll a very high compliment on his own account. Dr. Tobey then read a letter, written him by Mr. Brand Whitlock, Mayor of Toledo, who was prevented from attending the obsequies by reason of the critical illness of his aged mother. The letter, revealing as it does, the love of another author for Mr. Dunbar, and the high place he held in Mr. Whitlock's esteem, is given verbatim:

629 Winthrop Street, Toledo, Ohio,
11 February, 1906.

DEAR DOCTOR TOBEY:

I wish I could be with you all to-morrow to pay my tribute to poor Paul. But I cannot, and feeling as I do his loss, I cannot now attempt any estimate of his wonderful personality that would be at all worthy. If friendship knew obligation, I would acknowledge my debt to you for the boon of knowing Paul Dunbar. It is one of the countless good deeds to your credit that you were among the first to recognize the poet in him and help him to a larger and freer life.

For Paul was a poet: and I find that when I have said that I have said the greatest and most splendid thing that can be said about a man. Men call this or that man great and load him with what the world holds to be honors— its soldiers and its statesmen, its scholars and its scientists. This may all be very well, but I think we know that after all the soldiers and the statesmen and the savants are not concerned with the practical things of life, the things that are really worth while. Nature, who knows so much better than man about everything, cares nothing at all for the little distinctions, and when she elects one of her children for her most important work, bestows on him the rich gift of poesy, and assigns him a post in the greatest of the arts, she invariably seizes the opportunity to show her contempt of rank and title and race and land and creed. She took Burns from a plow and Paul from an elevator, and Paul has done for his own people what Burns did for the peasants of Scotland—he has expressed them in their own way and in their own words. There are many analogies between these two poets, just as there are many analogies between Paul and Shelley and Keats and Byron and Pushkin. They all died very young, they knew little of the joys that are common to common men, but they had their griefs, their sorrows, their sufferings, far beyond the common lot. But the terms on which Nature lets her darlings become poets are always obdurate. To the poet, as Whitman says, agonies must become as changes of garment, he must suffer all things, hope all things, endure all things, and knowledge is not otherwise obtained. He must go through torments and pain, he must feel the dreadful hunger of the soul, and usually he must die young—all for the sake of being a poet. And that is enough for him after all, for if the common joys and satisfactions—rest and peace and home and all that—are denied him,. he has the joy of artistic creation, which is the highest man may know. It is enough for the poet that he is a poet, yet this is not his glory. His glory is that through this experience he expresses for the race all joy and grief, all the moods and emotions, exalted or depressed, of the human soul, and myriads of voiceless people, living about him and living after him, find the solace and relief that come of expression which, were it not for him, they would be compelled to go without and suffer dumbly.

I have spoken of our friend as a poet of his own people and this he was : he expressed his own race—its humor, its kindliness, its fancy, its love of grace and melody : he expressed, too, its great sufferings, and what race has suffered more, or more unjustly, or what race has borne its sufferings with sublimer patience? It is a race that has produced many great and worthy men, in the very face of untold opposition and prejudice, but the work of these men has been more or less confined to their race. But without the least disparagement, I think I can say that Paul's range and appeal were wider than those of any other of his race : if they had not been he would not have been a poet. For the true poet is universal as is the love he incarnates in himself, and Paul's best poetry has this quality of universality.

I am very glad that he was so thoroughly American and democratic. He might have been a poet without having been an American, but he could not have been a poet without having been democratic, and I believe I may safely add that he could not have been a poet without

having had at least the spirit of America.   For all poets
have had this spirit : they have loved liberty, equality
and fraternity.   You know Browning says :

> Shakespeare was of us, Milton was for us,
> Burns, Shelley were with us—they watch from their graves.

There was nothing foreign in Paul's poetry, nothing
imported, nothing imitated : it was all original, native and
indigenous. Thus he becomes the poet not of his own
race alone—I wish I could make people see this—but the
poet of you and of me and of all men everywhere.

You and I know something of his deeper sufferings,
something of the disease that really killed him.   I can
never forget the things he said about this that last even-
ing we spent together.   I know nothing anywhere so
pathetic as this brave, gentle, loving spirit with its poet's
heart, moving among men, who, though far his inferior
in intellectual and spiritual endowment, yet claimed to
be—but I must not recall such things now.   The deep
melancholy this caused him has been expressed over and
over in his poems.   "The Warrior's Prayer," "We wear
the Mask," and others are veritably steeped in it.   Let
that suffice.

That last evening he recited—oh, what a voice he
had !—his "Ships that Pass in the Night."   You will re-
member.   I sat and listened sadly conscious that I would
not hear him often again, knowing that voice would soon
be mute.   I can hear him now and see the expression on
his fine face as he said "Passing ! Passing !"   It was pro-
phetic.

We shall hear that deep, melodious voice no more : his
humor, his drollery, his exquisite mimicry—these are
gone.   And to-morrow you will lay his tired body away,
fittingly enough, on Lincoln's birthday.   But his songs
will live and give his beautiful personality an immortality
in this world, and we—we can remember that he is with
Theocritus to-night.   Yours very sincerely,

BRAND WHITLOCK.

Dr. Davis W. Clark, of the Methodist Episcopal Church, one of the most scholarly men of that communion, offered the final prayer at Mr. Dunbar's funeral. Dr. Clark was so impressed by the occasion that he soon after set about securing funds for a monument to the poet's memory. Speaking of the event a few weeks afterwards Dr. Clark said:

"When I saw him lying there in his casket, he seemed to me a prince."

The remains of Paul Laurence Dunbar were placed in the vault at the beautiful Woodland Cemetery in Dayton, and two months later, he was buried. The site of his grave is well chosen, being at the summit of a little hill, and in selecting it his mother endeavored to follow as nearly as might be, the wishes voiced by her son in his "Death Song." She will plant a willow near the mound, so that by and by he will be lying "neaf de willers in de grass." He is near also to "de noises in de road," for the grave is in view of one of the entrances to the cemetery. . . .

Summing it all up, this short, feverish, brilliant life—an honest observer can but agree with the poet's best beloved friend Dr. Tobey, who when a sympathetic admirer of Mr. Dunbar's said: "It is such a pity he had to die,"—exclaimed:

"No, thank God, I'm glad he's gone—this world was too sad a place for him."

PART II

The Poems of Paul Laurence Dunbar

ERE SLEEP COMES DOWN TO SOOTHE THE WEARY EYES

This poem is one of the most profound that Mr. Dunbar ever wrote, though it is one of his early productions. It attracted the attention of many learned persons before the poet became famous. Among those who spoke of it especially, were the playwright James A. Herne and Colonel Robert G. Ingersoll.

ERE sleep comes down to soothe the weary
    eyes,
  Which all the day with ceaseless care
    have sought
The magic gold which from the seeker
    flies ;
  Ere dreams put on the gown and cap
    of thought,
And make the waking world a world of
    lies,—
Of lies most palpable, uncouth, forlorn,
That say life's full of aches and tears and
    sighs,—
  Oh, how with more than dreams the
    soul is torn,
Ere sleep comes down to soothe the weary
    eyes.

Ere sleep comes down to soothe the weary
    eyes,
  How all the griefs and heartaches we
    have known
Come up like pois'nous vapors that arise
  From some base witch's caldron, when
    the crone,
To work some potent spell, her magic plies.
  The past which held its share of bitter
    pain,

Whose ghost we prayed that Time might
    exorcise,
Comes up, is lived and suffered o'er
    again,
Ere sleep comes down to soothe the weary
    eyes.

Ere sleep comes down to soothe the weary
    eyes,
  What phantoms fill the dimly lighted
    room ;
What ghostly shades in awe-creating guise
  Are bodied forth within the teeming
    gloom.
What echoes faint of sad and soul-sick
    cries,
  And pangs of vague inexplicable pain
That pay the spirit's ceaseless enterprise,
  Come thronging through the chambers
    of the brain,
Ere sleep comes down to soothe the weary
    eyes.

Ere sleep comes down to soothe the weary
    eyes,
  Where ranges forth the spirit far and
    free ?
Through what strange realms and unfa-
    miliar skies
  Tends her far course to lands of mys-
    tery ?
To lands unspeakable—beyond surmise,
  Where shapes unknowable to being
    spring,
Till, faint of wing, the Fancy fails and dies
  Much wearied with the spirit's journey-
    ing,
Ere sleep comes down to soothe the weary
    eyes.

137

Ere sleep comes down to soothe the weary
    eyes,
    How questioneth the soul that other
        soul,—-
The inner sense which neither cheats nor
    lies,
But self exposes unto self, a scroll
Full writ with all life's acts unwise or
    wise,
    In characters indelible and known;
So, trembling with the shock of sad sur-
        prise,
The soul doth view its awful self alone,
Ere sleep comes down to soothe the weary
    eyes.

When sleep comes down to seal the weary
    eyes,
    The last dear sleep whose soft embrace
        is balm,
And whom sad sorrow teaches us to prize
For kissing all our passions into calm,
Ah, then, no more we heed the sad world's
    cries,
Or seek to probe th' eternal mystery,
Or fret our souls at long-withheld replies,
    At glooms through which our visions
        cannot see,
When sleep comes down to seal the weary
    eyes.

THE POET AND HIS SONG

A song is but a little thing,
And yet what joy it is to sing!
In hours of toil it gives me zest,
And when at eve I long for rest;
When cows come home along the bars,
    And in the fold I hear the bell,
As Night, the shepherd, herds his stars,
    I sing my song, and all is well.

There are no ears to hear my lays,
No lips to lift a word of praise;
But still, with faith unfaltering,
I live and laugh and love and sing.
What matters yon unheeding throng?
    They cannot feel my spirit's spell,
Since life is sweet and love is long,
    I sing my song, and all is well.

My days are never days of ease;
I till my ground and prune my trees.

When ripened gold is all the plain,
I put my sickle to the grain.
I labor hard, and toil and sweat,
    While others dream within the dell;
But even while my brow is wet,
    I sing my song, and all is well.

Sometimes the sun, unkindly hot,
My garden makes a desert spot;
Sometimes a blight upon the tree
Takes all my fruit away from me;
And then with throes of bitter pain
    Rebellious passions rise and swell;
But—life is more than fruit or grain,
    And so I sing, and all is well.

RETORT

" Thou art a fool," said my head to my
    heart,
" Indeed, the greatest of fools thou art,
    To be led astray by the trick of a tress,
By a smiling face or a ribbon smart;"
    And my heart was in sore distress.

Then Phyllis came by, and her face was
    fair,
The light gleamed soft on her raven hair;
    And her lips were blooming a rosy red.
Then my heart spoke out with a right bold
    air:
    " Thou art worse than a fool, O head!"

ACCOUNTABILITY

Folks ain't got no right to censuah othah
    folks about dey habits;
Him dat giv' de squir'ls de bushtails made
    de bobtails fu' de rabbits.
Him dat built de gread big mountains hol-
    lered out de little valleys,
Him dat made de streets an' driveways
    wasn't shamed to make de alleys.

We is all constructed diff'ent, d'ain't no
    two of us de same;
We cain't he'p ouah likes an' dislikes, ef
    we'se bad we ain't to blame.
Ef we'se good, we needn't show off, case
    you bet it ain't ouah doin'
We gits into su'ttain channels dat we jes'
    cain't he'p pu'suin'.

But we all fits into places dat no othah
ones could fill,
An' we does the things we has to, big er
little, good er ill.
John cain't tek de place o' Henry, Su an'
Sally ain't alike ;
Bass ain't nuthin' like a suckah, chub ain't
nuthin' like a pike.

When you come to think about it, how it's
all planned out it's splendid,
Nuthin's done er evah happens, 'dout hit's
somefin' dat's intended ;
Don't keer whut you does, you has to, an'
hit sholy beats de dickens,—
Viney, go put on de kittle, I got one o'
mastah's chickens.

FREDERICK DOUGLASS

A hush is over all the teeming lists,
  And there is pause, a breath-space in
    the strife ;
A spirit brave has passed beyond the mists
  And vapors that obscure the sun of life.
And Ethiopia, with bosom torn,
Laments the passing of her noblest born.

She weeps for him a mother's burning
    tears —
  She loved him with a mother's deepest
    love.
He was her champion thro' direful years,
  And held her weal all other ends above.
When Bondage held her bleeding in the
    dust,
He raised her up and whispered, " Hope
    and Trust."

For her his voice, a fearless clarion, rung
  That broke in warning on the ears of
    men ;
For her the strong bow of his power he
    strung,
  And sent his arrows to the very den
Where grim Oppression held his bloody
    place
And gloated o'er the mis'ries of a race.

And he was no soft-tongued apologist ;
  He spoke straightforward, fearlessly un-
    cowed ;

The sunlight of his truth dispelled the
    mist,
  And set in bold relief each dark-hued
    cloud ;
To sin and crime he gave their proper
    hue,
And hurled at evil what was evil's due.

Through good and ill report he cleaved
    his way
  Right onward, with his face set toward
    the heights,
Nor feared to face the foeman's dread
    array,—
  The lash of scorn, the sting of petty
    spites.
He dared the lightning in the lightning's
    track,
And answered thunder with his thunder
    back.

When men maligned him, and their torrent
    wrath
  In furious imprecations o'er him broke,
He kept his counsel as he kept his path ;
  'Twas for his race, not for himself, he
    spoke.
He knew the import of his Master's call,
And felt himself too mighty to be small.

No miser in the good he held was he,—
  His kindness followed his horizon's rim.
His heart, his talents, and his hands were
    free
  To all who truly needed aught of him.
Where poverty and ignorance were rife,
He gave his bounty as he gave his life.

The place and cause that first aroused his
    might
  Still proved its power until his latest
    day.
In Freedom's lists and for the aid of Right
  Still in the foremost rank he waged the
    fray ;
Wrong lived ; his occupation was not
    gone.
He died in action with his armor on !

We weep for him, but we have touched
    his hand,

And felt the magic of his presence nigh,
The current that he sent throughout the
	land,
The kindling spirit of his battle-cry.
O'er all that holds us we shall triumph yet,
And place our banner where his hopes
	were set!

Oh, Douglass, thou hast passed beyond the
	shore,
	But still thy voice is ringing o'er the
	gale!
Thou'st taught thy race how high her
	hopes may soar,
	And bade her seek the heights, nor
	faint, nor fail.
She will not fail, she heeds thy stirring
	cry,
She knows thy guardian spirit will be nigh,
And, rising from beneath the chast'ning
	rod,
She stretches out her bleeding hands to
	God!

LIFE

It is doubtful if any modern poem has
had a wider reading than this. It was a
favorite selection of Mr. Dunbar's when
reciting, and his reading of it was very
impressive. It is peculiarly typical of his
own experiences in life as well as of those
of us all. In spite of his frank acknowl-
edgment of the predominance of the
"groans," however, he would not end the
poem without a bit of exhortation and a
crumb of comfort—for, after all, it is true,
as he sings, that

" Joy seems sweeter when cares come after,
	And a moan is the finest of foils for laughter,"

and the man of sorrows is the man who
wins the ear and the heart of the world.

A crust of bread and a corner to sleep in,
A minute to smile and an hour to weep in,
A pint of joy to a peck of trouble,
And never a laugh but the moans come
	double;
		And that is life!

A crust and a corner that love makes
	precious,
With the smile to warm and the tears to
	refresh us;
And joy seems sweeter when cares come
	after,
And a moan is the finest of foils for
	laughter;
		And that is life!

THE LESSON

My cot was down by a cypress grove,
	And I sat by my window the whole
	night long,
And heard well up from the deep dark
	wood
	A mocking-bird's passionate song.

And I thought of myself so sad and lone,
	And my life's cold winter that knew no
	spring;
Of my mind so weary and sick and wild,
	Of my heart too sad to sing.

But e'en as I listened the mock-bird's
	song,
	A thought stole into my saddened heart,
And I said, " I can cheer some other soul
	By a carol's simple art."

For oft from the darkness of hearts and
	lives
	Come songs that brim with joy and
	light,
As out of the gloom of the cypress grove
	The mocking-bird sings at night.

So I sang a lay for a brother's ear
	In a strain to soothe his bleeding heart
And he smiled at the sound of my voice
	and lyre,
	Though mine was a feeble art.

But at his smile I smiled in turn,
	And into my soul there came a ray:
In trying to soothe another's woes
	Mine own had passed away.

THE RISING OF THE STORM

The lake's dark breast
Is all unrest,
It heaves with a sob and a sigh.
Like a tremulous bird,
From its slumber stirred,
The moon is a-tilt in the sky.

From the silent deep
The waters sweep,
But faint on the cold white stones,
And the wavelets fly
With a plaintive cry
O'er the old earth's bare, bleak bones.

And the spray upsprings
On its ghost-white wings,
And tosses a kiss at the stars ;
While a water-sprite,
In sea-pearls dight,
Hums a sea-hymn's solemn bars.

Far out in the night,
On the wavering sight
I see a dark hull loom ;
And its light on high,
Like a Cyclops' eye,
Shines out through the mist and gloom.

Now the winds well up
From the earth's deep cup,
And fall on the sea and shore,
And against the pier
The waters rear
And break with a sullen roar.

Up comes the gale,
And the mist-wrought veil
Gives way to the lightning's glare,
And the cloud-drifts fall,
A sombre pall,
O'er water, earth, and air.

The storm-king flies,
His whip he plies,
And bellows down the wind.
The lightning rash
With blinding flash
Comes pricking on behind.

Rise, waters, rise,
And taunt the skies
With your swift-flitting form.
Sweep, wild winds, sweep,
And tear the deep
To atoms in the storm.

And the waters leapt,
And the wild winds swept,
And blew out the moon in the sky,
And I laughed with glee,
It was joy to me
As the storm went raging by !

SUNSET

The river sleeps beneath the sky,
And clasps the shadows to its breast;
The crescent moon shines dim on high;
And in the lately radiant west
The gold is fading into gray.
Now stills the lark his festive lay,
And mourns with me the dying day.

While in the south the first faint star
Lifts to the night its silver face,
And twinkles to the moon afar
Across the heaven's graying space,
Low murmurs reach me from the
town,
As Day puts on her sombre crown,
And shakes her mantle darkly down.

THE OLD APPLE-TREE

There's a memory keeps a-runnin'
Through my weary head to-night,
An' I see a picture dancin'
In the fire-flames' ruddy light ;
'Tis the picture of an orchard
Wrapped in autumn's purple haze,
With the tender light about it
That I loved in other days.
An' a-standin' in a corner
Once again I seem to see
The verdant leaves an' branches
Of an old apple-tree.

You perhaps would call it ugly,
An' I don't know but it's so,
When you look the tree all over

Unadorned by memory's glow ;
For its boughs are gnarled an' crooked,
An' its leaves are gettin' thin,
An' the apples of its bearin'
Wouldn't fill so large a bin
As they used to. But I tell you,
When it comes to pleasin' me,
It's the dearest in the orchard,—
Is that old apple-tree.

I would hide within its shelter,
Settlin' in some cozy nook,
Where no calls nor threats could stir me
From the pages o' my book.
Oh, that quiet, sweet seclusion
In its fulness passeth words !
It was deeper than the deepest
That my sanctum now affords.
Why, the jaybirds an' the robins,
They was hand in glove with me,
As they winked at me an' warbled
In that old apple-tree.

It was on its sturdy branches
That in summers long ago
I would tie my swing an' dangle
In contentment to an' fro,
Idly dreamin' childish fancies,
Buildin' castles in the air,.
Makin' o' myself a hero
Of romances rich an' rare.
I kin shet my eyes an' see it
Jest as plain as plain kin be,
That same old swing a-danglin'
To the old apple-tree.

There's a rustic seat beneath it
That I never kin forget.
It's the place where me an' Hallie —
Little sweetheart—used to set,
When we'd wander to the orchard
So's no listenin' ones could hear
As I whispered sugared nonsense
Into her little willin' ear.
Now my gray old wife is Hallie,
An' I'm grayer still than she,
But I'll not forget our courtin'
'Neath the old apple-tree.

Life for us ain't all been summer,
But I guess we've had our share

Of its flittin' joys an' pleasures,
An' a sprinklin' of its care.
Oft the skies have smiled upon us ;
Then again we've seen 'em frown,
Though our load was ne'er so heavy
That we longed to lay it down.
But when death does come a-callin',
This my last request shall be,—
That they'll bury me an' Hallie
'Neath the old apple-tree.

A PRAYER

O Lord, the hard-won miles
Have worn my stumbling feet :
Oh, soothe me with thy smiles,
And make my life complete.

The thorns were thick and keen
Where'er I trembling trod ;
The way was long between
My wounded feet and God.

Where healing waters flow
Do thou my footsteps lead.
My heart is aching so ;
Thy gracious balm I need.

PASSION AND LOVE

A maiden wept and, as a comforter,
Came one who cried, " I love thee," and
he seized
Her in his arms and kissed her with hot
breath,
That dried the tears upon her flaming
cheeks.
While evermore his boldly blazing eye
Burned into hers ; but she uncomforted
Shrank from his arms and only wept the
more.

Then one came and gazed mutely in her
face
With wide and wistful eyes ; but still
aloof
He held himself ; as with a reverent fear,
As one who knows some sacred presence
nigh.
And as she wept he mingled tear with
tear,

That cheered her soul like dew a dusty
flower,—
Until she smiled, approached, and touched
his hand !

THE SEEDLING

As a quiet little seedling
Lay within its darksome bed,
To itself it fell a-talking,
And this is what it said :

" I am not so very robust,
But I'll do the best I can ; "
And the seedling from that moment
Its work of life began.

So it pushed a little leaflet
Up into the light of day,
To examine the surroundings
And show the rest the way.

The leaflet liked the prospect,
So it called its brother, Stem ;
Then two other leaflets heard it,
And quickly followed them.

To be sure, the haste and hurry
Made the seedling sweat and pant ;
But almost before it knew it
It found itself a plant.

The sunshine poured upon it,
And the clouds they gave a shower;
And the little plant kept growing
Till it found itself a flower.

Little folks, be like the seedling,
Always do the best you can ;
Every child must share life's labor
Just as well as every man.

And the sun and showers will help you
Through the lonesome, struggling
hours,
Till you raise to light and beauty
Virtue's fair, unfading flowers.

9

PROMISE AND FULFILMENT

This pair of poems was so admired by
Minnie Maddern Fiske that she wrote the
author asking permission to use them on
the stage. This was granted, and the
lines were read many times with flattering
applause. It is pathetic to reflect upon
the fact that this very thing came in after
years, to be a real part of the poet's heart
history. At the moment when his joy
should have been at its height, and his
rose of love was ready for the blooming,
it was discovered, alas, that, in very deed,
a " worm was at its heart."

I grew a rose within a garden fair,
And, tending it with more than loving
care,
I thought how, with the glory of its bloom,
I should the darkness of my life illume ;
And, watching, ever smiled to see the
lusty bud
Drink freely in the summer sun to tinct
its blood.

My rose began to open, and its hue
Was sweet to me as to it sun and dew ;
I watched it taking on its ruddy flame
Until the day of perfect blooming came,
Then hasted I with smiles to find it blush-
ing red —
Too late ! Some thoughtless child had
plucked my rose and fled !

FULFILMENT

I grew a rose once more to please mine
eyes.
All things to aid it—dew, sun, wind, fair
skies —
Were kindly ; and to shield it from de-
spoil,
I fenced it safely in with grateful toil.
No other hand than mine shall pluck this
flower, said I,
And I was jealous of the bee that hovered
nigh.

It grew for days ; I stood hour after hour
To watch the slow unfolding of the flower,

And then I did not leave its side at all,
Lest some mischance my flower should
    befall.
At last, oh, joy! the central petals burst
    apart.
It blossomed—but, alas! a worm was at
    its heart!

SONG

My heart to thy heart,
    My hand to thine;
My lips to thy lips,
    Kisses are wine
Brewed for the lover in sunshine and
    shade;
Let me drink deep, then, my African maid.

Lily to lily,
    Rose unto rose;
My love to thy love
    Tenderly grows.
Rend not the oak and the ivy in twain,
Nor the swart maid from her swarthier
    swain.

AN ANTE-BELLUM SERMON

We is gathahed hyeah, my brothahs,
    In dis howlin' wildaness,
Fu' to speak some words of comfo't
    To each othah in distress.
An' we chooses fu' ouah subjic'
    Dis—we'll 'splain it by an' by;
" An' de Lawd said, ' Moses, Moses,'
    An' de man said, ' Hyeah am I.' "

Now ole Pher'oh, down in Egypt,
    Was de wuss man evah bo'n,
An' he had de Hebrew chillun
    Down dah wukin' in his co'n;
'Twell de Lawd got tiahed o' his foolin',
    An' sez he: " I'll let him know —
Look hyeah, Moses, go tell Pher'oh
    Fu' to let dem chillun go."

" An' ef he refuse to do it,
    I will make him rue de houah,
Fu' I'll empty down on Egypt
    All de vials of my powah."

Yes, he did—an' Pher'oh's ahmy
    Wasn't wuth a ha'f a dime;
Fu' de Lawd will he'p his chillun,
    You kin trust him evah time.

An' yo' enemies may 'sail you
    In de back an' in de front;
But de Lawd is all aroun' you,
    Fu' to ba' de battle's brunt,
Dey kin fo'ge yo' chains an' shackles
    F'om de mountains to de sea;
But de Lawd will sen' some Moses
    Fu' to set his chillun free.

An' de lan' shall hyeah his thundah,
    Lak a blas' f'om Gab'el's ho'n,
Fu' de Lawd of hosts is mighty
    When he girds his ahmor on.
But fu' feah some one mistakes me,
    I will pause right hyeah to say,
Dat I'm still a-preachin' ancient,
    I ain't talkin' 'bout to-day.

But I tell you, fellah christuns,
    Things 'll happen mighty strange;
Now, de Lawd done dis fu' Isrul,
    An' his ways don't nevah change,
An' de love he showed to Isrul
    Wasn't all on Isrul spent;
Now don't run an' tell yo' mastahs
    Dat I's preachin' discontent.

'Cause I isn't; I'se a-judgin'
    Bible people by deir ac's;
I'se a-givin' you de Scriptuah,
    I'se a-handin' you de fac's.
Cose ole Pher'oh b'lieved in slav'ry,
    But de Lawd he let him see,
Dat de people he put bref in,—
    Evah mothah's son was free.

An' dahs othahs thinks lak Pher'oh,
    But dey calls de Scriptuah liar,
Fu' de Bible says " a servant
    Is a-worthy of his hire."
An' you cain't git roun' nor thoo dat,
    An' you cain't git ovah it,
Fu' whatevah place you git in,
    Dis hyeah Bible too 'll fit.

So you see de Lawd's intention,
  Evah sence de worl' began,
Was dat his almighty freedom
  Should belong to evah man,
But I think it would be bettah,
  Ef I'd pause agin to say,
Dat I'm talkin' 'bout ouah freedom
  In a Bibleistic way.

But de Moses is a-comin',
  An' he's comin', suah and fas'
We kin hyeah his feet a-trompin',
  We kin hyeah his trumpit blas'.
But I want to wa'n you people,
  Don't you git too brigity ;
An' don't you git to braggin'
  'Bout dese things, you wait an' see.

But when Moses wit his powah
  Comes an' sets us chillun free,
We will praise de gracious Mastah
  Dat has gin us liberty ;
An' we'll shout ouah halleluyahs,
  On dat mighty reck'nin' day,
When we's reco'nized ez citiz'—
  Huh uh! Chillun, let us pray !

ODE TO ETHIOPIA

O Mother Race ! to thee I bring
This pledge of faith unwavering,
  This tribute to thy glory.
I know the pangs which thou didst feel,
When Slavery crushed thee with its
  heel,
  With thy dear blood all gory.

Sad days were those—ah, sad indeed !
But through the land the fruitful seed
  Of better times was growing.
The plant of freedom upward sprung,
And spread its leaves so fresh and
  young—
  Its blossoms now are blowing.

On every hand in this fair land,
Proud Ethiope's swarthy children stand
  Beside their fairer neighbor ;
The forests flee before their stroke,
Their hammers ring, their forges
  smoke,—
  They stir in honest labour.

They tread the fields where honor calls ;
Their voices sound through senate halls
  In majesty and power.
To right they cling ; the hymns they sing
Up to the skies in beauty ring,
  And bolder grow each hour.

Be proud, my Race, in mind and soul :
Thy name is writ on Glory's scroll
  In characters of fire.
High 'mid the clouds of Fame's bright
  sky
Thy banner's blazoned folds now fly,
  And truth shall lift them higher.

Thou hast the right to noble pride,
Whose spotless robes were purified
  By blood's severe baptism.
Upon thy brow the cross was laid,
And labor's painful sweat-beads made
  A consecrating chrism.

No other race, or white or black,
When bound as thou wert, to the rack,
  So seldom stooped to grieving ;
No other race, when free again,
Forgot the past and proved them men
  So noble in forgiving.

Go on and up ! Our souls and eyes
Shall follow thy continuous rise ;
  Our ears shall list thy story
From bards who from thy root shall
  spring,
And proudly tune their lyres to sing
  Of Ethiopia's glory.

THE CORN-STALK FIDDLE

When the corn's all cut and the bright
  stalks shine
  Like the burnished spears of a field of
  gold ;
When the field-mice rich on the nubbins
  dine,
  And the frost comes white and the wind
  blows cold ;
Then it's heigho ! fellows and hi-diddle-
  diddle,
For the time is ripe for the corn-stalk
  fiddle.

And you take a stalk that is straight and
    long,
With an expert eye to its worthy points,
And you think of the bubbling strains of
    song
    That are bound between its pithy
    joints —
Then you cut out strings, with a bridge in
    the middle,
With a corn-stalk bow for a corn-stalk
    fiddle.

Then the strains that grow as you draw
    the bow
    O'er the yielding strings with a prac-
    ticed hand !
And the music's flow never loud but low
    Is the concert note of a fairy band.
Oh, your dainty songs are a misty riddle
To the simple sweets of the corn-stalk
    fiddle.

When the eve comes on, and our work is
    done,
    And the sun drops down with a tender
    glance,
With their hearts all prime for the harm-
    less fun,
    Come the neighbor girls for the evening's
    dance,
And they wait for the well-known twist
    and twiddle —
More time than tune—from the corn-stalk
    fiddle.

Then brother Jabez takes the bow,
    While Ned stands off with Susan Bland,
Then Henry stops by Milly Snow,
    And John takes Nellie Jones's hand,
While I pair off with Mandy Biddle,
And scrape, scrape, scrape goes the corn-
    stalk fiddle.

" Salute your partners," comes the call,
    " All join hands and circle round,"
" Grand train back," and " Balance all,"
    Footsteps lightly spurn the ground.
" Take your lady and balance down the
    middle "
To the merry strains of the corn-stalk
    fiddle.

So the night goes on and the dance is o'er
    And the merry girls are homeward gone
But I see it all in my sleep once more,
    And I dream till the very break of dawn
Of an impish dance on a red-hot griddle
To the screech and scrape of a corn-stalk
    fiddle.

THE MASTER-PLAYER

An old, worn harp that had been played
Till all its strings were loose and frayed,
Joy, Hate, and Fear, each one essayed,
To play.   But each in turn had found
No sweet responsiveness of sound.

Then Love the Master-Player came
With heaving breast and eyes aflame ;
The Harp he took all undismayed,
Smote on its strings, still strange to song,
And brought forth music sweet and strong.

THE MYSTERY

I was not; now I am—a few days hence
I shall not be ; I fain would look before
And after, but can neither do ; some Power
Or lack of power says " no " to all I would.
I stand upon a wide and sunless plain,
Nor chart nor steel to guide my steps
    aright.
Whene'er, o'ercoming fear, I dare to move,
I grope without direction and by chance.
Some feign to hear a voice and feel a hand
That draws them ever upward thro' the
    gloom.
But I—I hear no voice and touch no hand,
Tho' oft thro' silence infinite I list,
And strain my hearing to supernal sounds ;
Tho' oft thro' fateful darkness do I reach,
And stretch my hand to find that other
    hand.
I question of th' eternal bending skies
That seem to neighbor with the novice
    earth ;
But they roll on, and daily shut their eyes
On me, as I one day shall do on them,
And tell me not the secret that I ask.

TWO SONGS

A bee that was searching for sweets one
    day
Through the gate of a rose garden hap-
    pened to stray.
In the heart of a rose he hid away,
And forgot in his bliss the light of day,
As sipping his honey he buzzed in song;
Though day was waning, he lingered long,
    For the rose was sweet, so sweet.

A robin sits pluming his ruddy breast,
And a madrigal sings to his love in her
    nest:
" Oh, the skies they are blue, the fields are
    green,
And the birds in your nest will soon be
    seen ! "
She hangs on his words with a thrill of
    love,
And chirps to him as he sits above,
    For the song is sweet, so sweet.

A maiden was out on a summer's day
With the winds and the waves and the
    flowers at play;
And she met with a youth of gentle air,
With the light of the sunshine on his hair.
Together they wandered the flowers
    among;
They loved, and loving they lingered long,
    For to love is sweet, so sweet.

Bird of my lady's bower,
    Sing her a song;
Tell her that every hour,
    All the day long,
Thoughts of her come to me,
    Filling my brain
With the warm ecstasy
    Of love's refrain.

Little bird ! happy bird !
    Being so near,
Where e'en her slightest word
    Thou mayest hear,
Seeing her glancing eyes,
    Sheen of her hair,

Thou art in paradise,—
    Would I were there.

I am so far away,
    Thou art so near;
Plead with her, birdling gay,
    Plead with my dear.
Rich be thy recompense,
    Fine be thy fee,
If through thine eloquence
    She hearken me.

THE PATH

There are no beaten paths to Glory's
    height,
There are no rules to compass greatness
    known;
Each for himself must cleave a path alone,
And press his own way forward in the
    fight.
Smooth is the way to ease and calm de-
    light,
And soft the road Sloth chooseth for her
    own;
But he who craves the flower of life full-
    blown,
Must struggle up in all his armor dight !
What though the burden bear him sorely
    down
And crush to dust the mountain of his
    pride,
Oh, then, with strong heart let him still
    abide;
For rugged is the roadway to renown,
Nor may he hope to gain the envied
    crown
Till he hath thrust the looming rocks
    aside.

THE LAWYER'S WAYS

This poem, written in the earlier years
of Paul Laurence Dunbar's life is doubt-
less the fruit of his observations when a
page in the Dayton court-house, and the
discoveries that it shows he made even in
his youth of the instability of the law,
may have been one reason why he gave
up his chances and his ambitions to be-

come a lawyer, preferring to be a poet and an inspiration for his race.

I've been list'nin' to them lawyers
  In the court house up the street,
An' I've come to the conclusion
  That I'm most completely beat.
Fust one feller riz to argy,
  An' he boldly waded in
As he dressed the tremblin' pris'ner
  In a coat o' deep-dyed sin.

Why, he painted him all over
  In a hue o' blackest crime,
An' he smeared his reputation
  With the thickest kind o' grime,
Tell I found myself a-wond'rin',
  In a misty way and dim,
How the Lord had come to fashion
  Sich an awful man as him.

Then the other lawyer started,
  An', with brimmin', tearful eyes,
Said his client was a martyr
  That was brought to sacrifice.
An' he give to that same pris'ner
  Every blessed human grace,
Tell I saw the light o' virtue
  Fairly shinin' from his face.

Then I own 'at I was puzzled
  How sich things could rightly be ;
An' this aggervatin' question
  Seems to keep a-puzzlin' me.
So, will some one please inform me,
  An' this mystery unroll —
How an angel an' a devil
  Can persess the self-same soul ?

LONGING

If you could sit with me beside the sea to-
    day,
And whisper with me sweetest dreamings
    o'er and o'er ;
I think I should not find the clouds so dim
    and gray,
And not so loud the waves complaining at
    the shore.

If you could sit with me upon the shore
    to-day,
And hold my hand in yours as in the days
    of old,
I think I should not mind the chill baptis-
    mal spray,
Nor find my hand and heart and all the
    world so cold.

If you could walk with me upon the strand
    to-day,
And tell me that my longing love had won
    your own,
I think all my sad thoughts would then be
    put away,
And I could give back laughter for the
    Ocean's moan !

A BANJO SONG

Oh, dere's lots o' keer an' trouble
  In dis world to swaller down ;
An' ol' Sorrer's purty lively
  In her way o' gittin' roun'.
Yet dere's times when I furgit 'em,—
  Aches an' pains an' troubles all,—
An' it's when I tek at ebenin'
  My ol' banjo f'om de wall.

'Bout de time dat night is fallin'
  An' my daily wu'k is done,
An' above de shady hilltops
  I kin see de settin' sun ;
When de quiet, restful shadders
  Is beginnin' jes' to fall,—
Den I take de little banjo
  F'om its place upon de wall.

Den my fam'ly gadders roun' me
  In de fadin' o' de light,
Ez I strike de strings to try 'em
  Ef dey all is tuned er-right.
An' it seems we're so nigh heaben
  We kin hyeah de angels sing
When de music o' dat banjo
  Sets my cabin all er-ring.

OH, DERE'S LOTS O' KEER AN' TROUBLE

MALE AN' FEMALE, SMALL AN' BIG——

An' my wife an' all de othahs,—
  Male an' female, small an' big,—
Even up to gray-haired granny,
  Seem jes' boun' to do a jig;
'Twell I change de style o' music,
  Change de movement an' de time,
An' de ringin' little banjo
  Plays an ol' hea't-feelin' hime.

An' somehow my th'oat gits choky,
  An' a lump keeps tryin' to rise
Lak it wan'ed to ketch de water
  Dat was flowin' to my eyes;
An' I feel dat I could sorter
  Knock de socks clean off o' sin
Ez I hyeah my po' ol' granny
  Wif huh tremblin' voice jine in.

Den we all th'ow in our voices
  Fu' to he'p de chune out too,
Lak a big camp-meetin' choiry
  Tryin' to sing a mou'nah th'oo.
An' our th'oahts let out de music,
  Sweet an' solemn, loud an' free,
'Twell de raftahs o' my cabin
  Echo wif de melody.

Oh, de music o' de banjo,
  Quick an' deb'lish, solemn, slow,
Is de greates' joy an' solace
  Dat a weary slave kin know!
So jes' let me hyeah it ringin',
  Dough de chune be po' an' rough,
It's a pleasure; an' de pleasures
  O' dis life is few enough.

Now, de blessed little angels
  Up in heaben, we are told,
Don't do nothin' all dere lifetime
  'Ceptin' play on ha'ps o' gold.
Now I think heaben 'd be mo' home-
    like
Ef we'd hyeah some music fall
F'om a real ol'-fashioned banjo,
  Like dat one upon de wall.

NOT THEY WHO SOAR

Not they who soar, but they who plod
Their rugged way, unhelped, to God
Are heroes; they who higher fare,
And, flying, fan the upper air,

Miss all the toil that hugs the sod.
'Tis they whose backs have felt the rod,
Whose feet have pressed the path unshod,
May smile upon defeated care,
  Not they who soar.

High up there are no thorns to prod,
Nor boulders lurking 'neath the clod
To turn the keenness of the share,
For flight is ever free and rare;
But heroes they the soil who've trod,
  Not they who soar!

WHITTIER

Not o'er thy dust let there be spent
The gush of maudlin sentiment;
Such drift as that is not for thee,
Whose life and deeds and songs agree,
Sublime in their simplicity.

Nor shall the sorrowing tear be shed.
O singer sweet, thou art not dead!
In spite of time's malignant chill,
With living fire thy songs shall thrill,
And men shall say, " He liveth still!"

Great poets never die, for Earth
Doth count their lives of too great worth
To lose them from her treasured store;
So shalt thou live for evermore —
Though far thy form from mortal ken —
Deep in the hearts and minds of men.

ODE FOR MEMORIAL DAY

Done are the toils and the wearisome
    marches,
  Done is the summons of bugle and
    drum.
Softly and sweetly the sky overarches,
  Shelt'ring a land where Rebellion is
    dumb.
Dark were the days of the country's de-
    rangement,
  Sad were the hours when the conflict
    was on,
But through the gloom of fraternal es-
    trangement
  God sent his light, and we welcome the
    dawn.
O'er the expanse of our mighty dominions,

Sweeping away to the uttermost parts,
Peace, the wide-flying, on untiring pin-
    ions,
    Bringeth her message of joy to our
        hearts.

Ah, but this joy which our minds cannot
        measure,—
    What did it cost for our fathers to gain!
Bought at the price of the heart's dearest
        treasure,
    Born out of travail and sorrow and pain;
Born in the battle where fleet Death was
        flying,
    Slaying with sabre-stroke bloody and
        fell;
Born where the heroes and martyrs were
        dying,
    Torn by the fury of bullet and shell.
Ah, but the day is past: silent the rattle,
    And the confusion that followed the
        fight.
Peace to the heroes who died in the battle,
    Martyrs to truth and the crowning of
        Right!

Out of the blood of a conflict fraternal,
    Out of the dust and the dimness of death,
Burst into blossoms of glory eternal
    Flowers that sweeten the world with
        their breath.
Flowers of charity, peace, and devotion
    Bloom in the hearts that are empty of
        strife;
Love that is boundless and broad as the
        ocean
    Leaps into beau y and fulness of life.
So, with the singing of pæans and chorals,
    And with the flag flashing high in the
        sun,
Place on the graves of our heroes the
        laurels
    Which their unfaltering valor has won!

PREMONITION

Dear heart, good-night!
Nay, list awhile that sweet voice singing
    When the world is all so bright,
And the sound of song sets the heart
        a-ringing,

Oh, love, it is not right—
    Not then to say, " Good-night."

Dear heart, good-night!
The late winds in the lake weeds shiver,
    And the spray flies cold and white.
And the voice that sings gives a telltale
        quiver—
    " Ah, yes, the world is bright,
    But, dearest heart, good-night!"

Dear heart, good-night!
And do not longer seek to hold me!
    For my soul is in affright
As the fearful glooms in their pall enfold
        me.
    See him who sang how white
        And still; so, dear, good-night.

Dear heart, good-night!
Thy hand I'll press no more forever,
    And mine eyes shall lose the light;
For the great white wraith by the winding
        river
    Shall check my steps with might.
        So, dear, good-night, good-night!

RETROSPECTION

When you and I were young, the days
    Were filled with scent of pink and rose,
    And full of joy from dawn till close,
From morning's mist till evening's haze.
    And when the robin sung his song
    The verdant woodland ways along,
    We whistled louder than he sung.
And school was joy, and work was sport
For which the hours were all too short,
    When you and I were young, my boy,
        When you and I were young.

When you and I were young, the woods
    Brimmed bravely o'er with every joy
    To charm the happy-hearted boy.
The quail turned out her timid broods;
    The prickly copse, a hostess fine,
    Held high black cups of harmless wine;
    And low the laden grape-vine swung
With beads of night-kissed amethyst
Where buzzing lovers held their tryst,
    When you and I were young, my boy,
        When you and I were young.

When you and I were young, the cool
  And fresh wind fanned our fevered
    brows
When tumbling o'er the scerted mows,
Or stripping by the dimpling pool,
  Sedge-fringed about its shimmering face,
  Save where we'd worn an ent'ring place.
    How with our shouts the calm banks
      rung!
How flashed the spray as we plunged in,—
Pure gems that never caused a sin!
  When you and I were young, my boy,
    When you and I were young.

When you and I were young, we heard
  All sounds of Nature with delight,—
    The whirr of wing in sudden flight,
The chirping of the baby-bird.
  The columbine's red bells were rung;
  The locust's vested chorus sung;
    While every wind his zithern strung
To high and holy-sounding keys,
And played sonatas in the trees—
  When you and I were young, my boy,
    When you and I were young.

When you and I were young, we knew
  To shout and laugh, to work and play,
  And night was partner to the day
In all our joys. So swift time flew
  On silent wings that, ere we wist,
  The fleeting years had fled unmissed;
    And from our hearts this cry was
      wrung—
To fill with fond regret and tears
The days of our remaining years—
  "When you and I were young, my boy,
    When you and I were young."

UNEXPRESSED

Deep in my heart that aches with the re-
    pression,
  And strives with plenitude of bitter pain,
There lives a thought that clamors for ex-
    pression,
  And spends its undelivered force in vain.

What boots it that some other may have
    thought it?

The right of thoughts' expression is
    divine;
The price of pain I pay for it has bought it,
  I care not who lays claim to it—'tis
    mine!

And yet not mine until it be delivered;
  The manner of its birth shall prove the
    test.
Alas, alas, my rock of pride is shivered—
  I beat my brow—the thought still unex-
    pressed.

SPRING SONG

A blue-bell springs upon the ledge,
A lark sits singing in the hedge;
Sweet perfumes scent the balmy air,
And life is brimming everywhere.
What lark and breeze and bluebird sing,
  Is Spring, Spring, Spring!

Nor more the air is sharp and cold;
The planter wends across the wold,
And, glad, beneath the shining sky
We wander forth, my love and I.
And ever in our hearts doth ring
  This song of Spring, Spring!

For life is life and love is love,
'Twixt maid and man or dove and dove.
Life may be short, life may be long,
But love will come, and to its song
Shall this refrain forever cling
  Of Spring, Spring, Spring!

SONG OF SUMMER

Dis is gospel weathah sho'—
  Hills is sawt o' hazy.
Meddahs level ez a flo'
  Callin' to de lazy.
Sky all white wif streaks o' blue,
  Sunshine softly gleamin',
D'ain't no wuk hit's right to do,
  Nothin' 's right but dreamin'.

Dreamin' by de rivah side
  Wif de watahs glist'nin',
Feelin' good an' satisfied
  Ez you lay a-list'nin'

To the little nakid boys
  Splashin' in de watah,
Hollerin' fu' to spress deir joys
  Jes' lak youngsters ought to.

Squir'l a-tippin' on his toes,
  So's to hide an' view you ;
Whole flocks o' camp-meetin' crows
  Shoutin' hallelujah.
Peckahwood erpon de tree
  Tappin' lak a hammah ;
Jaybird chattin' wif a bee,
  Tryin' to teach him grammah.

Breeze is blowin' wif perfume,
  Jes' enough to tease you ;
Hollyhocks is all in bloom,
  Smellin' fu' to please you.
Go 'way, folks, an' let me 'lone,
  Times is gettin' dearah —
Summah's settin' on de th'one,
  An' I'm a-layin' neah huh !

TO LOUISE

When Paul Laurence Dunbar, young and full of timidity, was trying to sell his little book " Majors & Minors," from house to house, he sometimes became greatly discouraged. Upon the evening of a particularly disheartening day, he went to the home of his patron, Dr. H. A. Tobey, in Toledo, Ohio, and told him that he would never again have the courage to offer a book for sale to any man. His friend endeavored to encourage him, but he was despondent, and left the doctor with tears streaming down his cheeks. Just as poor Dunbar was leaving, the little daughter of his host, Miss Louise Tobey, ran to him and in the sweet, half-bashful way of a child, gave him a beautiful rose. The next morning, the young poet sought the " wee lassie," and handed her a bit of paper. Upon this sheet was written one of the most perfect of his poems—" Lines to Louise."

Oh, the poets may sing of their Lady Irenes,

And may rave in their rhymes about wonderful queens ;
But I throw my poetical wings to the bree.e,
And soar ın a song to my Lady Louise.
A sweet little maid, who is dearer, I ween,
Than any fair duchess, or even a queen.
When speaking of her I can't plod in my prose,
For she's the wee lassie who gave me a rose.

Since poets, from seeing a lady's lip curled,
Have written fair verse that has sweetened the world ;
Why, then, should not I give the space of an hour
To making a song in return for a flower ?
I have found in my life—it has not been so long —
There are too few of flowers—too little of song.
So out of that blossom, this lay of mine grows,
For the dear little lady who gave me the rose.

I thank God for innocence, dearer than Art,
That lights on a by-way which leads to the heart,
And led by an impulse no less than divine,
Walks into the temple and sits at the shrine.
I would rather pluck daisies that grow in the wild,
Or take one simple rose from the hand of a child,
Than to breathe the rich fragrance of flowers that bide
In the gardens of luxury, passion, and pride.

I know not, my wee one, how came you to know
Which way to my heart was the right way to go ;
Unless in your purity, soul-clean and clear,
God whispers his messages into your ear.
You have now had my song, let me end with a prayer

That your life may be always sweet,
  happy, and fair ;
That your joys may be many, and absent
  your woes,
O dear little lady who gave me the rose !

THE RIVALS

'Twas three an' thirty year ago
When I was ruther young, you know,
I had my last an' only fight
About a gal one summer night.
'Twas me an' Zekel Johnson ; Zeke
'N' me'd be'n spattin' 'bout a week,
Each of us tryin' his best to show
That he was Liza Jones's beau.
We couldn't neither prove the thing,
Fur she was fur too sharp to fling
One over fur the other one
An' by so doin' stop the fun
That we chaps didn't have the sense
To see she got at our expense,
But that's the way a feller does,
Fur boys is fools an' allus was.
An' when they's females in the game
I reckon men's about the same.
Well, Zeke an' me went on that way
An' fussed an' quarreled day by day ;
While Liza, mindin' not the fuss,
Jest kep' a-goin' with both of us,
Tell we pore chaps, that's Zeke an' me,
Was jest plum mad with jealousy.
Well, fur a time we kep' our places,
An' only showed by frownin' faces
An' looks 'at well our meanin' boded
How full o' fight we both was loaded.
At last it come, the thing broke out,
An' this is how it come about.
One night ('twas fair, you'll all agree)
I got Eliza's company,
An' leavin' Zekel in the lurch,
Went trottin' off with her to church.
An' jest as we had took our seat
(Eliza lookin' fair an' sweet),
Why, I jest couldn't help but grin
When Zekel come a bouncin' in
As furious as the law allows.
He'd jest be'n up to Liza's house,
To find her gone, then come to church
To have this end put to his search.
I guess I laffed that meetin' through,

An' not a mortal word I knew
Of what the preacher preached er read
Er what the choir sung er said.
Fur every time I'd turn my head
I couldn't skeercely help but see
'At Zekel had his eye on me.
An' he 'ud sort o' turn an' twist
An' grind his teeth an' shake his fist.
I laughed, fur la ! the hull church seen
  us,
An' knowed that suthin' was between us.
Well, meetin' out, we started hum,
I sorter feelin' what would come.
We'd jest got out, when up stepped Zeke,
An' said, " Scuse me, I'd like to speak
To you a minute." " Cert," said I —
A-nudgin' Liza on the sly
An' laughin' in my sleeve with glee,
I asked her, please, to pardon me.
We walked away a step or two,
Jest to git out o' Liza's view,
An' then Zeke said, " I want to know
Ef you think you're Eliza's beau,
An' 'at I'm goin' to let her go
Hum with sich a chap as you ? "
An' I said bold, " You bet I do."
Then Zekel, sneerin', said 'at he
Didn't want to hender me.
But then he 'lowed the gal was his
An' 'at he guessed he knowed his biz,
An' wasn't feared o' all my kin
With all my friends an' chums throwed
  in.
Some other things he mentioned there
That no born man could noways bear
Er think o' ca'mly tryin' to stan'
Ef Zeke had be'n the bigges' man
In town, an' not the leanest runt
'At time an' labor ever stunt.
An' so I let my fist go " bim,"
I thought I'd mos' nigh finished him.
But Zekel didn't take it so.
He jest ducked down an' dodged my
  blow
An' then come back at me so hard,
I guess I must 'a' hurt the yard,
Er spilet the grass plot where I fell,
An' sakes alive it hurt me ; well,
It wouldn't be'n so bad, you see,
But he jest kep' a-hittin' me.
An' I hit back an' kicked an' pawed,

But 't seemed 'twas mostly air I clawed,
While Zekel used his science well
A-makin' every motion tell.
He punched an' hit, why, goodness
    lands,
Seemed like he had a dozen hands.
Well, afterwhile they stopped the fuss,
An' some one kindly parted us.
All beat an' cuffed an' clawed an'
    scratched,
An' needin' both our faces patched,
Each started hum a different way;
An' what o' Liza, do you say,
Why, Liza—little humbug—dern her,
Why, she'd gone home with Hiram
    Turner.

THE LOVER AND THE MOON

A lover whom duty called over the wave,
    With himself communed: " Will my
        love be true
If left to herself? Had I better not sue
Some friend to watch over her, good and
        grave?
    But my friend might fail in my need,"
        he said,
" And I return to find love dead.
Since friendships fade like the flow'rs of
        June,
I will leave her in charge of the stable
        moon."

Then he said to the moon: " O dear old
        moon,
    Who for years and years from thy throne
        above
Hast nurtured and guarded young lovers
        and love,
My heart has but come to its waiting June,
    And the promise time of the budding
        vine;
Oh, guard thee well this love of mine."
And he harked him then while all was
        still,
    And the pale moon answered and said,
        " I will."

And he sailed in his ship o'er many seas,
    And he wandered wide o'er strange far
        strands:

In isles of the south and in Orient lands,
Where pestilence lurks in the breath of the
        breeze.
But his star was high, so he braved the
        main,
    And sailed him blithely home again;
And with joy he bended his footsteps
        soon
To learn of his love from the matron
        moon.

She sat as of yore, in her olden place,
    Serene as death, in her silver chair.
A white rose gleamed in her whiter hair,
And the tint of a blush was on her face.
    At sight of the youth she sadly bowed
    And hid her face 'neath a gracious cloud.
She faltered faint on the night's dim
        marge,
    But " How," spoke the youth, " have
        you kept your charge? "

The moon was sad at a trust ill-kept;
    The blush went out in her blanching
        cheek,
    And her voice was timid and low and
        weak,
As she made her plea and sighed and
        wept.
    " Oh, another prayed and another plead,
    And I couldn't resist," she answering
        said;
    " But love still grows in the hearts of
        men:
Go forth, dear youth, and love again."

But he turned him away from her proffered
        grace.
    " Thou art false, O moon, as the hearts
        of men,
I will not, will not love again."
And he turned sheer 'round with a soul-
        sick face
    To the sea, and cried: " Sea, curse the
        moon,
    Who makes her vows and forgets so
        soon."
And the awful sea with anger stirred,
    And his breast heaved hard as he lay
        and heard.

And ever the moon wept down in rain,
  And ever her sighs rose high in wind;
But the earth and sea were deaf and
    blind,
And she wept and sighed her griefs in
    vain.
  And ever at night, when the storm is
    fierce,
  The cries of a wraith through the thun-
    ders pierce;
  And the waves strain their awful hands
    on high
To tear the false moon from the sky.

CONSCIENCE AND REMORSE

" Good-bye," I said to my conscience —
  " Good-bye for aye and aye,"
And I put her hands off harshly,
  And turned my face away;
And conscience smitten sorely
  Returned not from that day.

But a time came when my spirit
  Grew weary of its pace;
And I cried : " Come back, my conscience;
  I long to see thy face."
But conscience cried : "I cannot;
  Remorse sits in my place."

IONE

I

Ah, yes, 'tis sweet still to remember,
  Though 'twere less painful to forget;
For while my heart glows like an ember,
  Mine eyes with sorrow's drops are wet,
  And, oh, my heart is aching yet.
It is a law of mortal pain
  That old wounds, long accounted well,
  Beneath the memory's potent spell,
Will wake to life and bleed again.

So 'tis with me; it might be better
  If I should turn no look behind,—
If I could curb my heart, and fetter
  From reminiscent gaze my mind,
  Or let my soul go blind—go blind!
But would I do it if I could?
  Nay! ease at such a price were spurned;
  For, since my love was once returned,
All that I suffer seemeth good.

I know, I know it is the fashion,
  When love has left some heart distressed,
To weight the air with wordful passion!
  But I am glad that in my breast
  I ever held so dear a guest.
Love does not come at every nod,
  Or every voice that calleth " hasten ";
  He seeketh out some heart to chasten,
And whips it, wailing, up to God!

Love is no random road wayfarer
  Who where he may must sip his glass.
Love is the King, the Purple-Wearer,
  Whose guard recks not of tree or grass
  To blaze the way that he may pass.
What if my heart be in the blast
  That heralds his triumphant way;
  Shall I repine, shall I not say :
" Rejoice, my heart, the King has passed!"

In life, each heart holds some sad story —
  The saddest ones are never told.
I, too, have dreamed of fame and glory,
  And viewed the future bright with gold;
  But that is as a tale long told.
Mine eyes hav' lost their youthful flash,
  My cunning hand has lost its art;
  I am not old, but in my heart
The ember lies beneath the ash.

I loved! Why not? My heart was
    youthful,
  My mind was filled with healthy thought.
He doubts not whose own self is truthful,
  Doubt by dishonesty is taught;
  So loved I boldly, fearing naught.
I did not walk this lowly earth;
  Mine was a newer, higher sphere,
  Where youth was long and life was dear,
And all save love was little worth.

Her likeness! Would that I might limn it,
  As Love did, with enduring art;
Nor dust of days nor death may dim it,
  Where it lies graven on my heart,
  Of this sad fabric of my life a part.
I would that I might paint her now
  As I beheld her in that day,
  Ere her first bloom had passed away,
And left the lines upon her brow.

A face serene that, beaming brightly,
   Disarmed the hot sun's glances bold.
A foot that kissed the ground so lightly,
   He frowned in wrath and deemed her
      cold,
   But loved her still though he was old.
A form where every maiden grace
   Bloomed to perfection's richest flower,—
   The statued pose of conscious power,
Like lithe-limbed Dian's of the chase.

Beneath a brow too fair for frowning,
   Like moonlit deeps that glass the skies
Till all the hosts above seem drowning,
   Looked forth her steadfast hazel eyes,
   With gaze serene and purely wise.
And over all, her tresses rare,
   Which, when, with his desire grown
      weak,
   The Night bent down to kiss her cheek,
Entrapped and held him captive there.

This was Ione ; a spirit finer
   Ne'er burned to ash its house of clay ;
A soul instinct with fire diviner
   Ne'er fled athwart the face of day,
   And tempted Time with earthly stay.
Her loveliness was not alone
   Of face and form and tresses' hue ;
For aye a pure, high soul shone through
Her every act : this was Ione.

II

'Twas in the radiant summer weather,
   When God looked, smiling, from the
      sky ;
And we went wand'ring much together
   By wood and lane, Ione and I,
   Attracted by the subtle tie
Of common thoughts and common tastes,
   Of eyes whose vision saw the same,
   And freely granted beauty's claim
Where others found but worthless wastes.

We paused to hear the far bells ringing
   Across the distance, sweet and clear.
We listened to the wild bird's singing
   The song he meant for his mate's ear,
   And deemed our chance to do so dear
We loved to watch the warrior Sun,

With flaming shield and flaunting crest,
   Go striding down the gory West,
When Day's long fight was fought and
     won.

And life became a different story ;
   Where'er I looked, I saw new light.
Earth's self assumed a greater glory,
   Mine eyes were cleared to fuller sight.
   Then first I saw the need and might
Of that fair band, the singing throng,
   Who, gifted with the skill divine,
   Take up the threads of life, spun fine,
And weave them into soulful song.

They sung for me, whose passion pressing
   My soul, found vent in song nor line.
They bore the burden of expressing
   All that I felt, with art's design,
   And every word of theirs was mine.
I read them to Ione, ofttimes,
   By hill and shore, beneath fair skies,
   And she looked deeply in mine eyes,
And knew my love spoke through their
     rhymes.

Her life was like the stream that floweth,
   And mine was like the waiting sea ;
Her love was like the flower that bloweth,
   And mine was like the searching bee —
   I found her sweetness all for me.
God plied him in the mint of time,
   And coined for us a golden day,
   And rolled it ringing down life's way
With love's sweet music in its chime.

And God unclasped the Book of Ages,
   And laid it open to our sight ;
Upon the dimness of its pages,
   So long consigned to rayless night,
   He shed the glory of his light.
We read them well, we read them long,
   And ever thrilling did we see
   That love ruled all humanity,—
The master passion, pure and strong.

III

To-day my skies are bare and ashen,
   And bend on me without a beam.
Since love is held the master-passion,

Its loss must be the pain supreme —
And grinning Fate has wrecked my
    dream.
But pardon, dear departed Guest,
  I will not rant, I will not rail;
  For good the grain must feel the flail;
There are whom love has never blessed.

I had and have a younger brother,
  One whom I loved and love to-day
As never fond and doting mother
  Adored the babe who found its way
From heavenly scenes into her day.
Oh, he was full of youth's new wine,—
  A man on life's ascending slope,
  Flushed with ambition, full of hope ;
And every wish of his was mine.

A kingly youth ; the way before him
  Was thronged with victories to be won ;
So joyous, too, the heavens o'er him
  Were bright with an unchanging sun,—
  His days with rhyme were overrun.
Toil had not taught him Nature's prose,
  Tears had not dimmed his brilliant eyes,
  And sorrow had not made him wise ;
His life was in the budding rose.

I know not how I came to waken,
  Some instinct pricked my soul to sight ;
My heart by some vague thrill was
    shaken,—
  A thrill so true and yet so slight,
  I hardly deemed I read aright.
As when a sleeper, ign'rant why,
  Not knowing what mysterious hand
  Has called him out of slumberland,
Starts up to find some danger nigh.

Love is a guest that comes, unbidden,
  But, having come, asserts his right ;
He will not be repressed nor hidden.
  And so my brother's dawning plight
Became uncovered to my sight.
Some sound-mote in his passing tone
  Caught in the meshes of my ear ;
  Some little glance, a shade too dear,
Betrayed the love he bore Ione.

What could I do ?   He was my brother,
  And young, and full of hope and trust ;

I could not, dared not try to smother
  His flame, and turn his heart to dust.
  I knew how oft life gives a crust
To starving men who cry for bread ;
  But he was young, so few his days,
  He had not learned the great world's
      ways,
Nor Disappointment's volumes read.

However fair and rich the booty,
  I could not make his loss my gain.
For love is dear, but dearer, duty,
  And here my way was clear and plain.
  I saw how I could save him pain.
And so, with all my day grown dim,
  That this loved brother's sun might
      shine,
  I joined his suit, gave over mine,
And sought Ione, to plead for him.

I found her in an eastern bower,
  Where all day long the am'rous sun
Lay by to woo a timid flower.
  This day his course was well-nigh run,
  But still with lingering art he spun
Gold fancies on the shadowed wall.
  The vines waved soft and green above,
  And there where one might tell his love,
I told my griefs—I told her all!

I told her all, and as she hearkened,
  A tear-drop fell upon her dress.
With grief her flushing brow was darkened ;
  One sob that she could not repress
  Betrayed the depths of her distress.
Upon her grief my sorrow fed,
  And I was bowed with unlived years,
  My heart swelled with a sea of tears,
The tears my manhood could not shed.

The world is Rome, and Fate is Nero,
  Disporting in the hour of doom.
God made us men ; times make the hero —
  But in that awful space of gloom
  I gave no thought but sorrow's room.
All—all was dim within that bower,
  What time the sun divorced the day ;
  And all the shadows, glooming gray,
Proclaimed the sadness of the hour.

She could not speak—no word was needed ;
  Her look, half strength and half despair,

Told me I had not vainly pleaded,
　　That she would not ignore my prayer.
And so she turned and left me there,
And as she went, so passed my bliss;
　　She loved me, I could not mistake —
　　But for her own and my love's sake,
Her womanhood could rise to this!

My wounded heart fled swift to cover,
　　And life at times seemed very drear.
My brother proved an ardent lover —
　　What had so young a man to fear?
He wed Ione within the year.
No shadow clouds her tranquil brow,
　　Men speak her husband's name with
　　　　pride,
　　While she sits honored at his side —
She is—she must be happy now!

I doubt the course I took no longer,
　　Since those I love seem satisfied.
The bond between them will grow stronger
　　As they go forward side by side;
Then will my pains be justified.
Their joy is mine, and that is best —
　　I am not totally bereft;
　　For I have still the mem'ry left —
Love stopped with me—a Royal Guest!

RELIGION

It was doubtless about the time that
Mr. Dunbar reached his final decision not
to enter the ministry that he wrote these
lines, which have at least the ring of sin-
cerity to recommend them.   One of Mr.
Dunbar's marked characteristics was fear-
lessness, and he usually wrote to the point
regardless of public prejudices or opinions.

I am no priest of crooks nor creeds,
For human wants and human needs
Are more to me than prophets' deeds;
And human tears and human cares
Affect me more than human prayers.

Go, cease your wail, lugubrious saint!
You fret high Heaven with your plaint.
Is this the " Christian's joy " you paint?
Is this the Christian's boasted bliss?
Avails your faith no more than this?

Take up your arms, come out with me,
Let Heav'n alone; humanity
Needs more and Heaven less from thee.
With pity for mankind look 'round;
Help them to rise—and Heaven is found.

DEACON JONES' GRIEVANCE

I've been watchin' of 'em, parson,
　　An' I'm sorry fur to say
'At my mind is not contented
　　With the loose an' keerless way
'At the young folks treat the music;
　　'Tain't the proper sort o' choir.
Then I don't believe in Christuns
　　A-singin' hymns for hire.

But I never would 'a' murmured
　　An' the matter might 'a' gone
Ef it wasn't fur the antics
　　'At I've seen 'em kerry on;
So I thought it was my dooty
　　Fur to come to you an' ask
Ef you wouldn't sort o' gently
　　Take them singin' folks to task.

Fust, the music they've be'n singin'
　　Will disgrace us mighty soon;
It's a cross between a opry
　　An' a ol' cotillion tune.
With its dashes an' its quavers
　　An' its highfalutin style —
Why, it sets my head to swimmin'
　　When I'm comin' down the aisle.

Now it might be almost decent
　, Ef it wasn't fur the way
'At they git up there an' sing it,
　　Hey dum diddle, loud and gay.
Why, it shames the name o' sacred
　　In its brazen worldliness,
An' they've even got " Ol' Hundred "
　　In a bold, new-fangled dress.

You'll excuse me, Mr. Parson,
　　Ef I seem a little sore;
But I've sung the songs of Isr'el
　　For threescore years an' more,
An' it sort o' hurts my feelin's

Fur to see 'em put away
Fur these harum-scarum ditties
'At is capturin' the day.

There's anuther little happ'nin'
'At I'll mention while I'm here,
Jes' to show 'at my objections
All is offered sound and clear.
It was one day they was singin'
An' was doin' well enough —
Singin' good as people could sing
Sich an awful mess o' stuff —

When the choir give a holler,
An' the organ give a groan,
An' they left one weak-voiced feller
A-singin' there alone !
But he stuck right to the music,
Tho' 'twas tryin' as could be ;
An' when I tried to help him,
Why, the hull church scowled at me.

You say that's so-low singin',
Well, I pray the Lord that I
Growed up when folks was willin'
To sing their hymns so high.
Why, we never had sich doin's
In the good ol' Bethel days,
When the folks was all contented
With the simple songs of praise.

Now I may have spoke too open,
But 'twas too hard to keep still,
An' I hope you'll tell the singers
'At I bear 'em no ill-will.
'At they all may git to glory
Is my wish an' my desire,
But they'll need some extry trainin'
'Fore they jine the heavenly choir.

ALICE

Know you, winds that blow your course
Down the verdant valleys,
That somewhere you must, perforce,
Kiss the brow of Alice ?
When her gentle face you find,
Kiss it softly, naughty wind.

Roses waving fair and sweet
Thro' the garden alleys,
10

Grow into a glory meet
For the eye of Alice ;
Let the wind your offering bear
Of sweet perfume, faint and rare.

Lily holding crystal dew
In your pure white chalice,
Nature kind hath fashioned you
Like the soul of Alice ;
It of purest white is wrought,
Filled with gems of crystal thought.

AFTER THE QUARREL

So we, who've supped the self-same cup,
To-night must lay our friendship by ;
Your wrath has burned your judgment up,
Hot breath has blown the ashes high.
You say that you are wronged—ah, well,
I count that friendship poor, at best
A bauble, a mere bagatelle,
That cannot stand so slight a test.

I fain would still have been your friend,
And talked and laughed and loved with
you ;
But since it must, why, let it end ;
The false but dies, 'tis not the true.
So we are favored, you and I,
Who only want the living truth.
It was not good to nurse the lie ;
'Tis well it died in harmless youth.

I go from you to-night to sleep.
Why, what's the odds ? why should I
grieve ?
I have no fund of tears to weep
For happenings that undeceive.
The days shall come, the days shall go
Just as they came and went before.
The sun shall shine, the streams shall flow
Though you and I are friends no more.

And in the volume of my years,
Where all my thoughts and acts shall be,
The page whereon your name appears
Shall be forever sealed to me.
Not that I hate you over-much,
'Tis less of hate than love defied ;

Howe'er, our hands no more shall touch,
  We'll go our ways, the world is wide.

BEYOND THE YEARS

I

Beyond the years the answer lies,
Beyond where brood the grieving skies
    And Night drops tears.
Where Faith rod-chastened smiles to rise
    And doff its fears,
And carping Sorrow pines and dies —
    Beyond the years.

II

Beyond the years the prayer for rest
Shall beat no more within the breast ;
    The darkness clears,
And Morn perched on the mountain's
    crest
    Her form uprears —
The day that is to come is best,
    Beyond the years.

III

Beyond the years the soul shall find
That endless peace for which it pined,
    For light appears,
And to the eyes that still were blind
    With blood and tears,
Their sight shall come all unconfined
    Beyond the years.

AFTER A VISIT

I be'n down in ole Kentucky
    Fur a week er two, an' say,
'Twuz ez hard ez breakin' oxen
    Fur to tear myse'f away.
Allus argerin' 'bout fren'ship
    An' yer hospitality —
Y' ain't no right to talk about it
    Tell you be'n down there to see.

See jest how they give you welcome
    To the best that's in the land,
Feel the sort o' grip they give you
    When they take you by the hand.
Hear 'em say, " We're glad to have you,
    Better stay a week er two ; "

An' the way they treat you makes you
    Feel that ev'ry word is true.

Feed you tell you hear the buttons
    Crackin' on yore Sunday vest ;
Haul you roun' to see the wonders
    Tell you have to cry for rest.
Drink yer health an' pet an' praise you
    Tell you git to feel ez great
Ez the Sheriff o' the county
    Er the Gov'ner o' the State.

Wife, she sez I must be crazy
    'Cause I go on so, an' Nelse
He 'lows, " Goodness gracious ! daddy,
    Cain't you talk about nuthin' else ? "
Well, pleg-gone it, I'm jes' tickled,
    Bein' tickled ain't no sin ;
I be'n down in ole Kentucky,
    An' I want o' go ag'in.

CURTAIN

Villain shows his indiscretion,
Villain's partner makes confession.
Juvenile, with golden tresses,
Finds her pa and dons long dresses.
Scapegrace comes home money-laden,
Hero comforts tearful maiden,
Soubrette marries loyal chappie
Villain skips, and all are happy.

THE SPELLIN'-BEE

I never shall furgit that night when father
    hitched up Dobbin,
An' all us youngsters clambered in an'
    down the road went bobbin'
To school where we was kep' at work in
    every kind o' weather,
But where that night a spellin'-bee was
    callin' us together.
'Twas one o' Heaven's banner nights, the
    stars was all a glitter,
The moon was shinin' like the hand o'
    God had jest then lit her.
The ground was white with spotless snow,
    the blast was sort o' stingin' ;
But underneath our round-abouts, you bet
    our hearts was singin'.
That spellin'-bee had be'n the talk o' many
    a precious moment,

The youngsters all was wild to see jes'
    what the precious show meant,
An' we whose years was in their teens was
    little less desirous
O' gittin' to the meetin' so's our sweet-
    hearts could admire us.
So on we went so anxious fur to satisfy our
    mission
That father had to box our ears, to smother
    our ambition.
But boxin' ears was too short work to hin-
    der our arrivin',
He jest turned roun' an' smacked us all,
    an' kep' right on a-drivin'.
Well, soon the schoolhouse hove in sight,
    the winders beamin' brightly;
The sound o' talkin' reached our ears, and
    voices laffin' lightly.
It puffed us up so full an' big 'at I'll jest
    bet a dollar,
There wa'n't a feller there but felt the
    strain upon his collar.
So down we jumped an' in we went ez
    sprightly ez you make 'em,
But somethin' grabbed us by the knees an'
    straight began to shake 'em.
Fur once within the lighted room, our
    feelin's took a canter,
An' scurried to the zero mark ez quick ez
    Tam O'Shanter.
'Cause there was crowds o' people there,
    both sexes an' all stations;
It looked like all the town had come an'
    brought all their relations.
The first I saw was Nettie Gray, I thought
    that girl was dearer
'N' gold; an' when I got a chance, you
    bet I aidged up near her.
An' Farmer Dobbs's girl was there, the one
    'at Jim was sweet on,
An' Cyrus Jones an' Mandy Smith an'
    Faith an' Patience Deaton.
Then Parson Brown an' Lawyer Jones
    were present—all attention,
An' piles on piles of other folks too nu-
    merous to mention.
The master rose an' briefly said : " Good
    friends, dear brother Crawford,
To spur the pupils' minds along, a little
    prize has offered.
To him who spells the best to-night—or 't
    may be ' her '—no tellin'—

He offers ez a jest reward, this precious
    work on spellin'."
A little blue-backed spellin'-book with
    fancy scarlet trimmin',
We boys devoured it with our eyes—so did
    the girls an' women.
He held it up where all could see, then on
    the table set it,
An' ev'ry speller in the house felt mortal
    bound to get it.
At his command we fell in line, prepared
    to do our dooty,
Outspell the rest an' set 'em down, an'
    carry home the booty.
'Twas then the merry times began, the
    blunders, an' the laffin',
The nudges an' the nods an' winks an'
    stale good-natured chaffin'.
Ole Uncle Hiram Dane was there, the
    clostest man a-livin',
Whose only bugbear seemed to be the
    dreadful fear o' givin'.
His beard was long, his hair uncut, his
    clothes all bare an' dingy ;
It wasn't 'cause the man was pore, but jest
    so mortal stingy.
An' there he sot by Sally Riggs a-smilin'
    an' a-smirkin',
An' all his childern lef' to home a diggin'
    an' a-workin'.
A widower he was, an' Sal was thinkin'
    'at she'd wing him ;
I reckon he was wond'rin' what them
    rings o' hern would bring him.
An' when the spellin'-test commenced, he
    up an' took his station,
A-spellin' with the best o' them to beat
    the very nation.
An' when he'd spell some youngster
    down, he'd turn to look at Sally,
An' say : " The teachin' nowadays can't
    be o' no great vally."
But true enough the adage says, " Pride
    walks in slipp'ry places,"
Fur soon a thing occurred that put a smile
    on all our faces.
The laffter jest kep' ripplin' 'roun' an'
    teacher couldn't quell it,
Fur when he give out " charity " ole
    Hiram couldn't spell it.
But laffin' 's ketchin' an' it throwed some
    others off their bases,

An' folks 'u'd miss the very word that
  seemed to fit their cases.
Why, fickle little Jessie Lee come near
  the house upsettin'
By puttin' in a double " kay " to spell the
  word " coquettin'."
An' when it come to Cyrus Jones, it
  tickled me all over —
Him settin' up to Mandy Smith an' got
  sot down on " lover."
But Lawyer Jones of all gone men did
  shorely look the gonest,
When he found out that he'd furgot to put
  the " h " in " honest."
An' Parson Brown, whose sermons were
  too long fur toleration,
Caused lots o' smiles by missin' when they
  give out " condensation."
So one by one they giv' it up—the big
  words kep' a-landin',
Till me àn' Nettie Gray was left, the only
  ones a-standin',
An' then my inward strife began—I guess
  my mind was petty—
I did so want that spellin'-book ; but then
  to spell down Nettie
Jest sort o' went ag'in my grain—I some-
  how couldn't do it,
An' when I git a notion fixed, I'm great
  on stickin' to it.
So when they giv' the next word out—I
  hadn't orter tell it,
But then 'twas all fur Nettie's sake—I
  missed so's she could spell it.
She spelt the word, then looked at me so
  lovin'-like an' mello',
I tell you 't sent a hunderd pins a-shootin
  through a fello'.
O' course I had to stand the jokes an'
  chaffin' of the fello's,
But when they handed her the book I vow
  I wasn't jealous.
We sung a hymn, an' Parson Brown dis-
  missed us like he orter,
Fur, la ! he'd learned a thing er two an'
  made his blessin' shorter.
'Twas late an' cold when we got out, but
  Nettie liked cold weather,
An' so did I, so we agreed we'd jest walk
  home together.
We both wuz silent, fur of words we
  nuther had a surplus,

'Til she spoke out quite sudden like,
  " You missed that word on purpose."
Well, I declare it frightened me ; at first
  I tried denyin',
But Nettie, she jest smiled an' smiled, she
  knowed that I was lyin'.
Sez she : " That book is yourn by right ; "
  sez I : " It never could be —
I—I—you—ah ——" an' there I stuck,
  an' well she understood me.
So we agreed that later on when age had
  giv' us tether,
We'd jine our lots an' settle down to own
  that book together.

KEEP A-PLUGGIN' AWAY

I've a humble little motto
That is homely, though it's true,—
  Keep a-pluggin' away.
It's a thing when I've an object
That I always try to do,—
  Keep a-pluggin' away.
When you've rising storms to quell,
When opposing waters swell,
It will never fail to tell,—
  Keep a-pluggin' away.

If the hills are high before
And the paths are hard to climb,
  Keep a-pluggin' away.
And remember that successes
Come to him who bides his time,—
  Keep a pluggin' away.
From the greatest to the least,
None are from the rule released.
Be thou toiler, poet, priest,
  Keep a-pluggin' away.

Delve away beneath the surface,
There is treasure farther down,—
  Keep a-pluggin' away.
Let the rain come down in torrents,
Let the threat'ning heavens frown,
  Keep a-pluggin' away.
When the clouds have rolled away,
There will come a brighter day
All your labor to repay,—
  Keep a-pluggin' away.

There'll be lots of sneers to swallow,
There'll be lots of pain to bear,—
  Keep a-pluggin' away.
If you've got your eye on heaven,
Some bright day you'll wake up there,—
  Keep a-pluggin' away.
Perseverance still is king;
Time its sure reward will bring;
Work and wait unwearying,—
  Keep a-pluggin' away.

NIGHT OF LOVE

The moon has left the sky, love,
  The stars are hiding now,
And frowning on the world, love,
  Night bares her sable brow.
The snow is on the ground, love,
  And cold and keen the air is.
I'm singing here to you, love;
  You're dreaming there in Paris.

But this is Nature's law, love,
  Though just it may not seem,
That men should wake to sing, love,
  While maidens sleep and dream.
Them care may not molest, love,
  Nor stir them from their slumbers,
Though midnight find the swain, love,
  Still halting o'er his numbers.

I watch the rosy dawn, love,
  Come stealing up the east,
While all things round rejoice, love,
  That Night her reign has ceased.
The lark will soon be heard, love,
  And on his way be winging;
When Nature's poets wake, love,
  Why should a man be singing?

COLUMBIAN ODE

I

Four hundred years ago a tangled waste
  Lay sleeping on the west Atlantic's side;
Their devious ways the Old World's mil-
    lions traced
  Content, and loved, and labored, dared
    and died,

While students still believed the charts
  they conned,
  And reveled in their thriftless igno-
    rance,
Nor dreamed of other lands that lay be-
  yond
  Old Ocean's dense, indefinite expanse.

II

But deep within her heart old Nature
  knew
  That she had once arrayed, at Earth's
    behest,
Another offspring, fine and fair to view,—
  The chosen suckling of the mother's
    breast.
The child was wrapped in vestments soft
  and fine,
  Each fold a work of Nature's matchless
    art;
The mother looked on it with love divine,
  And strained the loved one closely to
    her heart.
And there it lay, and with the warmth
  grew strong
  And hearty, by the salt sea breezes
    fanned,
Till Time with mellowing touches passed
  along,
  And changed the infant to a mighty
    land.

III

But men knew naught of this, till there
  arose
  That mighty mariner, the Genoese,
Who dared to try, in spite of fears and
  foes,
  The unknown fortunes of unsounded
    seas.
O noblest of Italia's sons, thy bark
  Went not alone into that shrouding
    night!
O dauntless darer of the rayless dark,
  The world sailed with thee to eternal
    light!
The deer-haunts that with game were
  crowded then
  To-day are tilled and cultivated lands;
The schoolhouse tow'rs where Bruin had
  his den,

And where the wigwam stood the chapel
stands ;
The place that nurtured men of savage
mien
Now teems with men of Nature's noblest
types ;
Where moved the forest-foliage banner
green,
Now flutters in the breeze the stars and
stripes !

A BORDER BALLAD

Oh, I haven't got long to live, for we all
Die soon, e'en those who live longest ;
And the poorest and weakest are taking
their chance
Along with the richest and strongest.
So it's heigho for a glass and a song,
And a bright eye over the table,
And a dog for the hunt when the game is
flush,
And the pick of a gentleman's stable.

There is Dimmock o' Dune, he was here
yesternight,
But he's rotting to-day on Glen Arragh ;
'Twas the hand o' MacPherson that gave
him the blow,
And the vultures shall feast on his mar-
row.
But it's heigho for a brave old song
And a glass while we are able ;
Here's a health to death and another cup
To the bright eye over the table.

I can show a broad back and a jolly deep
chest,
But who argues now on appearance ?
A blow or a thrust or a stumble at best
May send me to-day to my clearance.
Then it's heigho for the things I love,
My mother'll be soon wearing sable,
But give me my horse and my dog and my
glass,
And a bright eye over the table.

AN EASY-GOIN' FELLER

Ther' ain't no use in all this strife,
An' hurryin', pell-mell, right thro' life.

I don't believe in goin' too fast
To see what kind o' road you've passed.
It ain't no mortal kind o' good,
'N' I wouldn't hurry ef I could.
I like to jest go joggin' 'long,
To limber up my soul with song ;
To stop awhile 'n' chat the men,
'N' drink some cider now an' then.

Do' want no boss a-standin' by
To see me work ; I allus try
To do my dooty right straight up,
An' earn what fills my plate an' cup.
An' ez fur boss, I'll be my own,
I like to jest be let alone,
To plough my strip an' tend my bees,
An' do jest like I doggoned please.
My head's all right, an' my heart's meller,
But I'm a easy-goin' feller.

THE DILETTANTE : A MODERN
TYPE

He scribbles some in prose and verse,
And now and then he prints it ;
He paints a little,—gathers some
Of nature's gold and mints it.

He plays a little, sings a song,
Acts tragic rôles, or funny ;
He does, because his love is strong,
But not, oh, not for money !

He studies almost everything
From social art to science ;
A thirsty mind, a flowing spring,
Demand and swift compliance.

He looms above the sordid crowd —
At least through friendly lenses ;
While his mamma looks pleased and
proud,
And kindly pays expenses.

BY THE STREAM

By the stream I dream in calm delight,
and watch as in a glass,
How the clouds like crowds of snowy-hued
and white-robed maidens pass,
And the water into ripples breaks and
sparkles as it spreads,

Like a host of armored knights with silver
    helmets on their heads.
And I deem the stream an emblem fit of
    human life may go,
For I find a mind may sparkle much and
    yet but shallows show,
And a soul may glow with myriad lights
    and wondrous mysteries,
When it only lies a dormant thing and
    mirrors what it sees.

NATURE AND ART

TO MY FRIEND CHARLES BOOTH NET-
TLETON

I

The young queen Nature, ever sweet and
    fair,
    Once on a time fell upon evil days.
    From hearing oft herself discussed with
        praise,
There grew within her heart the longing
    rare
To see herself; and every passing air
    The warm desire fanned into lusty blaze.
Full oft she sought this end by devious
    ways,
But sought in vain, so fell she in despair.
For none within her train nor by her side
    Could solve the task or give the envied
        boon.
    So day and night, beneath the sun and
        moon,
She wandered to and fro unsatisfied,
Till Art came by, a blithe inventive elf,
And made a glass wherein she saw her-
    self.

II

Enrapt, the queen gazed on her glorious
    self,
    Then trembling with the thrill of sudden
        thought,
    Commanded that the skilful wight be
        brought
That she might dower him with lands and
    pelf.
Then out upon the silent sea-lapt shelf
    And up the hills and on the downs they
        sought

Him who so well and wondrously had
    wrought;
And with much search found and brought
    home the elf.
But he put by all gifts with sad replies,
And from his lips these words flowed forth
    like wine :
    " O queen, I want no gift but thee,"
    he said.
She heard and looked on him with love-lit
    eyes,
Gave him her hand, low murmuring, " I
    am thine,"
And at the morrow's dawning they were
    wed.

AFTER WHILE

A POEM OF FAITH

I think that though the clouds be dark,
That though the waves dash o'er the bark,
Yet after while the light will come,
And in calm waters safe at home
    The bark will anchor.
Weep not, my sad-eyed, gray-robed maid,
Because your fairest blossoms fade,
That sorrow still o'erruns your cup,
And even though you root them up,
    The weeds grow ranker.

For after while your tears shall cease,
And sorrow shall give way to peace ;
The flowers shall bloom, the weeds shall
    die,
And in that faith seen, by and by
    Thy woes shall perish.
Smile at old Fortune's adverse tide,
Smile when the scoffers sneer and chide.
Oh, not for you the gems that pale,
And not for you the flowers that fail ;
    Let this thought cherish :

That after while the clouds will part,
And then with joy the waiting heart
Shall feel the light come stealing in,
That drives away the cloud of sin
    And breaks its power.
And you shall burst your chrysalis,
And wing away to realms of bliss,
Untrammeled, pure, divinely free,
Above all earth's anxiety
    From that same hour.

A NEGRO LOVE SONG

This poem illustrates the way in which Mr. Dunbar utilized the most humble of happenings as material for his verses. During the World's Fair he served for a short time as hotel waiter. When the negroes were not busy they had a custom of congregating and talking about their sweethearts. Then a man with a tray would come along and, as the dining-room was frequently crowded, he would say, when in need of passing-room: "Jump back, honey, jump back." Out of these commonplace confidences, he wove the musical little composition—"A Negro Love Song."

Seen my lady home las' night,
    Jump back, honey, jump back.
Hel' huh han' an' sque'z it tight,
    Jump back, honey, jump back.
Hyeahd huh sigh a little sigh,
Seen a light gleam f'om huh eye,
An' a smile go flittin' by —
    Jump back, honey, jump back.

Hyeahd de win' blow thoo de pine,
    Jump back, honey, jump back.
Mockin'-bird was singin' fine,
    Jump back, honey, jump back.
An' my hea't was beatin' so,
When I reached my lady's do',
Dat I couldn't ba' to go —
    Jump back, honey, jump back.

Put my ahm aroun' huh wais',
    Jump back, honey, jump back.
Raised huh lips an' took a tase,
    Jump back, honey, jump back.
Love me, honey, love me true?
Love me well ez I love you?
An' she answe'd, " 'Cose I do"—
    Jump back, honey, jump back.

THE COLORED SOLDIERS

If the muse were mine to tempt it
And my feeble voice were strong,
If my tongue were trained to measures,
    I would sing a stirring song.

I would sing a song heroic
    Of those noble sons of Ham,
Of the gallant colored soldiers
    Who fought for Uncle Sam!

In the early days you scorned them,
    And with many a flip and flout
Said "These battles are the white man's,
    And the whites will fight them out."
Up the hills you fought and faltered,
    In the vales you strove and bled,
While your ears still heard the thunder
    Of the foes' advancing tread.

Then distress fell on the nation,
    And the flag was drooping low;
Should the dust pollute your banner?
    No! the nation shouted, No!
So when War, in savage triumph,
    Spread abroad his funeral pall —
Then you called the colored soldiers,
    And they answered to your call.

And like hounds unleashed and eager
    For the life blood of the prey,
Sprung they forth and bore them bravely
    In the thickest of the fray.
And where'er the fight was hottest,
    Where the bullets fastest fell,
There they pressed unblanched and fearless
    At the very mouth of hell.

Ah, they rallied to the standard
    To uphold it by their might;
None were stronger in the labors,
    None were braver in the fight.
From the blazing breach of Wagner
    To the plains of Olustee,
They were foremost in the fight
    Of the battles of the free.

And at Pillow! God have mercy
    On the deeds committed there,
And the souls of those poor victims
    Sent to Thee without a prayer.
Let the fulness of Thy pity
    O'er the hot wrought spirits sway
Of the gallant colored soldiers
    Who fell fighting on that day!

SEEN MY LADY HOME LAS' NIGHT

WHEN DE CO'N PONE'S HOT

Yes, the Blacks enjoy their freedom,
    And they won it dearly, too ;
For the life blood of their thousands
    Did the southern fields bedew.
In the darkness of their bondage,
    In the depths of slavery's night,
Their muskets flashed the dawning,
    And they fought their way to light.

They were comrades then and brothers,
    Are they more or less to-day ?
They were good to stop a bullet
    And to front the fearful fray.
They were citizens and soldiers,
    When rebellion raised its head ;
And the traits that made them worthy,—
    Ah ! those virtues are not dead.

They have shared your nightly vigils,
    They have shared your daily toil ;
And their blood with yours commingling
    Has enriched the Southern soil.
They have slept and marched and suffered
    'Neath the same dark skies as you,
They have met as fierce a foeman,
    And have been as brave and true.

And their deeds shall find a record
    In the registry of Fame ;
For their blood has cleansed completely
    Every blot of Slavery's shame.
So all honor and all glory
    To those noble sons of Ham —
The gallant colored soldiers
    Who fought for Uncle Sam !

WHEN DE CO'N PONE'S HOT

Dey is times in life when Nature
    Seems to slip a cog an' go,
Jes' a-rattlin' down creation,
    Lak an ocean's overflow ;
When de worl' jes' stahts a-spinnin'
    Lak a picaninny's top,
An' yo' cup o' joy is brimmin'
    'Twell it seems about to slop,
An' you feel jes' lak a racah,
    Dat is trainin' fu' to trot —
When yo' mammy says de blessin'
    An' de co'n pone's hot.

When you set down at de table,
    Kin' o' weary lak an' sad,
An' you'se jes' a little tiahed
    An' purhaps a little mad ;
How yo' gloom tu'ns into gladness,
    How yo' joy drives out de doubt
When de oven do' is opened,
    An' de smell comes po'in' out ;
Why, de 'lectric light o' Heaven
    Seems to settle on de spot,
When yo' mammy says de blessin'
    An' de co'n pone's hot.

When de cabbage pot is steamin'
    An' de bacon good an' fat,
When de chittlins is a-sputter'n'
    So's to show you whah dey's at ;
Tek away yo' sody biscuit,
    Tek away yo' cake an' pie,
Fu' de glory time is comin',
    An' it's 'proachin' mighty nigh,
An' you want to jump an' hollah,
    Dough you know you'd bettah not,
When yo' mammy says de blessin',
    An' de co'n pone's hot.

I have hyeahd o' lots o' sermons,
    An' I've hyeahd o' lots o' prayers,
An' I've listened to some singin'
    Dat has tuk me up de stairs
Of de Glory-Lan' an' set me
    Jes' below de Mahstah's th'one,
An' have lef' my hea't a-singin'
    In a happy aftah tone ;
But dem wu'ds so sweetly murmured
    Seem to tech de softes' spot,
When my mammy says de blessin',
    An' de co'n pone's hot.

THE OL' TUNES

You kin talk about yer anthems
    An' yer arias an' sich,
An' yer modern choir-singin'
    That you think so awful rich ;
But you orter heerd us youngsters
    In the times now far away,
A-singin' o' the ol' tunes
    In the ol'-fashioned way.

There was some of us sung treble
    An' a few of us growled bass,
An' the tide o' song flowed smoothly

With its 'comp'niment o' grace;
There was spirit in that music,
   An' a kind o' solemn sway,
A-singin' o' the ol' tunes
   In the ol'-fashioned way.

I remember oft o' standin'
   In my homespun pantaloons —
On my face the bronze an' freckles
   O' the suns o' youthful Junes —
Thinkin' that no mortal minstrel
   Ever chanted sich a lay
As the ol' tunes we was singin'
   In the ol'-fashioned way.

The boys 'ud always lead us,
   An' the girls 'ud all chime in,
Till the sweetness o' the singin'
   Robbed the list'nin' soul o' sin;
An' I used to tell the parson
   'Twas as good to sing as pray,
When the people sung the ol' tunes
   In the ol'-fashioned way.

How I long ag'in to hear 'em
   Pourin' forth from soul to soul,
With the treble high an' meller,
   An' the bass's mighty roll;
But the times is very diff'rent,
   An' the music heerd to-day
Ain't the singin' o' the ol' tunes
   In the ol'-fashioned way.

Little screechin' by a woman,
   Little squawkin' by a man,
Then the organ's twiddle-twaddle,
   Jest the empty space to span, —
An' ef you should even think it,
   'Tisn't proper fur to say
That you want to hear the ol' tunes
   In the ol'-fashioned way.

But I think that some bright mornin',
   When the toils of life air o'er,
An' the sun o' heaven arisin'
   Glads with light the happy shore,
I shall hear the angel chorus,
   In the realms of endless day,
A-singin' o' the ol' tunes
   In the ol'-fashioned way.

MELANCHOLIA

Silently without my window,
   Tapping gently at the pane,
   Falls the rain.
Through the trees sighs the breeze
   Like a soul in pain.
Here alone I sit and weep;
Thought hath banished sleep.

Wearily I sit and listen
   To the water's ceaseless drip.
   To my lip
Fate turns up the bitter cup,
   Forcing me to sip;
'Tis a bitter, bitter drink,
Thus I sit and think,—

Thinking things unknown and awful,
   Thoughts on wild, uncanny themes,
   Waking dreams.
Spectres dark, corpses stark,
   Show the gaping seams
Whence the cold and cruel knife
Stole away their life.

Bloodshot eyes all strained and staring,
   Gazing ghastly into mine;
   Blood like wine
On the brow—clotted now —
   Shows death's dreadful sign.
Lonely vigil still I keep;
Would that I might sleep!

Still, oh, still, my brain is whirling!
   Still runs on my stream of thought;
   I am caught
In the net fate hath set.
   Mind and soul are brought
To destruction's very brink;
Yet I can but think!

Eyes that look into the future,—
   Peeping forth from out my mind,
   They will find
Some new weight, soon or late,
   On my soul to bind,
Crushing all its courage out,—
Heavier than doubt.

Dawn, the Eastern monarch's daughter,
  Rising from her dewy bed,
  Lays her head
'Gainst the clouds' sombre shrouds
  Now half fringed with red.
O'er the land she 'gins to peep;
Come, O gentle Sleep!

Hark! the morning cock is crowing;
  Dreams, like ghosts, must hie away;
  'Tis the day.
Rosy morn now is born;
  Dark thoughts may not stay.
Day my brain from foes will keep;
Now, my soul, I sleep.

THE WOOING

A youth went faring up and down,
  Alack and well-a-day.
He fared him to the market town,
  Alack and well-a-day.
And there he met a maiden fair,
With hazel eyes and auburn hair;
His heart went from him then and there,
  Alack and well-a-day.

She posies sold right merrily,
  Alack and well-a-day;
But not a flower was fair as she,
  Alack and well-a-day.
He bought a rose and sighed a sigh,
" Ah, dearest maiden, would that I
Might dare the seller too to buy!"
  Alack and well-a-day.

She tossed her head, the coy coquette,
  Alack and well-a-day.
" I'm not, sir, in the market yet,"
  Alack and well-a-day.
" Your love must cool upon a shelf;
Tho' much I sell for gold and pelf,
I'm yet too young to sell myself,"
  Alack and well-a-day.

The youth was filled with sorrow sore,
  Alack and well-a-day;
And looked he at the maid once more,
  Alack and well-a-day.
Then loud he cried, " Fair maiden, if
Too young to sell, now as I live,
You're not too young yourself to give,"
  Alack and well-a-day.

The little maid cast down her eyes,
  Alack and well-a-day,
And many a flush began to rise,
  Alack and well-a-day.
" Why, since you are so bold," she said,
" I doubt not you are highly bred,
So take me!" and the twain were wed,
  Alack and well-a-day.

MERRY AUTUMN

It's all a farce,—these tales they tell
  About the breezes sighing,
And moans astir o'er field and dell,
  Because the year is dying.

Such principles are most absurd,—
  I care not who first taught 'em;
There's nothing known to beast or bird
  To make a solemn autumn.

In solemn times, when grief holds sway
  With countenance distressing,
You'll note the more of black and gray
  Will then be used in dressing.

Now purple tints are all around;
  The sky is blue and mellow;
And e'en the grasses turn the ground
  From modest green to yellow.

The seed burrs all with laughter crack
  On featherweed and jimson;
And leaves that should be dressed in black
  Are all decked out in crimson.

A butterfly goes winging by;
  A singing bird comes after;
And Nature, all from earth to sky,
  Is bubbling o'er with laughter.

The ripples wimple on the rills,
  Like sparkling little lasses;
The sunlight runs along the hills,
  And laughs among the grasses.

The earth is just so full of fun
  It really can't contain it;
And streams of mirth so freely run
  The heavens seem to rain it.

Don't talk to me of solemn days
In autumn's time of splendor,
Because the sun shows fewer rays,
And these grow slant and slender.

Why, it's the climax of the year,—
The highest time of living!—
Till naturally its bursting cheer
Just melts into thanksgiving.

BALLAD

I know my love is true,
And oh the day is fair.
The sky is clear and blue,
The flowers are rich of hue,
The air I breathe is rare,
I have no grief or care;
For my own love is true,
And oh the day is fair.

My love is false I find,
And oh the day is dark.
Blows sadly down the wind,
While sorrow holds my mind;
I do not hear the lark,
For quenched is life's dear spark,—
My love is false I find,
And oh the day is dark!

For love doth make the day
Or dark or doubly bright;
Her beams along the way
Dispel the gloom and gray.
She lives and all is bright,
She dies and life is night.
For love doth make the day,
Or dark or doubly bright.

THE CHANGE HAS COME

The change has come, and Helen sleeps—
Not sleeps; but wakes to greater deeps
Of wisdom, glory, truth, and light,
Than ever blessed her seeking sight,
In this low, long, lethargic night,
Worn out with strife
Which men call life.

The change has come, and who would say
" I would it were not come to-day " ?

What were the respite till to-morrow ?
Postponement of a certain sorrow,
From which each passing day would
borrow !
Let grief be dumb,
The change has come.

COMPARISON

The sky of brightest gray seems dark
To one whose sky was ever white.
To one who never knew a spark,
Thro' all his life, of love or light,
The grayest cloud seems over-bright.

The robin sounds a beggar's note
Where one the nightingale has heard,
But he for whom no silver throat
Its liquid music ever stirred,
Deems robin still the sweetest bird.

DISCOVERED

Seen you down at chu'ch las' night,
Nevah min', Miss Lucy.
What I mean ? oh, dat's all right,
Nevah min', Miss Lucy.
You was sma't ez sma't could be,
But you couldn't hide f'om me.
Ain't I got two eyes to see!
Nevah min', Miss Lucy.

Guess you thought you's awful keen ;
Nevah min', Miss Lucy.
Evahthing you done, I seen ;
Nevah min', Miss Lucy.
Seen him tek yo' ahm jes' so,
When he got outside de do'—
Oh, I know dat man's yo' beau!
Nevah min', Miss Lucy.

Say now, honey, wha'd he say ?—
Nevah min', Miss Lucy!
Keep yo' secrets—dat's yo' way—
Nevah min', Miss Lucy.
Won't tell me an' I'm yo' pal—
I'm gwine tell his othah gal,—
Know huh, too, huh name is Sal;
Nevah min', Miss Lucy!

DISAPPOINTED

An old man planted and dug and tended,
  Toiling in joy from dew to dew;
The sun was kind, and the rain befriended;
  Fine grew his orchard and fair to view.
Then he said: " I will quiet my thrifty
    fears,
For here is fruit for my failing years."

But even then the storm-clou ls gathered,
  Swallowing up the azure sky;
The sweeping winds into white foam
    lathered
  The placid breast of the bay, hard by;
Then the spirits that raged in the dark-
    ened air
Swept o'er his orchard and left it bare.

The old man stood in the rain, uncaring,
  Viewing the place the storm had swept;
And then with a cry from his soul despair-
    ing,
  He bowed him down to the earth and
    wept.
But a voice cried aloud from the driving
    rain;
" Arise, old man, and plant again! "

INVITATION TO LOVE

Come when the nights are bright with
    stars
  Or when the moon is mellow;
Come when the sun his golden bars
  Drops on the hay-field yellow.
Come in the twilight soft and gray,
Come in the night or come in the day,
Come, O Love, whene'er you may,
  And you are welcome, welcome.

You are sweet, O Love, dear Love,
You are soft as the nesting dove.
Come to my heart and bring it rest
As the bird flies home to its welcome nest.

Come when my heart is full of grief
  Or when my heart is merry;
Come with the falling of the leaf
  Or with the redd'ning cherry.
Come when the year's first blossom blows,
Come when the summer gleams and glows,
Come with the winter's drifting snows,
  And you are welcome, welcome.

HE HAD HIS DREAM

He had his dream, and all through life,
Worked up to it through toil and strife.
Afloat fore'er before his eyes,
It colored for him all his skies:
    The storm-cloud dark
    Above his bark,
The calm and listless vault of blue
Took on its hopeful hue,
It tinctured every passing beam —
    He had his dream.

He labored hard and failed at last,
His sails too weak to bear the blast,
The raging tempests tore away
And sent his beating bark astray.
    But what cared he
    For wind or sea!
He said, " The tempest will be short,
My bark will come to port."
He saw through every cloud a gleam —
    He had his dream.

GOOD-NIGHT

The lark is silent in his nest,
  The breeze is sighing in its flight,
Sleep, Love, and peaceful be thy rest.
  Good-night, my love, good-night, good-
    night.

Sweet dreams attend thee in thy sleep,
  To soothe thy rest till morning's light,
And angels round thee vigil keep.
  Good-night, my love, good-night, good-
    night.

Sleep well, my love, on night's dark breast,
  And ease thy soul with slumber bright;
Be joy but thine and I am blest.
  Good-night, my love, good-night, good-
    night.

A COQUETTE CONQUERED

Yes, my ha't's ez ha'd ez stone —
Go 'way, Sam, an' lemme 'lone.

No; I ain't gwine change my min'—
Ain't gwine ma'y you—nuffin' de kin'.

Phiny loves you true an' deah?
Go ma'y Phiny; whut I keer?
Oh, you needn't mou'n an' cry—
I don't keer how soon you die.

Got a present! Whut you got?
Somef'n fu' de pan er pot!
Huh! yo' sass do sholy beat—
Think I don't git 'nough to eat?

Whut's dat un'neaf yo' coat?
Looks des lak a little shoat.
'Tain't no possum! Bless de Lamb!
Yes, it is, you rascal, Sam!

Gin it to me; whut you say?
Ain't you sma't now! Oh, go 'way!
Possum do look mighty nice,
But you ax too big a price.

Tell me, is you talkin' true,
Dat's de gal's whut ma'ies you?
Come back, Sam; now whah's you gwine?
Co'se you knows dat possum's mine!

NORA: A SERENADE

Ah, Nora, my Nora, the light fades away,
    While Night like a spirit steals up o'er
        the hills;
The thrush from his tree where he chanted
    all day,
    No longer his music in ecstasy trills.
Then, Nora, be near me; thy presence
    doth cheer me,
    Thine eye hath a gleam that is truer
        than gold.
I cannot but love thee; so do not reprove
    me,
    If the strength of my passion should
        make me too bold.

Nora, pride of my heart,—
    Rosy cheeks, cherry lips, sparkling with
        glee,—
Wake from thy slumbers, wherever thou
    art;
    Wake from thy slumbers to me.

Ah, Nora, my Nora, there's love in the
    air,—
    It stirs in the numbers that thrill in my
        brain;
Oh, sweet, sweet is love with its mingling
    of care,
    Though joy travels only a step before
        pain.
Be roused f om thy slumbers and list to
    my nu nbers;
    My heart i poured out in this song unto
        thee.
Oh, be thou not cruel, thou treasure, thou
    jewel;
    Turn thine ear to my pleading and
        hearken to me.

OCTOBER

October is the treasurer of the year,
    And all the months pay bounty to her
        store;
The fields and orchards still their tribute
    bear,
    And fill her brimming coffers more and
        more.
But she, with youthful lavishness,
Spends all her wealth in gaudy dress,
    And decks herself in garments bold
    Of scarlet, purple, red, and gold.

She heedeth not how swift the hours fly,
    But smiles and sings her happy life
        along;
She only sees above a shining sky;
    She only hears the breezes' voice in
        song.
Her garments trail the woodlands through,
And gather pearls of early dew
    That sparkle, till the roguish Sun
    Creeps up and steals them every one.

But what cares she that jewels should be
    lost,
    When all of Nature's bounteous wealth
        is hers?
Though princely fortunes may have been
    their cost,
    Not one regret her calm demeanor stirs.
Whole-hearted, happy, careless, free,
She lives her life out joyously,

Nor cares when Frost stalks o'er her way
And turns her auburn locks to gray.

A SUMMER'S NIGHT.

The night is dewy as a maiden's mouth,
  The skies are bright as are a maiden's
    eyes,
Soft as a maiden's breath the wind that
    flies
Up from the perfumed bosom of the South.

Like sentinels, the pines stand in the park ;
  And hither hastening, like rakes that
    roam,
  With lamps to light their wayward foot-
    steps home,
The fireflies come stagg'ring down the
    dark.

SHIPS THAT PASS IN THE NIGHT

Out in the sky the great dark clouds are
    massing ;
  I look far out into the pregnant night,
Where I can hear a solemn booming gun
And catch the gleaming of a random
    light,
That tells me that the ship I seek is pass-
    ing, passing.

My tearful eyes my soul's deep hurt are
    glassing ;
  For I would hail and check that ship of
    ships.
I stretch my hands imploring, cry aloud,
  My voice falls dead a foot from mine
    own lips,
And but its ghost doth reach that vessel,
    passing, passing.

O Earth, O Sky, O Ocean, both surpassing,
  O heart of mine, O soul that dreads the
    dark !
Is there no hope for me ? Is there no way
  That I may sight and check that speed-
    ing bark
Which out of sight and sound is passing,
    passing ?

THE DELINQUENT

Goo'-by, Jinks, I got to hump,
Got to mek dis pony jump ;

See dat sun a-goin' down
'N' me a-foolin' hyeah in town !
  Git up, Suke—go long !

Guess Mirandy'll think I's tight,
Me not home an' comin' on night.
What's dat stan'in' by de fence ?
Pshaw ! why don't I lu'n some sense ?
  Git up, Suke—go long !

Guess I spent down dah at Jinks'
Mos' a dollah fur de drinks.
Bless yo'r soul, you see dat star ?
Lawd, but won't Mirandy rar ?
  Git up, Suke—go long !

Went dis mo'nin', hyeah it's night,
Dah's de cabin dah in sight.
Who's dat stan'in' in de do' ?
Dat must be Mirandy, sho',
  Git up, Suke—go long !

Got de close-stick in huh han',
Dat look funny, goodness lan',
Sakes alibe, but she look glum !
Hyeah, Mirandy, hyeah I come !
  Git up, Suke—go long !
Ef 't hadn't a be'n fur you, you slow ole
fool, I'd a' be'n home long fo' now !

DAWN

An angel, robed in spotless white,
Bent down and kissed the sleeping Night.
Night woke to blush ; the sprite was gone.
Men saw the blush and called it Dawn.

A DROWSY DAY

This poem, written before its author
was twenty years of age, was greatly ad-
mired and brought him many encourag-
ing letters.   Among these was a note
from James Whitcomb Riley, mentioned
otherwhere in this volume, in which Mr.
Riley says :
"Certainly your gift as evidenced by
this ' Drowsy Day ' poem alone is a superior
one, and therefore its fortunate possessor
should bear it with a becoming sense of
gratitude and meekness, always feeling

that for any resultant good God is the glory, the singer his very humble instrument. Already you have many friends, and can have thousands more by being simply honest, unaffected and just to yourself and the high source of your endowment."

The air is dark, the sky is gray,
    The misty shadows come and go,
And here within my dusky room
Each chair looks ghostly in the gloom.
    Outside the rain falls cold and slow —
Half-stinging drops, half-blinding spray.

Each slightest sound is magnified,
    For drowsy quiet holds her reign;
The burnt stick in the fireplace breaks,
The nodding cat with start awakes,
    And then to sleep drops off again,
Unheeding Towser at her side.

I look far out across the lawn,
    Where huddled stand the silly sheep;
My work lies idle at my hands,
My thoughts fly out like scattered strands
    Of thread, and on the verge of sleep —
Still half awake—I dream and yawn.

What spirits rise before my eyes!
    How various of kind and form!
Sweet memories of days long past,
The dreams of youth that could not last,
    Each smiling calm, each raging storm,
That swept across my early skies.

Half seen, the bare, gaunt-fingered boughs
    Before my window sweep and sway,
And chafe in tortures of unrest.
My chin sinks down upon my breast;
    I cannot work on such a day,
But only sit and dream and drowse.

DIRGE

Place this bunch of mignonette
    In her cold, dead hand;
When the golden sun is set,
    Where the poplars stand,
Bury her from sun and day,
Lay my little love away
    From my sight.

She was like a modest flower
    Blown in sunny June,
Warm as sun at noon's high hour,
    Chaster than the moon.
Ah, her day was brief and bright,
Earth has lost a star of light;
    She is dead.

Softly breathe her name to me.—
    Ah, I loved her so.
Gentle let your tribute be;
    None may better know
Her true worth than I who weep
O'er her as she lies asleep —
    Soft asleep.

Lay these lilies on her breast,
    They are not more white
Than the soul of her, at rest
    'Neath their petals bright.
Chant your aves soft and low,
Solemn be your tread and slow,—
    She is dead.

Lay her here beneath the grass,
    Cool and green and sweet,
Where the gentle brook may pass
    Crooning at her feet.
Nature's bards shall come and sing,
And the fairest flowers shall spring
    Where she lies.

Safe above the water's swirl,
    She has crossed the bar;
Earth has lost a precious pearl,
    Heaven has gained a star,
That shall ever sing and shine,
Till it quells this grief of mine
    For my love.

HYMN

When storms arise
And dark'ning skies
    About me threat'ning lower,
To thee, O Lord, I raise mine eyes,
To thee my tortured spirit flies
    For solace in that hour.

Thy mighty arm
Will let no harm

Come near me nor befall me ;
Thy voice shall quiet my alarm,
When life's great battle waxeth warm —
No foeman shall appall me.

Upon thy breast
Secure I rest,
    From sorrow and vexation ;
No more by sinful cares oppressed,
But in thy presence ever blest,
    O God of my salvation.

PREPARATION

The little bird sits in the nest and sings
    A shy, soft song to the morning light ;
And it flutters a little and prunes its
        wings.
The song is halting and poor and brief,
And the fluttering wings scarce stir a
        leaf ;
But the note is a prelude to sweeter things,
    And the busy bill and the flutter slight
    Are proving the wings for a bolder
        flight !

THE SECRET

What says the wind to the waving trees ?
    What says the wave to the river ?
What means the sigh in the passing breeze ?
    Why do the rushes quiver ?
Have you not heard the fainting cry
Of the flowers that said " Good-bye, good-
    bye " ?

List how the gray dove moans and grieves
    Under the woodland cover ;
List to the drift of the falling leaves,
    List to the wail of the lover.
Have you not caught the message heard
Already by wave and breeze and bird ?

Come, come away to the river's bank,
    Come in the early morning ;
Come when the grass with dew is dank,
    There you will find the warning —
A hint in the kiss of the quickening air
Of the secret that birds and breezes bear.

11

THE WIND AND THE SEA

I stood by the shore at the death of day,
    As the sun sank flaming red ;
And the face of the waters that spread
        away
Was as gray as the face of the dead.

And I heard the cry of the wanton sea
    And the moan of the wailing wind ;
For love's sweet pain in his heart had he,
    But the gray old sea had sinned.

The wind was young and the sea was old
    But their cries went up together ;
The wind was warm and the sea was cold,
    For age makes wintry weather.

So they cried aloud and they wept amain
    Till the sky grew dark to hear it ;
And out of its folds crept the misty rain,
    In its shroud, like a troubled spirit.

For the wind was wild with a hopeless
        love,
    And the sea was sad at heart
At many a crime that he wot of,
    Wherein he had played his part.

He thought of the gallant ships gone down
    By the will of his wicked waves ;
And he thought how the churchyard in the
        town
    Held the sea-made widows' graves.

The wild wind thought of the love he had
        left
Afar in an Eastern land,
And he longed, as long the much bereft,
    For the touch of her perfumed hand.

In his winding wail and his deep-heaved
        sigh
    His aching grief found vent ;
While the sea looked up at the bending
        sky
    And murmured : " I repent."

But e'en as he spoke, a ship came by,
    That bravely ploughed the main,
And a light came into the sea's green eye,
    And his heart grew hard again.

Then he spoke to the wind: " Friend,
    seest thou not
Yon vessel is eastward bound ?
Pray speed with it to the happy spot
    Where thy loved one may be found.''

And the wind rose up in a dear delight,
    And after the good ship sped ;
But the crafty sea by his wicked might
    Kept the vessel ever ahead.

Till the wind grew fierce in his despair,
    And white on the brow and lip.
He tore his garments and tore his hair,
    And fell on the flying ship.

And the ship went down, for a rock was
    there,
    And the sailless sea loomed black ;
While burdened again with dole and care,
    The wind came moaning back.

And still he moans from his bosom hot
    Where his raging grief lies pent,
And ever when the ships come not,
    The sea says: " I repent."

THE DESERTED PLANTATION

Oh, de grubbin'-hoe's a-rustin' in de
    co'nah,
    An' de plow's a-tumblin' down in de
    fiel',
While de whippo'will's a-wailin' lak a
    mou'nah
    When his stubbo'n hea't is tryin' ha'd to
    yiel'.

In de furrers whah de co'n was allus
    wavin',
    Now de weeds is growin' green an' rank
    an' tall ;
An' de swallers roun' de whole place is
    a-bravin'
    Lak dey thought deir folks had allus
    owned it all.

An' de big house stan's all quiet lak an'
    solemn,
    Not a blessed soul in pa'lor, po'ch, er
    lawn;

Not a guest, ner not a ca'iage lef' to haul
    'em,
    Fu' de ones dat tu'ned de latch-string
    out air gone.

An' de banjo's voice is silent in de qua'ters,
    D'ain't a hymn ner co'n-song ringin' in
    de air ;
But de murmur of a branch's passin' waters
    Is de only soun' dat breks de stillness
    dere.

Whah's de da'kies, dem dat used to be
    a dancin'
    Evry night befo' de ole cabin do' ?
Whah's de chillun, dem dat used to be
    a-prancin'
    Er a-rollin' in de san' er on de flo' ?

Whah's ole Uncle Mordecai an' Uncle
    Aaron ?
    Whah's Aunt Doshy, Sam, an' Kit, an'
    all de res' ?
Whah's ole Tom de da'ky fiddlah, how's
    he farin' ?
    Whah's de gals dat used to sing an'
    dance de bes' ?

Gone ! not one o' dem is lef' to tell de
    story ;
    Dey have lef' de deah ole place to fall
    away.
Couldn't one o' dem dat seed it in its glory
    Stay to watch it in de hour of decay ?

Dey have lef' de ole plantation to de
    swallers,
    But it hol's in me a lover till de las' ;
Fu' I fin' hyeah in de memory dat follers
    All dat loved me an' dat I loved in de
    pas'.

So I'll stay an' watch de deah ole place
    an' tend it
    Ez I used to in de happy days gone by.
'Twell de othah Mastah thinks it's time to
    end it,
    An' calls me to my qua'ters in de sky.

DE PLOW'S A-TUMBLIN' DOWN IN DE FIEL'

O'er the Fields with Heavy Tread

A CORN-SONG

On the wide veranda white,
In the purple failing light,
Sits the master while the sun is slowly
burning;
And his dreamy thoughts are drowned
In the softly flowing sound
Of the corn-songs of the field-hands slow
returning.

Oh, we hoe de co'n
Since de ehly mo'n ;
Now de sinkin' sun
Says de day is done.

O'er the fields with heavy tread,
Light of heart and high of head,
Though the halting steps be labored, slow,
and weary ;
Still the spirits brave and strong
Find a comforter in song,
And their corn song rises ever loud and
cheery.

Oh, we hoe de co'n
Since de ehly mo'n ;
Now de sinkin' sun
Says de day is done.

To the master in his seat,
Comes the burden, full and sweet,
Of the mellow minor music growing
clearer,
As the toilers raise the hymn,
Thro' the silence dusk and dim,
To the cabin's restful shelter drawing
nearer.

Oh, we hoe de co'n
Since de ehly mo'n;
Now de sinkin' sun
Says de day is done.

And a tear is in the eye
Of the master sitting by,
As he listens to the echoes low-replying
To the music's fading calls
As it faints away and falls
Into silence, deep within the cabin dying.

Oh, we hoe de co'n
Since de ehly mo'n ;
Now de sinkin' sun
Says de day is done.

RIDING TO TOWN

When labor is light and the morning is
fair,
I find it a pleasure beyond all compare
To hitch up my nag and go hurrying down
And take Katie May for a ride into town ;
For bumpety-bump goes the wagon,
But tra-la-la-la our lay.
There's joy in a song as we rattle along
In the light of the glorious day.

A coach would be fine, but a spring
wagon's good ;
My jeans are a match for Kate's gingham
and hood ;
The hills take us up and the vales take us
down,
But what matters that ? we are riding to
town,
And bumpety-bump goes the wagon,
But tra-la-la-la sing we.
There's never a care may live in the air
That is filled with the breath of our
glee.

And after we've started, there's naught
can repress
The thrill of our hearts in their wild hap-
piness ;
The heavens may smile or the heavens
may frown,
And it's all one to us when we're riding to
town.
For bumpety-bump goes the wagon,
But tra-la-la-la we shout,
For our hearts they are clear and there's
nothing to fear,
And we've never a pain nor a doubt.

The wagon is weak and the roadway is
rough,
And tho' it is long it is not long enough,
For mid all my ecstasies this is the crown
To sit beside Katie and ride into town,
When bumpety-bump goes the wagon,
But tra-la-la-la our song ;

And if I had my way, I'd be willing to
    pay
If the road could be made twice as long.

WE WEAR THE MASK

We wear the mask that grins and lies,
It hides our cheeks and shades our eyes,—
This debt we pay to human guile;
With torn and bleeding hearts we smile,
And mouth with myriad subtleties.

Why should the world be over-wise,
In counting all our tears and sighs?
Nay, let them only see us, while
    We wear the mask.

We smile, but, O great Christ, our cries
To thee from tortured souls arise.
We sing, but oh the clay is vile
Beneath our feet, and long the mile;
But let the world dream otherwise,
    We wear the mask!

THE MEADOW LARK

Though the winds be dank,
    And the sky be sober,
        And the grieving Day
        In a mantle gray
Hath let her waiting maiden robe her,—
    All the fields along
    I can hear the song
Of the meadow lark,
        As she flits and flutters,
        And laughs at the thunder when it
            mutters.
        O happy bird, of heart most gay
        To sing when skies are gray!

When the clouds are full,
    And the tempest master
        Lets the loud winds sweep
        From his bosom deep
Like heralds of some dire disaster,
        Then the heart alone
        To itself makes moan;
And the songs come slow,
        While the tears fall fleeter,
        And silence than song by far seems
            sweeter.

Oh, few are they along the way
Who sing when skies are gray!

ONE LIFE

Oh, I am hurt to death, my Love;
    The shafts of Fate have pierced my
        striving heart,
And I am sick and weary of
    The endless pain and smart.
My soul is weary of the strife,
And chafes at life, and chafes at life.

Time mocks me with fair promises;
    A blooming future grows a barren past,
Like rain my fair full-blossomed trees
    Unburdened in the blast.
The harvest fails on grain and tree,
Nor comes to me, nor comes to me.

The stream that bears my hopes abreast
    Turns ever from my way its pregnant
        tide.
My laden boat, torn from its rest,
    Drifts to the other side.
So all my hopes are set astray,
And drift away, and drift away.

The lark sings to me at the morn,
    And near me wings her skyward-soaring
        flight;
But pleasure dies as soon as born,
    The owl takes up the night,
And night seems long and doubly dark;
I miss the lark, I miss the lark.

Let others labor as they may,
    I'll sing and sigh alone, and write my
        line.
Their fate is theirs, or grave or gay,
    And mine shall still be mine.
I know the world holds joy and glee,
But not for me,—'tis not for me.

CHANGING TIME

The cloud looked in at the window,
    And said to the day, "Be dark!"
And the roguish rain tapped hard on the
    pane,
    To stifle the song of the lark.

The wind sprang up in the tree tops
And shrieked with a voice of death,
But the rough-voiced breeze, that shook
the trees,
Was touched with a violet's breath.

DEAD

A knock is at her door, but she is weak;
Strange dews have washed the paint
streaks from her cheek;
She does not rise, but, ah, this friend is
known,
And knows that he will find her all alone.
So opens he the door, and with soft tread
Goes straightway to the richly curtained
bed.
His soft hand on her dewy head he lays.
A strange white light she gives him for his
gaze.
Then, looking on the glory of her charms,
He crushes her resistless in his arms.

Stand back! look not upon this bold em-
brace,
Nor view the calmness of the wanton's
face;
With joy unspeakable and 'bated breath,
She keeps her last, long liaison with death!

A CONFIDENCE

Uncle John, he makes me tired;
Thinks 'at he's jest so all-fired
Smart, 'at he kin pick up, so,
Ever'thing he wants to know.
Tried to ketch me up last night,
But you bet I wouldn't bite.
I jest kept the smoothes' face,
But I led him sich a chase,
Couldn't corner me, you bet —
I skipped all the traps he set.
Makin' out he wan'ed to know
Who was this an' that girl's beau;
So's he'd find out, don't you see,
Who was goin' 'long with me.
But I answers jest ez sly,
An' I never winks my eye,
Tell he hollers with a whirl,
"Look here, ain't you got a girl?"
Y' ought 'o seen me spread my eyes,
Like he'd took me by surprise,

An' I said, "Oh, Uncle John,
Never thought o' havin' one."
An' somehow that seemed to tickle
Him an' he shelled out a nickel.
Then you ought to seen me leave
Jest a-laffin' in my sleeve.
Fool him—well, I guess I did;
He ain't on to this here kid.
Got a girl! well, I guess yes,
Got a dozen more or less,
But I got one reely one,
Not no foolin' ner no fun;
Fur I'm sweet on her, you see,
An' I ruther guess 'at she
Must be kinder sweet on me,
So we're keepin' company.
Honest Injun! this is true,
Ever' word I'm tellin' you!
But you won't be sich a scab
Ez to run aroun' an' blab.
Mebbe 'tain't the way with you,
But you know some fellers do.
Spoils a girl to let her know
'At you talk about her so.
Don't you know her? her name's Liz,
Nicest girl in town she is.
Purty? ah, git out, you gilly —
Liz 'ud purt' nigh knock you silly.
Y' ought 'o see her when she's dressed
All up in her Sunday best,
All the fellers nudgin' me,
An' a-whisperin', gemunee!
Betcher life 'at I feel proud
When she passes by the crowd.
'T's kinder nice to be a-goin'
With a girl 'at makes some showin'—
One you know 'at hain't no snide,
Makes you feel so satisfied.
An' I'll tell you she's a trump,
Never even seen her jump
Like some silly girls 'ud do,
When I'd hide and holler "Boo!"
She'd jest laugh an' say "Git out!
What you hollerin' about?"
When some girls 'ud have a fit
That 'un don't git skeered a bit,
Never makes a bit o' row
When she sees a worm er cow.
Them kind's few an' far between;
Bravest girl I ever seen.
Tell you 'nuther thing she'll do,
Mebbe you won't think it's true,

But if she's jest got a dime
She'll go halvers ever' time.
Ah, you goose, you needn't laff;
That's the kinder girl to have.
If you knowed her like I do,
Guess you'd kinder like her too.
Tell you somep'n' if you'll swear
You won't tell it anywhere.
Oh, you got to cross yer heart
Earnest, truly, 'fore I start.
Well, one day I kissed her cheek;
Gee, but I felt cheap an' weak,
'Cause at first she kinder flared,
'N', gracious goodness! I was scared.
But I needn't been, fer la!
Why, she never told her ma.
That's what I call grit, don't you?
Sich a girl's worth stickin' to.

PHYLLIS

Phyllis, ah, Phyllis, my life is a gray day,
Few are my years, but my griefs are not
few,
Ever to youth should each day be a May-
day,
Warm wind and rose-breath and dia-
monded dew —
Phyllis, ah, Phyllis, my life is a gray day.

Oh, for the sunlight that shines on a May-
day!
Only the cloud hangeth over my life.
Love that should bring me youth's hap-
piest heyday
Brings me but seasons of sorrow and
strife;
Phyllis, ah, Phyllis, my life is a gray day.

Sunshine or shadow, or gold day or gray
day,
Life must be lived as our destinies rule;
Leisure or labor or work day or play day —
Feasts for the famous and fun for the
fool;
Phyllis, ah, Phyllis, my life is a gray day.

RIGHT'S SECURITY

What if the wind do howl without,
And turn the creaking weather-vane;
What if the arrows of the rain
Do beat against the window-pane?
Art thou not armored strong and fast
Against the sallies of the blast?
Art thou not sheltered safe and well
Against the flood's insistent swell?

What boots it, that thou stand'st alone,
And laughest in the battle's face
When all the weak have fled the place
And let their feet and fears keep pace?
Thou wavest still thine ensign, high,
And shoutest thy loud battle-cry;
Higher than e'er the tempest roared,
It cleaves the silence like a sword.

Right arms and armors, too, that man
Who will not compromise with wrong;
Though single, he must front the throng.
And wage the battle hard and long.
Minorities, since time began,
Have shown the better side of man;
And often in the lists of Time
One man has made a cause sublime!

IF

If life were but a dream, my Love,
And death the waking time;
If day had not a beam, my Love,
And night had not a rhyme,—
A barren, barren world were this
Without one saving gleam;
I'd only ask that with a kiss
You'd wake me from the dream.

If dreaming were the sum of days,
And loving were the bane;
If battling for a wreath of bays
Could soothe a heart in pain,—
I'd scorn the meed of battle's might,
All other aims above
I'd choose the human's higher right,
To suffer and to love!

THE SONG

My soul, lost in the music's mist,
Roamed, rapt, 'neath skies of amethyst.
The cheerless streets grew summer meads,
The Son of Phœbus spurred his steeds,

And, wand'ring down the mazy tune,
December lost its way in June,
While from a verdant vale I heard
The piping of a love-lorn bird.

A something in the tender strain
Revived an old, long conquered pain,
And as in depths of many seas,
My heart was drowned in memories.
The tears came welling to my eyes,
Nor could I ask it otherwise;
For, oh! a sweetness seems to last
Amid the dregs of sorrows past.

It stirred a chord that here of late
I'd grown to think could not vibrate.
It brought me back the trust of youth,
The world again was joy and truth.
And Avice, blooming like a bride,
Once more stood trusting at my side.
But still, with bosom desolate,
The 'lorn bird sang to find his mate.

Then there are trees, and lights and stars,
The silv'ry tinkle of guitars;
And throbs again as throbbed that waltz,
Before I knew that hearts were false.
Then like a cold wave on a shore,
Comes silence and she sings no more.
I wake, I breathe, I think again,
And walk the sordid ways of men.

SIGNS OF THE TIMES

Air a-gittin' cool an' coolah,
    Frost a-comin' in de night,
Hicka'nuts an' wa'nuts fallin',
    Possum keepin' out o' sight.
Tu'key struttin' in de ba'nya'd
    Nary step so proud ez his;
Keep on struttin', Mistah Tu'key,
    Yo' do' know whut time it is.

Cidah press commence a-squeakin'
    Eatin' apples sto'ed away,
Chillun swa'min' 'roun' lak ho'nets,
    Huntin' aigs ermung de hay.
Mistah Tu'key keep on gobblin'
    At de geese a-flyin' souf,
Oomph! dat bird do' know whut's
        comin';
    Ef he did he'd shet his mouf.

Pumpkin gittin' good an' yallah
    Mek me open up my eyes;
Seems lak it's a-lookin' at me
    Jes' a-la'in' dah sayin' " Pies."
Tu'key gobbler gwine 'roun' blowin',
    Gwine 'roun' gibbin' sass an' slack;
Keep on talkin', Mistah Tu'key,
    You ain't seed no almanac.

Fa'mer walkin' th'oo de ba'nya'd
    Seein' how things is comin' on,
Sees ef all de fowls is fatt'nin'—
    Good times comin' sho's you bo'n.
Hyeahs dat tu'key gobbler braggin',
    Den his face break in a smile —
Nebbah min', you sassy rascal,
    He's gwine nab you atter while.

Choppin' suet in de kitchen,
    Stonin' raisins in de hall,
Beef a-cookin' fu' de mince meat,
    Spices groun'—I smell 'em all.
Look hyeah, Tu'key, stop dat gobblin',
    You ain' luned de sense ob feah,
You ol' fool, yo' naik's in dangah,
    Do' you know Thanksgibbin's hyeah?

WHY FADES A DREAM?

Why fades a dream?
    An iridescent ray
Flecked in between the tryst
    Of night and day.
Why fades a dream? —
Of consciousness the shade
Wrought out by lack of light and made
    Upon life's stream.
Why fades a dream?

That thought may thrive,
    So fades the fleshless dream;
Lest men should learn to trust
    The things that seem.
So fades a dream,
That living thought may grow
And like a waxing star-beam glow
    Upon life's stream —
So fades a dream.

THE SPARROW

A little bird, with plumage brown,
Beside my window flutters down,
A moment chirps its little strain,
Then taps upon my window-pane,
And chirps again, and hops along,
To call my notice to its song;
But I work on, nor heed its lay,
Till, in neglect, it flies away.

So birds of peace and hope and love
Come fluttering earthward from above,
To settle on life's window-sills,
And ease our load of earthly ills;
But we, in traffic's rush and din
Too deep engaged to let them in,
With deadened heart and sense plod on,
Nor know our loss till they are gone.

SPEAKIN' O' CHRISTMAS

Breezes blowin' middlin' brisk,
Snow-flakes thro' the air a-whisk,
Fallin' kind o' soft an' light,
Not enough to make things white,
But jest sorter siftin' down
So's to cover up the brown
Of the dark world's rugged ways
'N' make things look like holidays.
Not smoothed over, but jest specked,
Sorter strainin' fur effect,
An' not quite a-gittin' through
What it started in to do.
Mercy sakes! it does seem queer
Christmas day is 'most nigh here.
Somehow it don't seem to me
Christmas like it used to be,—
Christmas with its ice an' snow,
Christmas of the long ago.
You could feel its stir an' hum
Weeks an' weeks before it come;
Somethin' in the atmosphere
Told you when the day was near,
Didn't need no almanacs;
That was one o' Nature's fac's.
Every cottage decked out gay —
Cedar wreaths an' holly spray —
An' the stores, how they were drest,
Tinsel tell you couldn't rest;
Every winder fixed up pat,

Candy canes, an' things like that;
Noah's arks, an' guns, an' dolls,
An' all kinds o' fol-de-rols.
Then with frosty bells a-chime,
Slidin' down the hills o' time,
Right amidst the fun an' din
Christmas come a-bustlin' in,
Raised his cheery voice to call
Out a welcome to us all,
Hale and hearty, strong an' bluff,
That was Christmas, sure enough.
Snow knee-deep an' coastin' fine,
Frozen mill-ponds all ashine,
Seemin' jest to lay in wait,
Beggin' you to come an' skate.
An' you'd git your gal an' go
Stumpin' cheerily thro' the snow,
Feelin' pleased an' skeert an' warm
'Cause she had a-holt yore arm.
Why, when Christmas come in, we
Spent the whole glad day in glee,
Havin' fun an' feastin' high
An' some courtin' on the sly.
Bustin' in some neighbor's door
An' then suddenly, before
He could give his voice a lift,
Yellin' at him, "Christmas gift."
Now sich things are never heard,
"Merry Christmas" is the word.
But it's only change o' name,
An' means givin' jest the same.
There's too many new-styled ways
Now about the holidays.
I'd jest like once more to see
Christmas like it used to be!

LONESOME

Mother's gone a-visitin' to spend a month
    er two,
An', oh, the house is lonesome ez a nest
    whose birds has flew
To other trees to build ag'in; the rooms
    seem jest so bare
That the echoes run like sperrits from the
    kitchen to the stair.
The shetters flap more lazy-like 'n what
    they used to do,
Sence mother's gone a-visitin' to spend a
    month er two.

We've killed the fattest chicken an' we've
   cooked her to a turn;
We've made the richest gravy, but I jest
   don't give a durn
Fur nothin' 'at I drink er eat, er nothin'
   'at I see.
The food ain't got the pleasant taste it
   used to have to me.
They's somep'n' stickin' in my throat ez
   tight ez hardened glue,
Sence mother's gone a-visitin' to spend a
   month er two.

The hollyhocks air jest ez pink, they're
   double ones at that,
An' I wuz prouder of 'em than a baby of a
   cat.
But now I don't go near 'em, though
   they nod an' blush at me,
Fur they's somep'n' seems to gall me in
   their keerless sort o' glee
An' all their fren'ly noddin' an' their
   blushin' seems to say:
" You're purty lonesome, John, old boy,
   sence mother's gone away."

The neighbors ain't so fren'ly ez it seems
   they'd ort to be ;
They seem to be a-lookin' kinder side-
   ways like at me,
A kinder feared they'd tech me off ez ef I
   wuz a match,
An' all because 'at mother's gone an' I'm
   a-keepin' batch !
I'm shore I don't do nothin' worse'n what
   I used to do
'Fore mother went a-visitin' to spent a
   month er two.

The sparrers ac's more fearsome like an'
   won't hop quite so near,
The cricket's chirp is sadder, an' the sky
   ain't ha'f so clear ;
When ev'nin' comes, I set an' smoke tell
   my eyes begin to swim,
An' things aroun' commence to look all
   blurred an' faint an' dim.
Well, I guess I'll have to own up 'at I'm
   feelin' purty blue
Sence mother's gone a-visitin' to spend a
   month er two.

GROWIN' GRAY

Hello, ole man, you're a-gittin' gray,
An' it beats ole Ned to see the way
'At the crow's feet's a-getherin' aroun' yore
   eyes ;
Tho' it oughtn't to cause me no su'prise,
Fur there's many a sun 'at you've seen
   rise
An' many a one you've seen go down
Sence yore step was light an' yore hair was
   brown,
An' storms an' snows have had their
   way —
Hello, ole man, you're a-gittin' gray.

Hello, ole man, you're a-gittin' gray,
An' the youthful pranks 'at you used to
   play
Are dreams of a far past long ago
That lie in a heart where the fires burn
   low —
That has lost the flame though it kept the
   glow,
An' spite of drivin' snow an' storm,
Beats bravely on forever warm.
December holds the place of May —
Hello, ole man, you're a-gittin' gray.

Hello, ole man, you're a-gittin' gray —
Who cares what the carpin' youngsters
   say ?
For, after all, when the tale is told,
Love proves if a man is young or old !
Old age can't make the heart grow cold
When it does the will of an honest mind ;
When it beats with love fur all mankind ;.
Then the night but leads to a fairer day —
Hello, ole man, you're a-gittin' gray !

TO THE MEMORY OF MARY YOUNG

God has his plans, and what if we
With our sight be too blind to see
Their full fruition ; cannot he,
Who made it, solve the mystery ?
One whom we loved has fall'n asleep,
Not died ; although her calm be deep,
Some new, unknown, and strange surprise
In Heaven holds enrapt her eyes.

And can you blame her that her gaze
Is turned away from earthly ways,
When to her eyes God's light and love
Have giv'n the view of things above?
A gentle spirit sweetly good,
The pearl of precious womanhood;
Who heard the voice of duty clear,
And found her mission soon and near.

She loved all nature, flowers fair,
The warmth of sun, the kiss of air,
The birds that filled the sky with song,
The stream that laughed its way along.
Her home to her was shrine and throne,
But one love held her not alone;
She sought out poverty and grief,
Who touched her robe and found relief.

So sped she in her Master's work,
Too busy and too brave to shirk,
When through the silence, dusk and dim,
God called her and she fled to him.
We wonder at the early call,
And tears of sorrow can but fall
For her o'er whom we spread the pall;
But faith, sweet faith, is over all.

The house is dust, the voice is dumb,
But through undying years to come,
The spark that glowed within her soul
Shall light our footsteps to the goal.
She went her way; but oh, she trod
The path that led her straight to God.
Such lives as this put death to scorn;
They lose our day to find God's morn.

WHEN MALINDY SINGS

This poem has been adjudged as the best of his dialect pieces. It has been set to music and sung in homes all over the land. It was dedicated to his mother whose name Matilda, was slightly modified to suit the rhythm and melody of the verses.

Mr. Dunbar recited this poem before a critical audience in London, England, and it was given very complimentary mention in the London *Daily News*.

While in New York in 1896, Mr. Dunbar was tendered a reception by the entire staff of the *Century Magazine*, and was asked to read a few of his poems. This poem was among those recited that day. His hearers were loud in their applause, and showered compliments and congratulations upon its author.

Several of Mr. Dunbar's poems had been published in the *Century* before that date, but, full of the spirit of mischief, the young black man turned to Mr. Gilder, the editor of the *Century*, and said:

"That's one you returned."

Mr. Gilder was a bit embarrassed, but gallantly said:

"We'll take it yet."

"Sorry," replied Dunbar laughingly, "but you're too late. It has now been accepted by another magazine."

G'way an' quit dat noise, Miss Lucy —
    Put dat music book away;
What's de use to keep on tryin'?
    Ef you practise twell you're gray,
You cain't sta't no notes a-flyin'
    Lak de ones dat rants and rings
F'om de kitchen to de big woods
    When Malindy sings.

You ain't got de nachel o'gans
    Fu' to make de soun' come right,
You ain't got de tu'ns an' twistin's
    Fu' to make it sweet an' light.
'Tell you one thing now, Miss Lucy,
    An' I'm tellin' you fu' true,
When hit comes to raal right singin',
    Tain't no easy thing to do.

Easy 'nough fu' folks to hollah,
    Lookin' at de lines an' dots,
When dey ain't no one kin sence it,
    An' de chune comes in, in spots;
But fu' real melojous music,
    Dat jes' strikes yo' hea't and clings,
Jes' you stan' an' listen wif me
    When Malindy sings.

Ain't you nevah hyeahd Malindy?
    Blessed soul, tek up de cross!
Look hyeah, ain't you jokin', honey?
    Well, you don't know whut you los'.
Y' ought to hyeah dat gal a-wa'blin',
    Robins, la'ks, an' all dem things,

PUT DAT MUSIC BOOK AWAY

WHILE MALINDY SINGS

Heish dey moufs an' hides dey faces
　When Malindy sings.

Fiddlin' man jes' stop his fiddlin',
　Lay his fiddle on de she'f;
Mockin'-bird quit tryin' to whistle,
　'Cause he jes' so shamed hisse'f.
Folks a-playin' on de banjo
　Draps dey fingahs on de strings —
Bless yo' soul—fu'gits to move 'em,
　When Malindy sings.

She jes' spreads huh mouf and hollahs,
　" Come to Jesus," twell you hyeah
Sinnahs' tremblin' steps and voices,
　Timid-lak a-drawin' neah;
Den she tu'ns to " Rock of Ages,"
　Simply to de cross she clings,
An' you fin' yo' teahs a-drappin'
　When Malindy sings.

Who dat says dat humble praises
　Wif de Master nevah counts ?
Heish yo' mouf, I hyeah dat music,
　Ez hit rises up an' mounts —
Floatin' by de hills an' valleys,
　Way above dis buryin' sod,
Ez hit makes its way in glory
　To de very gates of God !

Oh, hit's sweetah dan de music
　Of an edicated band ;
An' hit's dearah dan de battle's
　Song o' triumph in de lan'.
It seems holier dan evenin'
　When de solemn chu'ch bell rings,
Ez I sit an' ca'mly listen
　While Malindy sings.

Towsah, stop dat ba'kin', hyeah me !
　Mandy, mek dat chile keep still;
Don't you hyeah de echoes callin'
　F'om de valley to de hill ?
Let me listen, I can hyeah it,
　Th'oo de bresh of angel's wings,
Sof' an' sweet, " Swing Low, Sweet
　　Chariot,"
Ez Malindy sings.

THE PARTY

Of this production William Dean Howells said in his notable article in Harper's Weekly :

" I wish I could give the whole of the piece which he calls ' The Pahty,' but I must content myself with a passage or two. They will impart some sense of the jolly rush of movement, its vivid picturesqueness, its broad characterization, and will perhaps suffice to show what vistas into the simple, sensuous, joyous nature of his race Mr. Dunbar's work opens." He then quoted a number of the lines.

" One sees," continued Mr. Howells, " how the poet exults in his material as the artist always does. It is not for him to blink its commonness, or to be ashamed of its rudeness : and in his treatment of it he has been able to bring us nearer to the heart of primitive human nature in his race than any one else has yet done."

(These quotations from Mr. Howells' article are used by permission and courtesy of Messrs. Harper & Brothers.)

Dey had a gread big pahty down to Tom's
　de othah night ;
Was I dah ? You bet ! I nevah in my
　life see sich a sight ;
All de folks f'om fou' plantations was in-
　vited, an' dey come,
Dey come troopin' thick ez chillun when
　dey hyeahs a fife an' drum.
Evahbody dressed deir fines'—Heish yo'
　mouf an' git away,
Ain't seen no sich fancy dressin' sence las'
　quah'tly meetin' day ;
Gals all dressed in silks an' satins, not a
　wrinkle ner a crease,
Eyes a-battin', teeth a-shinin', haih breshed
　back ez slick ez grease ;
Sku'ts all tucked an' puffed an' ruffled,
　evah blessed seam an' stitch ;
Ef you'd seen 'em wif deir mistus, couldn't
　swahed to which was which.
Men all dressed up in Prince Alberts,
　swallertails 'u'd tek yo' bref !
I cain't tell you nothin' 'bout it, yo' ought
　to seen it fu' yo'se'f.
Who was dah ? Now who you askin' ?
　How you 'spect I gwine to know ?
You mus' think I stood an' counted evah-
　body at de do'.

Ole man Babah's house boy Isaac, brung
   dat gal, Malindy Jane,
Huh a-hangin' to his elbow, him a struttin'
   wif a cane ;
My, but Hahvey Jones was jealous ! seemed
   to stick him lak a tho'n ;
But he laughed with Viney Cahteh, tryin'
   ha'd to not let on,
But a pusson would 'a' noticed f'om de
   d'rection of his look,
Dat he was watchin' ev'ry step dat Ike an'
   Lindy took.
Ike he foun' a cheer an' asked huh :
   " Won't you set down ? " wif a smile,
An' she answe'd up a-bowin', " Oh, I
   reckon 'tain't wuth while."
Dat was jes' fu' style, I reckon, 'cause she
   sot down jes' de same,
An' she stayed dah 'twell he fetched huh
   fu' to jine some so't o' game ;
Den I hyeahd huh sayin' propah, ez she
   riz to go away,
" Oh, you raly mus' excuse me, fu' I
   hardly keers to play."
But I seen huh in a minute wif de othahs
   on de flo',
An' dah wasn't any one o' dem a-playin'
   any mo';
Comin' down de flo' a-bowin' an' a-swayin'
   an' a-swingin',
Puttin' on huh high-toned mannahs all de
   time dat she was singin':
" Oh, swing Johnny up an' down, swing
   him all aroun',
Swing Johnny up an' down, swing him all
   aroun',
Oh, swing Johnny up an' down, swing
   him all aroun',
Fa' you well, my dahlin'."
Had to laff at ole man Johnson, he's a
   caution now, you bet —
Hittin' clost onto a hunderd, but he's spry
   an' nimble yet ;
He 'lowed how a-so't o' gigglin', " I ain't
   ole, I'll let you see,
D'ain't no use in gittin' feeble, now you
   youngstahs jes' watch me,"
An' he grabbed ole Aunt Marier—weighs
   th'ee hunderd mo' er less,
An' he spun huh 'roun' de cabin swingin'
   Johnny lak de res'.

Evahbody laffed an' hollahed : " Go it
   Swing huh, Uncle Jim ! "
An' he swung huh too, I reckon, lak a
   youngstah, who but him.
Dat was bettah'n young Scott Thomas,
   tryin' to be so awful smaht.
You know when dey gits to singin' an' dey
   comes to dat ere paht :
   " In some lady's new brick house,
  In some lady's gyahden.
    Ef you don't let me out, I will
     jump out,
  So fa' you well, my dahlin'."
Den dey's got a circle 'roun' you, an' you's
   got to break de line ;
Well, dat dahky was so anxious, lak to
   bust hisse'f a-tryin' ;
Kep' on blund'rin' 'roun' an' foolin' 'twell
   he giv' one gread big jump,
Broke de line, an' lit head-fo'most in de
   fiahplace right plump ;
Hit 'ad fiah in it, mind you ; well, I
   thought my soul I'd bust,
Tried my best to keep f'om laffin', but hit
   seemed like die I must !
Y' ought to seen dat man a-scramblin'
   f'om de ashes an' de grime.
Did it bu'n him ! Sich a question, why he
   didn't give it time' ;
Th'ow'd dem ashes and dem cindahs evah
   which-a-way I guess,
An' you nevah did, I reckon, clap yo'
   eyes on sich a mess ;
Fu' he sholy made a picter an' a funny
   one to boot,
Wif his clothes all full o' ashes an' his face
   all full o' soot.
Well, hit laked to stopped de pahty, an' I
   reckon lak ez not
Dat it would ef Tom's wife, Mandy, hadn't
   happened on de spot,
To invite us out to suppah—well, we
   scrambled to de table,
An' I'd lak to tell you 'bout it—what we
   had—but I ain't able,
Mention jes' a few things, dough I know I
   hadn't orter,
Fu' I know 'twill staht a hank'rin' an' yo'
   mouf 'll 'mence to worter.
We had wheat bread white ez cotton an' a
   egg pone jes' like gol',

Hog jole, bilin' hot an' steamin' roasted
   shoat an' ham sliced cold —
Look out! What's de mattah wif you?
   Don't be fallin' on de flo';
Ef it's go'n' to 'fect you dat way, I won't
   tell you nothin' mo'.
Dah now—well, we had hot chittlin's —
   now you's tryin' ag'in to fall,
Cain't you stan' to hyeah about it? S'pose
   you'd been an' seed it all;
Seed dem gread big sweet pertaters, layin'
   by de possum's side,
Seed dat coon in all his gravy, reckon den
   you'd up and died!
Mandy 'lowed " you all mus' 'scuse me, d'
   wa'n't much upon my she'ves,
But I's done my bes' to suit you, so set
   down an' he'p yo'se'ves."
Tom, he 'lowed : " I don't b'lieve in 'pol-
   ogizin' an' perfessin',
Let 'em tek it lak dey ketch it. Eldah
   Thompson, ask de blessin'."
Wish you'd seed dat colo'ed preachah
   cleah his th'oat an' bow his head;
One eye shet, an' one eye open,—dis is
   evah wud he said :
" Lawd, look down in tendah mussy on
   sich generous hea'ts ez dese;
Make us truly thankful, amen. Pass dat
   possum, ef you please ! "
Well, we eat and drunk ouah po'tion,
   'twell dah wasn't nothin' lef',
An' we felt jes' like new sausage, we was
   mos' nigh stuffed to def !
Tom, he knowed how we'd be feelin',
   so he had de fiddlah 'roun',
An' he made us cleah de cabin fu' to dance
   dat suppah down.
Jim, de fiddlah, chuned his fiddle, put
   some rosum on his bow,
Set a pine box on de table, mounted it an'
   let huh go !
He's a fiddlah, now I tell you, an' he made
   dat fiddle ring,
'Twell de ol'est an' de lamest had to give
   deir feet a fling.
Jigs, cotillions, reels an' break-downs,
   cordrills an' a waltz er two ;
Bless yo' soul, dat music winged 'em an'
   dem people lak to flew.
Cripple Joe, de ole rheumatic, danced dat
   flo' f'om side to middle,

Th'owed away his crutch an' hopped it,
   what's rheumatics 'ginst a fiddle ?
Eldah Thompson got so tickled dat he lak
   to los' his grace,
Had to tek bofe feet an' hol' dem so's to
   keep 'em in deir place.
An' de Christuns an' de sinnahs got so
   mixed up on dat flo',
Dat I don't see how dey'd pahted ef de
   trump had chanced to blow.
Well, we danced dat way an' capahed in
   de mos' redic'lous way,
'Twell de roostahs in de bahnyard cleahed
   deir th'oats an' crowed fu' day.
Y' ought to been dah, fu' I tell you evah-
   thing was rich an' prime,
An' dey ain't no use in talkin', we jes' had
   one scrumptious time !

LOVE'S APOTHEOSIS

Love me. I care not what the circling
     years
     To me may do.
If, but in spite of time and tears,
     You prove but true.

Love me—albeit grief shall dim mine eyes,
     And tears bedew,
I shall not e'en complain, for then my skies
     Shall still be blue.

Love me, and though the winter snow
     shall pile,
     And leave me chill,
Thy passion's warmth shall make for me,
     meanwhile,
     A sun-kissed hill.

And when the days have lengthened into
     years,
     And I grow old,
Oh, spite of pains and griefs and cares and
     fears,
     Grow thou not cold.

Then hand and hand we shall pass up
     the hill,
     I say not down;

That twain go up, of love, who've loved
      their fill,—
   To gain love's crown.

Love me, and let my life take up thine
      own,
   As sun the dew.
Come, sit, my queen, for in my heart a
      throne
   Awaits for you!

THE PARADOX

I am the mother of sorrows,
   I am the ender of grief;
I am the bud and the blossom,
   I am the late-falling leaf.

I am thy priest and thy poet,
   I am thy serf and thy king;
I cure the tears of the heartsick,
   When I come near they shall sing.

White are my hands as the snowdrop;
   Swart are my fingers as clay;
Dark is my frown as the midnight,
   Fair is my brow as the day.

Battle and war are my minions,
   Doing my will as divine;
I am the calmer of passions,
   Peace is a nursling of mine.

Speak to me gently or curse me,
   Seek me or fly from my sight;
I am thy fool in the morning,
   Thou art my slave in the night.

Down to the grave will I take thee,
   Out from the noise of the strife;
Then shalt thou see me and know me —
   Death, then, no longer, but life.

Then shalt thou sing at my coming,
   Kiss me with passionate breath,
Clasp me and smile to have thought me
   Aught save the foeman of Death.

Come to me, brother, when weary,
   Come when thy lonely heart swells;
I'll guide thy footsteps and lead thee
   Down   where   the   Dream   Woman
      dwells.

OVER THE HILLS

Over the hills and the valleys of dreaming
   Slowly I take my way.
Life is the night with its dream-visions
      teeming,
   Death is the waking at day.

Down thro' the dales and the bowers of
      loving,
   Singing, I roam afar.
Daytime or night-time, I constantly rov-
      ing,—
   Dearest one, thou art my star.

WITH THE LARK

Night is for sorrow and dawn is for joy,
Chasing the troubles that fret and annoy;
Darkness for sighing and daylight for
   song,—
Cheery and chaste the strain, heartfelt and
   strong.
All the night through, though I moan in
   the dark,
I wake in the morning to sing with the
   lark.

Deep in the midnight the rain whips the
   leaves,
Softly and sadly the wood-spirit grieves.
But when the first hue of dawn tints the
   sky,
I shall shake out my wings like the birds
   and be dry;
And though, like the rain-drops, I grieved
   through the dark,
I shall wake in the morning to sing with
   the lark.

On the high hills of heaven, some morning
   to be,
Where the rain shall not grieve thro' the
   leaves of the tree,
There my heart will be glad for the pain I
   have known,
For my hand will be clasped in the hand
   of mine own;
And though life has been hard and death's
   pathway been dark,
I shall wake in the morning to sing with
   the lark.

IN SUMMER

Oh, summer has clothed the earth
  In a cloak from the loom of the sun!
And a mantle, too, of the skies' soft blue,
  And a belt where the rivers run.

And now for the kiss of the wind,
  And the touch of the air's soft hands,
With the rest from strife and the heat of
    life,
  With the freedom of lakes and lands.

I envy the farmer's boy
  Who sings as he follows the plow;
While the shining green of the young
    blades lean
  To the breezes that cool his brow.

He sings to the dewy morn,
  No thought of another's ear;
But the song he sings is a chant for kings
  And the whole wide world to hear.

He sings of the joys of life,
  Of the pleasures of work and rest,
From an o'erfull heart, without aim or
    art;
  'Tis a song of the merriest.

O ye who toil in the town,
  And ye who moil in the mart,
Hear the artless song, and your faith
    made strong
  Shall renew your joy of heart.

Oh, poor were the worth of the world
  If never a song were heard,—
If the sting of grief had no relief,
  And never a heart were stirred.

So, long as the streams run down,
  And as long as the robins trill;
Let us taunt old Care with a merry air,
  And sing in the face of ill.

THE MYSTIC SEA

The smell of the sea in my nostrils,
  The sound of the sea in mine ears;
The touch of the spray on my burning face,
  Like the mist of reluctant tears.

The blue of the sky above me,
  The green of the waves beneath;
The sun flashing down on a gray-white sail
  Like a scimetar from its sheath.

And ever the breaking billows,
  And ever the rocks' disdain;
And ever a thrill in mine inmost heart
  That my reason cannot explain.

So I say to my heart, " Be silent,
  The mystery of time is here;
Death's way will be plain when we fathom
    the main,
  And the secret of life be clear."

A SAILOR'S SONG

Oh, for the breath of the briny deep,
  And the tug of a bellying sail,
With the sea-gull's cry across the sky
  And a passing boatman's hail.
For, be she fierce or be she gay,
The sea is a famous friend alway.

Ho! for the plains where the dolphins play,
  And the bend of the masts and spars,
And a fight at night with the wild sea-sprite
  When the foam has drowned the stars.
And, pray, what joy can the landsman feel
Like the rise and fall of a sliding keel?

Fair is the mead; the lawn is fair
  And the birds sing sweet on the lea;
But the echo soft of a song aloft
  Is the strain that pleases me;
And swish of rope and ring of chain
Are music to men who sail the main.

Then, if you love me, let me sail
  While a vessel dares the deep;
For the ship's my wife, and the breath of
    life
Are the raging gales that sweep;
And when I'm done with calm and blast,
A slide o'er the side, and rest at last.

THE BOHEMIAN

That Paul Dunbar—like all real artists
—scorned convention and believed in a

simple, natural existence, untrammeled by men's laws or foolish rules of etiquette, is shown in this brief bit of rhyme, which was composed after a conversation upon the subject with a sympathetic friend.

Bring me the livery of no other man.
    I am my own to robe me at my pleasure.
    Accepted rules to me disclose no treasure:
What is the chief who shall my garments
      plan?
No garb conventional but I'll attack it.
(Come, why not don my spangled jacket?)

ABSENCE

Good-night, my love, for I have dreamed
    of thee
    In waking dreams, until my soul is lost —
Is lost in passion's wide and shoreless sea,
    Where, like a ship, unruddered, it is tost
Hither and thither at the wild waves' will.
There is no potent Master's voice to still
This newer, more tempestuous Galilee!

The stormy petrels of my fancy fly
    In warning course across the darkening
      green,
And, like a frightened bird, my heart doth
      cry
    And seek to find some rock of rest be-
      tween
The threatening sky and the relentless
      wave.
It is not length of life that grief doth crave,
But only calm and peace in which to die.

Here let me rest upon this single hope,
    For oh, my wings are weary of the wind,
And with its stress no more may strive or
      cope.
    One cry has dulled mine ears, mine eyes
      are blind,—
Would that o'er all the intervening space,
I might fly forth and see thee face to face.
I fly; I search, but, love, in gloom I grope.

Fly home, far bird, unto thy waiting nest;
    Spread thy strong wings above the wind-
      swept sea.
Beat the grim breeze with thy unruffled
    breast

Until thou sittest wing to wing with me.
Then, let the past bring up its tales of
    wrong;
We shall chant low our sweet connubial
    song,
    Till storm and doubt and past no more
    shall be!

HER THOUGHT AND HIS

The gray of the sea, and the gray of the
    sky,
A glimpse of the moon like a half-closed
    eye.
The gleam on the waves and the light on
    the land,
A thrill in my heart,—and—my sweet-
    heart's hand.

She turned from the sea with a woman's
    grace,
And the light fell soft on her upturned
    face,
And I thought of the flood-tide of infinite
    bliss
That would flow to my heart from a single
    kiss.

But my sweetheart was shy, so I dared not
    ask
For the boon, so bravely I wore the mask.
But into her face there came a flame;—
I wonder could she have been thinking the
    same?

THE RIGHT TO DIE

One evening Mr. Dunbar and a friend of whom he was very fond, and in whose presence the poet felt no restraint, were talking of suicide. The friend took the orthodox and popular view of the dreadful practice.

Dunbar stood with his hands at his back before an open fire. Suddenly—with upturned eyes, and in earnest tones he began to improvise his reply in verse. So unusual was the sentiment and so daring the thought that his listener compelled him to take a seat at a desk and write it out ere the lines escaped him. Many of Dunbar's best poems came thus, and passed away with his breath, as he did not pause to set them down.

I have no fancy for that ancient cant
That makes us masters of our destinies,
And not our lives, to hold or give them up
As will directs; I cannot, will not think
That men, the subtle worms, who plot and
      plan
And scheme and calculate with such shrewd
      wit,
Are such great blund'ring fools as not to
      know
When they have lived enough.
                  Men court not death
When there are sweets still left in life to
      taste.
Nor will a brave man choose to live when
      he,
Full deeply drunk of life, has reached the
      dregs,
And knows that now but bitterness re-
      mains.
He is the coward who, outfaced in this,
Fears the false goblins of another life.
I honor him who being much harassed
Drinks of sweet courage until drunk of it,—
Then seizing Death, reluctant, by the hand,
Leaps with him, fearless, to eternal peace!

BEHIND THE ARRAS

As in some dim baronial hall restrained,
A prisoner sits, engirt by secret doors
And waving tapestries that argue forth
Strange passages into the outer air;
So in this dimmer room which we call life,
Thus sits the soul and marks with eye in-
      tent
That mystic curtain o'er the portal death;
Still deeming that behind the arras lies
The lambent way that leads to lasting
      light.
Poor fooled and foolish soul! Know now
      that death
Is but a blind, false door that nowhere
      leads,
And gives no hope of exit final, free.

12

WHEN THE OLD MAN SMOKES

In the forenoon's restful quiet,
   When the boys are off at school,
When the window lights are shaded
   And the chimney-corner cool,
Then the old man seeks his armchair,
   Lights his pipe and settles back;
Falls a-dreaming as he draws it
   Till the smoke-wreaths gather black.

And the tear-drops come a trickling
   Down his cheeks, a silver flow —
Smoke or memories you wonder,
   But you never ask him,—no;
For there's something almost sacred
   To the other family folks
In those moods of silent dreaming
   When the old man smokes.

Ah, perhaps he sits there dreaming
   Of the love of other days
And of how he used to lead her
   Through the merry dance's maze;
How he called her " little princess,"
   And, to please her, used to twine
Tender wreaths to crown her tresses,
   From the " matrimony vine."

Then before his mental vision
   Comes, perhaps, a sadder day,
When they left his little princess
   Sleeping with her fellow clay.
How his young heart throbbed, and pained
      him!
   Why, the memory of it chokes!
Is it of these things he's thinking
   When the old man smokes?

But some brighter thoughts possess him,
   For the tears are dried the while.
And the old, worn face is wrinkled
   In a reminiscent smile,
From the middle of the forehead
   To the feebly trembling lip,
At some ancient prank remembered
   Or some long unheard-of quip.

Then the lips relax their tension
   And the pipe begins to slide,
Till in little clouds of ashes,
   It falls softly at his side;

And his head bends low and lower
　　Till his chin lies on his breast,
And he sits in peaceful slumber
　　Like a little child at rest.

Dear old man, there's something sad'ning,
　　In these dreamy moods of yours,
Since the present proves so fleeting,
　　All the past for you endures.
Weeping at forgotten sorrows,
　　Smiling at forgotten jokes;
Life epitomized in minutes,
　　When the old man smokes.

THE GARRET

　　The poverty which befel Mr. Dunbar while in London, and which would have wholly discouraged many another sensitive soul, proved only a frame upon which he hung beautiful garlands of song.
　　The little poem, given herewith, shows that his English was a bit Londonized while in that city, but the philosophic cheerfulness was the same that came with him into the world, and forms the trimming of so many of his graceful poems. No doubt if he had been stranded on a desert island, he would have found abundant food for fun and would have written humorous verse at his own expense, to while the time away.

Within a London garret high,
Above the roofs and near the sky,
　　My ill-rewarding pen I ply
　　　　To win me bread.
This little chamber, six by four,
Is castle, study, den and more,—
　　Altho' no carpet decks the floor,
　　　　Nor down, the bed.

My room is rather bleak and bare;
I only have one broken chair,
But then, there's plenty of fresh air,—
　　Some light, beside.
What tho' I cannot ask my friends
To share with me my odds and ends,
A liberty my aerie lends,
　　To most denied.

The bore who falters at the stair
No more shall be my curse and care,
And duns shall fail to find my lair
　　With beastly bills.
When debts have grown and funds are
　　　　short,
I find it rather pleasant sport
To live " above the common sort "
　　With all their ills.

I write my rhymes and sing away,
And dawn may come or dusk or day:
Tho' fare be poor, my heart is gay,
　　And full of glee.
Though chimney-pots be all my views;
'Tis nearer for the winging Muse,
So I am sure she'll not refuse
　　To visit me.

LITTLE BROWN BABY

Little brown baby wif spa'klin' eyes,
　　Come to yo' pappy an' set on his knee.
What you been doin', suh—makin' san'
　　　　pies ?
　　Look at dat bib—you's ez du'ty ez me.
Look at dat mouf—dat's merlasses, I bet;
　　Come hyeah, Maria, an' wipe off his
　　　　han's.
Bees gwine to ketch you an' eat you up
　　　　yit,
　　Bein' so sticky an' sweet—goodness
　　　　lan's !

Little brown baby wif spa'klin' eyes,
　　Who's pappy's darlin' an' who's pappy's
　　　　chile ?
Who is it all de day nevah once tries
　　Fu' to be cross, er once loses dat smile ?
Whah did you git dem teef ?　My, you's a
　　　　scamp !
　　Whah did dat dimple come f'om in yo'
　　　　chin ?
Pappy do' know yo—I b'lieves you's a
　　　　tramp ;
　　Mammy, dis hyeah's some ol' straggler
　　　　got in !

WHO'S PAPPY'S DARLIN'

DEN YOU MEN'S DE MULE'S OL' HA'NESS

Let's th'ow him outen de do' in de san',
  We do' want stragglers a-layin' 'roun'
    hyeah ;
Let's gin him 'way to de big buggah-man ;
  I know he's hidin' erroun' hyeah right
    neah.
Buggah-man, buggah-man, come in de
    do',
  Hyeah's a bad boy you kin have fu' to
    eat.
Mammy an' pappy do' want him no mo',
  Swaller him down f'om his haid to his
    feet !

Dah, now, I t'ought dat you'd hug me up
    close.
  Go back, ol' buggah, you sha'n't have
    dis boy.
He ain't no tramp, ner no straggler, of
    co'se ;
  He's pappy's pa'dner an' playmate an'
    joy.
Come to you' pallet now—go to yo' res' ;
  Wisht you could allus know ease an'
    cleah skies ;
Wisht you could stay jes' a chile on my
    breas'—
  Little brown baby wif spa'klin' eyes !

TIME TO TINKER 'ROUN'

Summah's nice, wif sun a-shinin',
  Spring is good wif greens and grass,
An' dey's some t'ings nice 'bout wintah,
  Dough hit brings de freezin' blas' ;
But de time dat is the fines',
  Whethah fiel's is green or brown,
Is w'en de rain's a-po'in'
  An' dey's time to tinker 'roun'.

Den you men's de mule's ol' ha'ness,
  An' you men's de broken chair.
Hummin' all de time you's wo'kin'
  Some ol' common kind o' air.
Evah now an' then you looks out,
  Tryin' mighty ha'd to frown,
But you cain't, you's glad hit's rainin',
  An' dey's time to tinker 'roun'.

Oh, you 'ten's lak you so anxious
  Evah time it so't o' stops.
W'en hit goes on, den you reckon
  Dat de wet'll he'p de crops.
But hit ain't de crops you's aftah ;
  You knows w'en de rain comes **down**
Dat hit's too wet out fu' wo'kin',
  An' dey's time to tinker 'roun'.

Oh, dey's fun inside de co'n-crib,
  An' dey's laffin' at de ba'n ;
An' dey's allus some one jokin',
  Er some one to tell a ya'n.
Dah's a quiet in yo' cabin,
  Only fu' de rain's sof' soun' ;
So you's mighty blessed happy
  W'en dey's time to tinker 'roun' !

A BRIDAL MEASURE

Come, essay a sprightly measure,
Tuned to some light song of pleasure.
  Maidens, let your brows be crowned
  As we foot this merry round.

From the ground a voice is singing,
From the sod a soul is springing.
  Who shall say 'tis but a clod
  Quick'**ning** upward towards its God ?

Who **shall** say it ? Who may know it,
That the clod is not a poet
  Waiting but a gleam to waken
  In a spirit music-shaken ?

Phyllis, Phyllis, why be waiting ?
In the woods the birds are mating.
  From the tree beside the wall,
  Hear the am'rous robin call.

Listen to yon thrush's trilling ;
Phyllis, Phyllis, are you willing,
  When love speaks from cave and **tree,**
  Only we should silent be ?

When the year, itself renewing,
All the world with flowers is strewing,
  Then through Youth's Arcadian land,
  Love and song go hand in hand.

Come, unfold your vocal treasure.
Sing with me a nuptial measure,—
  Let this spring-time gambol be
  Bridal dance for you and me.

TO E. H. K.

ON THE RECEIPT OF A FAMILIAR POEM

To me, like hauntings of a vagrant breath
    From some far forest which I once have
      known,
    The perfume of this flower of verse is
      blown.
Tho' seemingly soul-blossoms faint to death,
Naught that with joy she bears e'er with-
    ereth.
    So, tho' the pregnant years have come
      and flown,
    Lives come and gone and altered like
      mine own,
This poem comes to me a shibboleth:

Brings sound of past communings to my
    ear,
    Turns round the tide of time and bears
      me back
      Along an old and long untraversed
        way;
Makes me forget this is a later year,
    Makes me tread o'er a reminiscent track,
      Half sad, half glad, to one forgotten
        day!

VENGEANCE IS SWEET

When I was young I longed for Love,
And held his glory far above
All other earthly things.   I cried:
" Come, Love, dear Love, with me abide; "
And with my subtlest art I wooed,
And eagerly the wight pursued.
But Love was gay and Love was shy,
He laughed at me and passed me by.

Well, I grew old and I grew gray,
When Wealth came wending down my
    way.
I took his golden hand with glee,
And comrades from that day were we.
Then Love came back with doleful face,
And prayed that I would give him place.
But, though his eyes with tears were dim,
I turned my back and laughed at him.

A HYMN

AFTER READING " LEAD, KINDLY LIGHT."

Lead gently, Lord, and slow,
    For oh, my steps are weak,
And ever as I go,
    Some soothing sentence speak;

That I may turn my face
    Through doubt's obscurity
Towards thine abiding-place,
    E'en tho' I cannot see.

For lo, the way is dark;
    Through mist and cloud I grope,
Save for that fitful spark,
    The little flame of hope.

Lead gently, Lord, and slow,
    For fear that I may fall;
I know not where to go
    Unless I hear thy call.

My fainting soul doth yearn
    For thy green hills afar;
So let thy mercy burn —
    My greater, guiding star!

JUST WHISTLE A BIT

Just whistle a bit, if the day be dark,
    And the sky be overcast:
If mute be the voice of the piping lark,
    Why, pipe your own small blast.

And it's wonderful how o'er the gray sky-
    track
The truant warbler comes stealing back.
But why need he come? for your soul's at
    rest,
And the song in the heart,—ah, that is
    best.

Just whistle a bit, if the night be drear
    And the stars refuse to shine:
And a gleam that mocks the starlight clear
    Within you glows benign.

Till the dearth of light in the glooming
    skies
Is lost to the sight of your soul-lit eyes.
What matters the absence of moon or star?
The light within is the best by far.

Just whistle a bit, if there's work to do,
  With the mind or in the soil.
And your note will turn out a talisman
    true
  To exorcise grim Toil.

It will lighten your burden and make you
    feel
That there's nothing like work as a sauce
  for a meal.
And with song in your heart and the meal
  in—its place,
There'll be joy in your bosom and light in
  your face.

Just whistle a bit, if your heart be sore
  'Tis a wonderful balm for pain.
Just pipe some old melody o'er and o'er
  Till it soothes like summer rain.

And perhaps 'twould be best in a later day,
When Death comes stalking down the way,
To knock at your bosom and see if you're
    fit,
Then, as you wait calmly, just whistle a
    bit.

THE BARRIER

The Midnight wooed the Morning-Star,
  And prayed her: " Love, come nearer;
Your swinging coldly there afar
  To me but makes you dearer ! "

The Morning-Star was pale with dole
  As said she, low replying:
" Oh, lover mine, soul of my soul,
  For you I too am sighing.

" But One ordained when we were born,
  In spite of Love's insistence,
That Night might only view the Morn
  Adoring at a distance."

But as she spoke the jealous Sun
  Across the heavens panted.
" Oh, whining fools," he cried, " have one;
  Your wishes shall be granted ! "

He hurled his flaming lances far;
  The twain stood unaffrighted —
And midnight and the Morning-Star
  Lay down in death united !

DREAMS

Dream on, for dreams are sweet :
  Do not awaken !
Dream on, and at thy feet
  Pomegranates shall be shaken.

Who likeneth the youth
  Of life to morning ?
'Tis like the night in truth,
  Rose-colored dreams adorning.

The wind is soft above,
  The shadows umber.
(There is a dream called Love.)
  Take thou the fullest slumber !

In Lethe's soothing stream,
  Thy thirst thou slakest.
Sleep, sleep ; 'tis sweet to dream.
  Oh, weep when thou awakest !

THE DREAMER

Temples he built and palaces of air,
  And, with the artist's parent-pride aglow,
  His fancy saw his vague ideals grow
Into creations marvelously fair ;
He set his foot upon Fame's nether stair.
  But ah, his dream,—it had entranced
    him so
  He could not move. He could no
    farther go ;
But paused in joy that he was even there !

He did not wake until one day there
    gleamed
  Thro' his dark consciousness a light
    that racked
His being till he rose, alert to act.
  But lo ! what he had dreamed, the while
    he dreamed,
  Another, wedding action unto thought,
  Into the living, pulsing world had
    brought.

WAITING

The sun has slipped his tether
  And galloped down the west.
(Oh, it's weary, weary waiting, love.)

The little bird is sleeping
  In the softness of its nest.
Night follows day, day follows dawn,
And so the time has come and gone :
  And it's weary, weary waiting, love.

The cruel wind is rising
  With a whistle and a wail.
(And it's weary, weary waiting, love.)
My eyes are seaward straining
  For the coming of a sail ;
But void the sea, and void the beach
Far and beyond where gaze can reach !
  And it's weary, weary waiting, love.

I heard the bell-buoy ringing —
  How long ago it seems !
(Oh, it's weary, weary waiting, love.)
And ever still, its knelling
  Crashes in upon my dreams.
The banns were read, my frock was sewn ;
Since then two seasons' winds have
    blown —
  And it's weary, weary waiting, love.

The stretches of the ocean
  Are bare and bleak to-day.
(Oh, it's weary, weary waiting, love.)
My eyes are growing dimmer —
  Is it tears, or age, or spray ?
But I will stay till you come home.
Strange ships come in across the foam !
  But it's weary, weary waiting, love.

THE END OF THE CHAPTER

So prone is humanity to "jump at conclusions " that when the newspaper chroniclers set about finding "things to say " about Paul Laurence Dunbar at the time of his death, they unanimously concluded that this poem referred to the end of Mr. Dunbar's married life, and so stated without reservation. A careful study of his work reveals the fact that these stanzas were written long before his marriage, and were no doubt suggested by the unhappy termination of some other man's connubial happiness.

That they proved startlingly prophetic in his own case cannot be denied, for, as he said for another he might well have said for himself —

    —" so close the book.
But brought it grief or brought it bliss,
No other page shall read like this ! "

No one will deny that while he had, like all poets, hundreds of "passing fancies " for fair woman, he was a man of one great passion, and that was for his estranged wife.

Ah, yes, the chapter ends to-day;
We even lay the book away ;
But oh, how sweet the moments sped
Before the final page was read !

We tried to read between the lines
The Author's deep-concealed designs ;
But scant reward such search secures ;
You saw my heart and I saw yours.

The Master,—he who penned the page
And bade us read it,—he is sage :
And what he orders, you and I
Can but obey, nor question why.

We read together and forgot
The world about us. Time was not.
Unheeded and unfelt, it fled.
We read and hardly knew we read.

Until beneath a sadder sun,
We came to know the book was done.
Then, as our minds were but new lit,
It dawned upon us what was writ ;

And we were startled. In our eyes,
Looked forth the light of great surprise.
Then as a deep-toned tocsin tolls,
A voice spoke forth : " Behold your souls ! "

I do, I do. I cannot look
Into your eyes : so close the book.
But brought it grief or brought it bliss,
No other page shall read like this !

SYMPATHY

I know what the caged bird feels, alas!
  When the sun is bright on the upland
    slopes;
When the wind stirs soft through the
    springing grass,
And the river flows like a stream of glass;
  When the first bird sings and the first
    bud opes,
And the faint perfume from its chalice
    steals —
I know what the caged bird feels!

I know why the caged bird beats his
    wing
  Till its blood is red on the cruel bars;
For he must fly back to his perch and
    cling
When he fain would be on the bough
    a-swing;
  And a pain still throbs in the old, old
    scars
And they pulse again with a keener
    sting —
I know why he beats his wing!

I know why the caged bird sings, ah me,
  When his wing is bruised and his
    bosom sore,—
When he beats his bars and he would be
    free;
It is not a carol of joy or glee,
  But a prayer that he sends from his
    heart's deep core,
But a plea, that upward to Heaven he
    flings —
I know why the caged bird sings!

LOVE AND GRIEF

Out of my heart, one treach'rous winter's
    day,
I locked young Love and threw the key
    away.
Grief, wandering widely, found the key,
And hastened with it, straightway, back
    to me,
With Love beside him. He unlocked the
    door
And bade Love enter with him there and
    stay.
And so the twain abide for evermore.

LOVE'S CHASTENING

Once Love grew bold and arrogant of air,
Proud of the youth that made him fresh
    and fair;
So unto Grief he spake, " What right hast
    thou
To part or parcel of this heart?" Grief's
    brow
Was darkened with the storm of inward
    strife;
Thrice smote he Love as only he might
    dare,
And Love, pride purged, was chastened
    all his life.

MORTALITY

Ashes to ashes, dust unto dust,
What of his loving, what of his lust?
What of his passion, what of his pain?
What of his poverty, what of his pride?
Earth, the great mother, has called him
    again:
Deeply he sleeps, the world's verdict de-
    fied.
Shall he be tried again? Shall he go free?
Who shall the court convene? Where
    shall it be?
No answer on the land, none from the sea.
Only we know that as he did, we must:
You with your theories, you with your
    trust, —
Ashes to ashes, dust unto dust!

LOVE

A life was mine full of the close concern
  Of many-voiced affairs. The world sped
    fast;
  Behind me, ever rolled a pregnant past.
A present came equipped with lore to learn.
Art, science, letters, in their turn,
  Each one allured me with its treasures
    vast;
  And I staked all for wisdom, till at last
Thou cam'st and taught my soul anew to
    yearn.
  I had not dreamed that I could turn
    away
From all that men with brush and pen had
    wrought;

But ever since that memorable day
When to my heart the truth of love was
     brought,
I have been wholly yielded to its sway,
And had no room for any other thought.

SHE GAVE ME A ROSE

She gave me a rose,
     And I kissed it and pressed it.
I love her, she knows,
     And my action confessed it.
She gave me a rose,
     And I kissed it and pressed it.

Ah, how my heart glows,
     Could I ever have guessed it ?
It is fair to suppose
     That I might have repressed it :
She gave me a rose,
     And I kissed it and pressed it.

'Twas a rhyme in life's prose
     That uplifted and blest it.
Man's nature, who knows
     Until love comes to test it ?
She gave me a rose,
     And I kissed it and pressed it.

DREAM SONG. I

Long years ago, within a distant clime,
Ere Love had touched me with his wand
     sublime,
I dreamed of one to make my life's calm
     May
The panting passion of a summer's day.
And ever since, in almost sad suspense,
I have been waiting with a soul intense
To greet and take unto myself the beams,
Of her, my star, the lady of my dreams.

O Love, still longed and looked for, come
     to me,
Be thy far home by mountain, vale, or sea.
My yearning heart may never find its rest
Until thou liest rapt upon my breast.
The wind may bring its perfume from the
     south,
Is it so sweet as breath from my love's
     mouth ?
Oh, naught that surely is, and naught that
     seems
May turn me from the lady of my dreams.

DREAM SONG. II

Pray, what can dreams avail
     To make love or to mar ?
The child within the cradle rail
     Lies dreaming of the star.
But is the star by this beguiled
To leave its place and seek the child ?

The poor plucked rose within its glass
     Still dreameth of the bee ;
But, tho' the lagging moments pass,
     Her Love she may not see.
If dream of child and flower fail,
Why should a maiden's dreams prevail ?

CHRISTMAS IN THE HEART

The snow lies deep upon the ground,
And winter's brightness all around
Decks bravely out the forest sere,
With jewels of the brave old year.
The coasting crowd upon the hill
With some new spirit seems to thrill ;
And all the temple bells achime
Ring out the glee of Christmas time.

In happy homes the brown oak-bough
Vies with the red-gemmed holly now ;
And here and there, like pearls, there show
The berries of the mistletoe.
A sprig upon the chandelier
Says to the maidens, " Come not here ! "
Even the pauper of the earth
Some kindly gift has cheered to mirth !

Within his chamber, dim and cold,
There sits a grasping miser old.
He has no thought save one of gain, —
To grind and gather and grasp and drain.
A peal of bells, a merry shout
Assail his ear : he gazes out
Upon a world to him all gray,
And snarls, " Why, this is Christmas Day ! "

No, man of ice,—for shame, for shame !
For " Christmas Day " is no mere name.
No, not for you this ringing cheer,
This festal season of the year.
And not for you the chime of bells
From holy temple rolls and swells.
In day and deed he has no part —
Who holds not Christmas in his heart !

THE KING IS DEAD

Aye, lay him in his grave, the old dead
    year!
His life is lived—fulfilled his destiny.
Have you for him no sad, regretful tear
To drop beside the cold, unfollowed bier?
Can you not pay the tribute of a sigh?

Was he not kind to you, this dead old year?
Did he not give enough of earthly store?
Enough of love, and laughter, and good
    cheer?
Have not the skies you scanned sometimes
    been clear?
How, then, of him who dies, could you ask
    more?

It is not well to hate him for the pain
He brought you, and the sorrows manifold.
To pardon him these hurts still I am fain;
For in the panting period of his reign,
He brought me new wounds, but he healed
    the old.

One little sigh for thee, my poor, dead
    friend —
One little sigh while my companions sing.
Thou art so soon forgotten in the end;
We cry e'en as thy footsteps downward
    tend:
"The king is dead! long live the king!"

THEOLOGY

There is a heaven, forever, day by day,
    The upward longing of my soul doth
        tell me so.
There is a hell, I'm quite as sure; for pray,
    If there were not, where would my
        neighbors go?

RESIGNATION

Long had I grieved at what I deemed
    abuse;
    But now I am as grain within the mill.
If so be thou must crush me for thy use,
    Grind on, O potent God, and do thy
        will!

LOVE'S HUMILITY

As some rapt gazer on the lowly earth,
    Looks up to radiant planets, ranging
        far,
So I, whose soul doth know thy wondrous
    worth
Look longing up to thee as to a star.

PRECEDENT

The poor man went to the rich man's
    doors,
"I come as Lazarus came," he said.
The rich man turned with humble head,—
"I will send my dogs to lick your sores!"

SHE TOLD HER BEADS

She told her beads with downcast eyes,
    Within the ancient chapel dim;
    And ever as her fingers slim
Slipt o'er th' insensate ivories,
My rapt soul followed, spaniel-wise.
    Ah, many were the beads she wore;
    But as she told them o'er and o'er,
They did not number all my sighs.
My heart was filled with unvoiced cries
    And prayers and pleadings unex-
        pressed;
    But while I burned with Love's unrest,
She told her beads with downcast eyes.

LITTLE LUCY LANDMAN

Oh, the day has set me dreaming
    In a strange, half solemn way
Of the feelings I experienced
    On another long past day,—
Of the way my heart made music
    When the buds began to blow,
And o' little Lucy Landman
    Whom I loved long years ago.

It's in spring, the poet tells us,
    That we turn to thoughts of love,
And our hearts go out a-wooing
    With the lapwing and the dove.
But whene'er the soul goes seeking
    Its twin-soul, upon the wing,
I've a notion, backed by mem'ry,
    That it's love that makes the spring.

I have heard a robin singing
  When the boughs were brown and bare,
And the chilling hand of winter
  Scattered jewels through the air.
And in spite of dates and seasons,
  It was always spring, I know,
When I loved Lucy Landman
  In the days of long ago.

Ah, my little Lucy Landman,
  I remember you as well
As if 'twere only yesterday
  I strove your thoughts to tell,—
When I tilted back your bonnet,
  Looked into your eyes so true,
Just to see if you were loving
  Me as I was loving you.

Ah, my little Lucy Landman
  It is true it was denied
You should see a fuller summer
  And an autumn by my side.
But the glance of love's sweet sunlight
  Which your eyes that morning gave
Has kept spring within my bosom,
  Though you lie within the grave.

THE KNIGHT

Our good knight, Ted, girds his broad-
    sword on
  (And he wields it well, I ween);
He's on his steed, and away has gone
  To the fight for king and queen.
What tho' no edge the broadsword hath?
What tho' the blade be made of lath?
    'Tis a valiant hand
    That wields the brand,
So, foeman, clear the path!

He prances off at a goodly pace;
  'Tis a noble steed he rides,
That bears as well in the speedy race
  As he bears in battle-tides.
What tho' 'tis but a rocking-chair
That prances with this stately air?
    'Tis a warrior bold
    The reins doth hold,
Who bids all foes beware!

LULLABY

Bedtime's come fu' little boys.
    Po' little lamb.
Too tiahed out to make a noise,
    Po' little lamb.
You gwine t' have to-morrer sho'?
Yes, you tole me dat befo',
Don't you fool me, chile, no mo',
    Po' little lamb.

You been bad de livelong day,
    Po' little lamb.
Th'owin' stones an' runnin' 'way,
    Po' little lamb.
My, but you's a-runnin' wil',
Look jes' lak some po' folks chile;
Mam' gwine whup you atter while,
    Po' little lamb.

Come hyeah! you mos' tiahed to def,
    Po' little lamb.
Played yo'se'f clean out o' bref,
    Po' little lamb.
See dem han's now—sich a sight!
Would you evah b'lieve dey's white?
Stan' still twell I wash 'em right,
    Po' little lamb.

Jes' cain't hol' yo' haid up straight,
    Po' little lamb.
Hadn't oughter played so late,
    Po' little lamb.
Mammy do' know whut she'd do,
Ef de chillun's all lak you;
You's a caution now fu' true,
    Po' little lamb.

Lay yo' haid down in my lap,
    Po' little lamb.
Y' ought to have a right good slap,
    Po' little lamb.
You been runnin' roun' a heap.
Shet dem eyes an' don't you peep,
Dah now, dah now, go to sleep,
    Po' little lamb.

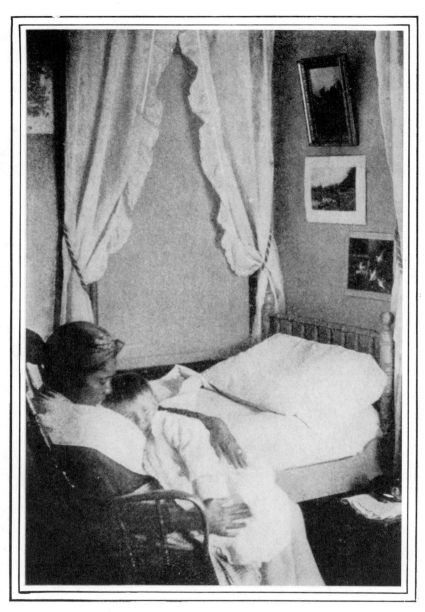

Po' Little Lamb

DAT'S MY GAL

THOU ART MY LUTE

Thou art my lute, by thee I sing,—
  My being is attuned to thee.
Thou settest all my words a-wing,
  And meltest me to melody.

Thou art my life, by thee I live,
  From thee proceed the joys I know;
Sweetheart, thy hand has power to give
  The meed of love—the cup of woe.

Thou art my love, by thee I lead
  My soul the paths of light along,
From vale to vale, from mead to mead,
  And home it in the hills of song.

My song, my soul, my life, my all,
  Why need I pray or make my plea,
Since my petition cannot fall ;
  For I'm already one with thee !

THE PHANTOM KISS

One night in my room, still and beamless,
  With will and with thought in eclipse,
I rested in sleep that was dreamless ;
  When softly there fell on my lips

A touch, as of lips that were pressing
  Mine own with the message of bliss —
A sudden, soft, fleeting caressing,
  A breath like a maiden's first kiss.

I woke—and the scoffer may doubt me —
  I peered in surprise through the gloom;
But nothing and none were about me,
  And I was alone in my room.

Perhaps 'twas the wind that caressed me
  And touched me with dew-laden breath ;
Or, maybe, close-sweeping, there passed
    me
  The low-winging Angel of Death.

Some sceptic may choose to disdain it,
  Or one feign to read it aright;
Or wisdom may seek to explain it —
  This mystical kiss in the night.

But rather let fancy thus clear it :
  That, thinking of me here alone,
The miles were made naught, and, in
    spirit,
  Thy lips, love, were laid on mine own.

THE PHOTOGRAPH

See dis pictyah in my han' ?
    Dat's my gal ;
Ain't she purty ? goodness lan' !
    Huh name Sal.
Dat's de very way she be
Kin' o' tickles me to see
Huh a-smilin' back at me.

She sont me dis photygraph
    Jes' las' week ;
An' aldough hit made me laugh —
    My black cheek
Felt somethin' a-runnin' queer ;
Bless yo' soul, it was a tear
Jes' f'om wishin' she was here.

Often when I's all alone
    Layin' here,
I git t'inkin' 'bout my own
    Sallie dear ;
How she say dat I's huh beau,
An' hit tickles me to know
Dat de gal do love me so.

Some bright day I's goin' back,
    Fo' de la !
An' ez sho' 's my face is black,
    Ax huh pa
Fu' de blessed little miss
Who's a-smilin' out o' dis
Pictyah, lak she wan'ed a kiss !

COMMUNION

In the silence of my heart,
  I will spend an hour with thee,
When my love shall rend apart
  All the veil of mystery :

All that dim and misty veil
  That shut in between our souls
When Death cried, " Ho, maiden, hail ! "
  And your barque sped on the shoals.

On the shoals ? Nay, wrongly said.
  On the breeze of Death that sweeps
Far from life, thy soul has sped
  Out into unsounded deeps.

I shall take an hour and come
  Sailing, darling, to thy side.
Wind nor sea may keep me from
  Soft communings with my bride.

I shall rest my head on thee
  As I did long days of yore,
When a calm, untroubled sea
  Rocked thy vessel at the shore.

I shall take thy hand in mine,
  And live o'er the olden days
When thy smile to me was wine,—
  Golden wine thy word of praise,

For the carols I had wrought
  In my soul's simplicity ;
For the petty beads of thought
  Which thine eyes alone could see.

Ah, those eyes, love-blind, but keen
  For my welfare and my weal !
Tho' the grave-door shut between,
  Still their love-lights o'er me steal.

I can see thee thro' my tears,
  As thro' rain we see the sun.
What tho' cold and cooling years
  Shall their bitter courses run,—

I shall see thee still and be
  Thy true lover evermore,
And thy face shall be to me
  Dear and helpful as before.

Death may vaunt and Death may boast,
  But we laugh his pow'r to scorn ;
He is but a slave at most,—
  Night that heralds coming morn.

I shall spend an hour with thee
  Day by day, my little bride.
True love laughs at mystery,
  Crying, " Doors of Death, fly wide."

THE GOURD

In the heavy earth the miner
  Toiled and labored day by day,
Wrenching from the miser mountain
  Brilliant treasure where it lay.
And the artist worn and weary
  Wrought with labor manifold
That the king might drink his nectar
  From a goblet made of gold.

On the prince's groaning table
  'Mid the silver gleaming bright
Mirroring the happy faces
  Giving back the flaming light,
Shine the cups of priceless crystal
  Chased with many a lovely line,
Glowing now with warmer color,
  Crimsoned by the ruby wine.

In a valley sweet with sunlight,
  Fertile with the dew and rain,
Without miner's daily labor,
  Without artist's nightly pain,
There there grows the cup I drink from,
  Summer's sweetness in it stored,
And my lips pronounce a blessing
  As they touch an old brown gourd.

Why, the miracle at Cana
  In the land of Galilee,
Tho' it puzzles all the scholars,
  Is no longer strange to me.
For the poorest and the humblest
  Could a priceless wine afford,
If they'd only dip up water
  With a sunlight-seasoned gourd.

So a health to my old comrade,
  And a song of praise to sing
When he rests inviting kisses
  In his place beside the spring.
Give the king his golden goblets,
  Give the prince his crystal hoard ;
But for me the sparkling water
  From a brown and brimming gourd !

MARE RUBRUM

In Life's Red Sea with faith I plant my
    feet,
  And wait the sound of that sustaining
    word

Which long ago the men of Israel
heard,
When Pharaoh's host behind them, fierce
and fleet,
Raged on, consuming with revengeful
heat.
Why are the barrier waters still un-
stirred? —
That struggling faith may die of hope
deferred?
Is God not sitting in his ancient seat?

The billows swirl above my trembling
limbs,
And almost chill my anxious heart to
doubt
And disbelief, long conquered and
defied.
But tho' the music of my hopeful hymns
Is drowned by curses of the raging
rout,
No voice yet bids th' opposing waves
divide!

IN AN ENGLISH GARDEN

In view of the fact that Mr. Dunbar
had left a sweetheart in America, and that
they had become betrothed just before he
sailed for England, it is not hard to under-
stand why the subtle scents and ancient
beauties of an old-world garden served
only to bring him a poignant heart-ache
and an overpowering longing for home
and love.

In this old garden, fair, I walk to-day
Heart-charmed with all the beauty of
the scene:
The rich, luxuriant grasses' cooling
green,
The wall's environ, ivy-decked and gray,
The waving branches with the wind at
play,
The slight and tremulous blooms that
show between,
Sweet all: and yet my yearning heart
doth lean
Towards Love's Egyptian flesh-pots far
away.

Beside the wall, the slim Laburnum
grows
And flings its golden flow'rs to every
breeze.
But e'en among such soothing sights as
these,
I pant and nurse my soul-devouring woes.
Of all the longings that our hearts wot of,
There is no hunger like the want of love!

THE CRISIS

A man of low degree was sore oppressed,
Fate held him under iron-handed sway,
And ever, those who saw him thus dis-
tressed
Would bid him bend his stubborn will
and pray.
But he, strong in himself and obdurate,
Waged, prayerless, on his losing fight
with Fate.

Friends gave his proffered hand their
coldest clasp,
Or took it not at all; and Poverty,
That bruised his body with relentless
grasp,
Grinned, taunting, when he struggled
to be free.
But though with helpless hands he beat
the air,
His need extreme yet found no voice in
prayer.

Then he prevailed; and forthwith snob-
bish Fate,
Like some whipped cur, came fawning
at his feet;
Those who had scorned forgave and called
him great —
His friends found out that friendship
still was sweet.
But he, once obdurate, now bowed his
head
In prayer, and trembling with its import,
said:

" Mere human strength may stand ill-
fortune's frown;
So I prevailed, for human strength was
mine;
But from the killing pow'r of great re-
nown,

Naught may protect me save a strength
    divine.
Help me, O Lord, in this my trembling
    cause ;
I scorn men's curses, but I dread ap-
    plause ! "

THE CONQUERORS

THE BLACK TROOPS IN CUBA

Round the wide earth, from the red field
    your valor has won,
Blown with the breath of the far-speaking
    gun,
    Goes the word.
Bravely you spoke through the battle cloud
    heavy and dun.
Tossed though the speech towards the mist-
    hidden sun,
    The world heard.

Hell would have shrunk from you seeking
    it fresh from the fray,
Grim with the dust of the battle, and gray
    From the fight.
Heaven would have crowned you, with
    crowns not of gold but of
    bay,
Owning you fit for the light of her day,
    Men of night.

Far through the cycle of years and of lives
    that shall come,
There shall speak voices long muffled and
    dumb,
    Out of fear.
And through the noises of trade and the
    turbulent hum,
Truth shall rise over the militant drum,
    Loud and clear.

Then on the cheek of the honester nation
    that grows,
All for their love of you, not for your
    woes,
    There shall lie
Tears that shall be to your souls as the dew
    to the rose;
Afterwards thanks, that the present yet
    knows
    Not to ply !

ALEXANDER CRUMMELL—DEAD

Back to the breast of thy mother,
Child of the earth !
E'en her caress cannot smother
What thou hast done.
Follow the trail of the westering sun
Over the earth.
Thy light and his were as one —
Sun, in thy worth.
Unto a nation whose sky was as night,
Camest thou, holily, bearing thy light:
And the dawn came,
In it thy fame
Flashed up in a flame.

Back to the breast of thy mother —
To rest.
Long hast thou striven;
Dared where the hills by the lightning of
    heaven were riven ;
Go now, pure shriven.
Who shall come after thee, out of the clay —
Learned one and leader to show us the
    way ?
Who shall rise up when the world gives
    the test ?
Think thou no more of this —
Rest !

WHEN ALL IS DONE

To any one who viewed the dead face
of Paul Laurence Dunbar, after the long,
hard race was done, there could but come
the memory of this poem, and one could
not but be grateful to him for having said
these so plainly and in such a simple way.

There was no trace of pain upon his
features, naught that could suggest any-
thing but peace and deep content. Those
who loved him could not keep back the
tears because of their loss, but no one who
saw him at the last feared that he was oth-
erwise than gloriously at rest ! He had
indeed " greeted the dawn," though it was
near the hour of the setting of an earthly
winter's sun that he broke the last of his
prison bars, and freedom found at last.

When all is done, and my last word is said,
And ye who loved me murmur, " He is
    dead,"
Let no one weep, for fear that I should
    know,
And sorrow too that ye should sorrow so.

When all is done and in the oozing clay,
Ye lay this cast-off hull of mine away,
Pray not for me, for, after long despair,
The quiet of the grave will be a prayer.

For I have suffered loss and grievous pain,
The hurts of hatred and the world's dis-
    dain,
And wounds so deep that love, well-tried
    and pure,
Had not the pow'r to ease them or to cure.

When all is done, say not my day is o'er,
And that thro' night I seek a dimmer
    shore :
Say rather that my morn has just begun,—
I greet the dawn and not a setting sun,
          When all is done.

THE POET AND THE BABY

This dainty bit of verse reflects the poet's
great love for children. What the inspira-
tion of that particular poem may have been,
it may have referred to almost any of his
child friendships. One of these was espe-
cially beautiful. A little baby boy of three,
with snow-white skin and golden curls,
loved Dunbar devotedly, and the people
who lived near the poet in Dayton, often
speak of how on bright days Mr. Dunbar
would sit on the front steps of his home
with little David Herr by his side. David
was only a baby, but he loved " Mr. Paul "
with an all-absorbing passion and always
sat as close as he could with one small arm
about the poet's waist. The sight was one
never to be forgotten—the black man and
the white poet, sitting for hours side by
side dumb in their mutual admiration.

When Mr. Dunbar lay dead, little David,
only half realizing the great change that
had come to his friend, came as usual with
a flower (he always brought a beautiful
flower to the poet), which strangely enough,
was a spotless white lily. A gentleman
who knew of the friendship existing be-
tween the baby and the dead man, carried
David into the chamber of Death.

" I want to div him my f'ower," said
the little fellow, and the man stooped low
until the dimpled fingers placed the white
lily in the poet's hand.

How's a man to write a sonnet, can you
    tell, —
How's he going to weave the dim, poetic
    spell, —
    When a-toddling on the floor
    Is the muse he must adore,
And this muse he loves, not wisely, but
    too well ?

Now, to write a sonnet, every one allows,
One must always be as quiet as a mouse ;
    But to write one seems to me
    Quite superfluous to be,
When you've got a little sonnet in the
    house.

Just a dainty little poem, true and fine,
That is full of love and life in every line,
    Earnest, delicate, and sweet,
    Altogether so complete
That I wonder what's the use of writing
    mine.

DISTINCTION

" I am but clay," the sinner plead,
    Who fed each vain desire.
" Not only clay," another said,
    " But worse, for thou art mire."

THE SUM

A little dreaming by the way,
A little toiling day by day ;
A little pain, a little strife,
A little joy,—and that is life.

A little short-lived summer's morn,
When joy seems all so newly born,
When one day's sky is blue above,
And one bird sings,—and that is love.

A little sickening of the years,
The tribute of a few hot tears,
Two folded hands, the failing breath,
And peace at last,—and that is death.

Just dreaming, loving, dying so,
The actors in the drama go —
A flitting picture on a wall,
Love, Death, the themes; but is that all?

SONNET

ON AN OLD BOOK WITH UNCUT LEAVES

Emblem of blasted hope and lost desire,
No finger ever traced thy yellow page
   Save Time's. Thou hast not wrought
     to noble rage
The hearts thou wouldst have stirred.
   Not any fire
Save sad flames set to light a funeral pyre
   Dost thou suggest. Nay,—impotent in
     age,
   Unsought, thou holdst a corner of the
     stage
And ceasest even dumbly to aspire.

How different was the thought of him that
   writ.
   What promised he to love of ease and
     wealth,
When men should read and kindle at his
   wit.
   But here decay eats up the book by
     stealth,
While it, like some old maiden, solemnly,
Hugs its incongruous virginity!

A DEATH SONG

At the time of Mr. Dunbar's death, many persons were of the opinion that this poem was of very recent date. The truth is that it was written as far back as 1898, while Mr. Dunbar was in Washington, D. C., and appeared in the *Congregationalist* in September or October of that year. These stanzas were printed in almost every newspaper in the country when the poet passed away, and the request embodied in the lines was followed, as nearly as possible, in the selection of a burial site.

Lay me down beneaf de willers in de
   grass,
   Whah de branch'll go a-singin' as it
     pass.
An' w'en I's a-layin' low,
   I kin hyeah it as it go
Singin', "Sleep, my honey, tek yo' res' at
   las'."

Lay me nigh to whah hit meks a little
   pool,
An' de watah stan's so quiet lak an'
   cool,
   Whah de little birds in spring,
   Ust to come an' drink an' sing,
An' de chillen waded on dey way to
   school.

Let me settle w'en my shouldahs draps
   dey load
Nigh enough to hyeah de noises in de
   road;
   Fu' I t'ink de las' long res'
   Gwine to soothe my sperrit bes'
Ef I's layin' 'mong de t'ings I's allus
   knowed.

CHRISMUS IS A-COMIN'

Bones a-gittin' achy,
Back a-feelin' col',
Han's a-growin' shaky,
Jes' lak I was ol'.
Fros' erpon de meddah
Lookin' mighty white;
Snowdraps lak a feddah
Slippin' down at night.
Jes' keep t'ings a-hummin'
Spite o' fros' an' showahs,
Chrismus is a-comin'
An' all de week is ouahs.

Little mas' a-axin',
"Who is Santy Claus?"
Meks it kin' o' taxin'
Not to brek de laws.
Chillun's pow'ful tryin'
To a pusson's grace
We'n dey go a pryin'
Right on th'oo you' face

Beneaf de Willers

Chris'mus is A-comin'

Down ermong yo' feelin's ;
Jes' 'pears lak dat you
Got to change you' dealin's
So's to tell 'em true.

An' my pickaninny —
Dreamin' in his sleep !
Come hyeah, Mammy Jinny,
Come an' tek a peep.
Ol' Mas' Bob an' Missis
In dey house up daih
Got no chile lak dis is,
D' ain't none anywhaih.
Sleep, my little lammy.
Sleep, you little limb,
He do' know whut mammy
Done saved up fu' him.

Dey'll be banjo pickin',
Dancin' all night thoo.
Dey'll be lots o' chicken,
Plenty tukky, too.
Drams to wet yo' whistles
So's to drive out chills.
Whut I keer fu' drizzles
Fallin' on de hills ?
Jes' keep t'ings a-hummin'
Spite o' col' an' showahs,
Chrismus day's a-comin',
An' all de week is ouahs.

ON THE SEA WALL

I sit upon the old sea wall,
　And watch the shimmering sea,
Where soft and white the moonbeams
　fall,
　Till, in a fantasy,
Some pure white maiden's funeral pall
　The strange light seems to me.

The waters break upon the shore
　And shiver at my feet,
While I dream old dreams o'er and o'er,
　And dim old scenes repeat ;
Tho' all have dreamed the same before,
　They still seem new and sweet.

13

The waves still sing the same old song
　That knew an elder time ;
The breakers' beat is not more strong,
　Their music more sublime ;
And poets thro' the ages long
　Have set these notes to rhyme.

But this shall not deter my lyre,
　Nor check my simple strain ;
If I have not the old-time fire,
　I know the ancient pain :
The hurt of unfulfilled desire, —
　The ember quenched by rain.

I know the softly shining sea
　That rolls this gentle swell
Has snarled and licked its tongues at me
　And bared its fangs as well ;
That 'neath its smile so heavenly,
　There lurks the scowl of hell !

But what of that ?　I strike my string
　(For songs in youth are sweet) ;
I'll wait and hear the waters bring
　Their loud resounding beat ;
Then, in her own bold numbers sing
　The Ocean's dear deceit !

TO A LADY PLAYING THE HARP

Thy tones are silver melted into sound,
　And as I dream
I see no walls around,
　But seem to hear
　A gondolier
Sing sweetly down some slow Venetian
　stream.

Italian skies—that I have never seen —
　I see above.
(Ah, play again, my queen ;
　Thy fingers white
　Fly swift and light
And weave for me the golden mesh of
　love.)

Oh, thou dusk sorceress of the dusky eyes
　And soft dark hair,
Tis thou that mak'st my skies
　So swift to change
　To far and strange ;
But far and strange, thou still dost make
　them fair.

Now thou dost sing, and I am lost in thee
　As one who drowns
In floods of melody.
　Still in thy art
　Give me this part,
Till　perfect love, the love of loving
　crowns.

CONFESSIONAL

Search thou my heart;
　If there be guile,
It shall depart
　Before thy smile.

Search thou my soul;
　Be there deceit,
'Twill vanish whole
　Before thee, sweet.

Upon my mind
　Turn thy pure lens;
Naught shalt thou find
　Thou canst not cleanse.

If I should pray,
　I scarcely know
In just what way
　My prayers would go.

So strong in me
　I feel love's leaven,
I'd bow to thee
　As soon as Heaven!

MISAPPREHENSION

Out of my heart, one day, I wrote a song,
　With my heart's blood imbued,
Instinct with passion, tremulously strong,
　With grief subdued;
　Breathing a fortitude
　　Pain-bought.
And one who claimed much love for what
　I wrought,
　Read and considered it,
　And spoke:
" Ay, brother,—'tis well writ,
　But where's the joke ? "

PROMETHEUS

Prometheus stole from Heaven the sacred
　fire
　And swept to earth with it o'er land and
　sea.
He lit the vestal flames of poesy,
Content, for this, to brave celestial ire.

Wroth were the gods, and with eternal
　hate
　Pursued the fearless one who ravished
　Heaven
　That earth might hold in fee the perfect
　leaven
To lift men's souls above their low estate.

But judge you now, when poets wield the
　pen,
　Think you not well the wrong has been
　repaired ?
　'Twas all in vain that ill Prometheus
　fared :
The fire has been returned to Heaven
　again !

We have no singers like the ones whose
　note
　Gave challenge to the noblest warbler's
　song.
　We have no voice so mellow, sweet,
　and strong
As that which broke from Shelley's golden
　throat.

The measure of our songs is our desires :
　We tinkle where old poets used to
　storm.
　We lack their substance tho' we keep
　their form:
We strum our banjo-strings and call them
　lyres.

LOVE'S PHASES

Love hath the wings of the butterfly,
　Oh, clasp him but gently,
Pausing and dipping and fluttering by
　Inconsequently.
Stir not his poise with the breath of a sigh;
Love hath the wings of the butterfly.

Love hath the wings of the eagle bold,
　　Cling to him strongly —
What if the look of the world be cold,
　　And life go wrongly?
Rest on his pinions, for broad is their
　　fold;
Love hath the wings of the eagle bold.

Love hath the voice of the nightingale,
　　Hearken his trilling —
List to his song when the moonlight is
　　pale,—
　　Passionate, thrilling.
Cherish the lay, ere the lilt of it fail;
Love hath the voice of the nightingale.

Love hath the voice of the storm at
　　night,
　　Wildly defiant.
Hear him and yield up your soul to his
　　might,
　　Tenderly pliant.
None shall regret him who heed him
　　aright;
Love hath the voice of the storm at night.

FOR THE MAN WHO FAILS

The world is a snob, and the man who
　　wins
　　Is the chap for its money's worth:
And the lust for success causes half of the
　　sins
　　That are cursing this brave old earth.
For it's fine to go up, and the world's ap-
　　plause
　　Is sweet to the mortal ear;
But the man who fails in a noble cause
　　Is a hero that's no less dear.

'Tis true enough that the laurel crown
　　Twines but for the victor's brow;
For many a hero has lain him down
　　With naught but the cypress bough.
There are gallant men in the losing fight,
　　And as gallant deeds are done
As ever graced the captured height
　　Or the battle grandly won.

We sit at life's board with our nerves
　　highstrung,
　　And we play for the stake of Fame,
And our odes are sung and our banners
　　hung
　　For the man who wins the game.
But I have a song of another kind
　　Than breathes in these fame-wrought
　　　gales,—
An ode to the noble heart and mind
　　Of the gallant man who fails!

The man who is strong to fight his fight,
　. And whose will no front can daunt,
If the truth be truth and the right be
　　right,
　　Is the man that the ages want.
Tho' he fail and die in grim defeat,
　　Yet he has not fled the strife,
And the house of Earth will seem more
　　sweet
　　For the perfume of his life.

HARRIET BEECHER STOWE

She told the story, and the whole world
　　wept
　　At wrongs and cruelties it had not
　　　known
But for this fearless woman's voice
　　alone.
She spoke to consciences that long had
　　slept:
Her message, Freedom's clear reveille,
　　swept
From heedless hovel to complacent
　　throne.
Command and prophecy were in the
　　tone
And from its sheath the sword of jus-
　　tice leapt.
Around two peoples swelled a fiery wave,
　　But both came forth transfigured from
　　　the flame.
Blest be the hand that dared be strong to
　　save,
　　And blest be she who in our weakness
　　　came —
Prophet and priestess! At one stroke
　　she gave
A race to freedom and herself to fame.

VAGRANTS

Long time ago, we two set out,
  My soul and I.
  I know not why,
For all our way was dim with doubt.
  I know not where
  We two may fare:
Though still with every changing weather,
We wander, groping on together.

We do not love, we are not friends,
  My soul and I.
  He lives a lie;
Untruth lines every way he wends.
  A scoffer he
  Who jeers at me:
And so, my comrade and my brother,
We wander on and hate each other.

Ay, there be taverns and to spare,
  Beside the road;
  But some strange goad
Lets me not stop to taste their fare.
  Knew I the goal
  Towards which my soul
And I made way, hope made life fragrant:
But no. We wander, aimless, vagrant!

A WINTER'S DAY

Across the hills and down the narrow
    ways,
  And up the valley where the free winds
    sweep,
  The earth is folded in an ermined sleep
That mocks the melting mirth of myriad
    Mays.
Departed her disheartening duns and
    grays,
  And all her crusty black is covered
    deep.
  Dark streams are locked in Winter's
    donjon-keep,
And made to shine with keen, unwonted
    rays.

O icy mantle, and deceitful snow!
  What world-old liars in your hearts ye
    are!
  Are there not still the darkened seam
    and scar
Beneath the brightness that you fain would
    show?

Come from the cover with thy blot and
    blur,
O reeking Earth, thou whited sepulchre!

MY LITTLE MARCH GIRL

Come to the pane, draw the curtain apart,
There she is passing, the girl of my heart;
See where she walks like a queen in the
    street,
Weather-defying, calm, placid and sweet.
Tripping along with impetuous grace,
Joy of her life beaming out of her face,
Tresses all truant-like, curl upon curl,
Wind-blown and rosy, my little March
    girl.

Hint of the violet's delicate bloom,
Hint of the rose's pervading perfume!
How can the wind help from kissing her
    face,—
Wrapping her round in his stormy em-
    brace?
But still serenely she laughs at his rout,
She is the victor who wins in the bout.
So may life's passions about her soul swirl,
Leaving it placid,—my little March girl.

What self-possession looks out of her eyes!
What are the wild winds, and what are
    the skies,
Frowning and glooming when, brimming
    with life,
Cometh the little maid ripe for the strife?
Ah! Wind, and bah! Wind, what might
    have you now?
What can you do with that innocent brow?
Blow, Wind, and grow, Wind, and eddy
    and swirl,
But bring her to me, Wind,—my little
    March girl.

REMEMBERED

She sang, and I listened the whole song
    thro'.
  (It was sweet, so sweet, the singing.)
The stars were out and the moon it grew
From a wee soft glimmer way out in the
    blue
  To a bird thro' the heavens winging.

She sang, and the song trembled down to
  my breast,—
(It was sweet, so sweet the singing.)
As a dove just out of its fledgling nest,
And, putting its wings to the first sweet
  test,
Flutters homeward so wearily winging.

She sang and I said to my heart, " That
  song,
That was sweet, so sweet i' the singing,
Shall live with us and inspire us long,
And thou, my heart, shalt be brave and
  strong
For the sake of those words a-winging.

The woman died and the song was still.
  (It was sweet, so sweet, the singing.)
But ever I hear the same low trill,
Of the song that shakes my heart with a
  thrill,
And goes forever winging.

LOVE DESPOILED

As lone I sat one summer's day,
  With mien dejected, Love came by ;
His face distraught, his locks astray,
  So slow his gait, so sad his eye,
  I hailed him with a pitying cry :

" Pray, Love, what has disturbed thee
  so ? "
  Said I, amazed. " Thou seem'st bereft ;
And see thy quiver hanging low,—
  What, not a single arrow left ?
  Pray, who is guilty of this theft ? "

Poor Love looked in my face and cried :
  " No thief were ever yet so bold
To rob my quiver at my side.
  But Time, who rules, gave ear to Gold,
  And all my goodly shafts are sold."

THE LAPSE

This poem must be done to-day ;
  Then, I'll e'en to it.
I must not dream my time away,—
  I'm sure to rue it.

The day is rather bright, I know
  The Muse will pardon
My half-defection, if I go
  Into the garden.
It must be better working there,—
  I'm sure it's sweeter ;
And something in the balmy air
  May clear my metre.

[*In the Garden.*]

Ah this is noble, what a sky !
  What breezes blowing !
The very clouds, I know not why,
  Call one to rowing.
The stream will be a paradise
  To-day, I'll warrant.
I know the tide that's on the rise
  Will seem a torrent ;
I know just how the leafy boughs
  Are all a-quiver ;
I know how many skiffs and scows
  Are on the river.
I think I'll just go out awhile
  Before I write it ;
When Nature shows us such a smile,
  We shouldn't slight it.
For Nature always makes desire
  By giving pleasure ;
And so 'twill help me put more fire
  Into my measure.

[*On the River.*]

The river's fine, I'm glad I came,
  That poem's teasing ;
But health is better far than fame,
  Though cheques are pleasing.
I don't know what I did it for,—
  This air's a poppy.
I'm sorry for my editor,—
  He 'll get no copy !

THE WARRIOR'S PRAYER

Long since, in sore distress, I heard one
  pray,
" Lord, who prevailest with resistless
  might,
Ever from war and strife keep me away,
  My battles fight ! "

I know not if I play the Pharisee,
  And if my brother after all be right;
But mine shall be the warrior's plea to
    thee —
      Strength for the fight.

I do not ask that thou shalt front the fray,
  And drive the warring foeman from my
    sight;
I only ask, O Lord, by night, by day,
    Strength for the fight!

When foes upon me press, let me not
    quail
  Nor think to turn me into coward flight.
I only ask, to make mine arms prevail,
    Strength for the fight!

Still let mine eyes look ever on the foe,
  Still let mine armor case me strong and
    bright;
And grant me, as I deal each righteous
    blow,
      Strength for the fight!

And when, at eventide, the fray is done,
  My soul to Death's bedchamber do thou
    light,
And give me, be the field or lost or won,
    Rest from the fight!

FAREWELL TO ARCADY

With sombre mien, the Evening gray
Comes nagging at the heels of Day,
And driven faster and still faster
Before the dusky-mantled Master,
The light fades from her fearful eyes,
She hastens, stumbles, falls, and dies.

Beside me Amaryllis weeps;
The swelling tears obscure the deeps
Of her dark eyes, as, mistily,
The rushing rain conceals the sea.
Here, lay my tuneless reed away,—
I have no heart to tempt a lay.

I scent the perfume of the rose
Which by my crystal fountain grows.
In this sad time, are roses blowing?
And thou, my fountain, art thou flowing,
While I who watched thy waters spring

Am all too sad to smile or sing?
Nay, give me back my pipe again,
It yet shall breathe this single strain:
    Farewell to Arcady!

THE VOICE OF THE BANJO

In a small and lonely cabin out of noisy
    traffic's way,
Sat an old man, bent and feeble, dusk of
    face, and hair of gray,
And beside him on the table, battered,
    old, and worn as he,
Lay a banjo, droning forth this reminiscent
    melody:

"Night is closing in upon us, friend of
    mine, but don't be sad;
Let us think of all the pleasures and the
    joys that we have had.
Let us keep a merry visage, and be happy
    till the last,
Let the future still be sweetened with the
    honey of the past.

"For I speak to you of summer nights
    upon the yellow sand,
When the Southern moon was sailing high
    and silvering all the land;
And if love tales were not sacred, there's
    a tale that I could tell
Of your many nightly wanderings with a
    dusk and lovely belle.

"And I speak to you of care-free songs
    when labor's hour was o'er,
And a woman waiting for your step out-
    side the cabin door,
And of something roly-poly that you took
    upon your lap,
While you listened for the stumbling,
    hesitating words, 'Pap, pap.'

"I could tell you of a 'possum hunt across
    the wooded grounds,
I could call to mind the sweetness of the
    baying of the hounds,
You could lift me up and smelling of the
    timber that's in me,
Build again a whole green forest with the
    mem'ry of a tree.

"So the future cannot hurt us while we
    keep the past in mind,
What care I for trembling fingers,—what
    care you that you are blind?
Time may leave us poor and stranded,
    circumstance may make us bend;
But they'll only find us mellower, won't
    they, comrade?—in the end."

THE STIRRUP CUP

Come, drink a stirrup cup with me,
    Before we close our rouse.
You're all aglow with wine, I know:
    The master of the house,
    Unmindful of our revelry,
Has drowned the carking devil care,
    And slumbers in his chair.

Come, drink a cup before we start;
    We've far to ride to-night.
And Death may take the race we make,
    And check our gallant flight:
    But even he must play his part,
And tho' the look he wears be grim,
    We'll drink a toast to him!

For Death,—a swift old chap is he,
    And swift the steed he rides.
He needs no chart o'er main or mart,
    For no direction bides,
    So, come a final cup with me,
And let the soldiers' chorus swell,—
    To hell with care, to hell!

A CHOICE

They please me not—these solemn songs
    That hint of sermons covered up.
'Tis true the world should heed its
    wrongs,
    But in a poem let me sup,
Not simples brewed to cure or ease
Humanity's confessed disease,
But the spirit-wine of a singing line,
    Or a dew-drop in a honey cup!

HUMOR AND DIALECT

THEN AND NOW

THEN

He loved her, and through many years,
    Had paid his fair devoted court,
Until she wearied, and with sneers
    Turned all his ardent love to sport.

That night within his chamber lone,
    He long sat writing by his bed
A note in which his heart made moan
    For love; the morning found him dead.

NOW

Like him, a man of later day
    Was jilted by the maid he sought,
And from her presence turned away,
    Consumed by burning, bitter thought.

He sought his room to write—a curse
    Like him before and die, I ween.
Ah, no, he put his woes in verse.
    And sold them to a magazine.

AT CHESHIRE CHEESE

When first of wise old Johnson taught,
My youthful mind its homage brought,
And made the pond'rous, crusty sage
The object of a noble rage.

Nor did I think (How dense we are!)
That any day, however far,
Would find me holding, unrepelled,
The place that Doctor Johnson held!

But change has come and time has moved,
And now, applauded, unreproved,
I hold, with pardonable pride,
The place that Johnson occupied.

Conceit! Presumption! What is this?
You surely read my words amiss!
Like Johnson I,—a man of mind!
How could you ever be so blind?

No. At the ancient "Cheshire Cheese,"
Blown hither by some vagrant breeze,
To dignify my shallow wit,
In Doctor Johnson's seat I sit!

MY CORN-COB PIPE

Men may sing of their Havanas, elevating
   to the stars
The real or fancied virtues of their foreign-
   made cigars;
But I worship Nicotina at a different sort
   of shrine,
And she sits enthroned in glory in this
   corn-cob pipe of mine.

It's as fragrant as the meadows when the
   clover is in bloom;
It's as dainty as the essence of the dainti-
   est perfume;
It's as sweet as are the orchards when the
   fruit is hanging ripe,
With the sun's warm kiss upon them—is
   this corn-cob pipe.

Thro' the smoke about it clinging, I de-
   light its form to trace,
Like an oriental beauty with a veil upon
   her face;
And my room is dim with vapor as a
   church when censers sway,
As I clasp it to my bosom—in a figurative
   way.

It consoles me in misfortune and it cheers
   me in distress,
And it proves a warm partaker of my
   pleasures in success;
So I hail it as a symbol, friendship's true
   and worthy type,
And I press my lips devoutly to my corn-
   cob pipe.

IN AUGUST

When August days are hot an' dry,
When burning copper is the sky,
I'd rather fish than feast or fly
In airy realms serene and high.

I'd take a suit not made for looks,
Some easily digested books,
Some flies, some lines, some bait, some
   hooks,
Then would I seek the bays and brooks.

I would eschew mine every task,
In Nature's smiles my soul should bask,
And I methinks no more could ask,
Except—perhaps—one little flask.

In case of accident, you know,
Or should the wind come on to blow,
Or I be chilled or capsized, so,
A flask would be the only go.

Then could I spend a happy time,—
A bit of sport, a bit of rhyme
(A bit of lemon, or of lime,
To make my bottle's contents prime).

When August days are hot an' dry,
I won't sit by an' sigh or die,
I'll get my bottle (on the sly)
And go ahead, and fish, and lie!

THE DISTURBER

Oh, what shall I do? I am wholly up-
   set;
I am sure I'll be jailed for a lunatic yet.
I'll be out of a job—it's the thing to ex-
   pect
When I'm letting my duty go by with
   neglect.
You may judge the extent and degree of
   my plight
When I'm thinking all day and a-dream-
   ing all night,
And a-trying my hand at a rhyme on the
   sly,
All on account of a sparkling eye.

There are those who say men should be
   strong, well-a-day!
But what constitutes strength in a man?
   Who shall say?
I am strong as the most when it comes to
   the arm.
I have aye held my own on the play-
   ground or farm.
And when I've been tempted, I haven't
   been weak;
But now—why, I tremble to hear a maid
   speak.
I used to be bold, but now I've grown
   shy,
And all on account of a sparkling eye.

There once was a time when my heart was
    devout,
But now my religion is open to doubt.
When parson is earnestly preaching of
    grace,
My fancy is busy with drawing a face,
Thro' the back of a bonnet most piously
    plain ;
" I draw it, redraw it, and draw it again."
While the songs and the sermon unheeded
    go by,—
All on account of a sparkling eye.

Oh, dear little conjurer, give o'er your
    wiles,
It is easy for you, you're all blushes and
    smiles ;
But, love of my heart, I am sorely per-
    plexed ;
I am smiling one minute and sighing the
    next ;
And if it goes on, I'll drop hackle and
    flail,
And go to the parson and tell him my tale.
I warrant he'll find me a cure for the sigh
That you're aye bringing forth with the
    glance of your eye.

EXPECTATION

You'll be wonderin' whut's de reason
    I's a grinnin' all de time,
An' I guess you t'ink my sperits
    Mus' be feelin' mighty prime.
Well, I 'fess up, I is tickled
    As a puppy at his paws.
But you needn't think I's crazy,
    I ain' laffin' 'dout a cause.

You's a wonderin' too, I reckon,
    Why I doesn't seem to eat,
An' I notice you a lookin'
    Lak you felt completely beat
When I 'fuse to tek de bacon,
    An' don' settle on de ham.
Don' you feel no feah erbout me,
    Jes' keep eatin', an' be ca'm.

Fu' I's waitin' an' I's watchin'
    'Bout a little t'ing I see —
D' othah night I's out a walkin'
    An' I passed a 'simmon tree.

Now I's whettin' up my hongry,
    An' I's laffin' fit to kill,
Fu' de fros' done turned de 'simmons,
    An' de possum's eat his fill.

He done go'ged hisse'f owdacious,
    An' he stayin' by de tree !
Don' you know, ol' Mistah Possum
    Dat you gittin' fat fu' me ?
'Tain't no use to try to 'spute it,
    'Case I knows you's gittin' sweet
Wif dat 'simmon flavoh thoo you,
    So I's waitin' fu' yo' meat.

An' some ebenin' me an' Towsah
    Gwine to come an' mek a call,
We jes' drap in onexpected
    Fu' to shek yo' han', dat's all.
Oh, I knows dat you'll be tickled,
    Seem lak I kin see you smile,
So pu'haps I mought pu'suade you
    Fu' to visit us a while.

LOVER'S LANE

Summah night an' sighin' breeze,
    'Long de lovah's lane ;
Frien'ly, shadder-mekin' trees,
    'Long de lovah's lane.
White folks' wo'k all done up gran'—
Me an' 'Mandy han'-in-han'
Struttin' lak we owned de lan',
    'Long de lovah's lane.

Owl a-settin' 'side de road,
    'Long de lovah's lane,
Lookin' at us lak he knowed
    Dis uz lovah's lane.
Go on, hoot yo' mou'nful tune,
You ain' nevah loved in June,
An' come hidin' f'om de moon
    Down in lovah's lane.

Bush it ben' an' nod an' sway,
    Down in lovah's lane,
Try'n' to hyeah me whut I say
    'Long de lovah's lane.
But I whispahs low lak dis,
An' my 'Mandy smile huh bliss —
Mistah Bush he shek his fis',
    Down in lovah's lane.

Whut I keer ef day is long,
　Down in lovah's lane.
I kin allus sing a song
　'Long de lovah's lane.
An' de wo'ds I hyeah an' say
Meks up fu' de weary day,
W'en I's strollin' by de way,
　Down in lovah's lane.

An' dis t'ought will allus rise
　Down in lovah's lane :
Wondah whethah in de skies
　Dey's a lovah's lane.
Ef dey ain't I tell you true,
'Ligion do look mighty blue,
'Cause I do' know whut I'd do
　'Dout a lovah's lane.

PROTEST

Who say my hea't ain't true to you ?
　Dey bettah heish dey mouf.
I knows I loves you thoo an' thoo
　In watah time er drouf.
I wush dese people 'd stop dey talkin',
Don't　mean　no　mo'　dan　chicken's
　　squawkin' :
I guess I knows which way I's walkin',
　I knows de norf f'om souf.

I does not love Elizy Brown,
　I guess I knows my min'.
You allus try to tek me down
　Wid evaht'ing you fin'.
Ef dese hyeah folks will keep on fillin'
Yo' haid wid nonsense, an' you's willin'
I bet some day dey'll be a killin'
　Somewhaih along de line.

O' cose I buys de gal ice-cream,
　Whut else I gwine to do?
I knows jes' how de t'ing 'u'd seem
　Ef I'd be sho't wid you.
On Sunday, you's at chu'ch a-shoutin',
Den all de week you go 'roun' poutin'—
I's mighty tiahed o' all dis doubtin',
　I tell you cause I's true.

HYMN

O li'l' lamb out in de col',
De Mastah call you to de fol',
　O l'i'l' lamb !

He hyeah you bleatin' on de hill ;
Come hyeah an' keep yo' mou'nin' still,
　O li'l' lamb !

De Mastah sen' de Shepud fo'f ;
He wandah souf, he wandah no'f,
　O li'l' lamb !
He wandah eas', he wandah wes' ;
De win' a-wrenchin' at his breas',
　O li'l' lamb !

Oh, tell de Shepud whaih you hide ;
He want you walkin' by his side,
　O l'l' lamb !
He know you weak, he know you so' ;
But come, don' stay away no mo',
　O li'l' lamb !

An' af'ah while de lamb he hyeah
De Shepud's voice a-callin' cleah—
　　Sweet li'l' lamb !
He answah f'om de brambles thick,
　" O Shepud, I's a-comin' quick "—
　　O li'l' lamb !

THE REAL QUESTION

Folks is talkin' 'bout de money, 'bout de
　silvah an' de gold ;
All de time de season's changin' an' de
　days is gittin' cold.
An' dey's wond'rin' 'bout de metals, whethah
　we'll have one er two,
While de price o' coal is risin' an' dey's two
　months' rent dat's due.

Some folks says dat gold's de only money
　dat is wuff de name,
Den de othahs rise an' tell 'em dat dey
　ought to be ashame,
An' dat silvah is de only thing to save us
　f'om de powah
Of de gold-bug ragin' 'roun' an' seekin'
　who he may devowah.

Well, you folks kin keep on shoutin' wif
　yo' gold er silvah cry,
But I tell you people hams is sceerce an'
　fowls is roostin' high.
An' hit ain't de so't o' money dat is pes-
　terin' my min',
But de question I want answehed's how tu
　get at any kin' !

JILTED

Lucy done gone back on me,
  Dat's de way wif life.
Evaht'ing was movin' free
  T'ought I had my wife.
Den some dahky comes along,
Sings my gal a little song,
Since den, evaht'ing's gone wrong,
  Evah day dey's strife.

Didn't answeh me to-day,
  W'en I called huh name,
Would you t'ink she'd ac' dat way
  W'en I ain't to blame?
Dat's de way dese women do,
W'en dey fin's a fellow true,
Den dey 'buse him thoo an' thoo;
  Well, hit's all de same.

Somep'n's wrong erbout my lung,
  An' I's glad hit's so.
Doctah says 'at I'll die young,
  Well, I wants to go!
Whut's de use o' livin' hyeah,
W'en de gal you loves so deah,
Goes back on you clean an' cleah —
  I sh'd like to know?

THE NEWS

Whut dat you whisperin' keepin' f'om me?
Don't shut me out 'cause I's ol' an' can't
  see.
Somep'n's gone wrong dat's a-causin' you
  dread, —
Don't be afeared to tell—Whut! mastah
  dead?

Somebody brung de news early to-day, —
One of de sojers he led, do you say?
Didn't he foller whah ol' mastah led?
How kin he live w'en his leadah is dead?

Let me lay down awhile, dah by his bed;
I wants to t'ink,—hit ain't cleah in my
  head: —
Killed while a-leadin' his men into fight, —
Dat's whut you said, ain't it, did I hyeah
  right?

Mastah, my mastah, dead dah in de fiel'?
Lif' me up some,—dah, jes' so I kin kneel.
I was too weak to go wid him, dey said,
Well, now I'll—fin' him—so—mastah is
  dead.

Yes, suh, I's comin' ez fas' ez I kin, —
'Twas kin' o' da'k, but hit's lightah agin:
P'omised yo' pappy I'd allus tek keer
Of you,—yes, mastah,—I's follerin' —
  hyeah!

CHRISMUS ON THE PLANTATION

It was Chrismus Eve, I mind hit fu' a
  mighty gloomy day —
Bofe de weathah an' de people—not a one
  of us was gay;
Cose you'll t'ink dat's mighty funny 'twell
  I try to mek hit cleah,
Fu' a da'ky's allus happy when de holi-
  days is neah.

But we wasn't, fu' dat mo'nin' mastah'd
  tol' us we mus' go,
He' been payin' us sence freedom, but he
  couldn't pay no mo';
He wa'n't nevah used to plannin' 'fo he
  got so po' an' ol',
So he gwine to give up tryin', an' de home-
  stead mus' be sol'.

I kin see him stan'in' now erpon de step
  ez cleah ez day,
Wid de win' a-kin' o' fondlin' thoo his haih
  all thin an' gray;
An' I 'membah how he trimbled when he
  said, "It's ha'd fu' me,
Not to mek yo' Chrismus brightah, but I
  'low it wa'n't to be."

All de women was a cryin', an' de men,
  too, on de sly,
An' I noticed somep'n shinin' even in ol'
  mastah's eye,
But we all stood still to listen ez ol' Ben
  come f'om de crowd
An' spoke up, a-tryin' to steady down his
  voice and mek it loud: —

" Look hyeah, Mastah, I's been servin'
  yo' fu' lo ! dese many yeahs,
An' now, sence we's got freedom an' you's
  kind o' po', hit 'pears
Dat you want us all to leave you 'cause
  you don't t'ink you can pay.
Ef my membry hasn't fooled me, seem dat
  whut I hyead you say.

" Er in othah wo'ds, you wants us to fu'git
  dat you's been kin',
An' ez soon ez you is he'pless, we's to leave
  you hyeah behin'.
Well, ef dat's de way dis freedom ac's on
  people, white er black,
You kin jes' tell Mistah Lincum fu' to tek
  his freedom back.

" We gwine to wo'k dis ol' plantation fu'
  whatevah we kin git,
Fu' I know hit did suppo't us, an' de place
  kin do it yit.
Now de land is yo's, de hands is ouahs, an'
  I reckon we'll be brave,
An' we'll bah ez much ez you do w'en we
  has to scrape an' save."

Ol' mastah stood dah trimblin', but a-smilin'
  thoo his teahs,
An' den hit seemed jes' nachul-like, de
  place fan rung wid cheahs,
An' soon ez dey was quiet, some one sta'ted
  sof' an' low :
" Praise God," an' den we all jined in,
  " from whom all blessin's flow ! "

Well, dey wasn't no use tryin', ouah min's
  was sot to stay,
An' po' ol' mastah couldn't plead ner baig,
  ner drive us 'way,
An' all at once, hit seemed to us, de day
  was bright agin,
So evah one was gay dat night, an' watched
  de Chrismus in.

FOOLIN' WID DE SEASONS

Seems lak folks is mighty curus
In de way dey t'inks an' ac's.
Dey jes' spen's dey days a-mixin'
Up de t'ings in almanacs.

Now, I min' my nex' do' neighbor,—
  He's a mighty likely man,
But he nevah t'inks o' nuffin
  'Ceptin' jes' to plot an' plan.

All de wintah he was plannin'
  How he'd gethah sassafras
Jes' ez soon ez evah Springtime
  Put some greenness in de grass.
An' he 'lowed a little soonah
  He could stan' a coolah breeze
So's to mek a little money
  F'om de sugah-watah trees.

In de summah, he'd be waihin'
  Out de linin' of his soul,
Try'n' to ca'ci'late an' fashion
  How he'd git his wintah coal ;
An' I b'lieve he got his jedgement
  Jes' so tuckahed out an' thinned
Dat he t'ought a robin's whistle
  Was de whistle of de wind.

Why won't folks gin up dey plannin',
  An' jes' be content to know
Dat dey's gittin' all dat's fu' dem
  In de days dat come an' go ?
Why won't folks quit movin' forrard ?
  Ain't hit bettah jes' to stan'
An' be satisfied wid livin'
  In de season dat's at han' ?

Hit's enough fu' me to listen
  W'en de birds is singin' 'roun',
'Dout a-guessin' whut'll happen
  W'en de snow is on de groun'.
In de Springtime an' de summah,
  I lays sorrer on de she'f ;
An' I knows ol' Mistah Wintah
  Gwine to hustle fu' hisse'f.

We been put hyeah fu' a pu'pose,
  But de questun dat has riz
An' made lots o' people diffah
  Is jes' whut dat pu'pose is.
Now, accordin' to my reas'nin',
  Hyeah's de p'int whaih I's arriv,
Sence de Lawd put life into us,
  We was put hyeah fu' to live !

I Lays Sorrer on de She'f

MEK DE SHADDERS ON DE WALL

AT CANDLE-LIGHTIN' TIME

When I come in f'om de co'n-fiel' aftah
    wo'kin' ha'd all day,
It's amazin' nice to fin' my suppah all
    erpon de way;
An' it's nice to smell de coffee bubblin'
    ovah in de pot,
An' it's fine to see de meat a-sizzlin'
    teasin'-lak an' hot.

But when suppah-time is ovah, an' de
    t'ings is cleahed away;
Den de happy hours dat foller are de
    sweetes' of de day.
When my co'ncob pipe is sta'ted, an' de
    smoke is drawin' prime,
My ole 'ooman says, "I reckon, Ike, it's
    candle lightin' time."

Den de chillun snuggle up to me, an' all
    commence to call,
"Oh, say, daddy, now it's time to mek de
    shadders on de wall."
So I puts my han's togethah—evah daddy
    knows de way,—
An' de chillun snuggle closer roun' ez I
    begin to say : —

"Fus' thing, hyeah come Mistah Rabbit;
    don' you see him wo'k his eahs ?
Huh, uh! dis mus' be a donkey,—look,
    how innercent he 'pears !
Dah's de ole black swan a-swimmin'—
    ain't she got a' awful neck ?
Who's dis feller dat's a-comin' ? Why,
    dat's ole dog Tray, I 'spec' ! "

Dat's de way I run on, tryin' fu' to please
    'em all I can ;
Den I hollahs, " Now be keerful—dis
    hyeah las' 's de buga-man ! "
An' dey runs an' hides dey faces ; dey
    ain't skeered—dey's lettin' on :
But de play ain't raaly ovah twell dat
    buga-man is gone.

So I jes' teks up my banjo, an' I plays a
    little chune,
An' you see dem haids come peepin' out
    to listen mighty soon.

Den my wife says, " Sich a pappy fu' to
    give you sich a fright !
Jes' you go to baid, an' leave him : say
    yo' prayers an' say good-night."

ANGELINA

When de fiddle gits to singin' out a ol'
    Vahginny reel,
An' you 'mence to feel a ticklin' in yo' toe
    an' in yo' heel ;
Ef you t'ink you got 'uligion an' you
    wants to keep it, too,
You jes' bettah tek a hint an' git yo'self
    clean out o' view.
Case de time is mighty temptin' when de
    chune is in de swing,
Fu' a darky, saint or sinner man, to cut de
    pigeon-wing.
An' you couldn't he'p f'om dancin' ef yo'
    feet was boun' wif twine,
When Angelina Johnson comes a-swingin'
    down de line.

Don't you know Miss Angelina? She's
    de da'lin' of de place.
W'y, dey ain't no high-toned lady wif sich
    mannahs an' sich grace.
She kin move across de cabin, wif its
    planks all rough an' wo';
Jes' de same's ef she was dancin' on ol'
    mistus' ball-room flo'.
Fact is, you do' see no cabin—evaht'ing
    you see look grand,
An' dat one ol' squeaky fiddle soun' to
    you jes' lak a ban';
Cotton britches look lak broadclof an' a
    linsey dress look fine,
When Angelina Johnson comes a-swingin'
    down de line.

Some folks say dat dancin's sinful, an' de
    blessed Lawd, dey say,
Gwine to purnish us fu' steppin' w'en we
    hyeah de music play.
But I tell you I don' b'lieve it, fu' de
    Lawd is wise and good,
An he made de banjo's metal an' he made
    de fiddle's wood,

An' he made de music in dem, so I don'
    quite t'ink he'll keer
Ef our feet keeps time a little to de
    melodies we hyeah.
W'y, dey's somep'n' downright holy in de
    way our faces shine,
When Angelina Johnson comes a-swingin'
    down de line.

Angelina steps so gentle, Angelina bows
    so low,
An' she lif' huh sku't so dainty dat huh
    sheetop skacely show :
An' dem teef o' huh'n a-shinin', ez she tek
    you by de han'—
Go 'way, people, d'ain't anothah sich a
    lady in de lan' !
When she's movin' thoo de figgers er
    a-dancin' by huhse'f,
Folks jes' stan' stock-still a-sta'in', an' dey
    mos' nigh hol's dey bref ;
An' de young mens, dey's a-sayin', " I's
    gwine mek dat damsel mine,"
When Angelina Johnson comes a-swingin'
    down de line.

MY SORT O' MAN

I don't believe in 'ristercrats
    An' never did, you see ;
The plain ol' homelike sorter folks
    Is good enough fur me.
O' course, I don't desire a man
    To be too tarnal rough,
But then, I think all folks should know
    When they air nice enough.

Now there is folks in this here world,
    From peasant up to king,
Who want to be so awful nice
    They overdo the thing.
That's jest the thing that makes me sick,
    An' quicker'n a wink
I set it down that them same folks
    Ain't half so good's you think.

I like to see a man dress nice,
    In clothes becomin' too ;
I like to see a woman fix
    As women orter to do ;

An' boys an' gals I like to see
    Look fresh an' young an' spry,—
We all must have our vanity
    An' pride before we die.

But I jedge no man by his clothes,—
    Nor gentleman nor tramp ;
The man that wears the finest suit
    May be the biggest scamp,
An' he whose limbs air clad in rags
    That make a mournful sight,
In life's great battle may have proved
    A hero in the fight.

I don't believe in 'ristercrats ;
    I like the honest tan
That lies upon the heathful cheek
    An' speaks the honest man ;
I like to grasp the brawny hand
    That labor's lips have kissed,
For he who has not labored here
    Life's greatest pride has missed :

The pride to feel that yore own strength
    Has cleaved fur you the way
To heights to which you were not born,
    But struggled day by day.
What though the thousands sneer an' scoff,
    An' scorn yore humble birth ?
Kings are but puppets ; you are king
    By right o' royal worth.

The man who simply sits an' waits
    Fur good to come along,
Ain't worth the breath that one would take
    To tell him he is wrong.
Fur good ain't flowin' round this world
    Fur every fool to sup ;
You've got to put yore see-ers on,
    An' go an' hunt it up.

Good goes with honesty, I say,
    To honor an' to bless ;
To rich an' poor alike it brings
    A wealth o' happiness.
The 'ristercrats ain't got it all,
    Fur much to their su'prise,
That's one of earth's most blessed things
    They can't monopolize.

POSSUM

Ef dey's anyt'ing dat riles me
  An' jes' gits me out o' hitch,
Twell I want to tek my coat off,
  So's to r'ar an' t'ar an' pitch,
Hit's to see some ign'ant white man
  'Mittin' dat owdacious sin —
W'en he want to cook a possum
  Tekin' off de possum's skin.

W'y, dey ain't no use in talkin',
  Hit jes' hu'ts me to de hea't
Fu' to see dem foolish people
  Th'owin' 'way de fines' pa't.
W'y, dat skin is jes' ez tendah
  An' ez juicy ez kin be;
I knows all erbout de critter —
  Hide an' haih—don't talk to me!

Possum skin is jes' lak shoat skin;
  Jes' you swinge an' scrope it down,
Tek a good sha'p knife an' sco' it,
  Den you bake it good an' brown.
Huh-uh! honey, you's so happy
  Dat yo' thoughts is 'mos' a sin
When you's settin' dah a-chawin'
  On dat possum's cracklin' skin.

White folks t'ink dey know 'bout eatin',
  An' I reckon dat dey do
Sometimes git a little idee
  Of a middlin' dish er two;
But dey ain't a t'ing dey knows of
  Dat I reckon cain't be beat
W'en we set down at de table
  To a unskun possum's meat!

ON THE ROAD

I's boun' to see my gal to-night —
  Oh, lone de way, my dearie!
De moon ain't out, de stars ain't bright —
  Oh, lone de way, my dearie!
Dis hoss o' mine is pow'ful slow,
But when I does git to yo' do'
Yo' kiss'll pay me back, an' mo',
  Dough lone de way, my dearie.

De night is skeery-lak an' still —
  Oh, lone de way, my dearie!
'Cept fu' dat mou'nful whippo-'will —
  Oh, lone de way, my dearie!

De way so long wif dis slow pace,
'T'u'd seem to me lak savin' grace
Ef you was on a nearer place,
  Fu' lone de way, my dearie.

I hyeah de hootin' of de owl —
  Oh, lone de way, my dearie!
I wish dat watch-dog wouldn't howl —
  Oh, lone de way, my dearie!
An' evaht'ing, bofe right an' lef',
Seem p'int'ly lak hit put itse'f
In shape to skeer me half to def —
  Oh, lone de way, my dearie!

I whistles so's I won't be feared —
  Oh, lone de way, my dearie!
But anyhow I's kin' o' skeered,
  Fu' lone de way, my dearie.
De sky been lookin' mighty glum,
But you kin mek hit lighten some,
Ef you'll jes' say you's glad I come,
  Dough lone de way, my dearie.

A BACK-LOG SONG

De axes has been ringin' in de woods de
    blessid day,
  An' de chips has been a-fallin' fa' an'
    thick;
Dey has cut de bigges' hick'ry dat de
    mules kin tote away,
  An' dey's laid hit down and soaked it in
    de crik.
Den dey tuk hit to de big house an' dey
    piled de wood erroun'
  In de fiahplace f'om ash-flo' to de
    flue,
While ol' Ezry sta'ts de hymn dat evah
    yeah has got to soun'
  When de back-log fus' commence
    a-bu'nin' thoo.

Ol' Mastah is a-smilin' on de da'kies f'om
    de hall,
  Ol' Mistus is a-stannin' in de do',
An' de young folks, males an' misses, is
    a-tryin', one an' all,
  Fu' to mek us feel hit's Chrismus time
    fu' sho'.

An' ouah hea'ts are full of pleasure, fu' we
    know de time is ouahs
Fu' to dance er do jes' whut we wants
    to do.
An' dey ain't no ovahseer an' no othah
    kind o' powahs
Dat kin stop us while dat log is bu'nin'
    thoo.

Dey's a-wokin' in de qua'tahs a-preparin'
    fu' de feas',
So de little pigs is feelin' kind o' shy.
De chickens ain't so trus'ful ez dey was, to
    say de leas',
An' de wise ol' hens is roostin' mighty
    high.
You couldn't git a gobblah fu' to look you
    in de face —
I ain't sayin' whut de tu'ky 'spects is
    true ;
But hit's mighty dange'ous trav'lin' fu' de
    critters on de place
F'om de time dat log commence
    a-bu'nin' thoo.

Some one's tunin' up his fiddle dah, I
    hyeah a banjo's ring,
An', bless me, dat's de tootin' of a
    ho'n !
Now dey'll evah one be runnin' dat has
    got a foot to fling,
An' dey'll dance an' frolic on f'om now
    'twell mo'n.
Plunk de banjo, scrap de fiddle, blow dat
    ho'n yo' level bes',
Keep yo' min' erpon de chune an' step
    it true.
Oh, dey ain't no time fu' stoppin' an' dey
    ain't no time fu' res',
Fu' hit's Chrismus an' de back-log's
    bu'nin' thoo !

JEALOUS

Hyeah come Cæsar Higgins,
    Don't he think he's fine ?
Look at dem new riggin's
    Ain't he tryin' to shine ?
Got a standin' collar
    An' a stovepipe hat,
I'll jes' bet a dollar
    Some one gin him dat.

Don't one o' you mention,
    Nothin' 'bout his cloes,
Don't pay no attention,
    Er let on you knows
Dat he's got 'em on him,
    Why, 't'll mek him sick,
Jes' go on an' sco'n him,
    My, ain't dis a trick !

Look hyeah, whut's he doin'
    Lookin' t'othah way ?
Dat ere move's a new one,
    Some one call him, " Say ! "
Can't you see no pusson —
    Puttin' on you' airs,
Sakes alive, you's wuss'n
    Dese hyeah millionaires.

Needn't git so flighty,
    Case you got dat suit.
Dem cloes ain't so mighty,—
    Second hand to boot,
I's a-tryin' to spite you!
    Full of jealousy !
Look hyeah, man, I'll fight you,
    Don't you fool wid me !

PARTED

De breeze is blowin' 'cross de bay,
    My lady, my lady ;
De ship hit teks me far away,
    My lady, my lady.
Ole Mas' done sol' me down de stream ;
Dey tell me 'tain't so bad's hit seem,
    My lady, my lady.

O' co'se I knows dat you'll be true,
    My lady, my lady ;
But den I do' know whut to do,
    My lady, my lady.
I knowed some day we'd have to pa't,
But den hit put' nigh breaks my hea't,
    My lady, my lady.

De day is long, de night is black,
    My lady, my lady ;
I know you'll wait twell I come back,
    My lady, my lady.
I'll stan' de ship, I'll stan' de chain,
But I'll come back, my darlin' Jane,
    My lady, my lady.

Jes' wait, jes' b'lieve in whut I say,
　My lady, my lady;
D'ain't nothin' dat kin keep me 'way,
　My lady, my lady.
A man's a man, an' love is love;
God knows ouah hea'ts, my little dove;
He'll he'p us f'om his th'one above,
　My lady, my lady.

TEMPTATION

I done got 'uligion, honey, an' I's happy
　ez a king;
Evahthing I see erbout me's jes' lak sun-
　shine in de spring;
An' it seems lak I do' want to do anothah
　blessid thing
But jes' run an' tell de neighbors, an' to
　shout an' pray an' sing.

I done shuk my fis' at Satan, an' I's gin
　de worl' my back;
I do' want no hendrin' causes now a-both-
　'rin' in my track;
Fu' I's on my way to glory, an' I feels too
　sho' to miss.
W'y, dey ain't no use in sinnin' when
　'uligion's sweet ez dis.

Talk erbout a man backslidin' w'en he's
　on de gospel way;
No, suh, I done beat de debbil, an' Temp-
　tation's los' de day.
Gwine to keep my eyes right straight up,
　gwine to shet my eahs, an' see
Whut ole projick Mistah Satan's gwine to
　try to wuk on me.

Listen, whut dat soun' I hyeah dah? 'tain't
　no one commence to sing;
It's a fiddle; git erway dah! don' you
　hyeah dat blessid thing?
W'y, dat's sweet ez drippin' honey, 'cause,
　you knows, I draws de bow,
An' when music's sho' 'nough music, I's
　de one dat's sho' to know.

W'y, I's done de double shuffle, twell a
　body couldn't res',
Jes' a-hyeahin' Sam de fiddlah play dat
　chune his level bes';
14

I could cut a mighty caper, I could gin a
　mighty fling
Jes' right now, I's mo' dan suttain I could
　cut de pigeon wing.

Look hyeah, whut's dis I's been sayin'?
　whut on urf's tuk holt o' me?
Dat ole music come nigh runnin' my 'uligion
　up a tree!
Cleah out wif dat dah ole fiddle, don' you
　try dat trick agin;
Didn't think I could be tempted, but you
　lak to made me sin!

POSSUM TROT

I've journeyed 'roun' consid'able, a-seein'
　men an' things,
An' I've learned a little of the sense that
　meetin' people brings;
But in spite of all my travelin', an' of all
　I think I know,
I've got one notion in my head, that I can't
　git to go;
An' it is that the folks I meet in any other
　spot
Ain't half so good as them I knowed back
　home in Possum Trot.

I know you've never heerd the name, it
　ain't a famous place,
An' I reckon ef you'd search the map you
　couldn't find a trace
Of any sich locality as this I've named to
　you;
But never mind, I know the place, an' I
　love it dearly, too.
It don't make no pretensions to bein' great
　or fine,
The circuses don't come that way, they
　ain't no railroad line.
It ain't no great big city, where the
　schemers plan an' plot,
But jest a little settlement, this place called
　Possum Trot.

But don't you think the folks that lived in
　that outlandish place
Were ignorant of all the things that go for
　sense or grace.

Why, there was Hannah Dyer, you may
  search this teemin' earth
An' never find a sweeter girl, er one o'
  greater worth;
An' Uncle Abner Williams, a-leanin' on
  his staff,
It seems like I kin hear him talk, an' hear
  his hearty laugh.
His heart was big an' cheery as a sunny
  acre lot,
Why, that's the kind o' folks we had down
  there at Possum Trot.

Good times? Well, now, to suit my
  taste,—an' I'm some hard to suit,—
There ain't been no sich pleasure sence, an'
  won't be none to boot,
With huskin' bees in Harvest time, an'
  dances later on,
An' singin' school, an' taffy pulls, an' fun
  from night till dawn.
Revivals come in winter time, baptizin's
  in the spring,
You'd ought to seen those people shout,
  an' heerd 'em pray an' sing;
You'd ought to've heard ole Parson Brown
  a-throwin' gospel shot
Among the saints an' sinners in the days
  of Possum Trot.

We live up in the city now, my wife was
  bound to come;
I hear aroun' me day by day the endless
  stir an' hum.
I reckon that it done me good, an' yet it
  done me harm,
That oil was found so plentiful down there
  on my ole farm.
We've got a new-styled preacher, our
  church is new-styled, too,
An' I've come down from what I knowed
  to rent a cushioned pew.
But often when I'm settin' there, it's fool-
  ish, like as not,
To think of them ol' benches in the church
  at Possum Trot.

I know that I'm ungrateful, an' sich
  thoughts must be a sin,
But I find myself a wishin' that the times
  was back agin.

With the huskin's an' the frolics, an' the
  joys I used to know,
When I lived at the settlement, a dozen
  years ago.
I don't feel this way often, I'm scarcely
  ever glum,
For life has taught me how to take her
  chances as they come.
But now an' then my mind goes back to
  that ol' buryin' plot,
That holds the dust of some I loved, down
  there at Possum Trot.

DELY

Jes' lak toddy wahms you thoo'
  Sets yo' haid a reelin',
Meks you ovah good and new,
  Dat's de way I's feelin'.
Seems to me hit's summah time,
  Dough hit's wintah reely,
I's a feelin' jes' dat prime —
  An' huh name is Dely.

Dis hyeah love's a cu'rus thing,
  Changes 'roun' de season,
Meks you sad or meks you sing,
  'Dout no urfly reason.
Sometimes I go mopin' 'roun',
  Den agin I's leapin';
Sperits allus up an' down
  Even when I's sleepin'.

Fu' de dreams comes to me den,
  An' dey keeps me pitchin',
Lak de apple dumplin's w'en
  Bilin' in de kitchen.
Some one sot to do me hahm,
  Tryin' to ovahcome me,
Ketchin' Dely by de ahm
  So's to tek huh f'om me.

Mon, you bettah b'lieve I fights
  (Dough hit's on'y seemin');
I's a hittin' fu' my rights
  Even w'en I's dreamin'.
But I'd let you have 'em all,
  Give 'em to you freely,
Good an' bad ones, great an' small,
  So's you leave me Dely.

Dely got dem meltin' eyes,
  Big an' black an' tendah.
Dely jes' a lady-size,
  Delikit an' slendah.
Dely brown ez brown kin be
  An' huh haih is curly;
Oh, she look so sweet to me,—
  Bless de precious girlie!

Dely brown ez brown kin be,
  She ain' no mullatter;
She pure cullud,—don' you see
  Dat's jes' whut's de mattah?
Dat's de why I love huh so,
  D' ain't no mix about huh,
Soon's you see huh face you know
  D' ain't no chanst to doubt huh.

Folks dey go to chu'ch an' pray
  So's to git a blessin'.
Oomph, dey bettah come my way,
  Dey could lu'n a lesson.
Sabbaf day I don' go fu',
  Jes' to see my pigeon;
I jes' sets an' looks at huh,
  Dat's enuff 'uligion.

BREAKING THE CHARM

Caught Susanner whistlin'; well,
It's most nigh too good to tell.
'Twould 'a' b'en too good to see
Ef it hadn't b'en fur me,
Comin' up so soft an' sly
That she didn' hear me nigh.
I was pokin' 'round that day,
An' ez I come down the way,
First her whistle strikes my ears,—
Then her gingham dress appears;
So with soft step up I slips.
Oh, them dewy, rosy lips!
Ripe ez cherries, red an' round,
Puckered up to make the sound.
She was lookin' in the spring,
Whistlin' to beat anything,—
"Kitty Dale" er "In the Sweet."
I was jest so mortal beat
That I can't quite ricoleck
What the toon was, but I 'speck
'Twas some hymn er other, fur
Hymny things is jest like her.
Well she went on fur awhile
With her face all in a smile,

An' I never moved, but stood
Stiller'n a piece o' wood —
Wouldn't wink ner wouldn't stir,
But a-gazin' right at her,
Tell she turns an' sees me—my!
Thought at first she'd try to fly.
But she blushed an' stood her ground.
Then, a-slyly lookin' round,
She says: "Did you hear me, Ben?"
"Whistlin' woman, crowin' hen,"
Says I, lookin' awful stern.
Then the red commenced to burn
In them cheeks o' hern. Why, la!
Reddest red you ever saw —
Pineys wa'n't a circumstance.
You'd 'a' noticed in a glance
She was pow'rful shamed an' skeart;
But she looked so sweet an' peart,
That a idee struck my head;
So I up an' slowly said:
"Woman whistlin' brings shore harm,
Jest one thing'll break the charm."
"And what's that?" "Oh, my!" says I,
"I don't like to tell you." "Why?"
Says Susanner. "Well, you see
It would kinder fall on me."
Course I knowed that she'd insist,—
So I says: "You must be kissed
By the man that heard you whistle;
Everybody says that this'll
Break the charm and set you free
From the threat'nin' penalty."
She was blushin' fit to kill,
But she answered, kinder still:
"I don't want to have no harm,
Please come, Ben, an' break the charm."
Did I break that charm?— oh, well,
There's some things I mustn't tell.
I remember, afterwhile,
Her a-sayin' with a smile:
"Oh, you quit,—you sassy dunce,
You jest caught me whistlin' once."
Ev'ry sence that when I hear
Some one whistlin' kinder clear,
I most break my neck to see
Ef it's Susy; but, dear me,
I jest find I've b'en to chase
Some blamed boy about the place.
Dad's b'en noticin' my way,
An' last night I heerd him say:
"We must send fur Dr. Glenn,
Mother; somethin's wrong with Ben!"

HUNTING SONG

Tek a cool night, good an' cleah,
Skiff o' snow upon de groun';
Jes' 'bout fall-time o' de yeah
W'en de leaves is dry an' brown;
Tek a dog an' tek a axe,
Tek a lantu'n in yo' han',
Step light whah de switches cracks,
Fu' dey's huntin' in de lan'.
Down thoo de valleys an' ovah de hills,
Into de woods whah de 'simmon-tree
grows,
Wakin' an' skeerin' de po' whippo'wills,
Huntin' fu' coon an' fu' 'possum we
goes.

Blow dat ho'n dah loud an' strong,
Call de dogs an' da'kies neah;
Mek its music cleah an' long,
So de folks at home kin hyeah.
Blow it twell de hills an' trees
Sen's de echoes tumblin' back;
Blow it twell de back'ard breeze
Tells de folks we's on de track.
Coons is a-ramblin' an' 'possums is out;
Look at dat dog; you could set on his
tail!
Watch him now—steady,—min'—what
you's about,
Bless me, dat animal's got on de trail!

Listen to him ba'kin' now!
Dat means bus'ness, sho's you bo'n;
Ef he's struck de scent I 'low
Dat ere 'possum's sholy gone.
Knowed dat dog fu' fo'teen yeahs,
An' I nevah seed him fail
W'en he sot dem flappin' eahs
An' went off upon a trail.
Run, Mistah 'Possum, an' run, Mistah
Coon,
No place is safe fu' yo' ramblin' to-
night;
Mas' gin' de lantu'n an' God gin de moon,
An' a long hunt gins a good appetite.

Look hyeah, folks, you hyeah dat
change?
Dat ba'k is sha'per dan de res'.
Dat ere soun' ain't nothin' strange,—
Dat dog's talked his level bes'.

Somep'n' 's treed, I know de soun'.
Dah now,—wha'd I tell you? see!
Dat ere dog done run him down;
Come hyeah, he'p cut down dis tree.
Ah, Mistah 'Possum, we got you at las'—
Needn't play daid, laying dah on de
groun';
Fros' an' de 'simmons has made you grow
fas',—
Won't he be fine when he's roasted up
brown!

A LETTER

DEAR MISS LUCY: I been t'inkin' dat
I'd write you long fo' dis,
But dis writin' 's mighty tejous, an' you
know jes' how it is.
But I's got a little lesure, so I teks my pen
in han'
Fu' to let you know my feelin's since I
retched dis furrin' lan'.
I's right well, I's glad to tell you (dough
dis climate ain't to blame),
An' I hopes w'en dese lines reach you, dat
dey'll fin' yo'se'f de same.
Cose I'se feelin' kin' o' homesick—dat's
ez nachul ez kin be,
W'en a feller's mo'n th'ee thousand miles
across dat awful sea.
(Don't you let nobidy fool you 'bout de
ocean bein' gran';
If you want to see de billers, you jes'
view dem f'om de lan'.)
'Bout de people? We been t'inkin' dat
all white folks was alak;
But dese Englishmen is diffunt, an' dey's
curus fu' a fac'.
Fust, dey's heavier an' redder in dey
make-up an' dey looks,
An' dey don't put salt nor pepper in a
blessed t'ing dey cooks!
W'en dey gin you good ol' tu'nips, ca'ots,
pa'snips, beets, an' sich,
Ef dey ain't some one to tell you, you
cain't 'stinguish which is which.
W'en I 't'ought I'se eatin' chicken—you
may b'lieve dis hyeah's a lie —
But de waiter beat me down dat I was
eatin' rabbit pie.

An' dey'd t'ink dat you was crazy—jes' a
 reg'lar ravin' loon,
Ef you'd speak erbout a 'possum or a piece
 o' good ol' coon.
O hit's mighty nice, dis trav'lin', an' I's
 kin' o' glad I come.
But, I reckon, now I's willin' fu' to tek my
 way back home.
I done see de Crystal Palace, an' I's
 hyeahd dey string-band play,
But I hasn't seen no banjos layin' nowhahs
 roun' dis way.
Jes' gin ol' Jim Bowles a banjo, an' he'd
 not go very fu',
'Fo' he'd outplayed all dese fiddlers, wif
 dey flourish and dey stir.
Evahbiddy dat I's met wif has been
 monst'ous kin' an' good ;
But I t'ink I'd lak it better to be down in
 Jones's wood,
Where we ust to have sich frolics, Lucy,
 you an' me an' Nelse,
Dough my appetite 'ud call me, ef dey
 wasn't nuffin else.
I'd jes' lak to have some sweet-pertaters
 roasted in de skin ;
I's a-longin' fu' my chittlin's an' my mus-
 tard greens ergin ;
I's a-wishin' fu' some buttermilk, an' co'n
 braid, good an' brown,
An' a drap o' good ol' bourbon fu' to wash
 my feelin's down !
An' I's comin' back to see you jes' as
 ehly as I kin,
So you better not go spa'kin' wif dat
 wuffless scoun'el Quin !
Well, I reckon, I mus' close now; write
 ez soon's dis reaches you;
Gi' my love to Sister Mandy an' to Uncle
 Isham, too.
Tell de folks I sen' 'em howdy; gin a kiss
 to pap an' mam ;
Closin' I is, deah Miss Lucy,
  Still Yo' Own True-Lovin' SAM.

P. S. Ef you cain't mek out dis letter,
   lay it by erpon de she'f,
  An' when I git home, I'll read it,
   darlin', to you my own se'f.

A CABIN TALE

THE YOUNG MASTER ASKS FOR A STORY

Whut you say, dah ? huh, uh ! chile,
You's enough to dribe me wile.
Want a sto'y ; jes' hyeah dat !
Whah' 'll I git a sto'y at ?
Di'n' I tell you th'ee las' night ?
Go 'way, honey, you ain't right.
I got somep'n' else to do,
'Cides jes' tellin' tales to you.
Tell you jes' one ? Lem me see
Whut dat one's a-gwine to be.
When you's ole, yo' membry fails ;
Seems lak I do' know no tales.
Well, set down dah in dat cheer,
Keep still ef you wants to hyeah.
Tek dat chin up off yo' han's,
Set up nice now. Goodness lan's !
Hol' yo'se'f up lak yo' pa.
Bet nobidy evah saw
Him scrunched down lak you was den —
High-tone boys meks high-tone men.

Once dey was a ole black bah,
Used to live 'roun' hyeah somewhah
In a cave. He was so big
He could ca'y off a pig
Lak you picks a chicken up,
Er yo' leetles' bit o' pup.
An' he had two gread big eyes,
Jes' erbout a saucer's size.
Why, dey looked lak balls o' fiah
Jumpin' 'roun' erpon a wiah
W'en dat bah was mad ; an' laws !
But you ought to seen his paws !
Did I see em ? How you 'spec
I's a-gwine to ricollec'
Dis hyeah ya'n I's try'n' to spin
Ef you keeps on puttin' in ?
You keep still an' don't you cheep
Less I'll sen' you off to sleep.
Dis hyeah bah'd go trompin' 'roun'
Eatin' evahthing he foun' ;
No one couldn't have a fa'm
But dat bah 'u'd do 'em ha'm ;
And dey couldn't ketch de scamp.
Anywhah he wan'ed to tramp,
Dah de scoun'el 'd mek his track,
Do his du't an' come on back.
He was sich a sly ole limb,
Traps was jes' lak fun to.him..

Now, down neah whah Mistah Bah
Lived, dey was a weasel dah ;
But dey wasn't fren's a-tall
Case de weasel was so small.
An' de bah 'u'd, jes' fu' sass,
Tu'n his nose up w'en he'd pass.
Weasels's small o' cose, but my !
Dem air animiles is sly.
So dis hyeah one says, says he,
" I'll jes' fix dat bah, you see."
So he fixes up his plan
An' hunts up de fa'merman.
When de fa'mer see him come,
He 'mence lookin' mighty glum,
An' he ketches up a stick ;
But de weasel speak up quick :
" Hol' on, Mistah Fa'mer man,
I wan' 'splain a little plan.
Ef you waits, I'll tell you whah
An' jes' how to ketch ol' Bah.
But I tell you now you mus'
Gin me one fat chicken fus'."
Den de man he scratch his haid,
Las' he say, " I'll mek de trade."
So de weasel et his hen,
Smacked his mouf and says, " Well, den,
Set yo' trap an' bait ternight,
An' I'll ketch de bah all right."
Den he ups an' goes to see
Mistah Bah, an' says, says he :
" Well, fren' Bah, we ain't been fren's,
But ternight ha'd feelin' 'en's.
Ef you ain't too proud to steal,
We kin git a splendid meal.
Cose I wouldn't come to you,
But it mus' be done by two ;
Hit's a trap, but we kin beat
All dey tricks an' git de meat."
" Cose I's wif you," says de bah,
" Come on, weasel, show me whah."
Well, dey trots erlong ontwell
Dat air meat beginned to smell
In de trap.   Den weasel say :
" Now you put yo' paw dis way
While I hol' de spring back so,
Den you grab de meat an' go."
Well, de bah he had to grin
Ez he put his big paw in,
Den he juked up, but—kerbing !
Weasel done let go de spring.
" Dah now," says de weasel, " dah,
I done cotched you, Mistah Bah ! "

O dat bah did sno't and spout,
Try'n' his bestes' to git out,
But de weasel say, " Goo'-bye !
Weasel small, but weasel sly."
Den he tu'ned his back an' run
Tol' de fa'mer whut he done.
So de fa'mer come down dah,
Wif a axe and killed de bah.

Dah now, ain't dat sto'y fine ?
Run erlong now, nevah mir.'.
Want some mo', you rascal, you ?
No, suh ! no, suh ! dat'll do.

WHISTLING SAM

I has hyeahd o' people dancin' an' I's
    hyeahd o' people singin'.
An' I's been 'roun' lots of othahs dat could
    keep de banjo ringin';
But of all de whistlin' da'kies dat have
    lived an' died since Ham,
De whistlin'est I evah seed was ol' Ike
    Bates's Sam.
In de kitchen er de stable, in de fiel' er
    mowin' hay,
You could hyeah dat boy a-whistlin' pu'ty
    nigh a mile erway,—
Puck'rin' up his ugly features 'twell you
    couldn't see his eyes,
Den you'd hyeah a soun' lak dis un f'om
    dat awful puckah rise :

When dey had revival meetin' an' de
    Lawd's good grace was flowin'
On de groun' dat needed wat'rin' whaih de
    seeds of good was growin',
While de othahs was a-singin' an' a-shoutin'
    right an' lef',
You could hyeah dat boy a-whistlin' kin'
    o' sof' beneaf his bref :

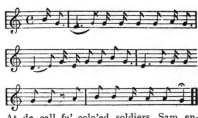

At de call fu' colo'ed soldiers, Sam en-
    listed 'mong de res'
Wid de blue o' Gawd's great ahmy wropped
    about his swellin' breas',
An' he laffed an' whistled loudah in his
    youfful joy an' glee
Dat de govament would let him he'p to
    mek his people free.
Daih was lots o' ties to bin' him, pappy,
    mammy, an' his Dinah, —
Dinah, min' you, was his sweethea't, an'
    dey wasn't nary finah;
But he lef' 'em all, I tell you, lak a king
    he ma'ched away,
Try'n' his level bes' to whistle, happy,
    solemn, choky, gay:

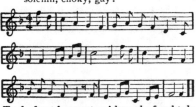

To de front he went an' bravely fought de
    foe an' kep' his sperrit,
An' his comerds said his whistle made 'em
    strong when dey could hyeah it.
When a saber er a bullet cut some frien'
    o' his'n down,
An' de time 'u'd come to trench him an'
    de boys 'u'd gethah 'roun',
An' dey couldn't sta't a hymn-tune, mebbe
    none o' dem 'u'd keer,
Sam 'u'd whistle "Sleep in Jesus," an' he
    knowed de Mastah 'd hyeah.
In de camp, all sad discouraged, he would
    cheer de hea'ts of all,
**When above de soun' of labor dey could
    hyeah his whistle call :**

When de cruel wah was ovah an' de boys
    come ma'chin' back,
Dey was shouts an' cries an' blessin's all
    erlong dey happy track,
An' de da'kies all was happy; souls an'
    bodies bofe was freed.
Why, hit seemed lak de Redeemah mus'
    'a' been on earf indeed.
Dey was gethahed all one evenin' jes' befo'
    de cabin do',
When dey hyeahd somebody whistlin' kin'
    o' sof' an' sweet an' low.
Dey couldn't see de whistlah, but de hymn
    was cleah and ca'm,
An' dey all stood daih a listenin' ontwell
    Dinah shouted, "Sam !"
An' dey seed a little da'ky way off yandah
    thoo de trees
Wid his face all in a puckah mekin' jes'
    sich soun's ez dese :

HOW LUCY BACKSLID

De times is mighty stirrin' 'mong de people
    up ouah way,
Dey 'sputin' an' dey argyin' an' fussin'
    night an' day;
An' all dis monst'ous trouble dat hit meks
    me tiahed to tell
Is 'bout dat Lucy Jackson dat was sich a
    mighty belle.

She was de preachah's favored, an' he tol'
    de chu'ch one night
Dat she traveled thoo de cloud o' sin
    a-bearin' of a light;
But, now, I 'low he t'inkin' dat she mus'
    'a' los' huh lamp,
Case Lucy done backslided an' dey trouble
    in de camp.

Huh daddy wants to beat huh, but huh
    mammy daihs him to,
Fu' she lookin' at de question f'om a
    ooman's pint o' view;
An' she say dat now she wouldn't have it
    diff'ent ef she could;
Dat huh darter only acted jes' lak any
    othah would.

Cose you know w'en women argy, dey is
    mighty easy led
By dey hea'ts an' don't go foolin' 'bout de
    reasons of de haid.
So huh mammy laid de law down (she
    ain' reckernizin' wrong),
But you got to mek erlowance fu' de cause
    dat go along.

Now de cause dat made Miss Lucy fu' to
    th'ow huh grace away
I's afeard won't baih no 'spection w'en hit
    come to jedgement day;
Do' de same t'ing been a-wo'kin' evah
    sence de worl' began,—
De ooman disobeyin' fu' to 'tice along a
    man.

Ef you 'tended de revivals which we held
    de wintah pas',
You kin rickolec' dat convuts was a-comin'
    thick an' fas';
But dey ain't no use in talkin', dey was all
    lef' in de lu'ch
W'en ol' Mis' Jackson's dartah foun' huh
    peace an' tuk de chu'ch.

W'y, she shouted ovah evah inch of Eben-
    ezah's flo';
Up into de preachah's pulpit an' f'om dah
    down to de do';
Den she hugged an' squeezed huh mammy,
    an' she hugged an' kissed huh dad,
An' she struck out at huh sistah, people
    said, lak she was mad.

I has 'tended some revivals dat was lively
    in my day,
An' I's seed folks git 'uligion in mos' evah
    kin' o' way;
But I tell you, an' you b'lieve me dat I's
    speakin' true indeed,
Dat gal tuk huh 'ligion ha'dah dan de
    ha'dest yit I's seed.

Well, f'om dat, 'twas "Sistah Jackson,
    won't you please do dis er dat?"
She mus' allus sta't de singin' w'en dey'd
    pass erroun' de hat,
An' hit seemed dey wasn't nuffin' in dat
    chu'ch dat could go by
'Dout sistah Lucy Jackson had a finger in
    de pie.

But de sayin' mighty trufeful dat hit easiah
    to sail
W'en de sea is ca'm an' gentle dan to
    weathah out a gale.
Dat's whut made dis ooman's trouble; ef
    de sto'm had kep' away,
She'd 'a' had enough 'uligion fu' to lasted
    out huh day.

Lucy went wid 'Lishy Davis, but w'en she
    jined chu'ch, you know
Dah was lots o' little places dat, of cose,
    she couldn't go;
An' she had to gin up dancin' an' huh
    singin' an' huh play.—
Now hit's nachul dat sich goin's-on 'u'd
    drive a man away.

So, w'en Lucy got so solemn, Ike he sta'ted
    fu' to go
Wid a gal who was a sinnah an' could mek
    a bettah show.
Lucy jes' went on to meetin' lak she didn't
    keer a rap,
But my 'sperunce kep' me t'inkin' dah was
    somep'n' gwine to drap.

Fu' a gal won't let 'uligion er no othah
    so't o' t'ing
Stop huh w'en she teks a notion dat she
    wants a weddin' ring.
You kin p'omise huh de blessin's of a happy
    aftah life
(An' hit's nice to be a angel), but she'd
    ravah be a wife.

So w'en Christmas come an' mastah gin a
    frolic on de lawn,
Didn't 'sprise me not de littlest seein' Lucy
    lookin' on.
An' I seed a wa'nin' lightnin' go a-flashin'
    f'om huh eye
Jest ez 'Lishy an' his new gal went a-galli-
    vantin' by.

An' dat Tildy, umph! she giggled, an' she
    gin huh dress a flirt
Lak de people she was passin' was ez com-
    mon ez de dirt ;
An' de minit she was dancin', w'y dat gal
    put on mo' aihs
Dan a cat a-tekin' kittens up a paih o'
    windin' staihs.

She could 'fo'd to show huh sma'tness, fu'
    she couldn't he'p but know
Dat wid jes' de present dancahs she was
    ownah of de flo' ;
But I t'ink she'd kin' o' cooled down ef
    she happened on de sly
Fu' to noticed dat 'ere lightnin' dat I seed
    in Lucy's eye.

An' she wouldn't been so 'stonished w'en
    de people gin a shout,
An' Lucy th'owed huh mantle back an'
    come a-glidin' out.
Some ahms was dah to tek huh an' she
    fluttahed down de flo'
Lak a feddah f'om a bedtick w'en de win'
    commence to blow

Soon as Tildy see de trouble, she jes' tu'n
    an' toss huh haid,
But seem lak she los' huh sperrit, all huh
    darin'ness was daid.
Didn't cut anothah capah nary time de
    blessid night ;
But de othah one, hit looked lak couldn't
    git enough delight.

W'en you keeps a colt a-stan'in' in de
    stable all along,
W'en he do git out hit's nachul he'll be
    pullin' mighty strong.
Ef you will tie up yo' feelin's, hyeah's de
    bes' advice to tek,
Look out fu' an awful loosin' w'en de string
    dat hol's 'em brek.

Lucy's mammy groaned to see huh, an'
    huh pappy sto'med an' to',
But she kep' right on a-hol'in' to de centah
    of de flo'.
So dey went an' ast de pastoh ef he
    couldn't mek huh quit,
But de tellin' of de sto'y th'owed de
    preachah in a fit.

Tildy Taylor chewed huh hank'cher twell
    she'd chewed it in a hole,—
All de sinnahs was rejoicin' 'cause a lamb
    had lef' de fol',
An' de las' I seed o' Lucy, she an' 'Lish
    was side an' side :
I don't blame de gal fu' dancin', an' I
    couldn't ef I tried.

Fu' de men dat wants to ma'y ain't
    a-growin' 'roun' on trees,
An de gal dat wants to git one sholy has
    to try to please.
Hit's a ha'd t'ing fu' a ooman fu' to pray
    an' jes' set down,
An' to sacafice a husban' so's to try to
    gain a crown.

Now, I don' say she was justified in fol-
    lowin' huh plan ;
But aldough she los' huh 'ligion, yit she
    sholy got de man.
Latah on, w'en she is suttain dat de preach-
    ah's made 'em fas'
She kin jes' go back to chu'ch an' ax fu'-
    giveness fu' de pas' !

TO THE ROAD

Cool is the wind, for the summer is waning,
    Who's for the road ?
Sun-flecked and soft, where the dead leaves
        are raining,
    Who's for the road ?
Knapsack and alpenstock press hand and
        shoulder,
Prick of the brier and roll of the boulder ;
This be your lot till the season grow older ;
    Who's for the road ?

Up and away in the hush of the morning,
    Who's for the road ?
Vagabond he, all conventions a-scorning,
    Who's for the road ?
Music of warblers·so merrily singing,
Draughts from the rill from the roadside
        upspringing,
Nectar of grapes from the vines lowly
        swinging,
    These on the road.

Now every house is a hut or a hovel,
  Come to the road :
Mankind and moles in the dark love to
    grovel,
  But to the road.
Throw off the loads that are bending you
    double ;
Love is for life, only labor is trouble ;
Truce to the town, whose best gift is a
    bubble :
  Come to the road !

TWO LITTLE BOOTS

In reading this touching little poem, one is constrained to compare it with Eugene Field's " Little Boy Blue "—the same sentiment, the same appeal to the world's heart which loves a baby and mourns its death—but there is a difference. Field wrote of a white baby who played with a little tin soldier and other toys—while Dunbar's " two little boots " belonged to some black woman's po' little lam'. Both are universal, each has its own special application, and the stanzas add one more argument to Dunbar's burden of proof that the negro is " more human than African."

Two little boots all rough an' wo',
  Two little boots !
Laws, I's kissed 'em times befo',
  Dese little boots !
Seems de toes a-peepin' thoo
Dis hyeah hole an' sayin' " Boo ! "
Evah time dey looks at you —
  Dese little boots.

Membah de time he put 'em on,
  Dese little boots ;
Riz an' called fu' 'em by dawn,
  Dese little boots ;
Den he tromped de livelong day,
Laffin' in his happy way,
Evaht'ing he had to say,
  " My little boots ! "

Kickin' de san' de whole day long,
  Dem little boots ;
Good de cobblah made 'em strong,
  Dem little boots !

Rocks was fu' dat baby's use,
I'on had to stan' abuse
W'en you tu'ned dese champeens loose,
  Dese little boots !

Ust to make de ol' cat cry,
  Dese little boots ;
Den you walked it mighty high,
  Proud little boots !
Ahms akimbo, stan'in' wide,
Eyes a-sayin' " Dis is pride ! "
Den de manny-baby stride !
  You little boots.

Somehow, you don' seem so gay,
  Po' little boots,
Sence yo' ownah went erway,
  Po' little boots !
Yo' bright tops don' look so red,
Dese brass tips is dull an' dead ;
" Goo'-by," whut de baby said ;
  Deah little boots !

Ain't you kin' o' sad yo'se'f,
  You little boots ?
Dis is all his mammy's lef',
  Two little boots.
Sence huh baby gone an' died,
Heav'n itse'f hit seem to hide
Des a little bit inside
  Two little boots.

IN MAY

Oh, to have you in May,
  To walk with you under the trees,
Dreaming throughout the day,
  Drinking the wine-like breeze,

Oh, it were sweet to think
  That May should be ours again,
Hoping it not, I shrink,
  Out of the sight of men.

May brings the flowers to bloom,
  It brings the green leaves to the tree,
And the fatally sweet perfume,
  Of what you once were to me.

DESE LITTLE BOOTS

COME ON WALKIN' WID ME, LUCY

A SPRING WOOING

Come on walkin' wid me, Lucy; 'tain't no
    time to mope erroun'
W'en de sunshine's shoutin' glory in de
    sky,
An' de little Johnny-Jump-Ups's jes'
    a-springin' f'om de groun',
Den a-lookin' roun' to ax each othah w'y.
Don' you hyeah dem cows a-mooin'?
    Dat's dey howdy to de spring;
    Ain' dey lookin' most oncommon satis-
    fied?
Hit's enough to mek a body want to spread
    dey mouf an' sing
Jes' to see de critters all so spa'klin'-
    eyed.

W'y dat squir'l dat jes' run past us, ef I
    didn' know his tricks,
    I could swaih he'd got 'uligion jes' to-
    day;
An' dem liza'ds slippin' back an' fofe
    ermong de stones an' sticks
    Is a-wigglin' 'cause dey feel so awful gay.
Oh, I see yo' eyes a-shinin' dough you try
    to mek me b'lieve
Dat you ain' so monst'ous happy 'cause
    you come;
But I tell you dis hyeah weathah meks it
    moughty ha'd to 'ceive
    Ef a body's soul ain' blin' an' deef an'
    dumb.

Robin whistlin' ovah yandah ez he buil'
    his little nes';
    Whut you reckon dat he sayin' to his
    mate?
He's a sayin' dat he love huh in de wo'ds
    she know de bes',
    An' she lookin' moughty pleased at whut
    he state.
Now, Miss Lucy, dat ah robin sholy got
    his sheer o' sense,
    An' de hen-bird got huh mothah-wit fu'
    true;
So I t'ink ef you'll ixcuse me, fu' I do'
    mean no erfence,
    Dey's a lesson in dem birds fu' me an'
    you.

I's a-buil'in' o' my cabin, an' I's vines
    erbove de do'
    Fu' to kin' o' gin it sheltah f'om de sun;
Gwine to have a little kitchen wid a reg'lar
    wooden flo',
    An' dey'll be a back verandy w'en hit's
    done.
I's a-waitin' fu' you, Lucy, tek de 'zample
    o' de birds,
    Dat's a-lovin' an' a-matin' eyahwhaih.
I cain' tell you dat I loves you in de robin's
    music wo'ds,
    But my cabin's talkin' fu' me ovah
    thaih!

JOGGIN' ERLONG

De da'kest hour, dey allus say,
Is des' befo' de dawn,
But it's moughty ha'd a-waitin'
W'ere de night goes frownin' on;
An' it's moughty ha'd a-hopin'
W'en de clouds is big an' black,
An' all de t'ings you's waited fu'
Has failed, er gone to wrack —
But des' keep on a joggin' wid a little bit
    o' song,
De mo'n is allus brightah w'en de night's
    been long.

Dey's lots o' knocks you's got to tek
Befo' yo' journey's done,
An' dey's times w'en you'll be wishin'
Dat de weary race was run;
W'en you want to give up tryin'
An' des' float erpon de wave,
W'en you don't feel no mo' sorrer
Ez you t'ink erbout de grave —
Den, des' keep on a-joggin' wid a little
    bit o' song,
De mo'n is allus brightah w'en de night's
    been long.

De whup-lash sting a good deal mo'
De back hit's knowed befo',
An' de burden's allus heavies'
Whaih hits weights has made a so';
Dey is times w'en tribulation
Seems to git de uppah han'
An' to whip de weary trav'lah

'Twell he ain't got stren'th to stan' —
But des' keep on a-joggin' wid a little bit
  o' song,
De mo'n is allus brightah w'en de night's
  been long.

DREAMS

What dreams we have and how they fly
Like rosy clouds across the sky ;
  Of wealth, of fame, of sure success,
  Of love that comes to cheer and bless ;
And how they wither, how they fade,
The waning wealth, the jilting jade —
  The fame that for a moment gleams,
  Then flies forever,—dreams, ah—
    dreams !

O burning doubt and long regret,
O tears with which our eyes are wet,
  Heart-throbs, heart-aches, the glut of
    pain,
  The sombre cloud, the bitter rain,
You were not of those dreams—ah ! well,
Your full fruition who can tell ?
  Wealth, fame, and love, ah ! love that
    beams
  Upon our souls, all dreams—ah !
    dreams.

THE TRYST

De night creep down erlong de lan',
  De shadders rise an' shake,
De frog is sta'tin' up his ban',
  De cricket is awake ;
My wo'k is mos' nigh done, Celes',
  To-night I won't be late,
I's hu'yin' thoo my level bes',
  Wait fu' me by de gate.

De mockin'-bird 'll sen' his glee
  A-thrillin' thoo and thoo,
I know dat ol' magnolia-tree
  Is smellin' des' fu' you ;
De jessamine erside de road
  Is bloomin' rich an' white,
My hea't's a-th'obbin' 'cause it knowed
  You'd wait fu' me to-night.

Hit's lonesome, ain't it, stan'in' thaih
  Wid no one nigh to talk ?

But ain't dey whispahs in de aih
  Erlong de gyahden walk ?
Don't somep'n' kin' o' call my name,
  An' say " he love you bes' " ?
Hit's true, I wants to say de same,
  So wait fu' me, Celes'.

Sing somep'n' fu' to pass de time,
  Outsing de mockin'-bird,
You got de music an' de rhyme,
  You beat him wid de word.
I's comin' now, my wo'k is done,
  De hour has come fu' res',
I wants to fly, but only run —
  Wait fu' me, deah Celes'.

A PLEA

Treat me nice, Miss Mandy Jane,
  Treat me nice.
Dough my love has tu'ned my brain,
  Treat me nice.
I ain't done a t'ing to shame,
Lovahs all ac's jes' de same :
Don't you know we ain't to blame ?
  Treat me nice !

Cose I know I's talkin' wild ;
  Treat me nice ;
I cain't talk no bettah, child,
  Treat me nice ;
Whut a pusson gwine to do,
W'en he come a-cou'tin' you
All a-trimblin' thoo and thoo ?
  Please be nice.

Reckon I mus' go de paf
  Othahs do :
Lovahs lingah, ladies laff ;
  Mebbe you
Do' mean all the things you say,
An' pu'haps some latah day
W'en I baig you-ha'd, you may
  Treat me nice !

THE DOVE

Out of the sunshine and out of the heat,
Out of the dust of the grimy street,
A song fluttered down in the form of a
  dove,
And it bore me a message, the one word —
  Love !

Ah, I was toiling, and oh, I was sad:
I had forgotten the way to be glad.
Now, smiles for my sadness and for my
toil, rest
Since the dove fluttered down to its home
in my breast!

A WARM DAY IN WINTER

" Sunshine on de medders,
  Greenness on de way;
Dat's de blessed reason
  I sing all de day."
Look hyeah! Whut you axin'?
  Whut meks me so merry?
'Spect to see me sighin'
  W'en hit's wa'm in Febawary?

'Long de stake an' rider
  Seen a robin set;
W'y, hit 'mence a-thawin',
  Groun' is monst'ous wet.
Den you stan' dah wond'rin',
  Lookin' skeert an' stary;
I's a right to caper
  W'en hit's wa'm in Febawary.

Missis gone a-drivin',
  Mastah gone to shoot;
Ev'ry da'ky lazin'
  In de sun to boot.
Qua'tah's moughty pleasant,
  Hangin' 'roun' my Mary;
Cou'tin' boun' to prospah
  W'en hit's wa'm in Febawary.

Cidah look so pu'ty
  Po'in' f'om de jug —
Don' you see it's happy?
  Hyeah it laffin'—glug?
Now's de time fu' people
  Fu' to try an' bury
All dey grief an' sorrer,
  W'en hit's wa'm in Febawary.

SNOWIN'

Dey is snow upon de meddahs, dey is
  snow upon de hill,
An' de little branch's watahs is all glis-
  tenin' an' still;
De win' goes roun' de cabin lak a sperrit
  wan'erin' 'roun',
An' de chillen shakes an' shivahs as dey
  listen to de soun'.
Dey is hick'ry in de fiahplace, whah de
  blaze is risin' high,
But de heat it meks ain't wa'min' up de
  gray clouds in de sky.
Now an' den I des peep outside, den I
  hurries to de do',
Lawd a mussy on my body, how I wish it
  wouldn't snow!

I kin stan' de hottes' summah, I kin stan'
  de wettes' fall,
I kin stan' de chilly springtime in de
  ploughland, but dat's all;
Fu' de ve'y hottes' fiah nevah tells my
  skin a t'ing,
W'en de snow commence a-flyin', an' de
  win' begin to sing.
Dey is plenty wood erroun' us, an' I chop
  an' tote it in,
But de t'oughts dat I's a t'inkin' while I's
  wo'kin' is a sin.
I kin keep f'om downright swahin' all de
  time I's on de go,
But my hea't is full o' cuss-wo'ds w'en I's
  trampin' thoo de snow.

What you say, you Lishy Davis, dat you
  see a possum's tracks?
Look hyeah, boy, you stop yo' foolin',
  bring ol' Spot, an' bring de ax.
Is I col'? Go way, now, Mandy, what you
  t'ink I's made of?—sho,
W'y dis win' is des ez gentle, an' dis ain't
  no kin' o' snow.
Dis hyeah weathah's des ez healthy ez de
  wa'mest summah days.
All you chillen step up lively, pile on wood
  an' keep a blaze.
What's de use o' gittin' skeery case dey's
  snow upon de groun'?
Huh-uh, I's a reg'lar snowbird ef dey's
  any possum 'roun'.

Go on, Spot, don' be so foolish; don' you
  see de signs o' feet.
What you howlin' fu'?   Keep still, suh,
  cose de col' is putty sweet;
But we goin' out on bus'ness, an' hit's
  bus'ness o' de kin'
Dat mus' put a dog an' dahky in a happy
  frame o' min'.
Yes, you's col'; I know it, Spotty, but you
  des stay close to me,
An' I'll mek you hot ez cotton w'en we
  strikes de happy tree.
No, I don' lak wintah weathah, an' I'd
  wush 't uz allus June,
Et it wasn't fu' de trackin' o' de possum
  an' de coon.

KEEP A SONG UP ON DE WAY

Mr. Dunbar was not one of those who
do not "practice what they preach."
Through all his troubles and trials,
through all his ill health and consequent
suffering he was always noted for his
cheerfulness, his love of fun, and his op-
timism. Indeed his very presence de-
noted that he was trying, at least, to
"Keep a Song Up on de Way."

Oh, de clouds is mighty heavy
An' de rain is mighty thick;
  Keep a song up on de way.
An' de waters is a rumblin'
On de boulders in de crick,
  Keep a song up on de way.
Fu' a bird ercross de road
Is a-singin' lak he knowed
Dat we people didn't daih
Fu' to try de rainy aih
  Wid a song up on de way.

What's de use o' gittin' mopy,
Case de weather ain' de bes'!
  Keep a song up on de way.
W'en de rain is fallin' ha'des',
Dey's de longes' time to res';
  Keep a song up on de way.
Dough de plough's a-stan'in' still
Dey'll be watah fu' de mill,
Rain mus' come ez well ez sun
'Fo' de weathah's wo'k is done,
  Keep a song up on de way.

W'y hit's nice to hyeah de showahs
Fallin' down ermong de trees:
  Keep a song up on de way.
Ef de birds don' bothah 'bout it,
But go singin' lak dey please,
  Keep a song up on de way.
You don' s'pose I's gwine to see
Dem ah fowls do mo' dan me?
No, suh, I'll des chase dis frown,
An' aldough de rain fall down,
  Keep a song up on de way.

THE TURNING OF THE BABIES IN THE BED

Woman's sho' a cur'ous critter, an' dey
  ain't no doubtin' dat.
She's a mess o' funny capahs f'om huh
  slippahs to huh hat.
Ef you tries to un'erstan' huh, an' you fails,
  des' up an' say:
" D' ain't a bit o' use to try to un'erstan' a
  woman's way."

I don' mean to be complainin', but I's jes'
  a-settin' down
Some o' my own obserwations, w'en I cas'
  my eye eroun'.
Ef you ax me fu' to prove it, I ken do it
  mighty fine,
Fu' dey ain't no bettah 'zample den dis
  ve'y wife o' mine.

In de ve'y hea't o' midnight, w'en I's
  sleepin' good an' soun',
I kin hyeah a so't o' rustlin' an' somebody
  movin' 'roun'.
An' I say, " Lize, whut you doin'?"   But
  she frown an' shek huh haid,
" Heish yo' mouf, I's only tu'nin' of de
  chillun in de bed.

" Don' you know a chile gits restless, layin'
  all de night one way?
An' you' got to kind o' 'range him sev'al
  times befo' de day?
So de little necks won't worry, an' de little
  backs won't break;
Don' you t'ink case chillun's chillun dey
  hain't got no pain an' ache."

So she shakes 'em, an' she twists 'em, an'
        she tu'ns 'em 'roun' erbout,
'Twell I don' see how de chillun evah
        keeps f'om hollahin' out.
Den she lif's 'em up head down'ards, so's
        dey won't git livah-grown,
But dey snoozes des' ez peaceful ez a liza'd
        on a stone.

W'en hit's mos' nigh time fu' wakin' on
        de dawn o' jedgment day,
Seems lak I kin hyeah ol' Gab'iel lay his
        trumpet down an' say,
" Who dat walkin' 'roun' so easy, down on
        earf ermong de dead ? " —
'Twill be Lizy up a-tu'nin' of de chillun
        in de bed.

THE DANCE

Heel and toe, heel and toe,
    That is the song we sing ;
Turn to your partner and curtsey low,
    Balance and forward and swing.
Corners are draughty and meadows are
        white,
This is the game for a winter's night.

Hands around, hands around,
    Trip it, and not too slow ;
Clear is the fiddle and sweet its sound,
    Keep the girls' cheeks aglow.
Still let your movements be dainty and
        light,
This is the game for a winter's night.

Back to back, back to back,
    Turn to your place again ;
Never let lightness nor nimbleness lack,
    Either in maidens or men.
Time hasteth ever, beware of its flight,
Oh, what a game for a winter's night !

Slower now, slower now,
    Softer the music sighs ;
Look, there are beads on your partner's
        brow
    Though there be light in her eyes.
Lead her away and her grace requite,
So goes the game on a winter's night.

SOLILOQUY OF A TURKEY

Dey's a so't o' threatenin' feelin' in de
        blowin' of de breeze,
    An' I's feelin' kin' o' squeamish in de
        night ;
I's a-walkin' 'roun' a-lookin' at de diffunt
        style o' trees,
    An' a-measurin' dey thickness an' dey
        height.
Fu' dey's somep'n' mighty 'spicious in de
        looks de da'kies give,
    Ez dey pass me an' my f⸗mbly on de
        groun',
So it 'curs to me dat lakly, ef I caihs to try
        an' live,
    It concehns me fu' to 'mence to look
        erroun'.

Dey's a cu'ious kin' o' shivah runnin' up
        an' down my back,
    An' I feel my feddahs rufflin' all de day,
An' my laigs commence to trimble evah
        blessid step I mek ;
    W'en I sees a ax, I tu'ns my head away.
Folks is go'gin' me wid goodies, an' dey's
        treatin' me wid caih,
    An' I's fat in spite of all dat I kin do.
I's mistrus'ful of de kin'ness dat's erroun'
        me evahwhaih,
    Fu' it's jes' too good, an' frequent, to be
        true.

Snow's a-fallin' on de medders, all erroun'
        me now is white,
    But I's still kep' on a-roostin' on de
        fence ;
Isham comes an' feels my breas'bone, an'
        he hefted me las' night,
    An' he's gone erroun' a-grinnin' evah
        sence.
'Tain't de snow dat meks me shivah ;
        'tain't de col' dat meks me shake ;
    'Tain't de wintah-time itse'f dat's 'fectin'
        me ;
But I t'ink de time is comin', an' I'd bet-
        tah mek a break,
    Fu' to set wid Mistah Possum in his tree.

W'en you hyeah de da'kies singin', an' de
        quahtahs all is gay,

'Tain't de time fu' birds lak me to be
    erroun';
W'en de hick'ry chips is flyin', an' de log's
    been ca'ied erway,
Den hit's dang'ous to be roostin' nigh de
    groun'.
Grin on, Isham! Sing on, da'kies! But
    I flop my wings an' go
Fu' de sheltah of de ve'y highest tree,
Fu' dey's too much close ertention—an'
    dey's too much fallin' snow —
    An' it's too nigh Chris'mus mo'nin' now
    fu' me.

THE VALSE

When to sweet music my lady is dancing
    My heart to mild frenzy her beauty
    inspires.
Into my face are her brown eyes a-glanc-
    ing,
    And swift my whole frame thrills with
    tremulous fires.
Dance, lady, dance, for the moments are
    fleeting,
    Pause not to place yon refractory curl;
Life is for love and the night is for sweet-
    ing;
    Dreamily, joyously, circle and whirl.

Oh, how those viols are throbbing and
    pleading;
    A prayer is scarce needed in sound of
    their strain.
Surely and lightly as round you are speed-
    ing,
    You turn to confusion my heart and my
    brain.
Dance, lady, dance to the viol's soft call-
    ing,
    Skip it and trip it as light as the air;
Dance, for the moments like rose leaves
    are falling,
    Strikes, now, the clock from its place on
    the stair.

Now sinks the melody lower and lower,
    The weary musicians scarce seeming to
    play.
Ah, love, your steps now are slower and
    slower,

The smile on your face is more sad and
    less gay.
Dance, lady, dance to the brink of our
    parting,
My heart and your step must not fail to
    be light.
Dance! Just a turn—tho' the tear-drop be
    starting.
    Ah—now it is done—so—my lady, good-
    night!

A PLANTATION PORTRAIT

Hain't you see my Mandy Lou,
    Is it true?
Whaih you been f'om day to day,
    Whaih, I say?
Dat you say you nevah seen
    Dis hyeah queen
Walkin' roun' f'om fiel' to street
    Smilin' sweet?

Slendah ez a saplin' tree;
    Seems to me
W'en de win' blow f'om de bay
    She jes' sway
Lak de reg'lar saplin' do
    Ef hit's grew
Straight an' graceful, 'dout a limb,
    Sweet an' slim.

Browner den de frush's wing,
    An' she sing
Lak he mek his wa'ble ring
    In de spring;
But she sholy beat de frush,
    Hyeah me, hush:
W'en she sing, huh teef kin show
    White ez snow.

Eyes ez big an' roun' an' bright
    Ez de light
Whut de moon gives in de prime
    Harvest time.
An' huh haih a woolly skein,
    Black an' plain.
Hol's you wid a natchul twis'
    Close to bliss.

Tendah han's dat mek yo' own
    Feel lak stone;

My Mandy Lou

Bring dat Basket, Nighah

Easy steppin', blessid feet,
    Small an' sweet.
Hain't you seen my Mandy Lou,
    Is it true?
Look at huh befo' she's gone,
    Den pass on!

THE VISITOR

Little lady at de do',
    W'y you stan' dey knockin'?
Nevah seen you ac' befo'
    In er way so shockin'.
        Don' you know de sin it is
        Fu' git my temper riz
        W'en I's got de rheumatiz
    An' my jints is lockin'?

No, ol' Miss ain't sont you down,
    Don' you tell no story;
I been seed you hangin' 'roun'
    Dis hyeah te'itory.
        You des come fu' me to tell
        You a tale, an' I ain'—well—
        Look hyeah, what is dat I smell?
    Steamin' victuals? Glory!

Come in, Missy, how you do?
    Come up by de fiah,
I was jokin', chile, wid you;
    Bring dat basket nighah.
        Huh uh, ain' dat lak ol' Miss,
        Sen'in' me a feas' lak dis?
        Rheumatiz cain't stop my bliss,
    Case I's feelin' spryah.

Chicken meat an' gravy, too,
    Hot an' still a-heatin';
Good ol' sweet pertater stew;
    Missy b'lieves in treatin'.
        Des set down, you blessed chile,
        Daddy got to t'ink a while,
        Den a story mek you smile
    W'en he git thoo eatin'.

FISHING

W'en I git up in de mo'nin' an' de clouds
    is big an' black,
Dey's a kin' o' wa'nin' shivah goes
    a-scootin' down my back;

Den I says to my ol' ooman ez I watches
    down de lane,
"Don't you so't o' reckon, Lizy, dat we
    gwine to have some rain?"

"Go on, man," my Lizy answah, "you
    cain't fool me, not a bit,
I don't see no rain a-comin', ef you's
    wishin' fu' it, quit;
Case de mo' you t'ink erbout it, an' de
    mo' you pràay an' wish,
W'y de rain stay 'way de longah, spechul
    ef you wants to fish."

But I see huh pat de skillet, an' I see huh
    cas' huh eye
Wid a kin' o' anxious motion to'ds de
    da'kness in de sky;
An' I knows whut she's a-t'inkin', dough
    she tries so ha'd to hide.
She's a-sayin', "Wouldn't catfish now tas'e
    monst'ous bully, fried?"

Den de clouds git black an' blackah, an'
    de thundah 'mence to roll,
An' de rain, it 'mence a-fallin'. Oh, I's
    happy, bless my soul!
Ez I look at dat ol' skillet, an' I 'magine I
    kin see
Jes' a slew o' new-ketched catfish sizzlin'
    daih fu' huh an' me.

'Tain't no use to go a-ploughin', fu' de
    groun' 'll be too wet,
So I puts out fu' de big house at a moughty
    pace, you bet,
An' ol' mastah say, "Well, Lishy, ef you
    t'ink hit's gwine to rain,
Go on fishin', hit's de weathah, an' I 'low
    we cain't complain."

Talk erbout a dahky walkin' wid his haid
    up in de aih!
Have to feel mine evah minute to be sho'
    I got it daih;
En' de win' is cuttin' capahs an' a-lashin'
    thoo de trees,
But de rain keeps on a-singin' blessed
    songs, lak "Tek yo' ease."

15

Wid my pole erpon my shouldah an' my
  wo'm can in my han',
I kin feel de fish a-waitin' w'en I strikes
  de rivah's san';
Nevah min', you ho'ny scoun'els, needn'
  swim erroun' an' grin,
I'll be grinnin' in a minute w'en I 'mence
  to haul you in.

W'en de fish begin to nibble, an' de co'k
  begin to jump,
I's erfeahed dat dey'll quit bitin', case dey
  hyeah my hea't go " thump,"
'Twell de co'k go way down undah, an' I
  raise a awful shout,
Ez a big ol' yallah belly comes a galli-
  vantin' out.

Needn't wriggle, Mistah Catfish, case I
  got you jes' de same,
You been eatin', I'll be eatin', an' we
  needah ain't to blame.
But you needn't feel so lonesome fu' I's
  th'owin' out to see
Ef dey ain't some of yo' comrades fu' to
  keep you company.

Spo't, dis fishin'! now you talkin', w'y dey
  ain't no kin' to beat;
I don' keer ef I is soakin', laigs, an' back,
  an' naik, an' feet,
It's de spo't I's lookin' aftah. Hit's de
  pleasure an' de fun,
Dough I knows dat Lizy's waitin' wid de
  skillet w'en I's done.

RESPONSE

When Phyllis sighs and from her eyes
The light dies out; my soul replies
With misery of deep-drawn breath,
E'en as it were at war with death.

When Phyllis smiles, her glance beguiles
My heart through love-lit woodland aisles,
And through the silence high and clear,
A wooing warbler's song I hear.

But if she frown, despair comes down,
I put me on my sack-cloth gown;
So frown not, Phyllis, lest I die,
But look on me with smile or sigh.

A LITTLE CHRISTMAS BASKET

No one can read this poem without ob-
serving that the author has little patience
with the " faith " that does not prove its
existence by " works."   He knew as well,
if not better, than any poet that ever lived•
the practical realization of Christmas with-
out money or fuel, or food, and he knew
also, for he was a regular attendant at
Sunday-school and church in boyhood
days, that too many professing Christians
are prone to tell the poor that the " Lord
will provide " and then close their purses
with an unpickable lock.

He does not fail in this remarkably fine
little jingle to give " 'ligion " its due mead
of respect, but it is very human, and very
natural for him to add —

" But I t'ink that 'ligion's sweeter w'en it kind o'
  mixes in
Wid a little Chrismus basket at de do'."

De win' is hollahin' " Daih you " to de
  shuttahs an' de fiah,
De snow's a-sayin' " Got you " to de
  groun',
Fu' de wintah weathah's come widout
  a-askin' ouah desiah,
An' he's laughin' in his sleeve at whut
  he foun';
Fu' dey ain't nobody eady wid dey fuel er
  dey food,
An' de money bag look timid lak, fu'
  sho',
So we want ouah Chrismus sermon, but
  we'd lak it ef you could
Leave a little Chrismus basket at de do'.

Wha's de use o' tellin' chillen 'bout a
  Santy er a Nick,
An' de sto'ies dat a body allus tol' ?
When de harf is gray wid ashes an' you
  hasn't got a stick
Fu' to warm dem when dey little toes is
  col' ?
Wha's de use o' preachin' 'ligion to a man
  dat's sta'ved to def,
An' a-tellin' him de Mastah will
  pu'vide ?

Ef you want to tech his feelin's, save yo'
    sermons an' yo' bref,
Tek a little Chrismus basket by yo'
    side.

'Tain't de time to open Bibles an' to lock
    yo' cellah do',
    'Tain't de time to talk o' bein' good to
    men;
Ef you want to preach a sermon ez you
    nevah preached befo',
    Preach dat sermon wid a shoat er wid
    er hen;
Bein' good is heap sight bettah den a-dal-
    lyin' wid sin,
    An' dey ain't nobody roun' dat knows it
    mo',
But I t'ink dat 'ligion's sweeter w'en it kind
    o' mixes in
    Wid a little Chrismus basket at de do'.

MY SWEET BROWN GAL

W'en de clouds is hangin' heavy in de
    sky,
An' de win's's a-taihin' moughty vig'rous
    by,
I don' go a-sighin' all erlong de way;
I des' wo'k a-waitin' fu' de close o' day.

Case I knows w'en evenin' draps huh
    shadders down,
I won' care a smidgeon fu' de weathah's
    frown;
Let de rain go splashin', let de thundah
    raih,
Dey's a happy sheltah, an' I's goin' daih.

Down in my ol' cabin wa'm ez mammy's
    toas',
'Taters in de fiah layin' daih to roas';
No one daih to cross me, got no talkin'
    pal,
But I's got de comp'ny o' my sweet brown
    gal.

So I spen's my evenin' listenin' to huh
    sing,
Lak a blessid angel; how huh voice do
    ring!
Sweetah den a bluebird flutterin' erroun',
W'en he sees de steamin' o' de new
    ploughed groun'.

Den I hugs huh closah, closah to my
    breas'.
Needn't sing, my da'lin', tek you' hones'
    res'.
Does I mean Malindy, Mandy, Lize er
    Sal?
No, I means my fiddle—dat's my sweet
    brown gal!

SPRING FEVER

Grass commence a-comin'
    Thoo de thawin' groun',
Evah bird dat whistles
    Keepin' noise erroun';
Cain't sleep in de mo'nin',
    Case befo' it's light
Bluebird an' de robin
    Done begun to fight.

Bluebird sass de robin,
    Robin sass him back,
Den de bluebird scol' him
    'Twell his face is black.
Would n' min' de quoilin'
    All de mo'nin' long,
'Cept it wakes me early,
    Case hit's done in song.

Anybody wo'kin'
    Wants to sleep ez late
Ez de folks 'll 'low him,
    An' I wish to state
(Co'se dis ain't to scattah,
    But 'twix' me an' you),
I could stan' de bedclothes,
    Kin' o' latah, too.

'Tain't my natchul feelin',
    Dis hyeah mopin' spell.
I stan's early risin'
    Mos'ly moughty well;
But de ve'y minute,
    I feel Ap'il's heat,
Bless yo' soul, de bedclothes
    Nevah seemed so sweet.

Mastah, he's a-scol'in',
    Case de han's is slow,
All de hosses balkin',
    Jes' cain't mek 'em go.

Don' know whut's de mattah,
Hit's a funny t'ing,
Less'n hit's de fevah
Dat you gits in spring.

TO A VIOLET FOUND ON ALL SAINTS' DAY

This poem found its inspiration in the actual finding of a late-blowing violet, found by the poet, under his library window at Washington. This was near the time when Mr. Dunbar's domestic tragedy occurred, and he said once in speaking of the incident:
" You know they say

" ' Flowers out of season,
Trouble without reason,'

and I really believe there is some truth in the rhyme. I found that one little solitary violet on All Saints' Day after all its sisters had long been dead, and "—with a deep sigh and a quick tear: " I never had much real happiness after that."

Belated wanderer of the ways of spring,
  Lost in the chill of grim November rain,
Would I could read the message that you bring
  And find in it the antidote for pain.

Does some sad spirit out beyond the day,
  Far looking to the hours forever dead,
Send you a tender offering to lay
  Upon the grave of us, the living dead?

Or does some brighter spirit, unforlorn,
  Send you, my little sister of the wood,
To say to some one on a cloudful morn,
  " Life lives through death, my brother, all is good " ?

With meditative hearts the others go
  The memory of their dead to dress anew.
But, sister mine, bide here that I may know,
  Life grows, through death, as beautiful as you.

THE COLORED BAND

W'en de colo'ed ban' comes ma'chin' down de street,
Don't you people stan' daih starin'; lif' yo' feet !
  Ain't dey playin' ? Hip, hooray !
  Stir yo' stumps an' cleah de way,
Fu' de music dat dey mekin' can't be beat.

Oh, de major man's a-swingin' of his stick,
An' de pickaninnies crowdin' roun' him thick ;
  In his go'geous uniform,
  He's de lightnin' of de sto'm,
An' de little clouds erroun' look mighty slick.

You kin hyeah a fine perfo'mance w'en de white ban's serenade,
An' dey play dey high-toned music mighty sweet,
But hit's Sousa played in rag-time, an' hit's Rastus on Parade,
  W'en de colo'ed ban' comes ma'chin' down de street.

W'en de colo'ed ban' comes ma'chin' down de street
You kin hyeah de ladies all erroun' repeat :
  " Ain't dey handsome ? Ain't dey gran' ?
  Ain't dey splendid ? Goodness, lan' !
W'y dey's pu'fect f'om dey fo'heads to dey feet ! "
An' sich steppin' to de music down de line,
'Tain't de music by itself dat meks it fine,
  Hit's de walkin', step by step,
  An' de keepin' time wid " Hep,"
Dat it mek a common ditty soun' divine.

Oh, de white ban' play hits music, an' hit's mighty good to hyeah,
An' it sometimes leaves a ticklin' in yo' feet ;
But de hea't goes into bus'ness fu' to he'p erlong de eah,
  W'en de colo'ed ban' goes ma'chin' down de street.

THE COLORED BAND

My 'Lias Went to Wah

WHEN DEY 'LISTED COLORED SOLDIERS

Dey was talkin' in de cabin, dey was
  talkin' in de hall ;
But I listened kin' o' keerless, not
  a-t'inkin' 'bout it all ;
An' on Sunday, too, I noticed, dey was
  whisp'rin' mighty much,
Stan'in' all erroun' de roadside w'en dey
  let us out o' chu'ch.
But I didn't t'ink erbout it 'twell de mid-
  dle of de week,
An' my 'Lias come to see me, an' somehow
  he couldn't speak.
Den I seed all in a minute whut he'd come
  to see me for ; —
Dey had 'listed colo'ed sojers, an' my 'Lias
  gwine to wah.

Oh, I hugged him, an' I kissed him, an' I
  baiged him not to go ;
But he tol' me dat his conscience, hit was
  callin' to him so,
An' he couldn't baih to lingah w'en he had
  a chanst to fight
For de freedom dey had gin him an' de
  glory of de right.
So he kissed me, an' he lef' me, w'en I'd
  p'omised to be true ;
An' dey put a knapsack on him, an' a coat
  all colo'ed blue.
So I gin him pap's ol' Bible f'om de bottom
  of de draw', —
W'en dey 'listed colo'ed sojers an' my
  'Lias went to wah.

But I t'ought of all de weary miles dat he
  would have to tramp,
An' I couldn't be contented w'en dey tuk
  him to de camp.
W'y my hea't nigh broke wid grievin'
  'twell I seed him on de street ;
Den I felt lak I could go an' th'ow my
  body at his feet.
For his buttons was a-shinin', an' his face
  was shinin', too,
An' he looked so strong an' mighty in his
  coat o' sojer blue,
Dat I hollahed, " Step up, manny," dough
  my th'oat was so' an' raw, —
W'en dey 'listed colo'ed sojers an' my 'Lias
  went to wah.·

Ol' Mis' cried w'en mastah lef' huh, young
  Miss mou'ned huh brothah Ned,
An' I didn't know dey feelin's is de ve'y
  wo'ds dey said
W'en I tol' 'em I was so'y. Dey had done
  gin up dey all ;
But dey only seemed mo' proudah dat dey
  men had hyeahd de call.
Bofe my mastahs went in gray suits, an' I
  loved de Yankee blue,
But I t'ought dat I could sorrer for de losin'
  of 'em too ;
But I couldn't, for I didn't know de ha'f
  o' whut I saw,
'Twell dey 'listed colo'ed sojers an' my
  'Lias went to wah.

Mastah Jack come home all sickly ; he was
  broke for life, dey said ;
An' dey let' my po' young mastah some'r's
  on de roadside, — dead.
W'en de women cried an' mou'ned 'em, I
  could feel it thoo an' thoo,
For I had a loved un fightin' in de way o'
  dangah, too.
Den dey tol' me dey had laid him some'r's
  way down souf to res',
Wid de flag dat he had fit for shinin' daih
  acrost his breas'.
Well, I cried, but den I reckon dat's whut
  Gawd had called him for,
W'en dey 'listed colo'ed sojers an' my 'Lias
  went to wah.

INSPIRATION

At the golden gate of song
Stood I, knocking all day long,
But the Angel, calm and cold,
Still refused and bade me, " Hold."

Then a breath of soft perfume,
Then a light within the gloom ;
Thou, Love, camest to my side,
And the gates flew open wide.

Long I dwelt in this domain,
Knew no sorrow, grief, or pain ;
Now you bid me forth and free,
Will you shut these gates on me ?

SONG

Wintah, summah, snow er shine,
　Hit's all de same to me,
Ef only I kin call you mine,
　An' keep you by my knee.

Ha'dship, frolic, grief er caih,
　Content by night an' day,
Ef only I kin see you whaih
　You wait beside de way.

Livin', dyin', smiles er teahs,
　My soul will still be free,
Ef only thoo de comin' yeahs
　You walk de worl' wid me.

Bird-song, breeze-wail, chune er moan
　What puny t'ings dey'll be,
Ef w'en I's seemin' all erlone,
　I knows yo' hea't's wid me.

MY LADY OF CASTLE GRAND

Gray is the palace where she dwells,
　Grimly the poplars stand
There by the window where she sits,
　My Lady of Castle Grand.

There does she bide the livelong day,
　Grim as the poplars are,
Ever her gaze goes reaching out,
　Steady, but vague and far.

Bright burn the fires in the castle hall,
　Brightly the fire-dogs stand;
But cold is the body and cold the heart
　Of my Lady of Castle Grand.

Blue are the veins in her lily-white hands,
　Blue are the veins in her brow;
Thin is the line of her blue drawn lips,
　Who would be haughty now?

Pale is the face at the window-pane,
　Pale as the pearl on her breast,
" Roderick, love, wilt come again?
　Fares he to east or west? "

The shepherd pipes to the shepherdess,
　The bird to his mate in the tree,
And ever she sighs as she hears their song,
　" Nobody sings for me."

The scullery maids have swains enow
　Who lead them the way of love,
But lonely and loveless their mistress sits
　At her window up above.

Loveless and lonely she waits and waits,
　The saddest in all the land;
Ah, cruel and lasting is love-blind pride,
　My Lady of Castle Grand.

DRIZZLE

Hit's been drizzlin' an' been sprinklin',
　Kin' o' techy all day long.
I ain't wet enough fu' toddy,
　I's too damp to raise a song,
An' de case have set me t'inkin',
　Dat dey's folk des lak de rain,
Dat goes drizzlin' w'en dey's talkin',
　An' won't speak out flat an' plain.

Ain't you nevah set an' listened
　At a body 'splain his min'?
W'en de t'oughts dey keep on drappin'
　Wasn't big enough to fin'?
Dem's whut I call drizzlin' people,
　Othahs call 'em mealy mouf,
But de fust name hits me bettah,
　Case dey nevah tech a drouf.

Dey kin talk from hyeah to yandah,
　An' f'om yandah hyeah ergain,
An' dey don' mek no mo' 'pression,
　Den dis powd'ry kin' o' rain.
En yo' min' is dry ez cindahs,
　Er a piece o' kindlin' wood,
'Tain't no use a-talkin' to 'em,
　Fu' dey drizzle ain't no good.

Gimme folks dat speak out nachul,
　Whut'll say des whut dey mean,
Whut don't set dey wo'ds so skimpy
　Dat you got to guess between.
I want talk des' lak de showahs
　Whut kin wash de dust erway,
Not dat sprinklin' convusation,
　Dat des drizzle all de day.

DE CRITTERS' DANCE

Ain't nobody nevah tol' you not a wo'd
   a-tall,
'Bout de time dat all de critters gin dey
   fancy ball ?
Some folks tell it in a sto'y, some folks
   sing de rhyme,
'Peahs to me you ought to hyeahed it, case
   hit's ol' ez time.

Well, de critters all was p'osp'ous, now
   would be de chance
Fu' to tease ol' Pa'son Hedgehog, givin' of
   a dance ;
Case, you know, de critter's preachah was
   de stric'est kin',
An' he nevah made no 'lowance fu' de
   frisky min'.

So dey sont dey inbitations, Raccoon writ
   'em all,
" Dis hyeah note is to inbite you to de
   Fancy Ball ;
Come erlong an' bring yo' ladies, bring yo'
   chillun too,
Put on all yo' bibs an' tuckahs, show whut
   you kin do."

W'en de night come, dey all gathahed in a
   place dey knowed,
Fu' enough erway f'om people, nigh
   enough de road,
All de critters had ersponded, Hop-Toad
   up to Baih,
An' I's hyeah to tell you, Pa'son Hedge-
   hog too, was daih.

Well, dey talked an' made dey 'bejunce,
   des lak critters do,
An' dey walked an' p'omenaded 'roun' an'
   thoo an' thoo ;
Jealous ol' Mis' Fox, she whispah, " See
   Mis' Wildcat daih,
Ain't hit scan'lous, huh a-comin' wid huh
   shouldahs baih ? "

Ol' man Tu'tle wasn't honin' fu' no dancin'
   tricks,
So he stayed by ol' Mis' Tu'tle, talkin'
   politics ;

Den de ban' hit 'mence a-playin' critters
   all to place,
Fou' ercross, an' fou' stan' sideways, smilin'
   face to face.

'Fessah Frog, he play de co'net, Cricket
   play de fife,
Slews o' Grasshoppahs a-fiddlin' lak to
   save dey life ;
Mistah Crow, he call de figgers, settin' in
   a tree,
Huh, uh ! how dose critters sasshayed was
   a sight to see.

Mistah Possom swing Mis' Rabbit up an'
   down de flo',
Ol' man Baih, he ain't so nimble, an' it
   mek him blow ;
Raccoon dancin' wid Mis' Squ'il squeeze
   huh little han',
She say, " Oh, now ain't you awful, quit it,
   goodness lan' ! "

Pa'son Hedgehog groanin' awful at his
   converts' shines,
'Dough he peepin' thoo his fingahs at dem
   movin' lines,
'Twell he cain't set still no longah w'en de
   fiddles sing,
Up he jump, an' bless you, honey, cut de
   pigeon-wing.

Well, de critters lak to fainted jes' wid dey
   su'prise,
Sistah Fox, she vowed she wasn't gwine
   to b'lieve huh eyes ;
But dey couldn't be no 'sputin' 'bout it
   any mo':
Pa'son Hedgehog was a-cape'in' all erroun'
   de flo'.

Den dey all jes' capahed scan'lous case
   dey didn't doubt,
Dat dey still could go to meetin' ; who
   could tu'n 'em out ?
So wid dancin' an' uligion, dey was in de
   fol',
Fu' a-dancin' wid de Pa'son couldn't hu't
   de soul.

LINCOLN

Hurt was the nation with a mighty wound,
And all her ways were filled with clam'-
    rous sound.
Wailed loud the South with unremitting
    grief,
And wept the North that could not find
    relief.
Then madness joined its harshest tone to
    strife :
A minor note swelled in the song of life.
Till, stirring with the love that filled his
    breast,
But still, unflinching at the right's behest,
Grave Lincoln came, strong handed, from
    afar,
The mighty Homer of the lyre of war.
'Twas he who bade the raging tempest
    cease,
Wrenched from his harp the harmony of
    peace,
Muted the strings that made the discord,—
    Wrong,
And gave his spirit up in thund'rous song.
Oh, mighty Master of the mighty lyre,
Earth heard and trembled at thy strains of
    fire :
Earth learned of thee what Heav'n already
    knew,
And wrote thee down among her treasured
    few.

ENCOURAGEMENT

Who dat knockin' at de do' ?
Why, Ike Johnson,—yes, fu' sho' !
Come in, Ike.   I's mighty glad
You come down.   I t'ought you's mad
At me 'bout de othah night,
An' was stayin' 'way fu' spite.
Say, now, was you mad fu' true
W'en I kin' o' laughed at you ?
    Speak up, Ike an' 'spress yo'se'f.

'Tain't no use a-lookin' sad,
An' a-mekin' out you's mad ;
Ef you's gwine to be so glum,
Wondah why you evah come.
I don't lak nobidy 'roun'
Dat jes' shet dey mouf an' frown,—
Oh, now, man, don't act a dunce !

Cain't you talk ?   I tol' you once,
    Speak up, Ike, an' 'spress yo'se'f.

Wha'd you come hyeah fu' to-night?
Body'd t'ink yo' haid ain't right.
I's done all dat I kin do,—
Dressed perticler, jes' fu' you ;
Reckon I'd 'a' bettah wo'
My ol' ragged calico.
Aftah all de pains I's took,
Cain't you tell me how I look ?
    Speak up, Ike, an' 'spress yo'se'f.

Bless my soul !   I 'mos' fu'got
Tellin' you 'bout Tildy Scott.
Don't you know, come Thu'sday night,
She gwine ma'y Lucius White ?
Miss Lize say I allus wuh
Heap sight laklier 'n huh ;
An' she'll git me somep'n new,
Ef I wants to ma'y too.
    Speak up, Ike, an' 'spress yo'se'f.

I could ma'y in a week,
Ef de man I wants 'ud speak.
Tildy's presents 'll be fine,
But dey wouldn't ekal mine.
Him whut gits me fu' a wife
'Ll be proud, you bet yo' life.
I's had offers ; some ain't quit ;
But I hasn't ma'ied yit !
    Speak up, Ike, an' 'spress yo'se'f.

Ike, I loves you,—yes, I does ;
You's my choice, and allus was.
Laffin' at you ain't no harm.—
Go 'way, dahky, whah's yo' arm ?
Hug me closer—dah, dat's right !
Wasn't you a awful sight,
Havin' me to baig you so ?
Now ax whut you want to know,—
    Speak up, Ike, an' 'spress yo'se'f!

THE BOOGAH MAN

W'en de evenin' shadders
    Come a-glidin' down,
Fallin' black an' heavy
    Ovah hill an' town,
Ef you listen keerful,
    Keerful ez you kin,

So's you boun' to notice
　Des a drappin' pin ;
Den you'll hyeah a funny
　Soun' ercross de lan' ;
Lay low ; dat's de callin'
　Of de Boogah Man !

Woo-oo, woo-oo !
　Hyeah him ez he go erlong de way ;
Woo-oo, woo-oo !
　Don' you wish de night 'ud tu'n to day ?
Woo-oo, woo-oo !
　Hide yo' little peepers 'hind yo' han' ;
Woo-oo, woo-oo !
　Callin' of de Boogah Man.

W'en de win's a-shiverin'
　Thoo de gloomy lane,
An' dey comes de patterin'
　Of de evenin' rain,
W'en de owl's a-hootin',
　Out daih in de wood,
Don' you wish, my honey,
　Dat you had been good ?
'Tain't no use to try to
　Snuggle up to Dan ;
Bless you, dat's de callin'
　Of de Boogah Man !

Ef you loves yo' mammy,
　An' you min's yo' pap,
Ef you nevah wriggles
　Outen Sukey's lap ;
Ef you says yo' " Lay me "
　Evah single night
'Fo' dey tucks de kivers
　An' puts out de light,
Den de rain kin pattah,
　Win' blow lak a fan,
But you need n' bothah
　'Bout de Boogah Man !

THE WRAITH

Ah me, it is cold and chill,
　And the fire sobs low in the grate,
While the wind rides by on the hill,
　And the logs crack sharp with hate.

And she, she is cold and sad
　As ever the sinful are,
But deep in my heart I am glad
　For my wound and the coming scar

Oh, ever the wind rides by
　And ever the rain-drops grieve ;
But a voice like a woman's sigh
　Says, " Do you believe, believe ? "

Ah, you were warm and sweet,
　Sweet as the May days be ;
Down did I fall at your feet,
　Why did you hearken to me ?

Oh, the logs they crack and whine,
　And the water drops from the eaves ;
But it is not rain but brine
　Where my dead darling grieves.

And a wraith sits by my side,
　A spectre grim and dark ;
Are you gazing here open-eyed
　Out to the lifeless dark ?

But ever the wind rides on,
　And we sit close within ;
Out of the face of the dawn,
　I and my darling,—sin.

SILENCE

This stanza was written on the same day as his " The Poet," and doubtless voices a feeling upon the part of the author that perhaps after all as Riley once wrote " The silent song is best, and the unsung worthiest ! "

In its more intimate application every reader will be led to think of some friend who does not misconstrue a silent mood, and who understands that there are times when the silence, lying between two human souls " is full of the deepest speech."

'Tis better to sit here beside the sea,
　Here on the spray-kissed beach,
In silence, that between such friends as we
　Is full of deepest speech.

WHIP-POOR-WILL AND KATY-DID

Slow de night's a-fallin',
An' I hyeah de callin'
    Out erpon de lonesome hill;
Soun' is moughty dreary,
Solemn-lak an' skeery,
    Sayin' fu' to " whip po' Will."
Now hit's moughty tryin',
Fu' to hyeah dis cryin',
    'Deed hit's mo' den I kin stan';
Sho' wid all our slippin',
Dey's enough of whippin'
    'Dout a bird a'visin' any man.

In de moons o' summah
Dey's anothah hummah
    Sings anothah song instid;
An' his th'oat's a-swellin'
Wid de joy o' tellin',
    But he says dat " Katy did."
Now I feels onsuhtain;
Won't you raise de cu'tain
    Ovah all de ti'ngs dat's hid?
W'y dat feathahed p'isen
Goes erbout a'visin'
    Whippin' Will w'en Katy did?

TO A CAPTIOUS CRITIC

Dear critic, who my lightness so deplores,
Would I might study to be prince of bores,
Right wisely would I rule that dull es-
    tate —
But, sir, I may not, till you abdicate.

'LONG TO'DS NIGHT

Daih's a moughty soothin' feelin'
    Hits a dahky man,
        'Long to'ds night.
W'en de row is mos' nigh ended,
    Den he stops to fan,
        'Long to'ds night.
De blue smoke f'om his cabin is a-callin'
    to him, " Come; "

He smell de bacon cookin', an' he hyeah
    de fiah hum;
An' he 'mence to sing, 'dough wo'kin'
    putty nigh done made him dumb,
        'Long to'ds night.

Wid his hoe erpon his shouldah
    Den he goes erlong,
        'Long to'ds night.
An' he keepin' time a-steppin'
    Wid a little song,
        'Long to'ds night.
De restin'-time's a-comin', an' de time to
    drink an' eat;
A baby's toddlin' to'ds him on hits little
    dusty feet,
An' a-goin' to'ds his cabin, an' his suppah's
    moughty sweet,
        'Long to'ds night.

Daih his Ca'line min' de kettle,
    Rufus min' de chile,
        'Long to'ds night;
An' de sweat roll down his forred,
    Mixin' wid his smile,
        'Long to'ds night.
He toss his piccaninny, an' he hum a little
    chune;
De wo'kin' all is ovah, an' de suppah
    comin' soon;
De wo'kin' time's Decembah, but de
    restin' time is June,
        'Long to'ds night.

Dey's a kin' o' doleful feelin',
    Hits a tendah place,
        'Long to'ds night;
Dey's a moughty glory in him
    Shinin' thoo his face,
        'Long to'ds night.
De cabin's lak de big house, an' de fiah's
    lak de sun;
His wife look moughty lakly, an' de chile
    de puttiest one;
W'y, hit's blessid, jes' a-livin' w'en a body's
    wo'k is done.
        'Long to'ds night.

HE TOSS HIS PICCANINNY

SHE DE ONLY HOSS FU' ME

DAT OL' MARE O' MINE

In 1899, when the poet was compelled to leave Washington, where his duties as librarian had been too hard for him, he and his wife and mother went to Denver. Here they lived in a cottage near the city, and Mr. Dunbar took long rides for his health. For this purpose he purchased a gray mare, and soon learned to love the animal devotedly. Desiring to pay a tribute to his faithful dumb friend he wrote the poem. He wrote to a friend about this time, that he sold this poem for a sum equal to half the price he had paid for the mare!

Want to trade me, do you, mistah? Oh, well, now, I reckon not,
W'y you couldn't buy my Sukey fu' a thousan' on de spot.
    Dat ol' mare o' mine?
Yes, huh coat ah long an' shaggy, an' she ain't no shakes to see;
Dat's a ring-bone, yes, you right, suh, an' she got a on'ry knee,
But dey ain't no use in talkin', she de only hoss fu' me,
    Dat ol' mare o' mine.

Co'se, I knows dat Suke's contra'y, an' she moughty ap' to vex;
But you got to mek erlowance fu' de nature of huh sex;
    Dat ol' mare o' mine.
Ef you pull her on de lef' han'; she plum 'termined to go right,
A 'cannon couldn't skeer huh, but she boun' to tek a fright
At a piece o' common paper, or anyt'ing whut's white,
    Dat ol' mare o' mine.

W'en my eyes commence to fail me, dough, I trus'es to huh sight,
An' she'll tote me safe an' hones' on de ve'y da'kes' night,
    Dat ol' mare o' mine.
Ef I whup huh, she jes' switch huh tail, an' settle to a walk,
Ef I whup huh mo', she shek huh haid, an' lak ez not, she balk.

But huh sense ain't no ways lackin', she do evaht'ing but talk,
    Dat ol' mare o' mine.

But she gentle ez a lady w'en she know huh beau kin see,
An' she sholy got mo' gumption any day den you or me,
    Dat ol' mare o' mine.
She's a leetle slow a-goin', an' she moughty ha'd to sta't,
But we's gittin' ol' togathah, an' she's closah to my hea't,
An' I doesn't reckon, mistah, dat she'd sca'cely keer to pa't;
    Dat ol' mare o' mine.

W'y I knows de time dat cidah's kin' o' muddled up my haid,
Ef it hadn't been fu' Sukey hyeah, I reckon I'd been daid;
    Dat ol' mare o' mine.
But she got me in de middle o' de road an' tuk me home,
An' she wouldn't let me wandah, ner she wouldn't let me roam,
Dat's de kin' o' hoss to tie to w'en you's seed de cidah's foam,
    Dat ol' mare o' mine.

You kin talk erbout yo' heaven, you kin talk erbout yo' hell,
Dey is people, dey is hosses, den dey's cattle, den dey's—well—
    Dat ol' mare o' mine;
She de beatenes' t'ing dat evah struck de medders o' de town,
An' aldough huh haid ain't fittin' fu' to waih no golden crown,
D' ain't a blessed way fu' Petah fu' to tu'n my Sukey down,
    Dat ol' mare o' mine.

A GRIEVANCE

W'en de snow's a-fallin'
  An' de win' is col'.
Mammy 'mence a-callin',
  Den she 'mence to scol',
"Lucius Lishy Brackett,
  Don't you go out do's,

Button up yo' jacket,
  Les'n you'll git froze."

I sit at de windah
  Lookin' at de groun',
Nuffin nigh to hindah,
  Mammy ain' erroun';
Wish't she wouldn' mek me
  Set down in dis chaih;
Pshaw, it wouldn't tek me
  Long to git some aih.

So I jump down nimble
  Ez a boy kin be,
Dough I's all a-trimble
  Feahed some one'll see;
Bet in a half a minute
  I fly out de do'
An' I's knee-deep in it,
  Dat dah blessed snow.

Den I hyeah a pattah
  Come acrost de flo'.
Den dey comes a clattah
  At de cabin do';
An' my mammy holler
  Spoilin' all my joy,
" Come in f'om dat waller,
  Don't I see you, boy?"

W'en de snow's a-sievin'
  Down ez sof' ez meal,
Whut's de use o' livin'
  'Cept you got de feel
Of de stuff dat's fallin'
  'Roun' an' white an' damp,
'Dout some one a-callin',
  " Come in hyeah, you scamp!"

DINAH KNEADING DOUGH

I have seen full many a sight
Born of day or drawn by night:
Sunlight on a silver stream,
Golden lilies all a-dream,
Lofty mountains, bold and proud,
Veiled beneath the lacelike cloud;
But no lovely sight I know
Equals Dinah kneading dough.

Brown arms buried elbow-deep
Their domestic rhythm keep,
As with steady sweep they go
Through the gently yielding dough.
Maids may vaunt their finer charms —
Naught to me like Dinah's arms;
Girls may draw, or paint, or sew —
I love Dinah kneading dough.

Eyes of jet and teeth of pearl,
Hair, some say, too tight a-curl;
But the dainty maid I deem
Very near perfection's dream.
Swift she works, and only flings
Me a glance—the least of things.
And I wonder, does she know
That my heart is in the dough?

IN THE MORNING

'Lias! 'Lias! Bless de Lawd!
Don' you know de day's erbroad?
Ef you don' git up, you scamp,
Dey'll be trouble in dis camp.
T'ink I gwine to let you sleep
W'ile I meks yo' boa'd an' keep?
Dat's a putty howdy-do —
Don' you hyeah me, 'Lias—you?

Bet ef I come crost dis flo'
You won' fin' no time to sno'.
Daylight all a-shinin' in
W'ile you sleep—w'y hit's a sin!
Ain't de can'le-light enough
To bu'n out widout a snuff,
But you go de mo'nin' thoo
Bu'nin' up de daylight too?

'Lias, don' you hyeah me call?
No use tu'nin' to'ds de wall;
I kin hyeah dat mattuss squeak;
Don' you hyeah me w'en I speak?
Dis hyeah clock done struck off six —
Ca'line, bring me dem ah sticks!
Oh, you down, suh; huh! you down —
Look hyeah, don' you daih to frown.

Ma'ch yo'se'f an' wash yo' face,
Don' you splattah all de place:
I got somep'n else to do,
'Sides jes' cleanin' aftah you.

Tek dat comb an' fix yo' haid —
Looks jes' lak a feddah baid.
Look hyeah, boy, I let you see
You sha'n't roll yo' eyes at me.

Come hyeah ; bring me dat ah strap !
Boy, I'll whup you 'twell you drap ;
You done felt yo'se'f too strong,
An' you sholy got me wrong.
Set down at dat table thaih ;
Jes' you whimpah ef you daih !
Evah mo'nin' on dis place,
Seem lak I mus' lose my grace.

Fol' yo' han's an' bow yo' haid —
Wait ontwell de blessin' 's said ;
" Lawd, have mussy on ouah souls —"
(Don' you daih to tech dem rolls —)
" Bless de food we gwine to eat —"
(You set still—I *see* yo' feet ;
You jes' try dat trick agin !)
" Gin us peace an' joy. Amen ! "

THE POET

These eight lines tell the story of Paul
Dunbar's greatest disappointment in con-
nection with his literary achievements.
He grew tired of writing jingles, in a
broken tongue, but the heedless world
wanted none of the almost fathomless
language poems, which reflected the real
soul of the poet. As the sheen of tinsel
pleases the eye of the ragged crowd who
seldom see pure gold, so the jingles, the
swing, and the laughter so apparent in
Dunbar's dialect satisfied the majority of
readers—the pure gold was left for the
thinking few.

He sang of life, serenely sweet,
  With, now and then, a deeper note.
From some high peak, nigh yet remote,
He voiced the world's absorbing beat.

He sang of love when earth was young,
  And Love, itself, was in his lays.
But ah, the world, it turned to praise
A jingle in a broken tongue.

A FLORIDA NIGHT

Win' a-blowin' gentle so de san' lay low,
  San' a little heavy f'om de rain,
All de pa'ms a-wavin' an' a-weavin' slow,
  Sighin' lak a sinnah-soul in pain.
Alligator grinnin' by de ol' lagoon,
Mockin'-bird a-singin' to de big full moon,
'Skeeter go a-skimmin' to his fightin'
    chune
  (Lizy Ann's a-waitin' in de lane !).

Moccasin a-sleepin' in de cyprus swamp ;
  Needn't wake de gent'man, not fu' me.
Mule, you needn't wake him w'en you
    switch an' stomp,
  Fightin' off a 'skeeter er a flea.
Florida is lovely, she's de fines' lan'
Evah seed de sunlight f'om de Mastah's
    han',
'Ceptin' fu' de varmints an' huh fleas an'
    san'
  An' de nights w'en Lizy Ann ain' free.

Moon's a-kinder shaddered on de melon
    patch ;
  No one ain't a-watchin' ez I go.
Climbin' of de fence so's not to click de
    latch
  Meks my gittin' in a little slow.
Watermelon smilin' as it say, " I's free ; "
Alligator boomin', but I let him be,
Florida, oh, Florida's de lan' fu' me —
  (Lizy Ann a-singin' sweet an' low).

DIFFERENCES

My neighbor lives on the hill,
  And I in the valley dwell,
My neighbor must look down on me,
  Must I look up ?—ah, well,
My neighbor lives on the hill,
  And I in the valley dwell.

My neighbor reads, and prays,
  And I—I laugh, God wot,
And sings like a bird when the grass is
    green
  In my small garden plot ;
But ah, he reads and prays,
  And I—I laugh, God wot.

His face is a book of woe,
  And mine is a song of glee;
A slave he is to the great " They say,"
  But I—I am bold and free;
No wonder he smacks of woe,
  And I have the tang of glee.

My neighbor thinks me a fool,
  " The same to yourself," say I;
" Why take your books and take your
    prayers,
  Give me the open sky; "
My neighbor thinks me a fool,
  " The same to yourself," say I.

LONG AGO

De ol' time's gone, de new time's hyeah
  Wid all hits fuss an' feddahs;
I done fu'got de joy an' cheah
  We knowed all kin's o' weddahs,
I done fu'got each ol'-time hymn
  We ust to sing in meetin';
I's leahned de prah's, so neat an' trim,
  De preachah keeps us 'peatin'.

  Hang a vine by de chimney side,
    An' one by de cabin do';
  An' sing a song fu' de day dat died,
    De day of long ergo.

My youf, hit's gone, yes, long ergo,
  An' yit I ain't a-moanin';
Hit's fu' somet'ings I ust to know
  I set to-night a-honin'.
De pallet on de ol' plank flo',
  De rain bar'l und' de eaves,
De live oak 'fo' de cabin do',
  Whaih de night dove comes an' grieves.

  Hang a vine by de chimney side,
    An' one by de cabin do';
  An' sing a song fu' de day dat died,
    De day of long ergo.

I'd lak a few ol' frien's to-night
  To come an' set wid me;
An' let me feel dat ol' delight
  I ust to in dey glee.
But hyeah we is, my pipe an' me,
  Wid no one else erbout;

We bote is choked ez choked kin be,
  An' bofe'll soon go out.

  Hang a vine by de chimney side,
    An' one by de cabin do';
  An' sing a song fu' de day dat died,
    De day of long ergo.

A PLANTATION MELODY

De trees is bendin' in de sto'm,
De rain done hid de mountain's fo'm,
  I's 'lone an' in distress.
But listen, dah's a voice I hyeah,
A-sayin' to me, loud an' cleah,
  " Lay low in de wildaness."

De lightnin' flash, de bough sway low,
My po' sick hea't is trimblin' so,
  It hu'ts my very breas'.
But him dat give de lightnin' powah
Jes' bids me in de tryin' howah
  " Lay low in de wildaness."

O brothah, w'en de tempes' beat,
An' w'en yo' weary head an' feet
  Can't fin' no place to res',
Jes' membah dat de Mastah's nigh,
An' putty soon you'll hyeah de cry,
  " Lay low in de wildaness."

O sistah, w'en de rain come down,
An' all yo' hopes is 'bout to drown,
  Don't trus' de Mastah less.
He smilin' w'en you t'ink he frown,
He ain' gwine let yo' soul sink down —
  Lay low in de wildaness.

A SPIRITUAL

De 'cession's stahted on de gospel way,
  De Capting is a-drawin' nigh:
Bettah stop a-foolin' an' a-try to pray;
  Lif' up yo' haid w'en de King go by!

Oh, sinnah mou'nin' in de dusty road,
  Hyeah's de minute fu' to dry yo' eye:
Dey's a moughty One a-comin' fu' to baih
    yo' load;
  Lif' up yo' haid w'en de King go by!

Oh, widder weepin' by yo' husban's
          grave,
    Hit's bettah fu' to sing den sigh:
Hyeah come de Mastah wid de powah to
          save;
    Lif' up yo' haid w'en de King go by!

Oh, orphans a-weepin' lak de widder do,
    An' I wish you'd tell me why:
De Mastah is a mammy an' a pappy too;
    Lif' up yo' haid w'en de King go by!

Oh, Moses sot de sarpint in de wildahness
    W'en de chillun had commenced to
          die:
Some 'efused to look, but hit cuohed de
          res';
    Lif' up yo' haid w'en de King go by!

Bow down, bow 'way down,
          Bow down,
But lif' up yo haid w'en de King go by!

THE MEMORY OF MARTHA

Out in de night a sad bird moans,
    An', oh, but hit's moughty lonely;
Times I kin sing, but mos' I groans,
    Fu' oh, but hit's moughty lonely!
Is you sleepin' well dis evenin', Marfy,
          deah?
W'en I calls you f'om de cabin, kin you
          hyeah?
    'Tain't de same ol' place to me,
    Nuffin' 's lak hit used to be,
W'en I knowed dat you was allus some'ers
          near.

Down by de road de shadders grows,
    An', oh, but hit's moughty lonely;
Seem lak de ve'y moonlight knows,
    An', oh, but hit's moughty lonely!
Does you know, I's cryin' fu' you, oh, my
          wife?
Does you know dey ain't no joy no mo' in
          life?
    An' my only t'ought is dis,
    Dat I's honin' fu' de bliss
Fu' to quit dis groun' o' worriment an'
          strife.

Dah on de baid my banjo lays,
    An', oh, but hit's moughty lonely;
Can't even sta't a chune o' praise,
    An', oh, but hit's moughty lonely!
Oh, hit's moughty slow a waitin' hyeah
          below.
Is you watchin' fu' me, Marfy, at de do'?
    Ef you is, in spite o' sin,
    Dey'll be sho' to let me in,
W'en dey sees yo' face a-shinin', den dey'll
          know.

W'EN I GITS HOME

It's moughty tiahsome layin' 'roun'
Dis sorrer-laden earfly groun',
An' oftentimes I thinks, thinks I,
'Twould be a sweet t'ing des to die,
    An' go 'long home.

Home whaih de frien's I loved'll say,
"We've waited fu' you many a day,
Come hyeah an' res' yo'se'f, an' know
You's done wid sorrer an' wid woe,
    Now you's at home."

W'en I gits home some blessid day,
I 'lows to th'ow my caihs erway,
An' up an' down de shinin' street,
Go singin' sof' an' low an' sweet,
    W'en I gits home.

I wish de day was neah at han',
I's tiahed of dis grievin' lan',
I's tiahed of de lonely yeahs,
I want to des dry up my teahs,
    An' go 'long home.

Oh, Mastah, won't you sen' de call?
My frien's is daih, my hope, my all.
I's waitin' whaih de road is rough,
I want to hyeah you say, " Enough,
    Ol' man, come home!"

"HOWDY, HONEY, HOWDY!"

Do' a-stan'in' on a jar, fiah a-shinin' thoo
Ol' folks drowsin' 'roun' de place, wide
          awake is Lou,
W'en I tap, she answeh, an' I see huh
          'mence to grin,

" Howdy, honey, howdy, won't you step
    right in ? "

Den I step erpon de log layin' at de do',
Bless de Lawd, huh mammy an' huh pap's
    done 'menced to sno',
Now's de time, ef evah, ef I's gwine to
    try an' win,
" Howdy, honey, howdy, won't you step
    right in ? "

No use playin' on de aidge, trimblin' on de
    brink,
W'en a body love a gal, tell huh whut he
    t'ink ;
W'en huh hea't is open fu' de love you
    gwine to gin,
Pull yo'se'f togethah, suh, an' step right
    in.

Sweetes' imbitation dat a body evah
    hyeahed,
Sweetah den de music of a love-sick
    mockin'-bird,
Comin' f'om de gal you loves bettah den
    yo' kin,
" Howdy, honey, howdy, won't you step
    right in ? "

At de gate o' heaven w'en de storm o' life
    is pas',
'Spec' I'll be a-stan'in', 'twell de Mastah
    say at las',
" Hyeah he stan' all weary, but he winned
    his fight wid sin.
Howdy, honey, howdy, won't you step
    right in ? "

THE UNSUNG HEROES

A song for the unsung heroes who rose in
    the country's need,
When the life of the land was threatened
    by the slaver's cruel greed,
For the men who came from the corn-field,
    who came from the plough and the
    flail,
Who rallied round when they heard the
    sound of the mighty man of the rail.

They laid them down in the valleys, they
    laid them down in the wood,
And the world looked on at the work they
    did, and whispered, " It is good."
They fought their way on the hillside, they
    fought their way in the glen,
And God looked down on their sinews
    brown, and said, " I have made them
    men."

They went to the blue lines gladly, and
    the blue lines took them in,
And the men who saw their muskets' fire
    thought not of their dusky skin.
The gray lines rose and melted beneath
    their scathing showers,
And they said, " 'Tis true, they have force
    to do, these old slave boys of ours."

Ah, Wagner saw their glory, and Pillow
    knew their blood,
That poured on a nation's altar, a sacrifi-
    cial flood.
Port Hudson heard their war-cry that
    smote its smoke-filled air,
And the old free fires of their savage sires
    again were kindled there.

They laid them down where the rivers the
    greening valleys gem,
And the song of the thund'rous cannon
    was their sole requiem,
And the great smoke wreath that mingled
    its hue with the dusky cloud,
Was the flag that furled o'er a saddened
    world, and the sheet that made their
    shroud.

Oh, Mighty God of the Battles who held
    them in thy hand,
Who gave them strength through the
    whole day's length, to fight for their
    native land,
They are lying dead on the hillsides, they
    are lying dead on the plain,
And we have not fire to smite the lyre and
    sing them one brief strain.

Give, thou, some seer the power to sing
    them in their might,
The men who feared the master's whip,
    but did not fear the fight ;

That he may tell of their virtues as min-
    strels did of old,
Till the pride of face and the hate of race
    grow obsolete and cold.

A song for the unsung heroes who stood
    the awful test,
When the humblest host that the land
    could boast went forth to meet the
    best;
A song for the unsung heroes who fell on
    the bloody sod,
Who fought their way from night to day
    and struggled up to God.

THE POOL.

By the pool that I see in my dreams, dear
    love,
I have sat with you time and again;
And listened beneath the dank leaves,
    dear love,
To the sibilant sound of the rain.

And the pool, it is silvery bright, dear
    love,
And as pure as the heart of a maid,
As sparkling and dimpling, it darkles and
    shines
In the depths of the heart of the glade.

But, oh, I've a wish in my soul, dear love,
    (The wish of a dreamer, it seems),
That I might wash free of my sins, dear
    love,
In the pool that I see in my dreams.

POSSESSION

Whose little lady is you, chile,
    Whose little gal is you?
What's de use o' kiver'n up yo' face?
Chile, dat ain't de way to do.
Lemme see yo' little eyes,
    Tek yo' little han's down nice,
Lawd, you wuff a million bills,
    Huh uh, chile, dat ain't yo' price.

Honey, de money ain't been made
    Dat dey could pay fu' you;
'Tain't no use a-biddin'; you too high
    Fu' de riches' Jap er Jew.
16

Lemme see you smilin' now,
    How dem teef o' yo'n do shine,
An' de t'ing dat meks me laff
    Is dat all o' you is mine.

How's I gwine to tell you how I feel,
    How's I gwine to weigh yo' wuff?
Oh, you sholy is de sweetes' t'ing
    Walkin' on dis blessed earf.
Possum is de sweetes' meat,
    Cidah is de nices' drink,
But my little lady-bird
    Is de bes' of all, I t'ink.

Talk erbout 'uligion he'pin' folks
    All thoo de way o' life,
Gin de res' 'uligion, des' gin me
    You, my little lady-wife.
Den de days kin come all ha'd,
    Den do nights kin come all black,
Des' you tek me by de han',
    An' I'll stumble on de track.

Stumble on de way to Gawd, my chile,
    Stumble on, an' mebbe fall;
But I'll keep a-trottin', while you lead
    on,
    Pickin' an' a-trottin', dat's all.
Hol' me mighty tight, dough, chile,
    Fu' hit's rough an' rocky lan',
Heaben's at de en', I know,
    So I's leanin' on yo' han'.

THE OLD FRONT GATE

W'en daih's chillun in de house,
    Dey keep on a-gittin' tall;
But de folks don' seem to see
    Dat dey's growin' up at all,
'Twell dey fin' out some fine day
    Dat de gals has 'menced to grow,
W'en dey notice as dey pass
    Dat de front gate's saggin' low.

W'en de hinges creak an' cry,
    An' de bahs go slantin' down,
You kin reckon dat hit's time
    Fu' to cas' yo' eye erroun',
'Cause daih ain't no 'sputin' dis,
    Hit's de trues' sign to show

Dat daih's cou'tin' goin' on
  W'en de ol' front gate sags low.

Oh, you grumble an' complain,
  An' you prop dat gate up right ;
But you notice right nex' day
  Dat hit's in de same ol' plight.
So you fin' dat hit's a rule,
  An' daih ain' no use to blow,
W'en de gals is growin' up,
  Dat de front gate will sag low.

Den you t'ink o' yo' young days,
  W'en you cou'ted Sally Jane,
An' you so't o' feel ashamed
  Fu' to grumble an' complain,
'Cause yo' ricerlection says,
  An' you know hits wo'ds is so,
Dat huh pappy had a time
  Wid his front gate saggin' low.

So you jes' looks on an' smiles
  At 'em leanin' on de gate,
Tryin' to t'ink whut he kin say
  Fu' to keep him daih so late,
But you lets dat gate erlone,
  Fu' yo' 'sperunce goes to show,
'Twell de gals is ma'ied off,
  It gwine keep on saggin' low.

DIRGE FOR A SOLDIER

In the east the morning comes,
Hear the rollin' of the drums
    On the hill.
But the heart that beat as they beat
In the battle's raging day heat
    Lieth still.
Unto him the night has come,
Though they roll the morning drum.

What is in the bugle's blast ?
It is : " Victory at last !
    Now for rest."
But, my comrades, come behold him
Where our colors now enfold him,
    And his breast
Bares no more to meet the blade,
But lies covered in the shade.

What a stir there is to-day !
They are laying him away
    Where he fell.
There the flag goes draped before him ;
Now they pile the grave sod o'er him
    With a knell.
And he answers to his name
In the higher ranks of fame.

There's a woman left to mourn
For the child that she has borne
    In travail.
But her heart beats high and higher,
With a patriot mother's fire,
    At the tale.
She has borne and lost a son,
But her work and his are done.

Fling the flag out, let it wave ;
They're returning from the grave —
    " Double quick ! "
And the cymbals now are crashing,
Bright his comrades' eyes are flashing
    From the thick
Battle-ranks which knew him brave,
No tears for a hero's grave.

In the east the morning comes,
Hear the rattle of the drums
    Far away.
Now no time for grief's pursuing,
Other work is for the doing,
    Here to-day.
He is sleeping, let him rest
With the flag across his breast.

A FROLIC

Swing yo' lady roun' an' roun',
  Do de bes' you know ;
Mek yo' bow an' p'omenade
  Up an' down de flo' ;
Mek dat banjo hump huhse'f,
  Listen at huh talk :
Mastah gone to town to-night ;
  'Tain't no time to walk.

Lif' yo' feet an' flutter thoo,
  Run, Miss Lucy, run ;
Reckon you'll be cotched an' kissed
  'Fo' de night is done.

You don't need to be so proud —
    I's a-watchin' you,
An' I's layin' lots o' plans
    Fu' to git you, too.

Moonlight on de cotton-fiel'
    Shinin' sof' an' white,
Whippo'will a-tellin' tales
    Out thaih in de night;
An' yo' cabin's 'crost de lot:
    Run, Miss Lucy, run;
Reckon you'll be cotched an' kissed
    'Fo' de night is done.

LOVE'S CASTLE

Key and bar, key and bar,
    Iron bolt and chain!
And what will you do when the King comes
    To enter his domain?

Turn key and lift bar,
    Loose, oh, bolt and chain!
Open the door and let him in,
    And then lock up again.

But, oh, heart, and woe, heart,
    Why do you ache so sore?
Never a moment's peace have you
    Since Love hath passed the door.

Turn key and lift bar,
    And loose bolt and chain;
But Love took in his esquire, Grief,
    And there they both remain.

MORNING SONG OF LOVE

Darling, my darling, my heart is on the
    wing,
    It flies to thee this morning like a bird,
Like happy birds in spring-time my spirits
    soar and sing,
    The same sweet song thine ears have
    often heard.

The sun is in my window, the shadow on
    the lea,
    The wind is moving in the branches
    green,

And all my life, my darling, is turning unto
    thee,
    And kneeling at thy feet, my own, my
    queen.

The golden bells are ringing across the
    distant hill,
    Their merry peals come to me soft and
    clear,
But in my heart's deep chapel all incense-
    filled and still
    A sweeter bell is sounding for thee, dear.

The bell of love invites thee to come and
    seek the shrine
    Whose altar is erected unto thee,
The offerings, the sacrifice, the prayers,
    the chants are thine,
    And I, my love, thy humble priest will
    be.

ON A CLEAN BOOK

TO F. N.

Like sea-washed sand upon the shore,
    So fine and clean the tale,
So clear and bright I almost see,
    The flashing of a sail.

The tang of salt is in its veins,
    The freshness of the spray
God give you love and lore and strength,
    To give us such alway.

TO THE EASTERN SHORE

I's feelin' kin' o' lonesome in my little
    room to-night,
    An' my min's done los' de minutes an'
    de miles,
W'ile it teks me back a-flyin' to de country
    of delight,
    Whaih de Chesapeake goes grumblin'
    er wid smiles.
    Oh, de ol' plantation's callin' to me,
    Come, come back,
    Hyeah's de place fu' you to labor an'
    to res',
    Fu' my sandy roads is gleamin' w'ile
    de city ways is black;

Come back, honey, case yo' country
   home is bes'.

I know de moon is shinin' down erpon de
      Eastern sho',
   An' de bay's a-sayin' " Howdy " to de
      lan';
An' de folks is all a-settin' out erroun' de
      cabin do',
   Wid dey feet a-restin' in de silvah san';
   An' de ol' plantation's callin' to me,
      Come, oh, come,
   F'om de life dat's des' a-waihin' you
      erway,
   F'om de trouble an' de bustle, an' de
      agernizin' hum
   Dat de city keeps ergoin' all de day.

I's tiahed of de city, tek me back to Sandy
      Side,
   Whaih de po'est ones kin live an' play
      an' eat;
Whaih we 'draws a simple livin' f'om de
      fo'est an' de tide,
   An' de days ah faih, an' evah night is
      sweet.
      Fu' de ol' plantation's callin' to me,
      Come, oh, come.
   An' the Chesapeake's a-sayin' " Dat's
      de t'ing,"
   W'ile my little cabin beckons, dough
      his mouf is closed an' dumb,
   I's a-comin', an' my hea't begins to
      sing.

BALLADE

By Mystics' banks I held my dream.
   (I held my fishing rod as well),
The vision was of dace and bream,
   A fruitless vision, sooth to tell.
But round about the sylvan dell
   Were other sweet Arcadian shrines,
   Gone now, is all the rural spell,
Arcadia has trolley lines.

Oh, once loved, sluggish, darkling stream,
   For me no more, thy waters swell,
Thy music now the engines' scream,
   Thy fragrance now the factory's smell;

Too near for me the clanging bell;
A false light in the water shines
   While Solitude lists to her knell,—
Arcadia has trolley lines.

Thy wooded lanes with shade and gleam
   Where bloomed the fragrant asphodel,
Now bleak commercially teem
   With signs " To Let," " To Buy," " To
      Sell."
And Commerce holds them fierce and
      fell;
With vulgar sport she now combines
   Sweet Nature's piping voice to quell.
Arcadia has trolley lines.

L'ENVOI

Oh, awful Power whose works repel
   The marvel of the earth's designs,—
I'll hie me otherwhere to dwell,
   Arcadia has trolley lines.

NODDIN' BY DE FIRE

Some folks t'inks hit's right an' p'opah,
   Soon ez bedtime come erroun',
   Fu' to scramble to de kiver,
   Lak dey'd hyeahed de trumpet soun'.
But dese people dey all misses
   Whut I mos'ly does desiah;
Dat's de settin' roun' an' dozin',
   An' a-noddin' by de fiah.

When you's tiahed out a-hoein',
   Er a-followin' de plough,
Whut's de use of des a-fallin'
   On yo' pallet lak a cow ?
W'y, de fun is all in waitin'
   In de face of all de tiah,
An' a-dozin' an' a-drowsin'
   By a good ol' hick'ry fiah.

Oh, you grunts an' groans an' mumbles
   Case yo' bones is full o' col',
Dough you feels de joy a-tricklin'
   Roun' de co'nahs of yo' soul.
An' you 'low anothah minute
   'S sho to git you wa'm an' dryah,
W'en you set up pas' yo' bedtime,
   Case you hates to leave de fiah.

By a Good Ol' Hick'ry Fiah

Li'l' Gal

Whut's de use o' downright sleepin' ?
  You can't feel it while it las',
An' you git up feelin' sorry
  W'en de time fu' it is pas'.
Seem to me dat time too precious,
  An' de houahs too short entiah,
Fu' to sleep, w'en you could spen' 'em
  Des a-noddin' by de fiah.

LI'L' GAL

Oh, de weathah it is balmy an' de breeze
    is sighin' low,
          Li'l' gal,
An' de mockin' bird is singin' in de locus'
    by de do',
          Li'l' gal ;
Dere's a hummin' an' a bummin' in de
    lan' f 'om eas' to wes',
I's a-sighin' fu' you, honey, an' I nevah
    know no res'.
Fu' dey's lots o' trouble brewin' an'
    a-stewin' in my breas',
          Li'l' gal.

Whut's de mattah wid de weathah, whut's
    de mattah wid de breeze,
          Li'l' gal ?
Whut's de mattah wid de locus' dat's
    a-singin' in de trees,
          Li'l' gal ?
W'y dey knows dey ladies love 'em, an'
    dey knows dey love 'em true,
An' dey love 'em back, I reckon, des' lak
    I's a-lovin' you ;
Dat's de reason dey's a-weavin' an'
    a-sighin', thoo an' thoo,
          Li'l' gal.

Don't you let no da'ky fool you 'cause de
    clo'es he waihs is fine,
          Li'l' gal.
Dey's a hones' hea't a-beatin' unnerneaf
    dese rags o' mine,
          Li'l' gal,
C'ose dey ain' no use in mockin' whut de
    birds an' weathah do,
But I's so'y I cain't 'spress it w'en I
    knows I loves you true,
Dat's de reason I's a-sighin' an' a-singin'
    now fu' you,
          Li'l' gal.

RELUCTANCE

Will I have some mo' dat pie ?
No, ma'am, thank-ee, dat is—I—
    Bettah quit daihin' me.
Dat ah pie look sutny good :
How'd you feel now ef I would ?
I don' reckon dat I should ;
    Bettah quit daihin' me.

Look hyeah, I gwine tell de truf,
Mine is sholy one sweet toof :
    Bettah quit daihin' me.
Yass'm, yass'm, dat's all right,
I's done tried to be perlite :
But dat pie's a lakly sight,
    Wha's de use o' daihin' me ?

My, yo' lips is full an' red,
Don't I wish you'd tu'n yo' haid ?
    Bettah quit daihin' me.
Dat ain't faih, now, honey chile,
I's gwine lose my sense erwhile
Ef you des set daih an' smile,
    Bettah quit daihin' me.

Nuffin' don' look ha'f so fine
Ez dem teef, deah, w'en dey shine :
    Bettah quit daihin' me.
Now look hyeah, I tells you dis ;
I'll give up all othah bliss
Des to have one little kiss,
    Bettah quit daihin' me.

Laws, I teks yo' little han',
Ain't it tendah ? bless de lan' —
    Bettah quit daihin' me.
I's so lonesome by myse'f,
'D ain't no fun in livin' lef' ;
Dis hyeah life's ez dull ez def :
    Bettah quit daihin' me.

Whyn't you tek yo' han' erway ?
Yass, I'll hol' it : but I say
    Bettah quit daihin' me.
Hol'in' han's is sholy fine.
Seems lak dat's de weddin' sign.
Wish you'd say dat you'd be mine ; —
    Dah you been daihin' me.

SPEAKIN' AT DE COU'T-HOUSE

Dey been speakin' at de cou't-house,
　An' laws-a-massy me,
'Twas de beatness kin' o' doin's
　Dat evah I did see.
Of cose I had to be dah
　In de middle o' de crowd,
An' I hallohed wid de othahs,
　W'en de speakah riz and bowed.

I was kind o' disapp'inted
　At de smallness of de man,
Case I'd allus pictered great folks
　On a mo' expansive plan;
But I t'ought I could respect him
　An' tek in de wo'ds he said,
Fu' dey sho was somep'n knowin'
　In de bald spot on his haid.

But hit did seem so't o' funny
　Aftah waitin' fu' a week
Dat de people kep' on shoutin'
　So de man des couldn't speak ;
De ho'ns dey blared a little,
　Den dey let loose on de drums,—
Some one tol' me dey was playin'
　" See de conkerin' hero comes."

" Well," says I, " you all is white folks,
　But you's sutny actin' queer,
What's de use of heroes comin'
　Ef dey cain't talk w'en dey's here ? "
Aftah while dey let him open,
　An' dat man he waded in,
An' he fit de wahs all ovah
　Winnin' victeries lak sin.

W'en he come down to de present,
　Den he made de feathahs fly.
He des waded in on money,
　An' he played de ta'iff high.
An' he said de colah question,
　Hit was ovah, solved, an' done,
Dat de dahky was his brothah,
　Evah blessed mothah's son.

Well he settled all de trouble
　Dat's been pesterin' de lan',
Den he set down mid de cheerin'
　An' de playin' of de ban'.

I was feelin' moughty happy
　'Twell I hyeahed somebody speak,
" Well, dat's his side of de bus'ness,
　But you wait for Jones nex' week."

BLACK SAMSON OF BRANDYWINE

" In the fight at Brandywine, Black Samson, a
giant negro armed with a scythe, sweeps his way
thro' the red ranks. . . ." C. M. SKINNER's
" *Myths and Legends of Our Own Land.*"

Gray are the pages of record,
　Dim are the volumes of eld ;
Else had old Delaware told us
　More that her history held.
Told us with pride in the story,
　Honest and noble and fine,
More of the tale of my hero,
　Black Samson of Brandywine.

Sing of your chiefs and your nobles,
　Saxon and Celt and Gaul,
Breath of mine ever shall join you,
　Highly I honor them all.
Give to them all of their glory,
　But for this noble of mine,
Lend him a tithe of your tribute,
　Black Samson of Brandywine.

There in the heat of the battle,
　There in the stir of the fight,
Loomed he, an ebony giant,
　Black as the pinions of night.
Swinging his scythe like a mower
　Over a field of grain,
Needless the care of the gleaners,
　Where he had passed amain.

Straight through the human harvest,
　Cutting a bloody swath,
Woe to you, soldier of Briton !
　Death is abroad in his path.
Flee from the scythe of the reaper,
　Flee while the moment is thine,
None may with safety withstand him,
　Black Samson of Brandywine.

Was he a freeman or bondman ?
　Was he a man or a thing ?
What does it matter ? His brav'ry
　Renders him royal—a king.

If he was only a chattel,
   Honor the ransom may pay
Of the royal, the loyal black giant
   Who fought for his country that day.

Noble and bright is the story,
   Worthy the touch of the lyre,
Sculptor or poet should find it
   Full of the stuff to inspire.
Beat it in brass and in copper,
   Tell it in storied line,
So that the world may remember
   Black Samson of Brandywine.

THE LOOKING-GLASS

Dinah stan' befo' de glass,
   Lookin' moughty neat,
An' huh purty shadder sass
   At huh haid an' feet.
While she sasshay 'roun' an' bow,
Smilin' den an' poutin' now,
An' de lookin'-glass, I 'low
   Say : " Now, ain't she sweet ? "

All she do, de glass it see,
   Hit des see, no mo',
Seems to me, hit ought to be
   Drappin' on de flo'.
She go w'en huh time git slack,
Kissin' han's an' smilin' back,
Lawsy, how my lips go smack,
   Watchin' at de do'.

Wisht I was huh lookin'-glass,
   W'en she kissed huh han' ;
Does you t'ink I'd let it pass,
   Settin' on de stan' ?
No ; I'd des' fall down an' break,
Kin' o' glad 't uz fu' huh sake ;
But de diffunce, dat whut make
   Lookin'-glass an' man.

A MISTY DAY

Heart of my heart, the day is chill,
The mist hangs low o'er the wooded hill,
The soft white mist and the heavy cloud
The sun and the face of heaven shroud.
The birds are thick in the dripping trees,
That drop their pearls to the beggar breeze ;

No songs are rife where songs are wont,
Each singer crouches in his haunt.

Heart of my heart, the day is chill,
Whene'er thy loving voice is still,
The cloud and mist hide the sky from me,
Whene'er thy face I cannot see.
My thoughts fly back from the chill with-
   out,
My mind in the storm drops doubt on
   doubt,
No songs arise. Without thee, love,
My soul sinks down like a frightened dove.

DOUGLASS

Ah, Douglass, we have fall'n on evil days,
   Such days as thou, not even thou didst
      know,
   When thee, the eyes of that harsh long
      ago
Saw, salient, at the cross of devious ways,
And all the country heard thee with amaze.
   Not ended then, the passionate ebb and
      flow,
   The awful tide that battled to and fro ;
We ride amid a tempest of dispraise.
Now, when the waves of swift dissension
      swarm,
   And Honor, the strong pilot, lieth stark,
Oh, for thy voice high-sounding o'er the
      storm,
   For thy strong arm to guide the shiver-
      ing bark,
The blast-defying power of thy form,
   To give us comfort through the lonely
      dark.

BOOKER T. WASHINGTON

The word is writ that he who runs may
      read.
What is the passing breath of earthly fame ?
But to snatch glory from the hands of
      blame —
That is to be, to live, to strive indeed.
A poor Virginia cabin gave the seed,
And from its dark and lowly door there
      came
A peer of princes in the world's acclaim,

A master spirit for the nation's need.
Strong, silent, purposeful beyond his kind,
   The mark of rugged force on brow and
     lip,
Straight on he goes, nor turns to look be-
     hind
   Where hot the hounds come baying at
     his hip;
With one idea foremost in his mind,
   Like the keen prow of some on-forging
     ship.

THE MONK'S WALK

This poem was written in autumn, at Washington, D. C., after the shadows of the death of his domestic peace had begun to fall. He sometimes spoke of becoming a priest of the Church, and this half-formed desire may be observed in several stanzas of the Monk's Walk. Reference to his henceforth lonely life is made thus —

     " Is it living thus to live?
      Has life nothing more to give?
      Ah, no more of smile or sigh —
      Life, the world, and love, good-bye."

The poem is one of a series of three whose direct inspiration was found in his discovery of a violet blooming in November.

In this sombre garden close
What has come and passed, who knows?
What red passion, what white pain
Haunted this dim walk in vain?

Underneath the ivied wall,
Where the silent shadows fall,
Lies the pathway chill and damp
Where the world-quit dreamers tramp.

Just across, where sunlight burns,
Smiling at the mourning ferns,
Stand the roses, side by side,
Nodding in their useless pride.

Ferns and roses, who shall say
What you witness day by day?
Covert smile or dropping eye,
As the monks go pacing by.

Has the novice come to-day
Here beneath the wall to pray?
Has the young monk, lately chidden,
Sung his lyric, sweet, forbidden?

Tell me, roses, did you note
That pale father's throbbing throat?
Did you hear him murmur, " Love!"
As he kissed a faded glove?

Mourning ferns, pray tell me why
Shook you with that passing sigh?
Is it that you chanced to spy
Something in the Abbot's eye?

Here no dream, nor thought of sin,
Where no worlding enters in;
Here no longing, no desire,
Heat nor flame of earthly fire.

Branches waving green above,
Whisper naught of life nor love;
Softened winds that seem a breath,
Perfumed, bring no fear of death.

Is it living thus to live?
Has life nothing more to give?
Ah, no more of smile or sigh —
Life, the world, and love, good-bye.

Gray, and passionless, and dim,
Echoing of the solemn hymn,
Lies the walk, 'twixt fern and rose,
Here within the garden close.

LOVE-SONG

If Death should claim me for her own to-
     day,
   And softly I should falter from your
     side,
Oh, tell me, loved one, would my memory
     stay,
   And would my image in your heart
     abide?
Or should I be as some forgotten dream,
   That lives its little space, then fades en-
     tire?
Should Time send o'er you its relentless
     stream,
   To cool your heart, and quench for aye
     love's fire?

I would not for the world, love, give you
  pain,
  Or ever compass what would cause you
    grief;
And, oh, how well I know that tears are
  vain!
  But love is sweet, my dear, and life is
    brief;
So if some day before you I should go
  Beyond the sound and sight of song and
    sea,
'Twould give my spirit stronger wings to
    know
  That you remembered still and wept for
    me.

SLOW THROUGH THE DARK

Slow moves the pageant of a climbing
  race;
  Their footsteps drag far, far below the
    height,
  And, unprevailing by their utmost
    might,
Seem faltering downward from each hard
  won place.
No strange, swift-sprung exception we; we
  trace
  A devious way thro' dim, uncertain
    light,—
  Our hope, through the long vistaed
    years, a sight
Of that our Captain's soul sees face to
  face.
  Who, faithless, faltering that the road is
    steep,
Now raiseth up his drear insistent cry?
  Who stoppeth here to spend a while in
    sleep
Or curseth that the storm obscures the
  sky?
  Heed not the darkness round you, dull
    and deep;
The clouds grow thickest when the sum-
  mit's nigh.

THE MURDERED LOVER

Say a mass for my soul's repose, my
  brother,
  Say a mass for my soul's repose, I need
    it,

Lovingly lived we, the sons of one mother,
  Mine was the sin, but I pray you not
    heed it.

Dark were her eyes as the sloe and they
  called me,
  Called me with voice independent of
    breath.
God! how my heart beat; her beauty ap-
  palled me,
  Dazed me, and drew to the sea-brink of
    death.

Lithe was her form like a willow. She
  beckoned,
  What could I do save to follow and fol-
    low,
Nothing of right or result could be
  reckoned;
  Life without her was unworthy and hol-
    low.

Ay, but I wronged thee, my brother, my
  brother;
  Ah, but I loved her, thy beautiful wife.
Shade of our father, and soul of our mother,
  Have I not paid for my love with my
    life?

Dark was the night when, revengeful, I
  met you,
  Deep in the heart of a desolate land.
Warm was the life-blood which angrily
  wet you,
  Sharp was the knife that I felt from your
    hand.

Wept you, oh, wept you, alone by the river,
  When my stark carcass you secretly sank.
Ha, now I see that you tremble and
  shiver;
  'Twas but my spirit that passed when
    you shrank!

Weep not, oh, weep not, 'tis over, 'tis
  over;
  Stir the dark weeds with the turn of the
    tide;
Go, thou hast sent me forth, ever a rover,
  Rest and the sweet realm of heaven
    denied.

Say a mass for my soul's repose, my
    brother,
  Say a mass for my soul, I need it.
Sin of mine was it, and sin of no other,
  Mine was it all, but I pray you not
    heed it.

PHILOSOPHY

I been t'inkin' 'bout de preachah ; whut he
    said de othah night,
  'Bout hit bein' people's dooty, fu' to
    keep dey faces bright ;
How one ought to live so pleasant dat
    ouah tempah never riles,
  Meetin' evahbody roun' us wid ouah
    very nicest smiles.

Dat's all right, I ain't a-sputin' not a t'ing
    dat soun's lak fac',
  But you don't ketch folks a-grinnin' wid
    a misery in de back ;
An' you don't fin' dem a-smilin' w'en dey's
    hongry ez kin be,
  Leastways, dat's how human natur' allus
    seems to 'pear to me.

We is mos' all putty likely fu' to have our
    little cares,
  An' I think we'se doin' fus' rate w'en
    we jes' go long and bears,
Widout breakin' up ouah faces in a sickly
    so't o' grin,
  W'en we knows dat in ouah innards we
    is p'intly mad ez sin.

Oh, dey's times fu' bein' pleasant an' fu'
    goin' smilin' roun',
  'Cause I don't believe in people allus
    totin' roun' a frown,
But it's easy 'nough to titter w'en de stew
    is smokin' hot,
  But hit's mighty ha'd to giggle w'en
    dey's nuffin' in de pot.

A PREFERENCE

Mastah drink his ol' Made'a,
  Missy drink huh sherry wine,
Ovahseah lak his whiskey,
  But dat othah drink is mine,

Des' 'lasses an' watah, 'lasses an'
    watah.

W'en you git a steamin' hoe-cake
  On de table, go way, man !
'D ain't but one t'ing to go wid it,
  'Sides de gravy in de pan,
    Dat's 'lasses an' watah, 'lasses an'
      watah.

W'en hit's 'possum dat you eatin',
  'Simmon beer is moughty sweet ;
But fu' evahday consumin'
  'D aint' no mo'tal way to beat
    Des' 'lasses an' watah, 'lasses an'
      watah.

W'y de bees is allus busy,
  An' ain' got no time to was' ?
Hit's beca'se dey knows de honey
  Dey's a makin', gwine to tas'
    Lak 'lasses an' watah, 'lasses an'
      watah.

Oh, hit's moughty mil' an' soothin',
  An' hit don' go to yo' haid ;
Dat's de reason I's a-backin'
  Up de othah wo'ds I said,
    " Des 'lasses an' watah, 'lasses an'
      watah."

THE DEBT

This is the debt I pay
Just for one riotous day,
Years of regret and grief,
Sorrow without relief.

Pay it I will to the end —
Until the grave, my friend,
Gives me a true release —
Gives me the clasp of peace.

Slight was the thing I bought,
Small was the debt I thought,
Poor was the loan at best —
God ! but the interest !

ON THE DEDICATION OF DOROTHY HALL

TUSKEEGEE, ALA., APRIL 22, 1901.

Not to the midnight of the gloomy past,
  Do we revert to-day; we look upon
The golden present and the future vast
  Whose vistas show us visions of the
    dawn.

Nor shall the sorrows of departed years
  The sweetness of our tranquil souls an-
    noy,
The sunshine of our hopes dispels the
    tears,
  And clears our eyes to see this later joy.

Not ever in the years that God hath given
  Have we gone friendless down the
    thorny way,
Always the clouds of pregnant black were
    riven
  By flashes from his own eternal day.

The women of a race should be its pride;
  We glory in the strength our mothers
    had,
We glory that this strength was not denied
  To labor bravely, nobly, and be glad.

God give to these within this temple here,
  Clear vision of the dignity of toil,
That virtue in them may its blossoms rear
  Unspotted, fragrant, from the lowly soil.

God bless the givers for their noble deed,
  Shine on them with the mercy of thy
    face,
Who come with open hearts to help and
    speed
  The striving women of a struggling
    race.

A ROADWAY

Let those who will stride on their barren
    roads
And prick themselves to haste with self-
    made goads,
Unheeding, as they struggle day by day,
If flowers be sweet or skies be blue or
  gray;

For me, the lone, cool way by purling
    brooks,
The solemn quiet of the woodland nooks,
A song-bird somewhere trilling sadly gay,
A pause to pick a flower beside the way.

BY RUGGED WAYS

By rugged ways and thro' the night
We struggle blindly towards the light;
And groping, stumbling, ever pray
For sight of long delaying day.
The cruel thorns beside the road
Stretch eager points our steps to goad,
And from the thickets all about
Detaining hands reach threatening out.

" Deliver us, oh, Lord," we cry,
Our hands uplifted to the sky.
No answer save the thunder's peal,
And onward, onward, still we reel.
" Oh, give us now thy guiding light; "
Our sole reply, the lightning's blight.
" Vain, vain," cries one, " in vain we
    call; "
But faith serene is over all.

Beside our way the streams are dried,
And famine mates us side by side.
Discouraged and reproachful eyes
Seek once again the frowning skies.
Yet shall there come, spite storm and
    shock,
A Moses who shall smite the rock,
Call manna from the Giver's hand,
And lead us to the promised land!

The way is dark and cold and steep,
And shapes of horror murder sleep,
And hard the unrelenting years;
But 'twixt our sighs and moans and tears,
We still can smile, we still can sing,
Despite the arduous journeying.
For faith and hope their courage lend,
And rest and light are at the end.

LOVE'S SEASONS

When the bees are humming in the hon-
    eysuckle vine
  And the summer days are in their
    bloom,

Then my love is deepest, oh, dearest
    heart of mine,
When the bees are humming in the hon-
    eysuckle vine.

When the winds are moaning o'er the
    meadows chill and gray,
And the land is dim with winter gloom,
Then for thee, my darling, love will have
    its way,
When the winds are moaning o'er the
    meadows chill and gray.

In the vernal dawning with the starting of
    the leaf,
In the merry-chanting time of spring,
Love steals all my senses, oh, the happy-
    hearted thiel!
In the vernal morning with the starting of
    the leaf.

Always, ever always, even in the autumn
    drear,
    When the days are sighing out their
        grief,
Thou art still my darling, dearest of the
    dear,
Always, ever always, even in the autumn
    drear.

TO A DEAD FRIEND

It is as if a silver chord
    Were suddenly grown mute,
And life's song with its rhythm warred
    Against a silver lute.

It is as if a silence fell
    Where bides the garnered sheaf,
And voices murmuring, " It is well,"
    Are stifled by our grief.

It is as if the gloom of night
    Had hid a summer's day,
And willows, sighing at their plight,
    Bent low beside the way.

For he was part of all the best
    That Nature loves and gives,
And ever more on Memory's breast
    He lies and laughs and lives.

TO THE SOUTH

ON ITS NEW SLAVERY

Heart of the Southland, heed me plead-
    ing now,
Who bearest, unashamed, upon my brow
The long kiss of the loving tropic sun,
And yet, whose veins with thy red current
    run.

Borne on the bitter winds from every
    hand,
Strange tales are flying over all the land,
And Condemnation, with his pinions foul,
Glooms in the place where broods the
    midnight owl.

What art thou, that the world should point
    at thee,
And vaunt and chide the weakness that
    they see ?
There was a time they were not wont to
    chide ;
Where is thy old, uncompromising pride ?

Blood-washed, thou shouldst lift up thine
    honored head,
White with the sorrow for thy loyal dead
Who lie on every plain, on every hill,
And whose high spirit walks the South-
    land still :

Whose infancy our mother's hands have
    nursed.
Thy manhood, gone to battle unaccursed,
Our fathers left to till th' reluctant field,
To rape the soil for what she would not
    yield ;

Wooing for aye, the cold unam'rous sod,
Whose growth for them still meant a mas-
    ter's rod ;
Tearing her bosom for the wealth that
    gave
The strength that made the toiler still a
    slave.

Too long we hear the deep impassioned
    cry
That echoes vainly to the heedless sky ;

Too long, too long, the Macedonian call
Falls fainting far beyond the outward wall,

Within whose sweep, beneath the shadow-
 ing trees,
A slumbering nation takes its dangerous
 ease;
Too long the rumors of thy hatred go
For those who loved thee and thy children
 so.

Thou must arise forthwith, and strong,
 thou must
Throw off the smirching of this baser
 dust,
Lay by the practice of this later creed,
And be thine honest self again indeed.

There was a time when even slavery's
 chain
Held in some joys to alternate with pain,
Some little light to give the night relief,
Some little smiles to take the place of
 grief.

There was a time when, jocund as the
 day,
The toiler hoed his row and sung his lay,
Found something gleeful in the very air,
And solace for his toiling everywhere.

Now all is changed, within the rude
 stockade,
A bondsman whom the greed of men has
 made
Almost too brutish to deplore his plight,
Toils hopeless on from joyless morn till
 night.

For him no more the cabin's quiet rest,
The homely joys that gave to labor zest;
No more for him the merry banjo's sound,
Nor trip of lightsome dances footing
 round.

For him no more the lamp shall glow at
 eve,
Nor chubby children pluck him by the
 sleeve;

No more for him the master's eyes be
 bright,—
He has nor freedom's nor a slave's de-
 light.

What, was it all for naught, those awful
 years
That drenched a groaning land with blood
 and tears?
Was it to leave this sly convenient hell,
That brother fighting his own brother fell?

When that great struggle held the world
 in awe,
And all the nations blanched at what they
 saw,
Did Sanctioned Slavery bow its conquered
 head
That this unsanctioned crime might rise
 instead?

Is it for this we all have felt the flame,—
This newer bondage and this deeper
 shame?
Nay, not for this, a nation's heroes bled,
And North and South with tears beheld
 their dead.

Oh, Mother South, hast thou forgot thy
 ways,
Forgot the glory of thine ancient days,
Forgot the honor that once made thee
 great,
And stooped to this unhallowèd estate?

It cannot last, thou wilt come forth in
 might,
A warrior queen full armored for the
 fight;
And thou wilt take, e'en with thy spear in
 rest,
Thy dusky children to thy saving breast.

Till then, no more, no more the gladsome
 song,
Strike only deeper chords, the notes oɪ
 wrong;
Till then, the sigh, the tear, the oath, the
 moan,
Till thou, oh, South, and thine, come tυ
 thine own.

ROBERT GOULD SHAW

Why was it that the thunder voice of Fate
  Should call thee, studious, from the
    classic groves,
  Where calm-eyed Pallas with still foot-
    step roves,
And charge thee seek the turmoil of the
    state ?
What bade thee hear the voice and rise
    elate,

  Leave home and kindred and thy spicy
    loaves,
  To lead th' unlettered and despised
    droves
To manhood's home and thunder at the
    gate?

Far better the slow blaze of Learning's
    light,
  The cool and quiet of her dearer fane,
Than this hot terror of a hopeless fight,
  This cold endurance of the final pain,—
Since thou and those who with thee died
    for right
  Have died, the Present teaches, but in
    vain!

ROSES

Oh, wind of the spring-time, oh, free wind
    of May,
  When blossoms and bird-song are rife ;
Oh, joy for the season, and joy for the day,
  That gave me the roses of life, of life,
  That gave me the roses of life.

Oh, wind of the summer, sing loud in the
    night,
  When flutters my heart like a dove ;
One came from thy kingdom, thy realm of
    delight,
  And gave me the roses of love, of love,
  And gave me the roses of love.

Oh, wind of the winter, sigh low in thy
    grief,
  I hear thy compassionate breath ;
I wither, I fall, like the autumn-kissed leaf,
  He gave me the roses of death, of death,
  He gave me the roses of death.

WHEN SAM'L SINGS

Hyeah dat singin' in de medders
  Whaih de folks is mekin' hay ?
Wo'k is pretty middlin' heavy
  Fu' a man to be so gay.
You kin tell dey's somep'n special
  F'om de canter o' de song ;
Somep'n sholy pleasin' Sam'l,
  W'en he singin' all day long.

Hyeahd him wa'blin' 'way dis mo'nin'
  'Fo' 'twas light enough to see.
Seem lak music in de evenin'
  Allus good enough fu' me.
But dat man commenced to hollah
  'Fo' he'd even washed his face ;
Would you b'lieve, de scan'lous rascal
  Woke de birds erroun' de place ?

Sam'l took a trip a-Sad'day ;
  Dressed hisse'f in all he had,
Tuk a cane an' went a-strollin',
  Lookin' mighty pleased an' glad.
Some folks don' know whut de mattah,
  But I do, you bet yo' life ;
Sam'l smilin' an' a-singin'
  'Case he been to see his wife.

She live on de fu' plantation,
  Twenty miles erway er so ;
But huh man is mighty happy
  W'en he git de chanst to go.
Walkin' allus ain' de nices'—
  Mo'nin' fin's him on de way —
But he allus comes back smilin',
  Lak his pleasure was his pay.

Den he do a heap o' talkin', -
  Do' he mos'ly kin' o' still,
But de wo'ds, dey gits to runnin'
  Lak de watah fu' a mill.
" Whut's de use o' havin' trouble,
  Whut's de use o' havin' strife ? "
Dat's de way dis Sam'l preaches
  W'en he been to see his wife.

An' I reckon I git jealous,
  Fu' I laff an' joke an' sco'n,
An' I say, " Oh, go on, Sam'l,
  Des go on, an' blow yo' ho'n."

SAM'L TOOK A TRIP A-SAD'DAY

Don' Fiddle dat Chune no Mo'

But I know dis comin' Sad'day,
  Dey'll be brighter days in life ;
An' I'll be ez glad ez Sam'l
  W'en I go to see my wife.

ITCHING HEELS

Fu' de peace o' my eachin' heels, set
    down ;
  Don' fiddle dat chune no mo'.
Don' you see how dat melody stuhs me up
An' baigs me to tek to de flo' ?
You knows I's a Christian, good an'
    strong ;
  I wusship f'om June to June ;
My pra'ehs dey ah loud an' my hymns ah
    long :
  I baig you don' fiddle dat chune.

J's a crick in my back an' a misery hyeah
  Whaih de j'ints's gittin' ol' an' stiff,
But hit seems lak you brings me de bref
    o' my youf ;
  W'y, I's suttain I noticed a w'iff.
Don' fiddle dat chune no mo', my chile,
  Don't fiddle dat chune no mo' ;
I'll git up an' taih up dis groun' fu' a mile,
  An' den I'll be chu'ched fu' it, sho'.

Oh, fiddle dat chune some mo', I say,
  An' fiddle it loud an' fas' :
I's a youngstah ergin in de mi'st o' my sin ;
  De p'esent's gone back to de pas'.
I'll dance to dat chune, so des fiddle
    erway ;
  I knows how de backslidah feels ;
So fiddle it on 'twell de break o' de day
  Fu' de sake o' my eachin' heels.

THE HAUNTED OAK

Pray why are you so bare, so bare,
  Oh, bough of the old oak-tree ;
And why, when I go through the shade
    you throw,
  Runs a shudder over me ?

My leaves were green as the best, I trow,
  And sap ran free in my veins,
But I saw in the moonlight dim and weird
  A guiltless victim's pains.

I bent me down to hear his sigh ;
  I shook with his gurgling moan,
And I trembled sore when they rode away,
  And left him here alone.

They'd charged him with the old, old
    crime,
  And set him fast in jail :
Oh, why does the dog howl all night long,
  And why does the night wind wail ?

He prayed his prayer and he swore his
    oath,
  And he raised his hand to the sky ;
But the beat of hoofs smote on his ear,
  And the steady tread drew nigh.

Who is it rides by night, by night,
  Over the moonlit road ?
And what is the spur that keeps the pace,
  What is the galling goad ?

And now they beat at the prison door,
  " Ho, keeper, do not stay !
We are friends of him whom you hold
    within,
  And we fain would take him away

" From those who ride fast on our heels
  With mind to do him wrong ;
They have no care for his innocence,
  And the rope they bear is long."

They have fooled the jailer with lying
    words,
  They have fooled the man with lies ;
The bolts unbar, the locks are drawn,
  And the great door open flies.

Now they have taken him from the jail,
  And hard and fast they ride,
And the leader laughs low down in his
    throat,
  As they halt my trunk beside.

Oh, the judge, he wore a mask of black,
  And the doctor one of white,
And the minister, with his oldest son,
  Was curiously bedight.

Oh, foolish man, why weep you now?
   'Tis but a little space,
And the time will come when these shall
     dread
   The mem'ry of your face.

I feel the rope against my bark,
   And the weight of him in my grain,
I feel in the throe of his final woe
   The touch of my own last pain.

And never more shall leaves come forth
   On a bough that bears the ban;
I am burned with dread, I am dried and
     dead,
   From the curse of a guiltless man.

And ever the judge rides by, rides by,
   And goes to hunt the deer,
And ever another rides his soul
   In the guise of a mortal fear.

And ever the man he rides me hard,
   And never a night stays he;
For I feel his curse as a haunted bough,
   On the trunk of a haunted tree.

WELTSCHMERTZ

The poet once told this author that he wrote the poem "Weltschmertz" not long before his great sorrow came into his life, and in anticipated comradeship he could "sympathize" with the falling leaf, the bare tree, the bird leaving her wind-swept nest, and with those who had lost friends. His sorrow was to be greater than death, a living grief, an ever-present remorse.

Foreknowing is one of the gifts of the poetic mind, and a poet is no more philosopher than prophet or seer. Many times a beautiful concept will take possession of the mind only to be later verified in actual happenings.

Every picture of Dunbar's Weltschmertz was afterwards painted on the canvas of Dunbar's own experience. Did not the falling leaf and the bare tree anti-type his deserted hearthstone? the wind-swept nest his home after the fires of anger had burned out and the two human singers who had sung there had flown to other climes? Were not his "unbidden tears" at the sight of a passing hearse, bearing a child to the cemetery, forewarnings of the time when he would come to feel as did his brother-poet Riley upon the death of a friend's baby —

    "Oh, how much sadder I
    Who have no child to die!"

And so one might follow the poem through, and at the end decide that it proved a flawless prophecy.

You ask why I am sad to-day,
I have no cares, no griefs, you say?
Ah, yes, 'tis true, I have no grief —
But—is there not the falling leaf?

The bare tree there is mourning left
With all of autumn's gray bereft;
It is not what has happened me,
Think of the bare, dismantled tree.

The birds go South along the sky,
I hear their lingering, long good-bye.
Who goes reluctant from my breast?
And yet—the lone and wind-swept nest.

The mourning, pale-flowered hearse goes
    by,
Why does a tear come to my eye?
Is it the March rain blowing wild?
I have no dead, I know no child.

I am no widow by the bier
Of him I held supremely dear.
I have not seen the choicest one
Sink down as sinks the westering sun.

Faith unto faith have I beheld,
For me, few solemn notes have swelled
Love beckoned me out to the dawn,
And happily I followed on.

And yet my heart goes out to them
Whose sorrow is their diadem;
The falling leaf, the crying bird,
The voice to be, all lost, unheard —

Not mine, not mine, and yet too much
The thrilling power of human touch,
While all the world looks on and scorns
I wear another's crown of thorns.

Count me a priest who understands
The glorious pain of nail-pierced hands;
Count me a comrade of the thief
Hot driven into late belief.

Oh, mother's tear, oh, father's sigh,
Oh, mourning sweetheart's last good-bye,
I yet have known no mourning save
Beside some brother's brother's grave.

A LOVE SONG

Ah, love, my love is like a cry in the night,
A long, loud cry to the empty sky,
The cry of a man alone in the desert,
With hands uplifted, with parching lips,

Oh, rescue me, rescue me,
Thy form to mine arms,
The dew of thy lips to my mouth,
Dost thou hear me?—my call thro' the
    night?

Darling, I hear thee and answer,
Thy fountain am I,
All of the love of my soul will I bring to
    thee,
All of the pains of my being shall wring
    to thee,
Deep and forever the song of my loving
    shall sing to thee,
Ever and ever thro' day and thro' night
    shall I cling to thee.
Hearest thou the answer?
Darling, I come, I come.

TO AN INGRATE

This is to-day, a golden summer's day,
    And yet—and yet
    My vengeful soul will not forget
The past, forever now forgot, you say.

From that half height where I had sadly
    climbed,
    I stretched my hand,

I lone in all that land,
Down there, where, helpless, you were
    limed.

Our fingers clasped, and dragging me a
    pace,
    You struggled up.
    It is a bitter Cup,
That now for naught, you turn away your
    face.

I shall remember this for aye and aye.
    Whate'er may come,
    Although my lips are dumb,
My spirit holds you to that yesterday.

IN THE TENTS OF AKBAR

In the tents of Akbar
    Are dole and grief to-day,
For the flower of all the Indies
    Has gone the silent way.

In the tents of Akbar
    Are emptiness and gloom,
And where the dancers gather,
    The silence of the tomb.

Across the yellow desert,
    Across the burning sands,
Old Akbar wanders madly,
    And wrings his fevered hands.

And ever makes his moaning
    To the unanswering sky,
For Sutna, lovely Sutna,
    Who was so fair to die.

For Sutna danced at morning,
    And Sutna danced at eve;
Her dusky eyes half hidden
    Behind her silken sleeve.

Her pearly teeth out-glancing
    Between her coral lips,
The tremulous rhythm of passion
    Marked by her quivering hips.

As lovely as a jewel
    Of fire and dewdrop blent,

So danced the maiden Sutna
  In gallant Akbar's tent.

And one who saw her dancing,
  Saw her bosom's fall and rise
Put all his body's yearning
  Into his lovelit eyes.

Then Akbar came and drove him —
  A jackal—from his door,
And bade him wander far and look
  On Sutna's face no more.

Some day the sea disgorges,
  The wilderness gives back,
Those half-dead who have wandered,
  Aimless, across its track.

And he returned—the lover,
  Haggard of brow and spent;
He found fair Sutna standing
  Before her master's tent.

" Not mine, nor Akbar's, Sutna ! "
  He cried and closely pressed,
And drove his craven dagger
  Straight to the maiden's breast.

Oh, weep, oh, weep, for Sutna,
  So young, so dear, so fair,
Her face is gray and silent
  Beneath her dusky hair.

And wail, oh, wail, for Akbar,
  Who walks the desert sands,
Crying aloud for Sutna,
  Wringing his fevered hands.

In the tents of Akbar
  The tears of sorrow run,
But the corpse of Sutna's slayer,
  Lies rotting in the sun.

THE FOUNT OF TEARS

All hot and grimy from the road,
  Dust gray from arduous years,
I sat me down and eased my load
  Beside the Fount of Tears.

The waters sparkled to my eye,
  Calm, crystal-like, and cool,
And breathing there a restful sigh,
  I bent me to the pool.

When, lo ! a voice cried : " Pilgrim, rise,
  Harsh tho' the sentence be,
And on to other lands and skies —
  This fount is not for thee.

" Pass on, but calm thy needless fears,
  Some may not love or sin,
An angel guards the Fount of Tears;
  All may not bathe therein."

Then with my burden on my back
  I turned to gaze awhile,
First at the uninviting track,
  Then at the water's smile.

And so I go upon my way,
  Thro'out the sultry years,
But pause no more, by night, by day,
  Beside the Fount of Tears.

LIFE'S TRAGEDY

It may be misery not to sing at all
  And to go silent through the brimming
    day.
It may be sorrow never to be loved,
  But deeper griefs than these beset the
    way.

To have come near to sing the perfect song
  And only by a half-tone lost the key,
There is the potent sorrow, there the grief,
  The pale, sad staring of life's tragedy.

To have just missed the perfect love,
  Not the hot passion of untempered
    youth,
But that which lays aside its vanity
  And gives thee, for thy trusting worship,
    truth —

This, this it is to be accursed indeed ;
  For if we mortals love, or if we sing,
We count our joys not by the things we
    have,
  But by what kept us from the perfect
    thing.

DE WAY T'INGS COME

De way t'ings come, hit seems to me,
Is des' one monst'ous mystery;
De way hit seem to strike a man,
Dey ain't no sense, dey ain't no plan;
Ef trouble sta'ts a pilin' down,
It ain't no use to rage er frown,
It ain't no use to strive er pray,
Hit's mortal boun' to come dat way.

Now, ef you's hongry, an' yo' plate
Des' keep on sayin' to you, " Wait,"
Don't mek no diffunce how you feel,
'Twon't do no good to hunt a meal,
Fu' dat ah meal des' boun' to hide
Ontwell de devil's satisfied,
An' 'twell dey's somep'n by' to cyave
You's got to ease yo'se'f an' sta've.

But ef dey's co'n meal on de she'f
You needn't bothah 'roun' yo'se'f,
Somebody's boun' to amble in
An' 'vite you to dey co'n meal bin;
An' ef you's stuffed up to de froat
Wid co'n er middlin', fowl er shoat,
Des' look out an' you'll see fu' sho
A 'possum faint befo' yo' do'.

De way t'ings happen, huhuh, chile,
Dis worl' 's done puzzled me one w'ile;
I's mighty skeered I'll fall in doubt,
I des' won't try to reason out
De reason why folks strive an' plan
A dinnah fu' a full-fed man,
An' shet de do' an' cross de street
F'om one dat raally needs to eat.

NOON

Shadder in de valley
Sunlight on de hill,
Sut'ny wish dat locus'
Knowed how to be still.
Don't de heat already
Mek a body hum,
'Dout dat insec' sayin'
Hottah days to come ?

Fiel' 's a shinin' yaller
Wid de bendin' grain,
Guinea hen a callin',
Now's de time fu' rain;
Shet yo' mouf, you rascal,
Wha' 's de use to cry ?
You do' see no rain clouds
Up dah in de sky.

Dis hyeah sweat's been po'in'
Down my face sence dawn;
Ain't hit time we's hyeahin'
Dat ah dinnah ho'n ?
Go on, Ben an' Jaspah,
Lif' yo' feet an' fly,
Hit out fu' de shadder
Fo' I drap an' die.

Hongry, lawd a' mussy,
Hongry as a baih,
Seems lak I hyeah dinnah
Callin' evahwhaih;
Daih's de ho'n a blowin' !
Let dat cradle swing,
One mo' sweep, den da'kies,
Beat me to de spring!

AT THE TAVERN

A lilt and a swing,
And a ditty to sing,
Or ever the night grow old;
The wine is within,
And I'm sure 'twere a sin
For a soldier to choose to be cold, my dear,
For a soldier to choose to be cold.

We're right for a spell,
But the fever is—well,
No thing to be braved, at least;
So bring me the wine;
No low fever in mine,
For a drink is more kind than a priest, my dear,
For a drink is more kind than a priest.

DEATH

Storm and strife and stress,
Lost in a wilderness,
Groping to find a way,
Forth to the haunts of day

Sudden a vista peeps,
Out of the tangled deeps,
Only a point—the ray
But at the end is day.

Dark is the dawn and chill,
Daylight is on the hill,
Night is the flitting breath,
Day rides the hills of death.

NIGHT, DIM NIGHT

Night, dim night, and it rains, my love, it
    rains,
(Art thou dreaming of me, I wonder)
The trees are sad, and the wind complains,
    Outside the rolling of the thunder,
And the beat against the panes.

Heart, my heart, thou art mournful in the
    rain,
(Are thy redolent lips a-quiver?)
My soul seeks thine, doth it seek in vain?
    My love goes surging like a river,
Shall its tide bear naught save pain?

LYRICS OF LOVE AND SORROW

These sonnets were all born of Mr. Dun-
bar's own great love and his sorrow at the
loss of it. One can readily picture the
poet, bereft of the woman he loved so pas-
sionately—the " Alice," of his youthful
poem, and the wife of earlier years, sitting
alone some " winter's midnight " with his
bruised heart—on " Heart-break Hill."
The world's sweetest music and its
greatest poems have been the aftermaths
of human heart-breaks, and these little
fragments, so perfect in metrical form, so
melodious and so masterly are no excep-
tion to the rule. He wrote every word
with a mixture of life-blood and -bitter
tears.

I

Love is the light of the world, my dear,
    Heigho, but the world is gloomy;
The light has failed and the lamp down
    hurled,
    Leaves only darkness to me.

Love is the light of the world, my dear,
    Ah me, but the world is dreary;
The night is down, and my curtain furled
    But I cannot sleep, though weary.

Love is the light of the world, my dear,
    Alas for a hopeless hoping,
When the flame went out in the breeze
    that swirled,
    And a soul went blindly groping.

II

The light was on the golden sands,
    A glimmer on the sea;
My soul spoke clearly to thy soul,
    Thy spirit answered me.

Since then the light that gilds the sands,
    And glimmers on the sea,
But vainly struggles to reflect
    The radiant soul of thee.

III

The sea speaks to me of you
    All the day long;
Still as I sit by its side
    You are its song.

The sea sings to me of you
    Loud on the reef;
Always it moans as it sings,
    Voicing my grief.

IV

My dear love died last night;
    Shall I clothe her in white?
My passionate love is dead,
    Shall I robe her in red?
But nay, she was all untrue,
    She shall not go drest in blue;
Still my desolate love was brave,
    Unrobed let her go to her grave.

V

There are brilliant heights of sorrow
    That only the few may know;

And the lesser woes of the world, like
        waves,
    Break noiselessly, far below.
I hold for my own possessing,
    A mount that is lone and still —
The great high place of a hopeless grief,
    And I call it my " Heart-break Hill."
And once on a winter's midnight
    I found its highest crown,
And there in the gloom, my soul and I,
    Weeping, we sat us down.

But now when I seek that summit
    We are two ghosts that go ;
Only two shades of a thing that died,
    Once in the long ago.
So I sit me down in the silence,
    And say to my soul, " Be still,"
So the world may not know we died that
        night,
    From weeping on " Heart-break Hill."

A BOY'S SUMMER SONG

    'Tis fine to play
    In the fragrant hay,
And romp on the golden load ;
    To ride old Jack
    To the barn and back,
Or tramp by a shady road.
    To pause and drink,
    At a mossy brink ;
Ah, that is the best of joy,
    And so I say
    On a summer's day ?
What's so fine as being a boy ?
    Ha, Ha !

    With line and hook
    By a babbling brook,
The fisherman's sport we ply ;
    And list the song
    Of the feathered throng
That flit in the branches nigh.
    At last we strip
    For a quiet dip ;
Ah, that is the best of joy.
    For this I say
    On a summer's day,
What's so fine as being a boy ?
    Ha, Ha !

THE SAND-MAN

    I know a man
    With face of tan,
But who is ever kind ;
    Whom girls and boys
    Leave games and toys
Each eventide to find.

    When day grows dim,
    They watch for him,
He comes to place his claim ;
    He wears the crown
    Of Dreaming-town ;
The sand-man is his name.

    When sparkling eyes
    Droop sleepywise
And busy lips grow dumb ;
    When little heads
    Nod towards the beds,
We know the sand-man's come.

JOHNNY SPEAKS

The sand-man he's a jolly old fellow,
His face is kind and his voice is mellow,
But he makes your eyelids as heavy as
        lead,
And then you got to go off to bed ;
    I don't think I like the sand-man.

But I've been playing this livelong day ;
It does make a fellow so tired to play !
Oh, my, I'm a-yawning right here be-
        fore ma,
I'm the sleepiest fellow that ever you saw.
    I think I do like the sand-man.

WINTER SONG

Oh, who would be sad tho' the sky be
        a-graying,
    And meadow and woodlands are empty
        and bare ;
For softly and merrily now there come
        playing,
    The little white birds thro' the winter-
        kissed air.

The squirrel's enjoying the rest of the
    thrifty,
  He munches his store in the old hollow
    tree ;
Tho' cold is the blast and the snowflakes
    are drifty
  He fears the white flock not a whit more
    than we.

Chorus :

Then heigho for the flying snow !
Over the whitened roads we go,
  With pulses that tingle,
  And sleigh-bells a-jingle
For winter's white birds here's a cheery
    heigho !

THE FOREST GREETING

Good hunting !—aye, good hunting,
  Wherever the forests call ;
But ever a heart beats hot with fear,
  And what of the birds that fall ?

Good hunting !—aye, good hunting,
  Wherever the north winds blow ;
But what of the stag that calls for his
    mate ?
  And what of the wounded doe ?

Good hunting !—aye, good hunting,
  And ah ! we are bold and strong ;
But our triumph call through the forest
    hall
  Is a brother's funeral song.

For we are brothers ever,
  Panther and bird and bear ;
Man and the weakest that fear his face,
  Born to the nest or lair.

Yes, brothers, and who shall judge us ?
  Hunters and game are we ;
But who gave the right for me to smite ?
  Who boasts when he smiteth me ?

Good hunting !—aye, good hunting,
  And dim is the forest track ;
But the sportsman Death comes striding
    on :
  Brothers, the way is black.

A CHRISTMAS FOLKSONG

De win' is blowin' wahmah,
  An hit's blowin' f 'om de bay ;
Dey's a so't o' mist a-risin'
  All erlong de meddah way ;
Dey ain't a hint o' frostin'
  On de groun' ner in de sky,
An' dey ain't no use in hopin'
    Dat de snow'll 'mence to fly.
      It's goin' to be a green Christmas,
        An' sad de day fu' me.
      I wish dis was de las' one
        Dat evah I should see.

Dey's dancin' in de cabin,
  Dey's spahkin' by de tree ;
But dancin' times an' spahkin'
  Are all done pas' fur me.
Dey's feastin' in de big house,
  Wid all de windahs wide —
Is dat de way fu' people
    To meet de Christmas-tide ?
      It's goin' to be a green Christmas,
        No mattah what you say.
      Dey's us dat will remembah
        An' grieve de comin' day.

Dey's des a bref o' dampness
  A-clingin' to my cheek ;
De aihs been dahk an' heavy
  An' threatenin' fu' a week,
But not wid signs o' wintah,
  Dough wintah'd seem so deah —
De wintah's out o' season,
    An' Christmas eve is heah.
      It's goin' to be a green Christmas,
        An' oh, how sad de day !
      Go ax de hongry chu'chya'd,
        An' see what hit will say.

Dey's Allen on de hillside,
  An' Marfy in de plain ;
Fu' Christmas was like spring-time,
  An' come wid sun an' rain.
Dey's Ca'line, John, an' Susie,
  Wid only dis one lef' :
An' now de curse is comin'
  Wid murder in hits bref.
    It's goin' to be a green Christmas—
      Des hyeah my words an' see :
    Befo' de summah beckons
      Dey's many'll weep wid me.

IT'S GOIN' TO BE A GREEN CHRISTMAS

W'en You Says Yo' " Now I
Lay Me "

SCAMP

Ain't it nice to have a mammy
    W'en you kin' o' tiahed out
Wid a-playin' in de meddah,
    ·An' a-runnin' roun' about
Till hit's made you mighty hongry,
    An' yo' nose hit gits to know
What de smell means dat's a-comin'
    F'om de open cabin do' ?
        She wash yo' face,
        An' mek yo' place,
    You's hongry as a tramp;
Den hit's eat you suppah right away,
    You sta'vin' little scamp.

W'en you's full o' braid an' bacon,
    An' dey ain't no mo' to eat,
An' de lasses dat's a-stickin'
    On yo' face ta'se kin' o' sweet,
Don' you t'ink hit's kin' o' pleasin
    Fu' to have som'body neah
Dat'll wipe yo' han's an' kiss you
    Fo' dey lif' you f'om yo' cheah ?
        To smile so sweet,
        An' wash yo' feet,
    An' leave 'em co'l an' damp ;
Den hit's come let me undress you, now
    You lazy little scamp.

Don' yo' eyes git awful heavy,
    An' yo' lip git awful slack,
Ain't dey som'p'n' kin' o' weaknin'
    In de backbone of yo' back ?
Don' yo' knees feel kin' o' trimbly,
    An' yo' head go bobbin' roun',
W'en you says yo' " Now I lay me,"
    An' is sno'in' on de " down " ?
        She kiss yo' nose,
        She kiss yo' toes,
    An' den tu'n out de lamp,
Den hit's creep into yo' trunnel baid,
    You sleepy little scamp.

THE LILY OF THE VALLEY

Sweetest of the flowers a-blooming
    In the fragrant vernal days
Is the Lily of the Valley
    With its soft, retiring ways.

Well, you chose this humble blossom
    As the nurse's emblem flower,
Who grows more like her ideal
    Every day and every hour.

Like the Lily of the Valley
    In her honesty and worth,
Ah, she blooms in truth and virtue
    In the quiet nooks of earth.

Tho' she stands erect in honor
    When the heart of mankind bleeds,
Still she hides her own deserving
    In the beauty of her deeds.

In the silence of the darkness
    Where no eye may see and know,
There her footsteps shod with mercy,
    And fleet kindness come and go.

Not amid the sounds of plaudits,
    Nor before the garish day,
Does she shed her soul's sweet perfume,
    Does she take her gentle way.

But alike her ideal flower,
    With its honey-laden breath,
Still her heart blooms forth its beauty
    In the valley shades of death.

ENCOURAGED

This dainty verse was inscribed to a friend, who through his last years, was staunch and real and true, who understood him, scolded him when he needed it, praised him when he deserved it, and whose love was a ray of sunshine, wholesome, and warm and bright. Ever appreciative, he thanked his friend in this four-lined bit of verse.

Because you love me I have much
    achieved,
Had you despised me then I must have
    failed,
But since I knew you trusted and
    believed,
I could not disappoint you and so prevailed.

TO J. Q.

What are the things that make life bright ?
  A star gleam in the night.
What hearts us for the coming fray ?
  The dawn tints of the day.
What helps to speed the weary mile ?
  A brother's friendly smile.
What turns o' gold the evening gray ?
  A flower beside the way.

DIPLOMACY

Tell your love where the roses blow,
  And the hearts of the lilies quiver,
Not in the city's gleam and glow,
  But down by a half-sunned river.
Not in the crowded ballroom's glare,
  That would be fatal, Marie, Marie,
How can she answer you then and there ?
  So come then and stroll with me, my
    dear,
  Down where the birds call, Marie,
    Marie.

THE PLANTATION CHILD'S LULLABY

Wintah time hit comin'
  Stealin' thoo de night ;
Wake up in the mo'nin'
  Evaht'ing is white ;
Cabin lookin' lonesome
  Standin' in de snow,
Meks you kin' o' nervous,
  W'en de win' hit blow.

Trompin' back from feedin',
  Col' an' wet an' blue,
Homespun jacket ragged,
  Win' a-blowin' thoo.
Cabin lookin' cheerful,
  Unnerneaf de do',
Yet you kin' o' keerful
  W'en de win' hit blow.

Hickory log a-blazin'
  Light a-lookin' red,
Faith o' eyes o' peepin'
  F'om a trun'le bed,

Little feet a-patterin'
  Cleak across de flo' ;
Bettah had be keerful
  W'en de win' hit blow.

Suppah done an' ovah,
  Evaht'ing is still ;
Listen to de snowman
  Slippin' down de hill.
Ashes on de fiah,
  Keep it wa'm but low.
What's de use o' keerin'
  Ef de win' do blow ?

Smoke house full o' bacon,
  Brown an' sweet an' good ;
Taters in de cellah,
  'Possum roam de wood ;
Little baby snoozin'
  Des ez ef he know.
What's de use o' keerin'
  Ef de win' do blow ?

WADIN' IN DE CRICK

Days git wa'm an' wa'mah,
  School gits mighty dull,
Seems lak dese hyeah teachahs
  Mus' feel mussiful.
Hookey's wrong, I know it
  Ain't no gent'man's trick ;
But de aih's a-callin',
  " Come on to de crick."

Dah de watah's gu'glin'
  Ovah shiny stones,
Des hit's ve'y singin'
  Seems to soothe yo' bones.
W'at's de use o' waitin',
  Go on good an' quick :
Dain't no fun lak dis hyeah
  Wadin' in de crick.

W'at dat jay-bu'd sayin' ?
  Bettah shet yo' haid,
Fus' t'ing dat you fin' out,
  You'll be layin' daid.
Jay-bu'ds sich a tattlah,
  Des seem lak his trick
Fu' to tell on folkses
  Wadin' in de crick.

DAH DE WATAH'S GU'GLIN'

WHUT IS MAMMY COOKIN'

Willer boughs a-bendin',
    Hidin' of de sky,
Wavin' kin' o' frien'ly
    Ez de win' go by,
Elum trees a-shinin',
    Dahk an' green an' thick,
Seem to say, " I see yo'
    Wadin' in de crick."

But de trees don' chattah,
    Dey des look an' sigh
Lak hit's kin' o' peaceful
    Des a-bein' nigh,
An' yo' t'ank yo' Mastah
    Dat dey trunks is thick
W'en yo' mammy fin's you
    Wadin' in de crick.

Den yo' run behin' dem
    Lak yo' scaihed to def,
Mammy come a-flyin',
    Mos' nigh out o' bref;
But she set down gentle
    An' she drap huh stick,—
An' fus' t'ing, dey's mammy
    Wadin' in de crick.

CURIOSITY

Mammy's in de kitchen, an' de do' is shet ;
All de pickaninnies climb an' tug an'
    sweat,
Gittin' to de winder, stickin' dah lak flies,
Evah one ermong us des all nose an' eyes.
" Whut's she cookin', Isaac ? "   " Whut's
    she cookin', Jake ? "
" Is it sweet pertaters ? Is hit pie er
    cake ? "
But we couldn't mek out even whah we
    stood
Whut was mammy cookin' dat could smell
    so good.

Mammy spread de winder, an' she frown
    an' frown.
How de pickaninnies come a-tumblin'
    down !
Den she say : " Ef you-all keeps a-peepin'
    in,
How I'se gwine to whup you, my ! 't 'ill
    be a sin !

Need n' come a-sniffin' an' a-nosin' hyeah,
'Ca'se I knows my business, nevah feah."
Won't somebody tell us—how I wish dey
    would !—
Whut is mammy cookin' dat it smells so
    good ?

We know she means business, an' we das-
    sent stay,
Dough it's mighty tryin' fuh to go erway ;
But we goes a-troopin' down de ol' wood-
    track
'Twell dat steamin' kitchen brings us
    stealin' back,
Climbin' an' a-peepin' so's to see inside.
Whut on earf kin mammy be so sha'p to
    hide ?
I'd des up an' tell folks w'en I knowed I
    could,
Ef I was a-cookin' t'ings dat smelt so
    good.

Mammy in de oven, an' I see huh smile ;
Moufs mus' be a-wat'rin' roun' hyeah fuh
    a mile ;
Den we almos' hollah ez we hu'ies down,
'Ca'se hit's apple dumplin's, big an' fat
    an' brown !
W'en de do' is opened, solemn lak an'
    slow,
Wisht you see us settin' all dah in a row
Innercent an' p'opah, des lak chillun
    should
W'en dey mammy's cookin' t'ings dat
    smell so good.

OPPORTUNITY

Granny's gone a-visitin',
    Seen huh git huh shawl
W'en I was a-hidin' down
    Hime de gyahden wall.
Seen huh put her bonnet on,
    Seen huh tie de strings,
An' I'se gone to dreamin' now
    'Bout dem cakes an' t'ings.

On de she'f behime de do'—
    Mussy, what a feas' !

Soon ez she gits out o' sight,
  I kin eat in peace.
I bin watchin' fu' a week
  Des fu' dis hyeah chance.
Mussy, w'en I gits in daih,
  I'll des sholy dance.

Lemon pie an' gingah-cake,
  Let me set an' t'ink —
Vinegah an' sugah, too,
  Dat'll mek a drink;
Ef dey's one t'ing dat I loves
  Mos' pu'ticlahly,
It is eatin' sweet t'ings an'
  A-drinkin' Sangaree.

Lawdy, won' po' granny raih
  W'en she see de she'f;
W'en I t'ink erbout huh face,
  I's mos' 'shamed myse'f.
Well, she gone, an' hyeah I is,
  Back behime de do'—
Look hyeah! gran' 's done 'spected me,
  Dain't no sweets no mo'.

Evah sweet is hid erway,
  Job des done up brown;
Pusson t'ink dat some un t'ought
  Dey was t'eves erroun';
Dat des breaks my heart in two,
  Oh, how bad I feel!
Des to t'ink my own gramma
  B'lieved dat I 'u'd steal!

TWILIGHT

'Twixt a smile and a tear,
  'Twixt a song and a sigh,
'Twixt the day and the dark,
  When the night draweth nigh.

Ah, sunshine may fade
  From the heavens above,
No twilight have we
  To the day of our love.

THE FISHER CHILD'S LULLABY

The wind is out in its rage to-night,
  And your father is far at sea.
The rime on the window is hard and
      white
  But dear, you are near to me.
    Heave ho, weave low,
      Waves of the briny deep;
    Seethe low and breathe low,
      But sleep you, my little one,
        sleep, sleep.

The little boat rocks in the cove no more,
  But the flying sea-gulls wail;
I peer through the darkness that wraps
      the shore,
  For sight of a home set sail.
    Heave ho, weave low,
      Waves of the briny deep;
    Seethe low and breathe low,
      But sleep you, my little one,
        sleep, sleep.

Ay, lad of mine, thy father may die
  In the gale that rides the sea,
But we'll not believe it, not you and I,
  Who mind us of Galilee.
    Heave ho, weave low,
      Waves of the briny deep;
    Seethe low and breathe low,
      But sleep you, my little one,
        sleep, sleep.

FAITH

I's a-gittin' weary of de way dat people
    do,
De folks dat's got dey 'ligion in dey fiah-
    place an' flue;
Dey's allus somep'n' comin' so de spit'll
    have to turn,
An' hit tain't no p'oposition fu' to mke de
    hickory bu'n.
Ef de sweet pertater fails us an' de
    go'geous yallah yam,
We kin tek a bit o' comfo't f'om ouah sto'
    o' summah jam.
W'en de snow hit git to flyin', dat's de
    Mastah's own desiah,
De Lawd'll run de wintah an' yo'
    mammy'll run de fiah.

I ain' skeered because de win' hit staht
    to raih and blow,
I ain't bothahed w'en he come er rattlin'
    at de do',
Let him taih hisse't an' shout, let him
    blow an' bawl,

Dat's de time de branches shek an' bresh-
    wood 'mence to fall.
W'en de sto'm er railin' an' de shettahs
    blowin' 'bout,
Dat de time de fiahplace crack hits wel-
    come out.
Tain' my livin' business fu' to trouble ner
    enquiah,
De Lawd'll min' de wintah an' my
    mammy'll min' de fiah.

Ash-cake allus gits ez brown w'en
    February's hyeah
Ez it does in bakin' any othah time o'
    yeah.
De bacon smell ez callin'-like, de kittle
    rock an' sing,
De same way in de wintah dat dey do it
    in de spring ;
Dey ain't no use in mopin' 'round an'
    lookin' mad an' glum
Erbout de wintah season, fu' hit's des
    plumb boun' to come ·

An' ef it comes to runnin' t'ings I's willin'
    to retiah,
De Lawd'll min' de wintah an' my
    mammy'll min' de fiah.

THE FARM CHILD'S LULLABY

Oh, the little bird is rocking in the cradle
    of the wind,
And it's bye, my little wee one, bye ;
The harvest all is gathered and the pippins
    all are binned ;
Bye, my little wee one, bye ;
The little rabbit's hiding in the golden
    shock of corn,
The thrifty squirrel's laughing bunny's
    idleness to scorn ;
You are smiling with the angels in your
    slumber, smile till morn ;
    So it's bye, my little wee one, bye.

There'll be plenty in the cellar, there'll be
    plenty on the shelf ;
Bye, my little wee one, bye ;
There'll be goodly store of sweetings for a
    dainty little elf ;
Bye, my little wee one, bye.
The snow may be a-flying o'er the meadow
    and the hill,
The ice has checked the chatter of the
    little laughing rill,
But in your cosey cradle you are warm and
    happy still ;
    So bye, my little wee one, bye.

Why, the Bob White thinks the snowflake
    is a brother to his song ;
Bye, my little wee one, bye ;
And the chimney sings the sweeter when
    the wind is blowing strong ;
Bye my little wee one, bye ;
The granary's overflowing, full is cellar,
    crib, and bin,
The wood has paid its tribute and the ax
    has ceased its din ;
The winter may not harm you when you're
    sheltered safe within ;
    So bye, my little wee one, bye.

THE PLACE WHERE THE RAIN-
BOW ENDS

There's a fabulous story
Full of splendor and glory,
    That Arabian legends transcends ;
Of the wealth without measure,
The coffers of treasure,
    At the place where the rainbow ends.

Oh, many have sought it,
And all would have bought it,
    With the blood we so recklessly
    spend ;
But none has uncovered,
The gold, nor discovered
    The spot at the rainbow's end.

They have sought it in battle,
And e'en where the rattle
    Of dice with man's blasphemy
    blends ;

But howe'er persuasive,
It still proves evasive,
  This place where the rainbow ends.

I own for my pleasure,
I yearn not for treasure,
  Though gold has a power it lends;
And I have a notion,
To find without motion,
  The place where the rainbow ends.

The pot may hold pottage,
The place be a cottage,
  That a humble contentment defends,
Only joy fills its coffer,
But spite of the scoffer,
  There's the place where the rainbow
    ends.

Where care shall be quiet,
And love shall run riot,
  And I shall find wealth in my
    friends;
Then truce to the story,
Of riches and glory;
  There's the place where the rainbow
    ends.

HOPE

De dog go howlin' 'long de road,
  De night come shiverin' down;
My back is tiahed of its load,
  I cain't be fu' f'om town.
No mattah ef de way is long,
My haht is swellin' wid a song,
  No mattah 'bout de frownin' skies,
  I'll soon be home to see my Lize.

My shadder staggah on de way,
  It's monst'ous col' to-night;
But I kin hyeah my honey say
  "W'y bless me if de sight
O' you ain't good fu' my so' eyes."
(Dat talk's dis lak my lady Lize)
  I's so'y case de way was long
  But Lawd you bring me love an' song.

No mattah ef de way is long,
  An' ef I trimbles so'
I knows de fiah's burnin' strong,

Behime my Lizy's do'.
An' daih my res' an' joy shell be,
Whaih my ol' wife's awaitin' me —
  Why what I keer fu' stingin' blas',
  I see huh windah light at las'.

APPRECIATION

My muvver's ist the nicest one
  'At ever lived wiz folks;
She lets you have ze mostes' fun,
  An' laffs at all your jokes.

I got a ol' maid auntie, too,
  The worst you ever saw;
Her eyes ist bore you through and
    through,—
  She ain't a bit like ma.

She's ist as slim as slim can be,
  An' when you want to slide
Down on ze balusters, w'y she
  Says 'at she's harrified.

She ain't as nice as Uncle Ben,
  What says 'at little boys
Won't never grow to be big men
  Unless they're fond of noise.

But muvver's nicer zan 'em all,
  She calls you, " precious lamb,"
An' lets you roll your ten-pin ball,
  An' spreads your bread wiz jam.

An' when you're bad, she ist looks sad,
  You fink she's goin' to cry;
An' when she don't you're awful glad,
  An' den you're good, oh, my!

At night, she take ze softest hand,
  An' lays it on your head,
An' says " Be off to Sleepy-Land
  By way o' trundle-bed."

So when you fink what muvver knows
  An' aunts an' uncle tan't,
It skeers a feller; ist suppose
  His muvver 'd been a aunt.

DAY

The gray dawn on the mountain top
  Is slow to pass away.
Still lays him by in sluggish dreams,
  The golden God of day.

And then a light along the hills,
  Your laughter silvery gay;
The Sun God wakes, a bluebird trills,
  You come and it is day.

TO DAN

Step me now a bridal measure,
Work give way to love and leisure,
Hearts be free and hearts be gay —
Doctor Dan doth wed to-day.

Diagnosis, cease your squalling –
Check that scalpel's senseless bawling,
Put that ugly knife away —
Doctor Dan doth wed to-day.

'Tis no time for things unsightly,
Life's the day and life goes lightly;
Science lays aside her sway —
Love rules Dr. Dan to-day.

Gather, gentlemen and ladies,
For the nuptial feast now made is,
Swing your garlands, chant your lay
For the pair who wed to day.

Wish them happy days and many,
Troubles few and griefs not any,
Lift your brimming cups and say
God bless them who wed to-day.

Then a cup to Cupid daring,
Who for conquest ever faring,
With his arrows dares assail
E'en a doctor's coat of mail.

So with blithe and happy hymning
And with harmless goblets brimming,
Dance a step—musicians play —
Doctor Dan doth wed to-day.

WHAT'S THE USE

What's the use o' folks a-frownin'
  When the way's a little rough?
Frowns lay out the road fur smilin'
  You'll be wrinkled soon enough.
    What's the use?

What's the use o' folks a-sighin'?
  It's an awful waste o' breath,
An' a body can't stand wastin'
  What he needs so bad in death.
    What's the use?

What's the use o' even weepin'?
  Might as well go long an' smile.
Life, our longest, strongest arrow,
  Only lasts a little while.
    What's the use?

A LAZY DAY

The trees bend down along the stream,
  Where anchored swings my tiny boat.
The day is one to drowse and dream
  And list the thrush's throttling note.
When music from his bosom bleeds
Among the river's rustling reeds.

No ripple stirs the placid pool,
  When my adventurous line is cast,
A truce to sport, while clear and cool,
  The mirrored clouds slide softly past.
The sky gives back a blue divine,
And all the world's wide wealth is mine.

A pickerel leaps, a bow of light,
  The minnows shine from side to side.
The first faint breeze comes up the tide --
  I pause with half uplifted oar,
While night drifts down to claim the shore.

LIMITATIONS

Ef you's only got de powah fe' to blow a
  little whistle,
  Keep ermong de people wid de whistles.
Ef you don't, you'll fin' out sho'tly dat
  you's th'owed yo' fines' feelin'

In a place dat's all a bed o' thistles.
'Tain't no use a-goin' now, ez sho's you bo'n,
A-squeakin' of yo' whistle 'g'inst a gread
    big ho'n.

Ef you ain't got but a teenchy bit o'
    victuals on de table,
Whut's de use a-claimin' hit's a feas' ?
Fe' de folks is mighty 'spicious, an' dey's
    ap' to come a-peerin',
Lookin' fe' de scraps you lef' at leas'.
W'en de meal's a-hidin' f'om de meal-bin's
    top,
You needn't talk to hide it ; ef you sta'ts,
    des stop.

Ef yo' min' kin only carry half a pint o'
    common idees,
Don' go roun' a-sayin' hit's a bar'l ;
'Ca'se de people gwine to test you, an'
    dey'll fin' out you's a-lyin',
Den dey'll twis' yo' sayin's in a snarl.
Wuss t'ing in de country dat I evah
    hyahed —
A crow dot sat a-squawkin', " I's a
    mockin'-bird."

A GOLDEN DAY

I found you and I lost you,
    All on a gleaming day.
The day was filled with sunshine,
    And the land was full of May.

A golden bird was singing
    Its melody divine,
I found you and I loved you,
    And all the world was mine.

I found you and I lost you,
    All on a golden day,
But when I dream of you, dear,
    It is always brimming May.

THE UNLUCKY APPLE

'Twas the apple that in Eden
    Caused our father's primal fall ;
And the Trojan War, remember —
    'Twas an apple caused it all.

So for weeks I've hesitated,
    You can guess the reason why,
For I want to tell my darling
    She's the apple of my eye.

PUTTIN' THE BABY AWAY

Eight of 'em hyeah all tol' an' yet
Dese eyes o .nine is wringin' wet ;
My haht's a-achin' ha'd an' so',
De way hit nevah ached befo' ;
My soul's a-pleadin', " Lawd give back
Dis little lonesome baby black,
Dis one, dis las' po' he'pless one
Whose little race was too soon run."

Po' Little Jim, des fo' yeahs' ol'
A-layin' down so still an' col'.
Somehow hit don' seem ha'dly faih,
To have my baby lyin' daih
Wi'dout a smile upon his face,
Wi'dout a look erbout de place ;
He ust to be so full o' fun
Hit don' seem right dat all's done, done.

Des eight in all but I don' caih,
Dey wa'nt a single one to spaih ;
De worl' was big, so was my haht,
An' dis hyeah baby owned hits paht ;
De house was po', dey clothes was rough,
But daih was meat an' meal enough ;
An' daih was room fu' little Jim ;
Oh ! Lawd, what made you call fu' him ?

It do seem monst'ous ha'd to-day,
To lay dis baby boy away ;
I'd learned to love his teasin' smile,
He mought o' des been lef' erwhile ;
You wouldn't t'ought wid all de folks,
Dat's roun' hyeah mixin' teahs an' jokes,
De Lawd u'd had de time to see
Dis chile an' tek him 'way f'om me.

But let it go, I reckon Jim,
'll des go right straight up to him
Dat took him f'om his mammy's nest
An' lef' dis achin' in my breas',
An' lookin' in dat fathah's face
An' 'memberin' dis lone sorrerin' place,
He'll say, " Good Lawd, you ought to had
Do sumpin' fu' to comfo't dad ! "

Dese Eyes o' Mine is Wringin' Wet

DES DON' PET YO' WORRIES

ADVICE

W'en you full o' worry
  'Bout yo' wo'k an' sich,
W'en you kind o' bothered
  Case you can't get rich,
An' yo' neighboh p'ospah
  Past his jest desu'ts,
An' de sneer of comerds
  Stuhes yo' heaht an' hu'ts,
Des don' pet yo' worries,
  Lay 'em on de she'f,
Tek a little trouble
  Brothah, wid yo'se'f.

Ef a frien' comes mou'nin'
  'Bout his awful case,
You know you don' grieve him
  Wid a gloomy face,
But you wrassle wid him,
  Try to tek him in;
Dough hit cracks yo' features,
  Law, you smile lak sin,
Ain't you good ez he is?
  Don' you pine to def;
Tek a little trouble
  Brothah, wid yo'se'f.

Ef de chillun pestahs,
  An' de baby's bad,
Ef yo' wife gits narvous,
  An' you're gettin' mad,
Des you grab yo' boot-strops,
  Hol' yo' body down,
Stop a-t'inkin' cuss-w'rds,
  Chase away de frown,
Knock de haid o' worry,
  Twell dey ain' none lef';
Tek a little trouble,
  Brothah, wid yo'se'f.

THE DISCOVERY

These are the days of elfs and fays:
Who says that with the dreams of myth,
These imps and elves disport themselves?
Ah no, along the paths of song
Do all the tiny folk belong.

Round all our homes,
Kobolds and gnomes do daily cling,

Then nightly fling their lanterns out.
And shout on shout, they join the rout,
And sing, and sing, within the sweet en-
    chanted ring.

Where gleamed the guile of moonlight's
    smile,
Once paused I, listening for a while,
And heard the lay, unknown by day, —
The fairies' dancing roundelay.

Queen Mab was there, her shimmering
    hair
Each fairy prince's heart's despair.
She smiled to see their sparkling glee,
And once I ween, she smiled at me.

Since when, you may by night or day,
Dispute the sway of elf-folk gay;
But, hear me, stay!
I've learned the way to find Queen Mab
    and elf and fay.

Where'er by streams, the moonlight gleams,
Or on meadow softly beams,
There, footing round on dew-lit ground,
The fairy folk may all be found.

MORNING

The mist has left the greening plain,
The dew-drops shine like fairy rain,
The coquette rose awakes again
  Her lovely self adorning.
The Wind is hiding in the trees,
A sighing, soothing, laughing tease,
Until the rose says, " Kiss me, please,"
  'Tis morning, 'tis morning.

With staff in hand and careless-free,
The wanderer fares right jauntily,
For towns and houses are, thinks he,
  For scorning, for scorning.
My soul is swift upon the wing,
And in its deeps a song I bring;
Come, Love, and we together sing,
  " 'Tis morning, 'tis morning."

THE AWAKENING

I did not know that life could be so sweet,
I did not know the hours could speed so
　fleet,
Till I knew you, and life was sweet again.
The days grew brief with love and lack of
　pain —

I was a slave a few short days ago,
The powers of Kings and Princes now I
　know ;
I would not be again in bondage, save
I had your smile, the liberty I crave.

LOVE'S DRAFT

The draft of love was cool and sweet
　You gave me in the cup,
But, ah, love's fire is keen and fleet,
　And I am burning up.

Unless the tears I shed for you
　Shall quench this burning flame.
It will consume me through and through,
　And leave but ash—a name.

A MUSICAL

Outside the rain upon the street,
　The sky all grim of hue,
Inside, the music-painful sweet,
　And yet I heard but you.

As is a thrilling violin,
　So is your voice to me
And still above the other strains,
　It sang in ecstasy.

TWELL DE NIGHT IS PAS'

All de night long twell de moon goes down,
　Lovin' I set at huh feet,
Den fu' de long jou'ney back fom de town,
　Ha'd, but de dreams mek it sweet.

All de night long twell de break of de day,
　Dreamin' agin in my sleep,
Mandy comes drivin' my sorrers away,
　Axin' me, " Wha' fu' you weep ? "

All de day long twell de sun goes down,
　Smilin', I ben' to my hoe,
Fu' dough de weddah git nasty an' frown,
　One place I know I kin go.

All my life long twell de night has pas'
　Let de wo'k come ez it will,
So dat I fin' you, my honey, at las',
　Somewhaih des ovah de hill.

AT NIGHT

Whut time'd dat clock strike ?
Nine ? No—eight ;
I didn't think hit was so late.
Aer chew ! I must 'a' got a cough,
I raally b'lieve I did doze off —
Hit's mighty soothin' to de tiah,
A-dozin' dis way by de fiah ;
Oo oom—hit feels so good to stretch
I sutny is one weary wretch !

Look hyeah, dat boy done gone to sleep !
He des ain't wo'th his boa'd an' keep ;
I des don't b'lieve he'd bat his eyes
If Gab'el called him fom de skies !
But sleepin's good dey ain't no doubt —
Dis pipe o' mine is done gone out.
Don't bu'n a minute, bless my soul,
Des please to han' me dat ah coal.

You 'Lias git up now, my son,
Seems lak my nap is des begun ;
You sutny mus' ma'k down de day
W'en I treats comp'ny dis away !
W'y, Brother Jones, dat drowse come on,
An' laws ! I dremp dat you was gone !
You 'Lias, whaih yo' mannahs, suh,
To hyeah me call an' nevah stuh !

To-morrer mo'nin' w'en I call
Dat boy'll be sleepin' to beat all,
Don't mek no diffunce how I roah,
He'll des lay up an' sno' and sno'.
Now boy, you done hyeahed whut I said,
You bettah tek yo'se'f yo' baid,
Case ef you gits me good an' wrong
I'll mek dat sno' a diffunt song.

Dis wood fiah is invitin' dho',
Hit seems to wa'm de ve'y flo' —
An' nuffin' ain't a whit ez sweet,
Ez settin' toastin' of yo' feet.
Hit mek you drowsy, too, but La!
Hyeah, 'Lias, don't you hyeah yo' ma?
Ef I gits sta'ted f'om dis cheah
I' lay, you scamp, I'll mek you heah!

To-morrer mo'nin' I kin bawl
Twell all de neighbohs hyeah me call;
An' you'll be snoozin' des ez deep
Ez if de day was made fu' sleep;
Hit's funny when you got a cough
Somehow yo' voice seems too fu' off —
Can't wake dat boy fu' all I say,
I reckon he'll sleep daih twell day!

KIDNAPPED

I held my heart so far from harm,
    I let it wander far and free
In mead and mart, without alarm,
    Assured it must come back to me.

And all went well till on a day,
    Learned Dr. Cupid wandered by
A search along our sylvan way
    For some peculiar butterfly.

A flash of wings, a hurried drive,
    A flutter and a short-lived flit;
This Scientist, as I am alive
    Had seen my heart and captured it.

Right tightly now 'tis held among
    The specimens that he has trapped,
And sings (oh, love is ever young),
    'Tis passing sweet to be kidnapped.

COMPENSATION

Because I had loved so deeply,
    Because I had loved so long,
God in his great compassion
    Gave me the gift of song.

Because I have loved so vainly,
    And sung with such faltering
        breath,

The Master in infinite mercy
    Offers the boon of Death.

WINTER'S APPROACH

De sun hit shine an' de win' hit blow,
Ol' Brer Rabbit be a-layin' low,
    He know dat de wintah time
        a-comin',
De huntah man he walk an' wait,
He walk right by Brer Rabbit's gate —
    He know —

De dog he lick his sliverin' chop,
An' he tongue 'gin' his mouf go flop,
        flop —
    He —
He rub his nose fu' to clah his scent
So's to tell w'ich way dat cotton-tail went,
    He —

De huntah's wife she set an' spin
A good wahm coat fu' to wrop him in
    She —
She look at de skillet an' she smile, oh
        my!
An' ol' Brer Rabbit got to sholy fly.
    Dey know.

ANCHORED

If thro' the sea of night which here sur-
        rounds me,
    I could swim out beyond the farthest
        star,
Break every barrier of circumstance that
        bounds me,
    And greet the Sun of sweeter life afar,

Tho' near you there is passion, grief, and
        sorrow,
    And out there rest and joy and peace
        and all,
I should renounce that beckoning for to-
        morrow,
    I could not choose to go beyond your
        call.

18

THE VETERAN

Underneath the autumn sky,
Haltingly, the lines go by.
Ah, would steps were blithe and gay,
As when first they marched away,
Smile on lip and curl on brow,—
Only white-faced gray-beards now,
Standing on life's outer verge,
E'en the marches sound a dirge.

Blow, you bugles, play, you fife,
Rattle, drums, for dearest life.
Let the flags wave freely so,
As the marching legions go,
Shout, hurrah and laugh and jest,
This is memory at its best.
(Did you notice at your quip,
That old comrade's quivering lip?)

Ah, I see them as they come,
Stumbling with the rumbling drum;
But a sight more sad to me
E'en than these ranks could be
Was that one with cane upraised
Who stood by and gazed and gazed,
Trembling, solemn, lips compressed,
Longing to be with the rest.

Did he dream of old alarms,
As he stood, " presented arms " ?
Did he think of field and camp
And the unremitting tramp
Mile on mile—the lonely guard
When he kept his midnight ward?
Did he dream of wounds and scars
In that bitter war of wars?

What of that?   He stood and stands
In my memory—trembling hands,
Whitened beard and cane and all
As if waiting for the call
Once again: " To arms, my sons,"
And his ears hear far-off guns,
Roll of cannon and the tread
Of the legions of the Dead !

BLUE

Standin' at de winder,
   Feelin' kind o' glum,
Listenin' to de rain-drops
   Play de kettle drum,
Lookin' crost de medders
   Swimmin' lak a sea;
Lawd 'a' mussy on us,
   What's de good o' me ?

Can't go out a-hoein',
   Wouldn't ef I could ;
Groun' too wet fu' huntin',
   Fishin' ain't no good.
Too much noise fo' sleepin',
   No one hyeah to chat;
Des mus' stan' an' listen
   To dat pit-a-pat.

Hills is gittin' misty,
   Valley's gittin' dahk ;
Watch-dog's 'mence a-howlin',
   Rathah have 'em ba'k
Dan a-moanin' solemn
   Somewhaih out o' sight;
Rain-crow des a-chucklin' —
   Dis is his delight.

Mandy, bring my banjo,
   Bring de chillen in,
Come in f'om de kitchen,
   I feel sick ez sin.
Call in Uncle Isaac,
   Call Aunt Hannah, tco,
Tain't no use in talkin',
   Chile, I's sholy blue.

DREAMIN' TOWN

Come away to dreamin' town,
   Mandy Lou, Mandy Lou,
Whaih de skies don' nevah frown,
   Mandy Lou ;
Whaih de streets is paved with gol',
Whaih de days is nevah col',
An' no sheep strays f'om de fol',
   Mandy Lou.

Ain't you tiahed of every day,
   Mandy Lou, Mandy Lou,

CHILE, I'S SHOLY BLUE

In dat Dreamland of Delight

Tek my han' an' come away,
    Mandy Lou,
To the place whaih dreams is King,
Whaih my heart hol's everything,
An' my soul can allus sing,
    Mandy Lou.

Come away to dream wid me,
    Mandy Lou, Mandy Lou,
Whaih our hands an' hea'ts are free,
    Mandy Lou;
Whaih de sands is shinin' white,
In dat dreamland of delight,
Whaih de rivahs glistens bright,
    Mandy Lou.

Come away to dreamland town,
    Mandy Lou, Mandy Lou,
Whaih de fruit is bendin' down,
    Des fu' you.
Smooth your brow of lovin' brown,
An' my love will be its crown;
Come away to dreamin' town,
    Mandy Lou.

YESTERDAY AND TO-MORROW

Yesterday I held your hand,
    Reverently I pressed it,
And its gentle yieldingness
    From my soul I blessed it.

But to-day I sit alone,
    Sad and sore repining;
Must our gold forever know
    Flames for the refining?

Yesterday I walked with you,
    Could a day be sweeter?
Life was all a lyric song
    Set to tricksy meter.

Ah, to-day is like a dirge,—
    Place my arms around you,
Let me feel the same dear joy
    As when first I found you.

Let me once retrace my steps,
    From these roads unpleasant,
Let my heart and mind and soul
    All ignore the present.

Yesterday the iron seared
    And to-day means sorrow.
Pause, my soul, arise, arise,
    Look where gleams the morrow.

THE CHANGE

Love used to carry a bow, you know,
    But now he carries a taper;
It is either a length of wax aglow,
    Or a twist of lighted paper.

I pondered a little about the scamp,
    And then I decided to follow
His wandering journey to field and camp,
    Up hill, down dale or hollow.

I dogged the rollicking, gay, young blade
    In every species of weather;
Till, leading me straight to the home of a
        maid
He left us there together.

And then I saw it, oh, sweet surprise,
    The taper it set a-burning
The love-light brimming my lady's eyes,
    And my heart with the fire of yearning.

THE CHASE

The wind told the little leaves to hurry,
    And chased them down the way,
While the mother tree laughed loud in
        glee,
    For she thought her babes at play.

The cruel wind and the rain laughed
        loudly,
    We'll bury them deep, they said,
And the old tree grieves, and the little
    leaves
    Lie low, all chilled and dead.

SUPPOSE

If 'twere fair to suppose
    That your heart were not taken,
That the dew from the rose
    Petals still were not shaken,
I should pluck you,

Howe'er you should thorn me and
　　scorn me,
And wear you for life as the green of the
　　bower.

If 'twere fair to suppose
　　That that road was for vagrants,
That the wind and the rose,
　　Counted all in their fragrance;
Oh, my dear one,
　　My love, I should take you and make
　　　you,
The green of my life from the scintillant
　　hour.

THE DEATH OF THE FIRST-BORN

Cover him over with daisies white,
　　And eke with the poppies red,
Sit with me here by his couch to-night,
　　For the First-Born, Love, is dead.

Poor little fellow, he seemed so fair
　　As he lay in my jealous arms;
Silent and cold he is lying there
　　Stripped of his darling charms.

Lusty and strong he had grown forsooth,
　　Sweet with an infinite grace,
Proud in the force of his conquering
　　youth,
　　Laughter alight in his face.

Oh, but the blast, it was cruel and keen,
　　And ah, but the chill it was rare;
The look of the winter-kissed flow'r you've
　　seen
　　When meadows and fields were bare.

Can you not wake from this white, cold
　　sleep
　　And speak to me once again?
True that your slumber is deep, so deep,
　　But deeper by far is my pain.

Cover him over with daisies white,
　　And eke with the poppies red,
Sit with me here by his couch to-night,
　　For the First-Born, Love, is dead.

BEIN' BACK HOME

Wearying of his losing battle for health, assured that his days were numbered, and too weak to continue his literary labors, poor Paul Dunbar went home to Dayton to die.

Show me another, who, under such heart-breaking conditions, could have written such a poem as " Bein' Back Home."

The old settee to which he refers in the fourth stanza, actually exists, and was the poet's favorite seat. His mother counts it among the most precious relics of her son.

Home agin, an' home to stay —
Yes, it's nice to be away.
Plenty things to do an' see,
But the old place seems to me
Jest about the proper thing.
Mebbe 'ts 'cause the mem'ries cling
Closer 'round yore place o' birth
'N ary other spot on earth.

W'y it's nice jest settin' here,
Lookin' out an' seein' clear,
'Thout no smoke, ner dust, ner haze
In these sweet October days.
What's as good as that there lane,
Kind o' browned from last night's rain?
'Pears like home has got the start
When the goal's a feller's heart.

What's as good as that there jay
Screechin' up'ards towards the gray
Skies? An' tell me, what's as fine
As that full-leafed pumpkin vine?
Tow'rin' buildin's—yes, they're good;
But in sight o' field and wood,
Then a feller understan's
'Bout the house not made with han's.

Let the others rant an' roam
When they git away from home;
Jest gi' me my old settee
An' my pipe beneath a tree;
Sight o' medders green an' still,
Now and then a gentle hill,
Apple orchards, full o' fruit,
Nigh a cider press to boot—

That's the thing jest done up brown
D'want to be too nigh to town ;
Want to have the smells an' sights,
An' the dreams o' long still nights,
With the friends you used to know
In the keerless long ago —
Same old cronies, same old folks,
Same old cider, same old jokes.

Say, it's nice a-gittin' back,
When yore pulse is growin' slack,
An' yore breath begins to wheeze
Like a fair-set valley breeze ;
Kind o' nice to set aroun'
On the old familiar groun',
Knowin' that when Death does come,
That he'll find you right at home.

DESPAIR

Let me close the eyes of my soul
  That I may not see
What stands between thee and me.

Let me shut the ears of my heart
  That I may not hear
A voice that drowns yours, my dear.

Let me cut the cords of my life,
  Of my desolate being,
Since cursed is my hearing and seeing.

CIRCUMSTANCES ALTER CASES

Tim Murphy's gon' walkin' wid Maggie
  O'Neill,
      O chone !
If I was her muther, I'd frown on sich
  foolin',
      O chone !
I'm sure it's unmutherlike, darin' an' wrong
To let a gyrul hear tell the sass an' the
  song
Of every young felly that happens along,
      O chone !

An' Murphy, the things that's be'n sed of
  his doin',
      O chone !

'Tis a cud that no decent folks want to be
  chewin',
      O chone !
If he came to my door wid his cane on a
  twirl,
Fur to thry to make love to you, Biddy,
  my girl,
Ah, wouldn't I send him away wid a
  whirl,
      O chone !

They say the gossoon is indecent and
  dirty,
      O chone !
In spite of his dressin' so.
      O chone !
Let him dress up ez foine ez a king or a
  queen,
Let him put on more wrinkles than ever
  was seen,
You'll be sure he's no match for my little
  colleen,
      O chone !

Faith the two is comin' back an' their
  walk is all over,
      O chone !
'Twas a pretty short walk fur to take wid
  a lover,
      O chone !
Why, I believe that Tim Murphy's a
  kumin' this way,
Ah, Biddy, jest look at him steppin' so
  gay,
I'd niver belave what the gossipers say,
      O chone !

He's turned in the gate an' he's coming
  a-caperin',
      O chone !
Go, Biddy, go quick an' put on a clane
  apern,
      O chone !
Be quick as ye kin fur he's right at the
  dure ;
Come in, master Tim, fur ye're welcome
  I'm shure.
We were talkin' o' ye jest a minute be-
  fore.
      O chone !

TILL THE WIND GETS RIGHT

Oh, the breeze is blowin' balmy
    And the sun is in a haze ;
There's a cloud jest givin' coolness,
    To the laziest of days.
There are crowds upon the lakeside,
    But the fish refuse to bite,
So I'll wait and go a-fishin'
    When the wind gets right.

Now my boat tugs at her anchor,
    Eager now to kiss the spray,
While the little waves are callin'
    Drowsy sailor come away,
There's a harbor for the happy,
    And its sheen is just in sight,
But I won't set sail to get there,
    Till the wind gets right.

That's my trouble, too, I reckon,
    I've been waitin' all too long,
Tho' the days were always bright
    Still the wind is always wrong.
An' when Gabriel blows his trumpet,
    In the day o' in the night,
I will still be found waitin',
    Till the wind gets right.

A SUMMER NIGHT

Summah is de lovin' time —
    Do' keer what you say.
Night is allus peart an' prime,
    Bettah dan de day.
Do de day is sweet an' good,
    Birds a-singin' fine,
Pines a-smellin' in de wood,—
    But de night is mine.

Rivah whisperin' " howdy do,"
    Ez it pass you by —
Moon a-lookin' down at you,
    Winkin' on de sly.
Frogs a-croakin' f'om de pon',
    Singin' bass dey fill,
An' you listen way beyon'
    Ol' man whippo'will.

Hush up, honey, tek my han',
    Mek yo' footsteps light ;
Somep'n' kin' o' hol's de lan'
    On a summah night.
Somep'n' dat you nevah sees
    An' you nevah hyeahs,
But you feels it in de breeze,
    Somep'n' nigh to teahs.

Somep'n' nigh to teahs? dat's so ;
    But hit's nigh to smiles.
An' you feels it ez you go
    Down de shinin' miles.
Tek my han', my little dove ;
    Hush an' come erway —
Summah is de time fu' love,
    Night-time beats de day !

AT SUNSET TIME

A down the west a golden glow
    Sinks burning in the sea,
And all the dreams of long ago
    Come flooding back to me.
The past has writ a story strange
    Upon my aching heart,
But time has wrought a subtle change,
    My wounds have ceased to smart.

No more the quick delight of youth,
    No more the sudden pain,
I look no more for trust or truth
    Where greed may compass gain.
What, was it I who bared my heart
    Through unrelenting years,
And knew the sting of misery's dart,
    The tang of sorrow's tears ?

'Tis better now, I do not weep,
    I do not laugh nor care ;
My soul and spirit half asleep
    Drift aimless everywhere.
We float upon a sluggish stream,
    We ride no rapids mad,
While life is all a tempered dream
    And every joy half sad.

NIGHT

Silence, and whirling worlds afar
  Through all encircling skies.
What floods come o'er the spirit's bar,
  What wondrous thoughts arise.

The earth, a mantle falls away,
  And, winged, we leave the sod ;
Where shines in its eternal sway
  The majesty of God.

AT LOAFING-HOLT

Since I left the city's heat
For this sylvan, cool retreat,
High upon the hillside here
Where the air is clean and clear,
I have lost the urban ways.
Mine are calm and tranquil days,
Sloping lawns of green are mine,
Clustered treasures of the vine ;
Long forgotten plants I know,
Where the best wild berries grow,
Where the greens and grasses sprout,
When the elders blossom out.
Now I am grown weather-wise
With the lore of winds and skies.
Mine the song whose soft refrain
Is the sigh of summer rain.
Seek you where the woods are cool,
Would you know the shady pool
Where, throughout the lazy day,
Speckled beauties drowse or play ?
Would you find in rest or peace
Sorrow's permanent release ? —
Leave the city, grim and gray,
Come with me, ah, come away.
Do you fear the winter chill,
Deeps of snow upon the hill ?
'Tis a mantle, kind and warm,
Shielding tender shoots from harm.
Do you dread the ice-clad streams,—
They are mirrors for your dreams.
Here's a rouse, when summer's past
To the raging winter's blast.
Let him roar and let him rout,
We are armored for the bout.
How the logs are glowing, see !
Who sings louder, they or he ?
Could the city be more gay ?
Burn your bridges ! Come away !

WHEN A FELLER'S ITCHIN' TO BE SPANKED

W'en us fellers stomp around, makin' lots
    o' noise,
Gramma says, " There's certain times
    comes to little boys
W'en they need a shingle or the soft side
    of a plank ; "
She says, " we're a-itchin' for a right good
    spank."
  An' she says, " Now thes you wait,
  It's a-comin'—soon or late,
W'en a feller's itchin' fer a spank."

W'en a feller's out o' school, you know
    how he feels,
Gramma says we wriggle 'roun' like a lot
    o' eels.
W'y it's like a man that's thes home from
    out o' jail.
What's the use o' scoldin' if we pull Tray's
    tail ?
  Gramma says, tho', " thes you wait,
  It's a-comin'—soon or late,
You'se the boys that's itchin' to be
    spanked."

Cats is funny creatures an' I like to make
    'em yowl,
Gramma alwus looks at me with a awful
    scowl
An' she says, " Young gentlemen, mamma
    should be thanked
Ef you'd get your knickerbockers right
    well spanked."
  An' she says, " Now thes you wait,
  It's a-comin'—soon or late,"
W'en a feller's itchin' to be spanked.

Ef you fin' the days is gettin' awful hot in
    school
An' you know a swimmin' place where it's
    nice and cool,
Er you know a cat-fish hole brimmin' full
    o' fish,
Whose a-goin' to set around school and
    wish ?
  'Tain't no use to hide your bait,
  It's a-comin'—soon or late,
W'en a feller's itchin' to be spanked.

Ol' folks know most ever'thing 'bout the
    world, I guess,
Gramma does, we wish she knowed thes a
    little less,
But I alwus kind o' think it 'ud be as well
Ef they wouldn't alwus have to up an' tell;
    We kids wish 'at they'd thes wait,
    It's a-comin'—soon or late,
W'en a feller's itchin' to be spanked.

THE RIVER OF RUIN

Along by the river of ruin
They dally—the thoughtless ones,
They dance and they dream
By the side of the stream,
As long as the river runs.

It seems all so pleasant and cheery —
No thought of the morrow is theirs,
And their faces are bright
With the sun of delight,
And they dream of no night-brooding cares.

The women wear garlanded tresses,
The men have rings on their hands,
And they sing in their glee,
For they think they are free —
They that know not the treacherous sands.

Ah, but this be a venturesome journey,
Forever those sands are ashrift,
And a step to one side
Means a grasp of the tide,
And the current is fearful and swift.

For once in the river of ruin,
What boots it, to do or to dare,
For down we must go
In the turbulent flow,
To the desolate sea of Despair.

TO HER

Your presence like a benison to me
Wakes my sick soul to dreamful ecstasy,
I fancy that some old Arabian night
Saw you my houri and my heart's de-
    light.

And wandering forth beneath the passion-
    ate moon,
Your love-strung zither and my soul in
    tune,
We knew the joy, the haunting of the
    pain
That like a flame thrills through me now
    again.

To-night we sit where sweet the spice
    winds blow,
    A wind the northland lacks and ne'er
      shall know,
With clasped hands and spirits all aglow
    As in Arabia in the long ago.

A LOVE LETTER

Oh, I des received a letter f'om de sweet-
    est little gal;
    Oh, my; oh, my.
She's my lovely little sweetheart an' her
    name is Sal:
    Oh, my; oh, my.

She writes me dat she loves me, an' she
    loves me true,
She wonders ef I'll tell huh dat I loves
    huh too;
An' my heaht's so full o' music dat I do'
    know what to do;
    Oh, my; oh, my.

I got a man to read it an' he read it fine;
    Oh, my; oh, my.
Dey ain' no use denying dat her love is
    mine;
    Oh, my; oh, my.

But hyeah's de t'ing dat's puttin' me in
    such a awful plight,
I t'ink of huh at mornin' an' I dream of
    huh at night;
But how's I gwine to cou't huh w'en I do'
    know how to write?
    Oh, my; oh, my.

My heaht is bubblin' ovah wid de t'ings I
    want to say;
    Oh, my; oh, my.

A Letter f'om de Sweetes' Little Gal

I . . . Git to T'inkin' of de Pas'

An' dey's lots of folks to copy what I tell
    'em fu' de pay ;
        Oh, my ; oh, my.

But dey's t'ings dat I's a-t'inkin' dat is
    only fu' huh ears,
An' I couldn't lu'n to write 'em ef I took
    a dozen years ;
So to go down daih an' tell huh is de only
    way, it 'pears ;
        Oh, my ; oh, my.

THE OLD CABIN

In de dead of night I sometimes,
    Git to t'inkin' of de pas'
An' de days w'en slavery helt me
    In my mis'ry—ha'd an' fas'.
Dough de time was mighty tryin',
    In dese houahs somehow hit seem
Dat a brightah light come slippin'
    Thoo de kivahs of my dream.

An' my min' fu'gits de whuppins
    Draps de feah o' block an' lash
An' flies straight to somep'n' joyful
    In a secon's lightnin' flash.
Den hit seems I see a vision
    Of a dearah long ago
Of de childern tumblin' roun' me
    By my rough ol' cabin do'.

Talk about yo' go'geous mansions
    An' yo' big house great an' gran',
Des bring up de fines' palace
    Dat you know in all de lan'.
But dey's somep'n' dearah to me,
    Somep'n' faihah to my eyes
In dat cabin, less you bring me
    To yo' mansion in de skies.

I kin see de light a-shinin'
    Thoo de chinks atween de logs,
I kin hyeah de way-off bayin'
    Of my mastah's huntin' dogs,
An' de neighin' of de hosses
    Stampin' on de ol' bahn flo',
But above dese soun's de laughin'
    At my deah ol' cabin do'.

We would gethah daih at evenin',
    All my frien's 'ud come erroun'

An' hit wan't no time, twell, bless you,
    You could hyeah de banjo's soun'.
You could see de dahkies dancin'
    Pigeon wing an' heel an' toe,—
Joyous times I tell you people
    Roun' dat same ol' cabin do'.

But at times my t'oughts gits saddah,
    Ez I riccolec' de folks,
An' dey frolickin' an' talkin'
    Wid dey laughin' an' dey jokes.
An' hit hu'ts me w'en I membahs
    Dat I'll nevah see no mo'
Dem ah faces gethered smilin'
    Roun' dat po' ol' cabin do'.

AFTER MANY DAYS

I've always been a faithful man
    An' tried to live for duty,
But the stringent mode of life
    Has somewhat lost its beauty.

The story of the generous bread
    He sent upon the waters,
Which after many days returns
    To trusting sons and daughters,

Had oft impressed me, so I want
    My soul influenced by it,
And bought a loaf of bread and sought
    A stream where I could try it.

I cast my bread upon the waves
    And fancied then to await it ;
It had not floated far away
    When a fish came up and ate it.

And if I want both fish and bread,
    And surely both I'm wanting,
About the only way I see
    Is for me to go fishing.

LIZA MAY

Little brown face full of smiles,
And a baby's guileless wiles,
    Liza May, Liza May.

Eyes a-peeping thro' the fence
With an interest intense,
    Liza May.

Ah, the gate is just ajar,
And the meadow is not far,
    Liza May, Liza May.

And the road feels very sweet,
To your little toddling feet,
    Liza May.

Ah, you roguish runaway,
What will toiling mother say,
    Liza May, Liza May ?

What care you who smile to greet
Every one you chance to meet,
    Liza May ?

Soft the mill-race sings its song,
Just a little way along,
    Liza May, Liza May.

But the song is full of guile,
Turn, ah turn, your steps the while,
    Liza May.

You have caught the gleam and glow
Where the darkling waters flow,
    Liza May, Liza May.

Flash of ripple, bend of bough,
Where are all the angels now ?
    Liza May.

Now a mother's eyes intense
Gazing o'er a shabby fence,
    Liza May, Liza May.

Then a mother's anguished face
Peering all around the place,
    Liza May.

Hear the agonizing call
For a mother's all in all,
    Liza May, L za May.

Hear a mother's maddened prayer
To the calm unanswering air,
    Liza May.

What's become of—Liza May ?
What has darkened all the day ?
    Liza May, Liza May.

Ask the waters dark and fleet,
If they know the smiling, sweet
    Liza May.

Call her, call her as you will,
On the meadow, on the hill,
    Liza May, Liza May.

Through the brush or beaten track
Echo only gives you back,
    Liza May.

Ah, but you were loving—sweet,
On your little toddling feet,
    Liza May, Liza May.

But through all the coming years,
Must a mother breathe with tears,
    Liza May.

THE MASTERS

Oh, who is the Lord of the land of life,
    When hotly goes the fray ?
When, fierce we smile in the midst of
    strife
    Then whom shall we obey ?

Oh, Love is the Lord of the land of life
    Who holds a monarch's sway ;
He wends with wish of maid and wife,
    And him you must obey.

Then who is the Lord of the land of life,
    At setting of the sun ?
Whose word shall sway when Peace is
    rife
    And all the fray is done ?

Then Death is the Lord of the land of
    life,
    When your hot race is run.
Meet then his scythe and pruning-knife
    When the fray is lost or won.

TROUBLE IN DE KITCHEN

Dey was oncet a awful quoil 'twixt de
  skillet an' de pot;
De pot was des a-bilin' an' de skillet sho'
  was hot.
Dey slurred each othah's colah an' dey
  called each othah names,
W'ile de coal-oil can des gu gled, po'in' oil
  erpon de flames.

De pot, hit called de skillet des a flat, dis-
  figgered t'ing,
An' de skillet 'plied dat all de pot could
  do was set an' sing,
An' he 'lowed dat dey was 'lusions dat he
  wouldn't stoop to mek
'Case he reckernize his juty, an' he had
  too much at steak.

Well, at dis de pot biled ovah, case his
  tempah gittin' highah,
An' de skillet got to sputterin', den de fat
  was in de fiah.
Mistah fiah lay daih smokin' an' a-t'inkin'
  to hisse'f,
W'ile de peppah-box us nudgin' of de
  gingah on de she'f.

Den dey all des lef' hit to 'im, 'bout de
  trouble an' de talk;
An' howevah he decided, w'y dey bofe 'u'd
  walk de chalk;
But de fiah uz so 'sgusted how dey quoil
  an' dey shout
Dat he cooled 'em off, I reckon, w'en he
  puffed an' des went out.

THE QUILTING

Dolly sits a-quilting by her mother, stitch
  by stitch,
Gracious, how my pulses throb, how my
  fingers itch,
While I note her dainty waist and her
  slender hand,
As she matches this and that, she stitches
  strand by strand.
And I long to tell her Life's a quilt and
  I'm a patch;
Love will do the stitching if she'll only be
  my match.

PARTED

She wrapped her soul in a lace of lies,
  With a prime deceit to pin it;
And I thought I was gaining a fearsome
  prize,
  So I staked my soul to win it.

We wed and parted on her complaint,
  And both were a bit of barter,
Tho' I'll confess that I'm no saint,
  I'll swear that she's no martyr.

FOREVER

I had not known before
  Forever was so long a word.
The slow stroke of the clock of time
  I had not heard.

'Tis hard to learn so late;
  It seems no sad heart really learns,
But hopes and trusts and doubts and fears,
  And bleeds and burns.

The night is not all dark,
  Nor is the day all it seems,
But each may bring me this relief —
  My dreams and dreams.

I had not known before
  That Never was so sad a word,
So wrap me in forgetfulness —
  I have not heard.

CHRISTMAS

Step wid de banjo an' glide wid de fiddle,
  Dis ain' no time fu' to pottah an' pid-
  dle;
Fu' Christmas is comin', it's right on de
  way,
  An' dey's houahs to dance 'fo' de break
  o' de day.
What if de win' is taihin' an' whistlin'?
  Look at dat fiah how hit's spittin' an'
  bristlin'!
Heat in de ashes an' heat in de cindahs,
  Ol' mistah Fros' kin des look thoo de
  windahs.

Heat up de toddy an' pas' de wa'm glasses,
  Don' stop to shivah at blowin's an'
    blas'es,
Keep on de kittle an' keep it a-hummin',
  Eat all an' drink all, dey's lots mo'
    a-comin'.
Look hyeah, Maria, don't open dat oven,
  Want all dese people a-pushin' an'
    shovin'?

Res' f'om de dance?   Yes, you done
    cotch dat odah,
  Mammy done cotch it, an' law! hit nigh
    flo'h huh;
'Possum is monst'ous fu' mekin' folks fin'
    it!
  Come, draw yo' cheers up, I's sho' I do'
    min' it.
Eat up dem critters, you men folks an'
    wimmens,
  'Possums ain' skace w'en dey's lots o'
    pu'simmons.

ROSES AND PEARLS

Your spoken words are roses fine and
    sweet,
  The songs you sing are perfect pearls of
    sound.
How lavish nature is about your feet,
  To scatter flowers and jewels both
    around.

Blushing the stream of petal beauty flows,
  Softly the white strings trickle down
    and shine.
Oh! speak to me, my love, I crave a rose.
  Sing me a song, for I would pearls were
    mine.

RAIN-SONGS

The rain streams down like harp-strings
    from the sky;
  The wind, that world-old harpist, sitteth
    by;
And ever as he sings his low refrain,
  He plays upon the harp-strings of the
    rain.

A LOST DREAM

Ah, I have changed, I do not know
Why lonely hours affect me so.
In days of yore, this were not wont,
No loneliness my soul could daunt.

For me too serious for my age,
The weighty tome of hoary sage,
Until with puzzled heart astir,
One God-giv'n night, I dreamed of her.

I loved no woman, hardly knew
More of the sex that strong men woo
Than cloistered monk within his cell;
But now the dream is lost, and hell

Holds me her captive tight and fast
Who prays and struggles for the past.
No living maid has charmed my eyes,
But now, my soul is wonder-wise.

For I have dreamed of her and seen
Her red-brown tresses, ruddy sheen,
Have known her sweetness, lip to lip,
The joy of her companionship.

When days were bleak and winds were
    rude,
She shared my smiling solitude,
And all the bare hills walked with me
To hearken winter's melody.

And when the spring came o'er the land
We fared together hand in hand
Beneath the linden's leafy screen
That waved above us faintly green.

In summer, by the riverside,
Our souls were kindred with the tide
That floated onward to the sea
As we swept towards Eternity.

The bird's call and the water's drone
Were all for us and us alone.
The water fall that sang all night
Was her companion, my delight,

And e'en the squirrel, as he sped
Along the branches overhead,
Half kindly and half envious,
Would chatter at the joy of us.

'Twas but a dream, her face, her hair,
The spring-time sweet, the winter bare,
The summer when the woods we ranged,—
'Twas but a dream, but all is changed.

Yes, all is changed and all has fled,
The dream is broken, shattered, dead.
And yet, sometimes, I pray to know
How just a dream could hold me so.

A SONG

On a summer's day as I sat by a stream,
  A dainty maid came by,
And she blessed my sight like a rosy
    dream,
  And left me there to sigh, to sigh,
  And left me there to sigh, to sigh.

On another day as I sat by the stream,
  This maiden paused a while,
Then I made me bold as I told my dream,
  She heard it with a smile, a smile,
  She heard it with a smile, a smile.

Oh, the months have fled and the autumn's
    red,
  The maid no more goes by ;

For my dream came true and the maid I
    wed,
  And now no more I sigh, I sigh,
  And now no more I sigh.

A SONG

Thou art the soul of a summer's day,
Thou art the breath of the rose.
  But the summer is fled
  And the rose is dead
Where are they gone, who knows, who
    knows ?

Thou art the blood of my heart o' hearts,
Thou art my soul's repose,
  But my heart grows numb
  And my soul is dumb
Where art thou, love, who knows, who
    knows ?

Thou art the hope of my after years —
Sun for my winter snows
  But the years go by
  'Neath a clouded sky.
Where shall we meet, who knows, who
    knows ?

PART III

The Best Stories of Paul Laurence Dunbar

A FAMILY FEUD

I WISH I could tell you the story as I heard it from the lips of the old black woman as she sat bobbing her turbaned head to and fro with the motion of her creaky little rocking-chair, and droning the tale forth in the mellow voice of her race. So much of the charm of the story was in that voice, which even the cares of age had not hardened.

It was a sunny afternoon in late November, one of those days that come like a backward glance from a reluctantly departing summer. I had taken advantage of the warmth and brightness to go up and sit with old Aunt Doshy on the little porch that fronted her cottage. The old woman had been a trusted house-servant in one of the wealthiest of the old Kentucky families, and a visit to her never failed to elicit some reminiscence of the interesting past. Aunt Doshy was inordinately proud of her family, as she designated the Venables, and was never weary of detailing accounts of their grandeur and generosity. What if some of the harshness of reality was softened by the distance through which she looked back upon them ; what

339

if the glamour of memory did put a halo round the heads
of some people who were never meant to be canonized?
It was all plain fact to Aunt Doshy, and it was good to
hear her talk.   That day she began : —

"I reckon I hain't never tol' you 'bout ole Mas' an'
young Mas' fallin' out, has I?   Hit's all over now, an'
things is done change so dat I reckon eben ef ole Mas'
was libin', he wouldn't keer ef I tol', an' I knows young
Mas' Tho'nton wouldn't.   Dey ain't nuffin' to hide 'bout
it nohow, 'ca'se all quality families has de same kin' o'
'spectable fusses.

" Hit all happened 'long o' dem Jamiesons whut libed
jinin' places to our people, an' whut ole Mas' ain't spoke
to fu' nigh onto thutty years.   Long while ago, when
Mas' Tom Jamieson an' Mas' Jack Venable was bofe
young mans, dey had a qua'l 'bout de young lady dey
bofe was a-cou'tin', an' by an' by dey had a du'l an' Mas'
Jamieson shot Mas' Jack in de shouldah, but Mas' Jack
ma'ied de lady, so dey was eben.   Mas' Jamieson ma'ied
too, an' after so many years dey was bofe wid'ers, but
dey ain't fu'give one another yit.   When Mas' Tho'nton
was big enough to run erroun', ole Mas' used to try to
press on him dat a Venable mus'n' never put his foot on
de Jamieson lan' ; an' many a tongue-lashin' an' some-
times wuss de han's on our place got fu' mixin' wif de
Jamieson servants.   But, la! young Mas' Tho'nton was
wuss'n de niggers.   Evah time he got a chance he was
out an' gone, over lots an' fiel's an' into de Jamieson ya'd
a-playin' wif little Miss Nellie, whut was Mas' Tom's little
gal.   I never did see two chillun so 'tached to one an-
other.   Dey used to wander erroun', han' in han', lak
brother an' sister, an' dey'd cry lak dey little hea'ts

'u'd brek ef either one of dey pappys seed 'em an' pa'ted 'em.

"I 'member once when de young Mastah was erbout eight year ole, he was a-settin' at de table one mo'nin' eatin' wif his pappy, when all of er sudden he pause an' say, jes' ez solerm-lak, 'When I gits big, I gwine to ma'y Nellie.' His pappy jump lak he was shot, an' tu'n right pale, den he say kin' o' slow an' gaspy-lak, 'Don't evah let me hyeah you say sich a thing ergin, Tho'nton Venable. Why, boy, I'd raver let evah drap o' blood outen you, dan to see a Venable cross his blood wif a Jamieson.'

"I was jes' a-bringin' in de cakes whut Mastah was pow'ful fon' of, an' I could see bofe dey faces. But, la! honey, dat chile didn't look a bit skeered. He jes' sot dah lookin' in his pappy's face,—he was de spittin' image of him, all 'cept his eyes, dey was his mother's,—den he say, 'Why, Nellie's nice,' an' went on eatin' a aig. His pappy laid his napkin down an' got up an' went erway 'om de table. Mas' Tho'nton say, 'Why, father didn't, eat his cakes.' 'I reckon yo' pa ain't well,' says I, fu' I knowed de chile was innercent.

"Well, after dat day, ole Mas' tuk extry pains to keep de chillun apa't—but 'twa'n't no use. 'Tain't never no use in a case lak dat. Dey jes' would be together, an' ez de boy got older, it seemed to grieve his pappy mighty. I reckon he didn't lak to jes' fu'bid him seein' Miss Nellie fu' he know how haidstrong Mas' Tho'nton was, anyhow. So things kep' on dis way, an' de boy got handsomer evah day. My, but his pappy did set a lot o' sto' by him. Dey wasn't nuffin' dat boy eben wished fu' dat his pappy didn't gin him. Seemed lak he fa'ly wusshiped him.

19

He'd jes' watch him ez he went erroun' de house lak he
was a baby yit.   So hit mus' 'a' been putty ha'd wif Mas'
Jack when hit come time to sen' Mas' Tho'nton off to
college.   But he never showed it.   He seed him off wif
a cheerful face, an' nobidy would 'a' ever guessed dat it
hu't him ; but dat afternoon he shet hisse'f up an' hit was
th'ee days befo' anybody 'cept me seed him, an' nobidy
'cept me knowed how his vittels come back not teched.
But after de fus' letter come, he got better.   I hyeahd him
a-laffin' to hisse'f ez he read it, an' dat day he et his
dinner.

"Well, honey, dey ain't no tellin' whut Mas' Jack's
plans was, an' hit ain't fu' me to try an' guess 'em ; but ef
he had sont Mas' Tho'nton erway to brek him off f'om
Miss Nellie, he mout ez well 'a' let him stayed at home ;
fu' Jamieson's Sal whut nussed Miss Nellie tol' me dat
huh mistis got a letter f'om Mas' Tho'nton evah day er
so.   An' when he was home fu' holidays, you never seed
nuffin' lak it.   Hit was jes' walkin' er ridin' er dribin' wif
dat young lady evah day of his life.   An' dey did look so
sweet together dat it seemed a shame to pa't 'em—him wif
his big brown eyes an' sof' curly hair an' huh all white
an' gentle lak a little dove.   But de ole Mas' couldn't see
hit dat erway, an' I knowed dat hit was a-troublin' him
mighty bad.   Ez well ez he loved his son, hit allus
seemed lak he was glad when de holidays was over an'
de boy was back at college.

"Endurin' de las' year dat de young Mastah was to be
erway, his pappy seemed lak he was jes' too happy an'
res'less fu' anything.   He was dat proud of his son, he
didn't know whut to do.   He was allus tellin' visitors dat
come to de house erbout him, how he was a 'markable

boy an' was a-gwine to be a honor to his name. An' when 'long to'ds de ve'y end of de term, a letter come sayin' dat Mas' Tho'nton had done tuk some big honor at de college, I jes' thought sho Mas' Jack 'u'd plum bus' hisse'f, he was so proud an' tickled. I hyeahd him talkin' to his ole frien' Cunnel Mandrey an' mekin' great plans 'bout whut he gwine to do when his son come home. He gwine tek him trav'lin' fus' in Eur'p, so's to ' finish him lak a Venable ought to be finished by seein' somep'n' of de worl'—' dem's his ve'y words. Den he was a-gwine to come home an' 'model de house an' fit it up, ' fu' '—I never shell fu'git how he said it,—' fu' I 'spec' my son to tek a high place in de society of ole Kintucky an' to mo' dan surstain de reputation of de Venables.' Den when de las' day come an' young Mastah was home fu' sho, so fine an' clever lookin' wif his new mustache—sich times ez dey was erbout dat house nobidy never seed befo'. All de frien's an' neighbors, 'scusin', o' co'se, de Jamie-sons, was invited to a big dinner dat lasted fu' hours. Dey was speeches by de gent'men, an' evahbidy drinked de graderate's health an' wished him good luck. But all de time I could see dat Mas' Tho'nton wasn't happy, dough he was smilin' an' mekin' merry wif evahbidy. It 'pressed me so dat I spoke erbout hit to Aunt Emmerline. Aunt Emmerline was Mas' Tho'nton's mammy, an' sence he'd growed up, she didn't do much but he'p erroun' de house a little.

" ' You don' mean to tell me dat you noticed dat too ?' says she when I tol' huh erbout it.

" ' Yes, I did,' says I, ' an' I noticed hit strong.'

" ' Dey's somep'n' ain't gwine right wif my po' chile,' she say, ' an' dey ain't no tellin' whut it is.'

"'Hain't you got no idee, Aunt Emmerline?' I say.

"'La! chile,' she say in a way dat mek me think she keepin' somep'n' back, 'la! chile, don' you know young mans don' come to dey mammys wif dey secuts lak dey do when dey's babies? How I gwine to know whut's pesterin' Mas' Tho'nton?'

"Den I knowed she was hidin' somep'n', an' jes' to let huh know dat I'd been had my eyes open too, I say slow an' 'pressive lak, 'Aunt Emmerline, don' you reckon hit Miss Nellie Jamieson?' She jumped lak she was skeered, an' looked at me right ha'd; den she say, 'I ain' reck'nin' nuffin' 'bout de white folks' bus'ness.' An' she pinched huh mouf up right tight, an' I couldn't git another word outen huh; but I knowed dat I'd hit huh jes' erbout right.

"One mo'nin' erbout a week after de big dinner, jes' ez dey was eatin', Mas' Tho'nton say, 'Father, I'd lak to see you in de liberry ez soon ez you has de time. I want to speak to you 'bout somep'n' ve'y impo'tant.' De ole man look up right quick an' sha'p, but he say ve'y quiet lak, 'Ve'y well, my son, ve'y well; I's at yo' service at once.'

"Dey went into de liberry, an' Mas' Tho'nton shet de do' behin' him. I could hyeah dem talkin' kin' o' low while I was cl'arin' erway de dishes. After while dey 'menced to talk louder. I had to go out an' dus' de hall den near de liberry do', an' once I hyeahd ole Mas' say right sho't an' sha'p, 'Never!' Den young Mas' he say, 'But evah man has de right to choose fu' his own se'f.'

"'Man, man!' I hyeahd his pappy say in a way I had never hyeahd him use to his son befo', 'evah male bein' dat wahs men's clothes an' has a mustache ain't a man.'

"'Man er whut not,' po' young Mastah's voice was a

tremblin', ' I am at leas' my father's son an' I deserve bet-
ter dan dis at his han's.'   I hyeahd somebody a-walkin'
de flo', an' I was feared dey'd come out an' think dat I
was a-listenin', so I dus'es on furder down de hall, an'
didn't hyeah no mo' ontwell Mas' Tho'nton come hurryin'
out an' say, ' Ike, saddle my hoss.'   He was ez pale ez he
could be, an' when he spoke sho't an' rough lak dat, he
was so much lak his father dat hit skeered me.   Ez soon
ez his hoss was ready, he jumped into de saddle an' went
flyin' outen de ya'd lak mad, never eben lookin' back at
de house.   I didn't see Mas' Jack fu' de res' of de day,
an' he didn't come in to suppah.   But I seed Aunt Em-
merline an' I knowed dat she had been somewhah an'
knowed ez much ez I did erbout whut was gwine on, but
I never broached a word erbout hit to huh.   I seed she
was oneasy, but I kep' still 'twell she say, ' Whut you
reckon keepin' Mas' Tho'nton out so late ? '   Den I jes
say, ' I ain't reck'nin' 'bout de white folks' bus'ness.'   She
looked a little bit cut at fus', den she jes' go on lak nuffin'
hadn't happened : ' I's mighty 'sturbed 'bout young
Mas' ; he never stays erway f'om suppah 'dout sayin'
somep'n'.'

      " ' Oh, I reckon he kin fin' suppah somewhah else.'   I
says dis don't keer lak jes' fu' to lead huh on.

      " ' I ain't so much pestered 'bout his suppah,' she say ;
' I's feared he gwine do somep'n' he hadn't ought to do
after dat qua'l 'twixt him an' his pappy.'

      " ' Did dey have a qua'l ? ' says I.

      " ' G'long ! ' Aunt Emmerline say, ' you wasn't dus'in'
one place in de hall so long fu' nuffin'.   You knows an' I
knows eben ef we don't talk a heap.   I's troubled myse'f.
Hit jes' in dat Venable blood to go right straight an' git

Miss Nellie an' ma'y huh right erway, an' ef he do it, I p'intly know his pa 'll never fu'give him.' Den Aunt Emmerline 'mence to cry, an' I feel right sorry fu' huh, 'ca'se Mas' Tho'nton huh boy, an' she think a mighty heap o' him.

"Well, we hadn't had time to say much mo' when we hyeahd a hoss gallopin' into de ya'd. Aunt Emmerline jes' say, ' Dat's Gineral's lope ! ' an' she bus' outen de do.' I waits, 'spectin' huh to come back an' say dat Mas' Tho'nton done come at las'. But after while she come in wif a mighty long face an' say, ' Hit's one o' Jamieson's darkies ; he brung de hoss back an' a note Mas' gin him fu' his pappy. Mas' Tho'nton done gone to Lexin'ton wif Miss Nellie an' got ma'ied.' Den she jes' brek down an' 'mence a-cryin' ergin an' a-rockin' huhse'f back an' fofe an' sayin', ' Oh, my po' chile, my po' boy, whut's to 'come o' you ! '

"I went up-stairs an' lef' huh—we bofe stayed at de big house—but I didn't sleep much, 'ca'se all thoo de night I could hyeah ole Mas' a-walkin' back an' fofe ercross his flo', an' when Aunt Emmerline come up to baid, she mou'ned all night, eben in huh sleep. I tell you, honey, dem was mou'nin' times.

"Nex' mo'nin' when ole Mas' come down to brekfus', he looked lak he done had a long spell o' sickness. But he wasn't no man to 'spose his feelin's. He never let on, never eben spoke erbout Mas' Tho'nton bein' erway f'om de table. He didn't eat much, an' fin'ly I see him look right long an' stiddy at de place whah Mas' Tho'nton used to set an' den git up an' go 'way f'om de table. I knowed dat he was done filled up. I went to de liberry do' an' I could hyeah him sobbin' lak a chile. I tol'

Aunt Emmerline 'bout it, but she jes' shuck huh haid an' didn't say nuffin' a'-tall.

"Well, hit went dis erway fu' 'bout a week. Mas' Jack was gittin' paler an' paler evah day, an' hit jes' 'menced to come to my min' how ole he was. One day Aunt Emmerline say she gwine erway, an' she mek Jim hitch up de spring wagon an' she dribe on erway by huhse'f. Co'se, now, Aunt Emmerline she do putty much ez she please, so I don't think nuffin' 'bout hit. When she come back, 'long to'ds ebenin', I say, 'Aunt Emmerline, whah you been all day?'

"'Nemmine, honey, you see,' she say, an' laff. Well, I ain't seed nobidy laff fu' so long dat hit jes' mek me feel right wa'm erroun' my hea't, an' I laff an' keep on laffin' jes' at nuffin'.

"Nex' mo'nin' Aunt Emmerline mighty oneasy, an' I don' know whut de matter ontwell I hyeah some un say, 'Tek dat hoss, Ike, an' feed him, but keep de saddle on.' Aunt Emmerline jes' fa'ly fall out de do' an' I lak to drap, 'ca'se hit's Mas' Tho'nton's voice. In a minute he come to me an' say, 'Doshy, go tell my father I'd lak to speak to him.'

"I don' skeercely know how I foun' my way to de liberry, but I did. Ole Mas' was a-settin' dah wif a open book in his han', but his eyes was jes' a-starin' at de wall, an' I knowed he wasn't a-readin'. I say, 'Mas' Jack,' an' he sta't jes' lak he rousin' up, 'Mas' Jack, Mas' Tho'nton want to speak to you.' He jump up quick, an' de book fall on de flo', but he grab a cheer an' stiddy hisse'f. I done tol' you Mas' Jack wasn't no man to 'spose his feelin's. He jes' say, slow lak he hol'in' hisse'f, 'Sen' him in hyeah.' I goes back an' 'livers de message, den I

flies roun' to de po'ch whah de liberry winder opens out,
'ca'se, I ain't gwine lie erbout it, I was mighty tuk up wif
all dis gwine on an' I wanted to see an' hyeah,—an' who
you reckon 'roun' dah but Aunt Emmerline! She jes'
say, 'S-sh!' ez I come 'roun', an' clas' huh han's. In a
minute er so, de liberry do' open an' Mas' Tho'nton come
in. He shet hit behin' him, an' den stood lookin' at his
pa, dat ain't never tu'ned erroun' yit. Den he say sof',
'Father.' Mas' Jack tu'ned erroun' raal slow an' look at
his son fu' a while. Den he say, 'Do you still honor me
wif dat name?' Mas' Tho'nton got red in de face, but
he answer, 'I don' know no other name to call you.'

"'Will you set down?' Mas' speak jes' lak he was
a-talkin' to a stranger.

"'Ef you desiah me to.' I see Mas' Tho'nton was
a-bridlin' up too. Mas' jes' th'owed back his haid an'
say, 'Fa' be it f'om any Venable to fu'git cou'tesy to his
gues'.' Young Mas' moved erway f'om de cheer whah
he was a-gwine to set, an' his haid went up. He spoke
up slow an' delibut, jes' lak his pa, 'I do not come, suh,
in dat cha'acter, I is hyeah ez yo' son.'

"Well, ole Mas' eyes fa'ly snapped fiah. He was
white ez a sheet, but he still spoke slow an' quiet, hit
made me creep, 'You air late in 'memberin' yo' relation-
ship, suh.'

"'I hab never fu'got it.'

"'Den, suh, you have thought mo' of yo' rights dan
of yo' duties.' Mas' Jack was mad an' so was Mas'
Tho'nton; he say, 'I didn't come hyeah to 'scuss dat.'
An' he tu'ned to'ds de do'. I hyeah Aunt Emmerline
groan jes' ez Mas' say, 'Well, whut did you come fu'?'

"'To be insulted in my father's house by my father,

an' I's got all dat I come fu' !' Mas' Tho'nton was ez
white ez his pa now, an' his han' was on de do'-knob.
Den all of a sudden I hyeah de winder go up, an' I lak
to fall over gittin' outen de way to keep f'om bein' seed.
Aunt Emmerline done opened de winder an' gone in.
Dey bofe tu'ned an' looked at huh s'prised lak, an' Mas'
Jack sta'ted to say somep'n', but she th'owed up huh
han' an' say, ' Wait !' lak she owned de house. ' Mas'
Jack,' she say, ' you an' Mas' Tho'nton ain't gwine pa't
dis way. You mus'n't. You's father an' son. You
loves one another. I knows I ain't got no bus'ness
meddlin' in yo' 'fairs, but I cain't see you all qua'l dis
way. Mastah, you's bofe stiffnecked. You's bofe wrong.
I know Mas' Tho'nton didn't min' you, but he didn't
mean no ha'm—he couldn't he'p it—it was in de Venable
blood, an' you mus'n't 'spise him fu' it.'

" ' Emmerline '—ole Mas' tried to git in a word, but
she wouldn't let him.

" ' Yes, Mastah, yes, but I nussed dat boy an' tuk keer
o' him when he was a little bit of a he'pless thing; an'
when his po' mammy went to glory, I 'member how she
look up at me wif dem blessed eyes o' hern an' lay him
in my arms an' say, "Emmerline, tek keer o' my baby "
I's done it, Mastah, I's done it de bes' I could. I's
nussed him thoo sickness when hit seemed lak his little
soul mus' foller his mother anyhow, but I's seen de look
in yo' eyes, an' prayed to God to gin de chile back to
you. He done it, he done it, an' you sha'n't th'ow erway
de gif' of God !' Aunt Emmerline was a-cryin' an' so
was Mas' Tho'nton. Ole Mas' mighty red, but he clared
his th'oat an' said wif his voice tremblin', ' Emmerline,
leave de room.' De ole ooman come out a-cryin' lak

huh hea't 'u'd brek, an' jes' ez de do' shet behin' huh, ole
Mas' brek down an' hol' out his arms, cryin', 'My son,
my son.' An' in a minute he an' Mas' Tho'nton was
a-hol'in' one another lak dey'd never let go, an' his pa
was a-pattin' de boy's haid lak he was a baby. All of a
sudden ole Mas' hel' him off an' looked at him an' say,
'Dat ole fool talkin' to me erbout yo' mother's eyes, an'
you stannin' hyeah a-lookin' at me wif 'em.' An' den he
was a-cryin' ergin, an' dey was bofe huggin'.

"Well, after while dey got all settled down, an' Mas'
Tho'nton tol' his pa how Aunt Emmerline drib to Lexin'-
ton an' foun' him an' made him come home. 'I was
wrong, father,' he say, 'but I reckon ef it hadn't 'a' been
fu' Aunt Emmerline, I would 'a' stuck it out.'

"'It was in de Venable blood,' his pa say, an' dey bofe
laff. Den ole Mas' say, kin' o' lak it hu't him, 'An'
whah's yo' wife?' Young Mas' got mighty red ergin ez
he answer, 'She ain't fu' erway.'

"'Go bring huh,' Mas' Jack say.

"Well, I reckon Mas' Tho'nton lak to flew, an' he had
Miss Nellie dah in little er no time. When dey come,
Mas' he say, 'Come hyeah,' den he pause awhile—'my
daughter.' Den Miss Nellie run to him, an' dey was an-
other cryin' time, an' I went on to my work an' lef' 'em
talkin' an' laffin' an' cryin'.

"Well, Aunt Emmerline was skeered to def. She jes'
p'intly knowed dat she was gwine to git a tongue-lashin'.
I don' know whether she was mos' skeered er mos' happy.
Mas' sont fu' huh after while, an' I listened when she
went in. He was tryin' to talk an' look pow'ful stern,
but I seed a twinkle in his eye. He say, 'I want you to
know, Emmerline, dat hit ain't yo' place to dictate to yo'

mastah whut he shell do —— Shet up, shet up! I don'
want a word outen you. You been on dis place so long,
an' been bossin' de other darkies an' yo' Mas' Tho'nton
erroun' so long, dat I 'low you think you own de place.
Shet up, not a word outen you! Ef you an' yo' young
Mas' 's a-gwine to run dis place, I reckon I'd better step
out. Humph! You was so sma't to go to Lexin'ton de
other day, you kin go back dah ergin. You seem to
think you's white, an' hyeah's de money to buy a new
dress fu' de ole fool darky dat nussed yo' son an' made
you fu'give his foo'ishness when you wanted to be a fool
yo'se'f.' His voice was sof' ergin, an' he put de money
in Aunt Emmerline's han' an' pushed huh out de do', huh
a-cryin' an' him put' nigh it.

"After dis, Mas' Jack was jes' bent an' boun' dat de
young people mus' go on a weddin' trip. So dey got
ready, an' Miss Nellie went an' tol' huh pa goo'-bye.
Min' you, dey hadn't been nuffin' said 'bout him an' Mas'
not bein' frien's. He done fu'give Miss Nellie right
erway fu' runnin' off. But de mo'nin' dey went erway,
we all was out in de ya'd, an' Aunt Emmerline settin' on
de seat wif Jim, lookin' ez proud ez you please. Mastah
was ez happy ez a boy. 'Emmerline,' he hollahs ez dey
drib off, 'tek good keer o' dat Venable blood.' De
ca'iage stopped ez it went out de gate, an' Mas' Tom
Jamieson kissed his daughter. He had rid up de road to
see de las' of huh. Mastah seed him, an' all of a sudden
somep'n' seemed to tek holt o' him an' he hollahed,
'Come in, Tom.'

"'Don' keer ef I do,' Mas' Jamieson say, a-tu'nin' his
hoss in de gate. 'You Venables has got de res' o' my
fambly.' We all was mos' s'prised to def.

" Mas' Jamieson jumped offen his hoss, an' Mas' Venable come down de steps to meet him. Dey shuk han's, an' Mas' Jack say, 'Dey ain't no fool lak a ole fool.'

" ' An' fu' unekaled foo'ishness,' Mas' Tom say, ' recker-men' me to two ole fools.' Dey went into de house a-laffin', an' I knowed hit was all right 'twixt 'em, fu' putty soon I seed Ike out in de ya'd a-getherin' mint."

OLD AUNT DOSHY

MANDY MASON

IMSELLA

No one could ever have accused Mandy Mason of being thrifty. For the first twenty years of her life conditions had not taught her the necessity for thrift. But that was before she had come North with Jim. Down there at home one either rented or owned a plot of ground with a shanty set in the middle of it, and lived off the products of one's own garden and coop. But here it was all very different: one room in a crowded tenement house, and the necessity of grinding day after day to keep the wolf—a very terrible and ravenous wolf—from the door. No wonder that Mandy was discouraged and finally gave up to more than her old shiftless ways.

Jim was no less disheartened. He had been so hopeful when he first came, and had really worked hard. But he could not go higher than his one stuffy room, and the food was not so good as it had been at home. In this state of mind, Mandy's shiftlessness irritated him. He grew to look on her as the source of all his disappointments. Then, as he walked Sixth or Seventh Avenue, he saw other colored women who dressed gayer than Mandy, looked smarter, and did not wear such great shoes. These he contrasted with his wife, to her great disadvantage.

"Mandy," he said to her one day, "why don't you fix yo'se'f up an' look like people? You go 'roun' hyeah lookin' like I dunno what."

355

"Whyn't you git me somep'n' to fix myse'f up in?"
came back the disconcerting answer.

"Ef you had any git up erbout you, you'd git somep'n'
fu' yo'se'f an' not wait on me to do evahthing."

"Well, ef I waits on you, you keeps me waitin', fu' I
ain' had nothin' fit to eat ner waih since I been up
hyeah."

"Nev' min'! You's mighty free wid yo' talk now, but
some o' dese days you won't be so free. You's gwine to
wake up some mo'nin' an' fin' dat I's lit out; dat's what
you will."

"Well, I 'low nobody ain't got no string to you."

Mandy took Jim's threat as an idle one, so she could
afford to be independent. But the next day had found
him gone. The deserted wife wept for a time, for she had
been fond of Jim, and then she set to work to struggle on
by herself. It was a dismal effort, and the people about her
were not kind to her. She was hardly of their class. She
was only a simple, honest countrywoman, who did not go
out with them to walk the avenue.

When a month or two afterwards the sheepish Jim
returned, ragged and dirty, she had forgiven him and
taken him back. But immunity from punishment spoiled
him, and hence of late his lapses had grown more frequent
and of longer duration.

He walked in one morning, after one of his absences,
with a more than usually forbidding face, for he had heard
the news in the neighborhood before he got in. During
his absence a baby had come to share the poverty of his
home. He thought with shame at himself, which turned
into anger, that the child must be three months old and
he had never seen it.

" Back ag'in, Jim?" was all Mandy said as he entered and seated himself sullenly.

" Yes, I's back, but I ain't back fu' long. I jes' come to git my clothes. I's a-gwine away fu' good."

" Gwine away ag'in ! Why, you been gone fu' nigh on to fou' months a'ready. Ain't you nevah gwine to stay home no mo'?"

" I tol' you I was gwine away fu' good, didn't I? Well, dat's what I mean."

" Ef you didn't want me, Jim, I wish to Gawd dat you'd 'a' lef' me back home among my folks, whaih people knowed me an' would 'a' give me a helpin' han'. Dis hyeah No'f ain't no fittin' place fu' a lone colo'ed ooman less'n she got money."

" It ain't no place fu' nobody dat's jes' lazy an' no 'count."

" I ain't no 'count. I ain't wuffless. I does de bes' I kin. I been wo'kin' like a dog to try an' keep up while you trapsein' 'roun', de Lawd knows whaih. When I was single I could git out an' mek my own livin'. I didn't ax nobody no odds ; but you wa'n't satisfied ontwell I ma'ied you, an' now, when I's tied down wid a baby, dat's de way you treats me."

The woman sat down and began to cry, and the sight of her tears angered her husband the more.

" Oh, cry !" he exclaimed. " Cry all you want to. I reckon you'll cry yo' fill befo' you gits me back. What do I keer about de baby ! Dat's jes' de trouble. It wa'n't enough fu' me to have to feed an' clothe you a-layin' 'roun' doin' nothin', a baby had to go an' come too."

"It's yo'n, an' you got a right to tek keer of it, dat's

what you have. I ain't a-gwine to waih my soul-case out a-tryin' to pinch along an' sta've to def at las'. I'll kill myse'f an' de chile, too, fus'."

The man looked up quickly. "Kill yo'se'f," he said. Then he laughed. "Who evah hyeahed tell of a niggah killin' hisse'f ?"

"Nev' min', nev' min', you jes' go on yo' way rejoicin'. I 'spect you runnin' roun' aftah somebody else—dat's de reason you cain't nevah stay at home no mo'."

"Who tol' you dat?" exclaimed the man, fiercely. "I ain't runnin' aftah nobody else—'tain't none o' yo' business ef I is."

The denial and implied confession all came out in one breath.

"Ef hit ain't my bus'ness, I'd like to know whose it gwine to be. I's yo' lawful wife an' hit's me dat's a-sta'vin' to tek keer of yo' chile."

"Doggone de chile; I's tiahed o' hyeahin' 'bout huh."

"You done got tiahed mighty quick when you ain't nevah even seed huh yit. You done got tiahed quick, sho."

"No, an' I do' want to see huh, neithah."

"You do' know nothin' 'bout de chile, you do' know whethah you wants to see huh er not."

"Look hyeah, ooman, don't you fool wid me. I ain't right, nohow !"

Just then, as if conscious of the hubbub she had raised, and anxious to add to it, the baby awoke and began to wail. With quick mother instinct, the black woman went to the shabby bed, and, taking the child in her arms, began to croon softly to it: "Go s'eepy, baby; don' you be 'f'aid; mammy ain' gwine let nuffin' hu't you, even ef

pappy don' wan' look at huh li'l face. Bye, bye, go
s'eepy, mammy's li'l gal."   Unconsciously she talked to
the baby in a dialect that was even softer than usual.
For a moment the child subsided, and the woman turned
angrily on her husband : " I don' keer whethah you
evah sees dis chile er not.   She's a blessed li'l angel, dat's
what she is, an' I'll wo'k my fingahs off to raise huh, an'
when she grows up, ef any nasty niggah comes erroun'
mekin' eyes at huh, I'll tell huh 'bout huh pappy an' she'll
stay wid me an' be my comfo't."

" Keep yo' comfo't.   Gawd knows I do' want huh."

" De time 'll come, though, an' I kin wait fu' it. Hush-
a-bye, Jimsella."

The man turned his head slightly.

" What you call huh ? "

" I calls huh Jimsella, dat's what I calls huh, 'ca'se she
de ve'y spittin' image of you.   I gwine to jes' lun to huh
dat she had a pappy, so she know she's a hones' chile an'
kin' hol' up huh haid."

" Oomph ! "

They were both silent for a while, and then Jim said,
" Huh name ought to be Jamsella—don't you know Jim's
sho't fu' James ? "

" I don't keer what it's sho't fu'."   The woman was
holding the baby close to her breast and sobbing now.
" It wasn't no James dat come a-cou'tin' me down home.
It was jes' plain Jim.   Dat's what de mattah, I reckon
you done got to be James."   Jim didn't answer, and there
was another space of silence, only interrupted by two or
three contented gurgles from the baby.

" I bet two bits she don't look like me," he said finally,
in a dogged tone that was a little tinged with curiosity.

20

" I know she do.   Look at huh yo'se'f."

" I ain' gwine look at huh."

" Yes, you's 'fraid—dat's de reason."

" I ain' 'fraid nuttin' de kin'.   What I got to be 'fraid fu'?   I reckon a man kin look at his own darter.   I will look jes' to spite you."

He couldn't see much but a bundle of rags, from which sparkled a pair of beady black eyes.   But he put his finger down among the rags.   The baby seized it and gurgled.   The sweat broke out on Jim's brow.

" Cain't you let me hold de baby a minute?" he said angrily.   " You must be 'fraid I'll run off wid huh."   He took the child awkwardly in his arms.

The boiling over of Mandy's clothes took her to the other part of the room, where she was busy for a few minutes.   When she turned to look for Jim, he had slipped out, and Jimsella was lying on the bed trying to kick free of the coils which swaddled her.

At supper-time that evening Jim came in with a piece of " shoulder-meat " and a head of cabbage.

" You'll have to git my dinnah ready fu' me to ca'y to-morrer.   I's wo'kin' on de street, an' I cain't come home twell night."

" Wha', what!" exclaimed Mandy, " den you ain' gwine leave, aftah all."

" Don't bothah me, ooman," said Jim.   " Is Jimsella 'sleep?"

THE WALLS OF JERICHO

PARKER was sitting alone under the shade of a locust tree at the edge of a field. His head was bent and he was deep in thought. Every now and then there floated to him the sound of vociferous singing, and occasionally above the music rose the cry of some shouting brother or sister. But he remained in his attitude of meditation as if the singing and the cries meant nothing to him.

They did, however, mean much, and, despite his outward impassiveness, his heart was in a tumult of wounded pride and resentment. He had always been so faithful to his flock, constant in attendance and careful of their welfare. Now it was very hard, at the first call of the stranger to have them leave their old pastor and crowd to the new exhorter.

It was nearly a week before that a free negro had got permission to hold meetings in the wood adjoining the Mordaunt estate. He had invited the negroes of the surrounding plantations to come and bring their baskets with them that they might serve the body while they saved the soul. By ones and twos Parker had seen his congregation drop away from him until now, in the cabin meeting house where he held forth, only a few retainers, such as Mandy and Dinah and some of the older ones on the plantation, were present to hear him. It grieved his heart, for he had been with his flock in sickness and in distress, in sorrow and in trouble, but now, at the first approach of the rival they could and did desert him   He

felt it the more keenly because he knew just how power-
ful this man Johnson was. He was loud-voiced and
theatrical, and the fact that he invited all to bring their
baskets gave his scheme added influence; for his congre-
gations flocked to the meetings as to a holy picnic. It
was seldom that they were thus able to satisfy both the
spiritual and material longings at the same time.

Parker had gone once to the meeting and had hung
unobserved on the edge of the crowd; then he saw by
what power the preacher held the people. Every night,
at the very height of the service, he would command the
baskets to be opened and the people, following the ex-
ample of the children of Israel, to march, munching their
food, round and round the inclosure, as their Biblical
archetypes had marched around the walls of Jericho.
Parker looked on and smiled grimly. He knew, and the
sensational revivalist knew, that there were no walls there
to tumble down, and that the spiritual significance of the
performance was entirely lost upon the people. What-
ever may be said of the Mordaunt plantation exhorter, he
was at least no hypocrite, and he saw clearly that his rival
gave to the emotional negroes a breathing chance and
opportunity to eat and a way to indulge their dancing pro-
clivities by marching trippingly to a spirited tune.

He went away in disgust and anger, but thoughts
deeper than either burned within him. He was thinking
some such thoughts now as he sat there on the edge of
the field listening to the noise of the basket meeting. It
was unfortunate for his peace of mind that while he sat
there absorbed in resentful musings two of the young men
of his master's household should come along. They did
not know how Parker felt about the matter, or they never

would have allowed themselves to tease him on the score of his people's defection.

"Well, Parker," said Ralph, "seems mighty strange to me that you are not down there in the woods at the meeting."

The old man was silent.

"I am rather surprised at Parker myself," said Tom Mordaunt; "knowing how he enjoys a good sermon I expected him to be over there.   They do say that man Johnson is a mighty preacher."

Still Parker was silent.

"Most of your congregation are over there," Ralph resumed.   Then the old exhorter, stung into reply, raised his head and said quietly :

"Dat ain't nuffin' strange, Mas' Ralph.   I been preachin' de gospel on yo' father's plantation, night aftah night, nigh on to twenty-five years, an' spite o' dat, mos' o' my congregation is in hell."

"That doesn't speak very well for your preaching," said Ralph, and the two young fellows laughed heartily.

"Come, Parker, come, don't be jealous ; come on over to the meeting with us, and let us see what it is that Johnson has that you haven't.   You know any man can get a congregation about him, but it takes some particular power to hold them after they are caught."

Parker rose slowly from the ground and reluctantly joined his two young masters as they made their way towards the woods.   The service was in full swing.   At a long black log, far to the front, there knelt a line of mourners wailing and praying, while the preacher stood above them waving his hands and calling on them to believe and be saved.   Every now and then some one voluntarily broke into a song, either a stirring, marching spiritual or some soft crooning melody that took strange hold upon the hearts of even the most skeptical listeners. As they approached and joined the crowd some one had just swung into the undulating lilt of

> "Some one buried in de graveyard,
>   Some one buried in de sea,
> All come togethah in de mo'nin',
>   Go soun' de Jubilee."

Just the word "Jubilee" was enough to start the whole throng into agitated life, and they moaned and shouted and wailed until the forest became a pandemonium.

Johnson, the preacher, saw Parker approach with the two young men and a sudden spirit of conquest took possession of him. He felt that he owed it to himself to crystallize his triumph over the elder exhorter. So, with a glance that begged for approbation, he called aloud:

"Open de baskets! Rise up, fu' de Jericho walls o' sin is a-stan'in'. You 'member dey ma'ched roun' seven times, an' at de sevent' time de walls a-begun to shake an' shiver; de foundations a-begun to trimble; de chillen a-hyeahed de rum'lin' lak a thundah f'om on high, an' putty soon down come de walls a-fallin' an' a-crum lin'! Oh, brothahs an' sistahs, let us a-ma'ch erroun' de walls o' Jericho to-night seven times, an' a-eatin' o' de food dat de Lawd has pervided us wid. Dey ain't no walls o' brick an' stone a-stan'in' hyeah to-night, but by de eye o' Christian faif I see a great big wall o' sin a-stan'in' strong an' thick hyeah in ouah midst. Is we gwine to let it stan'?"

"Oh, no, no!" moaned the people.

"Is we gwine to ma'ch erroun' dat wall de same ez Joshuay an' his ban' did in de days of ol', ontwell we hyeah de cracklin' an' de rum'lin', de breakin' an' de taihin', de onsettlin' of de foundations an' de fallin' of de stones an' mo'tah?" Then raising his voice he broke into the song:

> "Den we'll ma'ch, ma'ch down, ma'ch, ma'ch down,
>   Oh, chillen, ma'ch down,
>   In de day o' Jubilee."

The congregation joined him in the ringing chorus, and springing to their feet began marching around and around the inclosure, chewing vigorously in the breathing spaces of the hymn.

The two young men, who were too used to such sights to be provoked to laughter, nudged each other and bent their looks upon Parker, who stood with bowed head, refusing to join in the performance, and sighed audibly.

After the march Tom and Ralph started for home, and Parker went with them.

"He's very effective, don't you think so, Tom?" said Ralph.

"Immensely so," was the reply. "I don't know that I have ever seen such a moving spectacle."

"The people seem greatly taken up with him."

"Personal magnetism, that's what it is. Don't you think so, Parker?"

"Hum," said Parker.

"It's a wonderful idea of his, that marching around the walls of sin."

"So original, too. It's a wonder you never thought of a thing like that, Parker. I believe it would have held your people to you in the face of everything.　They do love to eat and march."

"Well," said Parker, "you all may think what you please, but I ain't nevah made no business of mekin' a play show outen de Bible.　Dem folks don't know what dey're doin'.　Why, ef dem niggahs hyeahed anything commence to fall they'd taih dat place up gittin' erway f'om daih.　It's a wondah de Lawd don' sen' a jedgmen' on 'em fu' tu'nin' his wo'd into mockery."

The two young men bit their lips and a knowing glance flashed between them.　The same idea had leaped into both of their minds at once.　They said no word to Parker, however, save at parting, and then they only begged that he would go again the next night of the meeting.

"You must, Parker," said Ralph.　"You must represent the spiritual interest of the plantation.　If you don't, that man Johnson will think we are heathen or that our exhorter is afraid of him."

At the name of fear the old preacher bridled and said with angry dignity:

"Nemmine, nemmine; he shan't nevah think dat.　I'll be daih."

Parker went alone to his cabin, sore at heart; the young men, a little regretful that they had stung him a bit too far, went up to the big house, their heads close together, and in the darkness and stillness there came to them the hymns of the people.

On the next night Parker went early to the meeting-place and, braced by the spirit of his defiance, took a conspicuous front seat.　His face gave no sign, though his heart throbbed angrily as he saw the best and most trusted of his flock come in with intent faces and seat themselves anxiously · to await the advent of an alien. Why had those rascally boys compelled him for his own dignity's sake to come there ? Why had they forced him to be a living witness of his own degradation and of his own people's ingratitude?

But Parker was a diplomat, and when the hymns began he joined his voice with the voices of the rest.

Something, though, tugged at Parker's breast, a vague hoped-for something ; he knew not what—the promise of relief from the tension of his jealousy, the harbinger of revenge. It was in the air. Everything was tense as if awaiting the moment of catastrophe. He found himself joyous, and when Johnson arose on the wings of his elo- quence it was Parker's loud " Amen " which set fire to all the throng. Then, when the meeting was going well, when the spiritual fire had been thoroughly kindled and had gone from crackling to roaring ; when the hymns were loudest and the hand-clapping strongest, the reviv- alist called upon them to rise and march around the walls of Jericho. Parker rose with the rest, and, though he had no basket, he levied on the store of a solicitous sister and marched with them, singing, singing, but waiting, wait- ing for he knew not what.

It was the fifth time around and yet nothing had hap- pened. Then the sixth, and a rumbling sound was heard near at hand. A tree crashed down on one side. White eyes were rolled in the direction of the noise and the bur- den of the hymn was left to the few faithful. Half way around and the bellow of a horn broke upon the startled people's ears, and the hymn sank lower and lower. The preacher's face was ashen, but he attempted to inspire the people, until on the seventh turn such a rumbling and such a clattering, such a tumbling of rocks, such a falling of trees as was never heard before gave horror to the night. The people paused for one moment and then the remains of the bread and meat were cast to the winds, baskets were thrown away, and the congregation, thoroughly maddened with fear, made one rush for the road and the quarters. Ahead of them all, his long coat-tails flying and his legs making not steps but leaps, was the Rev. Mr. Johnson. He had no word of courage or hope to offer the frightened flock behind him. Only Parker, with some perception of the situation, stood his ground. He had leaped upon a log and was crying aloud :

"Stan' still, stan' still, I say, an' see de salvation," but he got only frightened, backward glances as the place was cleared.

When they were all gone, he got down off the log and went to where several of the trees had fallen. He saw that they had been cut nearly through during the day on the side away from the clearing, and ropes were still along the upper parts of their trunks. Then he chuckled softly to himself. As he stood there in the dim light of the fat-pine torches that were burning themselves out, two stealthy figures made their way out of the surrounding gloom into the open space. Tom and Ralph were holding their sides, and Parker, with a hand on the shoulder of each of the boys, laughed unrighteously.

"Well, he hyeahed de rum'lin' an' crum'lin'," he said, and Ralph gasped.

"You're the only one who stood your ground, Parker," said Tom.

" How erbout de walls o' Jericho now ?" was all Parker
could say as he doubled up.

When the people came back to their senses they began
to realize that the Rev. Mr. Johnson had not the qualities
of a leader.   Then they recalled how Parker had stood
still in spite of the noise and called them to wait and see
the salvation, and so, with a rush of emotional feeling,
they went back to their old allegiance.   Parker's meeting-
house again was filled, and for lack of worshipers Mr.
Johnson held no more meetings and marched no more
around the walls of Jericho.

"Stan' Still, Stan' Still, an' See de Salvation"

HIS EYES WERE BRIGHT, AND HE WAS BREATHING
QUICKLY

HOW BROTHER PARKER FELL
FROM GRACE

IT all happened so long ago that it has almost been
forgotten upon the plantation, and few save the older
heads know anything about it save from hearsay. It was
in Parker's younger days, but the tale was told on him
for a long time, until he was so old that every little dis-
paragement cut him like a knife. Then the young scape-
graces who had the story only from their mothers' lips
spared his dotage. Even to young eyes, the respect
which hedges about the form of eighty obscures many of
the imperfections that are apparent at twenty-eight, and
Parker was nearing eighty.

The truth of it is that Parker, armed with the authority
which his master thought the due of the plantation ex-
horter, was wont to use his power with rather too free a
rein. He was so earnest for the spiritual welfare of his
fellow servants that his watchful ministrations became a
nuisance and a bore.

Even Aunt Doshy, who was famous for her devotion to
all that pertained to the church, had been heard to state
that " Brothah Pahkah was a moughty powahful 'zortah,
but he sholy was monst'ous biggity." This from a mem-
ber of his flock old enough to be his mother, quite
summed up the plantation's estimate of this black disciple.

There was many a time when it would have gone hard
with Brother Parker among the young bucks on the
Mordaunt plantation but that there was scarcely one of
them but could remember a time when Parker had come

373

to his cabin to console some sick one, help a seeker, comfort the dying or close the eyes of one already dead, and it clothed him about with a sacredness, which, however much inclined, they dared not invade.

"Ain't it enough," Mandy's Jim used to say, "fu' Brothah Pahkah to 'tend to his business down at meetin' widout spookin' 'roun' all de cabins an' outhouses? Seems to me dey's enough dev'ment gwine on right undah his nose widout him gwine 'roun' tryin' to smell out what's hid."

Every secret sinner on the place agreed with this dictum, and it came to the preacher's ears. He smiled broadly.

"Uh, huh," he remarked, "hit's de stuck pig dat squeals. I reckon Jim's up to somep'n' right now, an' I lay I'll fin' out what dat somep'n' is." Parker was a subtle philosopher and Jim had by his remark unwittingly disclosed his interest in the preacher's doings. It then behooved his zealous disciple to find out the source of this unusual interest and opposition.

On the Sunday following his sermon was strong, fiery and convincing. His congregation gave themselves up to the joy of the occasion and lost all consciousness of time or place in their emotional ecstasy. But, although he continued to move them with his eloquence, not for one moment did Parker lose possession of himself. His eyes roamed over the people before him and took in the absence of several who had most loudly and heartily agreed with Jim's dictum. Jim himself was not there.

"Uh, huh," said the minister to himself even in the midst of his exhortations. "Uh, huh, erway on some dev'ment, I be boun'." He could hardly wait to hurry through his sermon. Then he seized his hat and almost

ran away from the little table that did duty as a pulpit
desk.   He brushed aside with scant ceremony those who
would have asked him to their cabins to share some
special delicacy, and made his way swiftly to the door.
There he paused and cast a wondering glance about the
plantation.

"I des wondah whaih dem scoun'els is mos' lakly to
be."   Then his eye fell upon an old half-ruined smoke-
house that stood between the kitchen and the negro
quarters, and he murmured to himself, "Lak ez not, lak
ez not."   But he did not start directly for the object of
his suspicions.   Oh, no, he was too deep a diplomat for
that.   He knew that if there were wrong-doers in that
innocent-looking ruin they would be watching in his
direction about the time when they expected meeting to
be out; so he walked off swiftly, but carelessly, in an op-
posite direction, and, instead of going straight past the
kitchen, began to circle around from the direction of the
quarters, whence no danger would be apprehended.

As he drew nearer and nearer the place, he thought he
heard the rise and fall of eager voices.   He approached
more cautiously.   Now he was perfectly sure that he
could hear smothered conversation, and he smiled grimly
as he pictured to himself the surprise of his quarry when
he should come up with them.   He was almost upon the
smoke-house now.   Those within were so absorbed that
the preacher was able to creep up and peer through a
crack at the scene within.

There, seated upon the earthen floor, were the un-
regenerate of the plantation.   In the very midst of them
was Mandy's Jim, and he was dealing from a pack of
greasy cards.

It is a wonder that they did not hear the preacher's gasp of horror as he stood there gazing upon the iniquitous performance. But they did not. The delight of High-Low-Jack was too absorbing for that, and they suspected nothing of Parker's presence until he slipped around to the door, pushed it open and confronted them like an accusing angel.

Jim leaped to his feet with a strong word upon his lips.

"I reckon you done fu'got, Brothah Jim, what day dis is," said the preacher.

"I ain't fu'got nuffin'," was the dogged reply; "I don't see what you doin' roun' hyeah nohow."

"I's a lookin' aftah some strayin' lambs," said Parker, "an' I done foun' 'em. You ought to be ashamed o' yo'se'ves, evah one o' you, playin' cyards on de Lawd's day."

There was the light of reckless deviltry in Jim's eyes.

"Dey ain't no ha'm in a little game o' cyards."

"Co'se not, co'se not," replied the preacher scornfully. "Dem's des de sins that's ca'ied many a man to hell wid his eyes wide open, de little no-ha'm kin'."

"I don't reckon you evah played cyards," said Jim sneeringly.

"Yes, I has played, an' I thought I was enjoyin' myse'f ontwell I foun' out dat it was all wickedness an' idleness."

"Oh, I don't reckon you was evah ve'y much of a player. I know lots o' men who has got uligion des case dey couldn't win at cyards."

The company greeted this sally with a laugh and then looked aghast at Jim's audacity.

"Uligion's a moughty savin' to de pocket," Jim went

on.   " We kin believe what we wants to, and I say you
nevah was no playah, an' dat's de reason you tuk up de
Gospel."

" Hit ain't so.   I 'low dey was a time when I could 'a'
outplayed any one o' you sinnahs hyeah, but ———"

" Prove it ! "   The challenge shot forth like a pistol's
report.

Parker hesitated.   " What you mean ? " he said.

" Beat me, beat all of us, an' we'll believe you didn't
quit playin' case you allus lost.   You a preachah now, an'
I daih you."

Parker's face turned ashen and his hands gripped to-
gether.   He was young then, and the hot blood sped
tumultuously through his veins.

" Prove it," said Jim ; " you cain't.   We'd play you
outen yo' coat an' back into de pulpit ag'in."

" You would, would you ? "   The light of battle was in
Parker's eyes, the desire for conquest throbbing in his
heart.   " Look a'hyeah, Jim, Sunday er no Sunday,
preachah er no preachah, I play you th'ee games fu' de
Gospel's sake."   And the preacher sat down in the circle,
his face tense with anger at his tormentor's insinuations.
He did not see the others around him.   He saw only Jim,
the man who had spoken against his cloth.   He did not
see the look of awe and surprise upon the faces of the
others, nor did he note that one of the assembly slipped
out of the shed just as the game began.

Jim found the preacher no mean antagonist, but it mat-
tered little to him whether he won or not.   His triumph
was complete when he succeeded in getting this man,
who kept the conscience of the plantation, to sin as others
sinned.

21

" I see you ain't fu'got yo' cunnin'," he remarked as the preacher dealt in turn.

" 'Tain't no time to talk now," said Parker fiercely.

The excitement of the onlookers grew more and more intense. They were six and six, and it was the preacher's deal. His eyes were bright, and he was breathing quickly. Parker was a born fighter and nothing gave him more joy than the heat of the battle itself. He riffled the cards. Jim cut. He dealt and turned Jack. Jim laughed.

" You know the trick," he said.

" Dat's one game," said Parker, and bent over the cards as they came to him. He did not hear a light step outside nor did he see a shadow that fell across the open doorway. He was just about to lead when a cold voice, full of contempt, broke upon his ear and made him keep the card he would have played poised in his hand.

" And so these are your after-meeting diversions, are they, Parker?" said his master's voice.

Stuart Mordaunt was standing in the door, his face cold and stern, while his informant grinned maliciously.

Parker brushed his hand across his brow as if dazed.

" Well, Mas' Stua't, he do play monst'ous well fu' a preachah," said his tempter.

The preacher at these words looked steadily at Jim, and then the realization of his position burst upon him. The tiger in him came uppermost and, with flaming eyes, he took a quick step towards Jim.

" Stop," said Mordaunt, coming between them ; " don't add anything more to what you have already done."

" Mas' Stua't, I—I——" Parker broke down, and, turning away from the exultant faces, rushed headlong out of the place.   His master followed more leisurely, angry and hurt at the hypocrisy of a trusted servant.

Of course the game was over for that day, but Jim and his companions hung around the smoke-house for some time, rejoicing in the downfall of their enemy.   Afterwards, they went to their cabins for dinner.   Then Jim made a mistake.   With much laughter and boasting he told Mandy all about it, and then suddenly awakened to the fact that she was listening to him with a face on which only horror was written.   Jim turned to his meal in silence and disgust.   A woman has no sense of humor.

"Whaih you gwine?" he asked, as Mandy began putting on her bonnet and shawl with ominous precision.

"I's gwine up to be big house, dat's whaih I's gwine."

"What you gwine daih fu'?"

"I's gwine to tell Mas' Stua't all erbout hit."

"Don't you daih."

"Heish yo' mouf.   Don't you talk to me, you nasty, low-life scamp.   I's gwine tell Mas' Stua't, an' I hope an' pray he'll tek all de hide offen yo' back."

Jim sat in bewildered misery as Mandy flirted out of the cabin ; he felt vaguely some of the hopelessness of defeat which comes to a man whenever he attempts to lay sacrilegious hands on a woman's religion or what stands to her for religion.

Parker was sitting alone in his cabin with bowed head when the door opened and his master came across the floor and laid his hand gently on the negro's shoulder.

"I didn't know how it was, Parker," he said softly.

"Oh, I's back-slid, I's fell from grace," moaned Parker.

"Nonsense," said his master, "you've fallen from nothing.   There are times when we've got to meet the devil on his own ground and fight him with his own weapons."

Parker raised his head gladly. " Say dem wo'ds ag'in, Mas' Stua't," he said.

His master repeated the words, but added : " But it isn't safe to go into the devil's camp too often, Parker."

" I ain't gwine into his camp no mo.' Aftah dis I's gwine to stan' outside an' hollah in." His face was beaming and his voice trembled with joy.

" I didn't think I'd preach to-night," he said timidly.

" Of course you will," said Mordaunt, "and your mistress and I are coming to hear you, so do your best."

His master went out and Parker went down on his knees.

He did preach that night and the plantation remembered the sermon.

JIM'S PROBATION

FOR so long a time had Jim been known as the hardest sinner on the plantation that no one had tried to reach the heart under his outward shell even in camp-meeting and revival times. Even good old Brother Parker, who was ever looking after the lost and straying sheep, gave him up as beyond recall.

"Dat Jim," he said, " Oomph, de debbil done got his stamp on dat boy, an' dey ain' no use in tryin' to scratch hit off."

"But Parker," said his master, "that's the very sort of man you want to save. Don't you know it's your business as a man of the gospel to call sinners to repentance ? "

"Lawd, Mas' Mordaunt," exclaimed the old man, "my v'ice done got hoa'se callin' Jim, too long ergo to talk erbout. You jes' got to let him go 'long, maybe some o' dese days he gwine slip up on de gospel an' fall plum' inter salvation."

Even Mandy, Jim's wife, had attempted to urge the old man to some more active efforts in her husband's behalf. She was a pillar of the church herself, and was woefully disturbed about the condition of Jim's soul. Indeed, it was said that half of the time it was Mandy's prayers and exhortations that drove Jim into the woods with his dog and his axe, or an old gun that he had come into possession of from one of the younger Mordaunts.

Jim was unregenerate. He was a fighter, a hard

381

drinker, fiddled on Sunday, and had been known to go
out hunting on that sacred day. So it startled the whole
place when Mandy announced one day to a few of her
intimate friends that she believed "Jim was under con-
viction." He had stolen out hunting one Sunday night
and in passing through the swamp had gotten himself
thoroughly wet and chilled, and this had brought on an
attack of acute rheumatism, which Mandy had pointed
out to him as a direct judgment of heaven. Jim scoffed
at first, but Mandy grew more and more earnest, and
finally, with the racking of the pain, he waxed serious and
determined to look to the state of his soul as a means to
the good of his body.

"Hit do seem," Mandy said, "dat Jim feel de weight
o' his sins mos' powahful."

"I reckon hit's de rheumatics," said Dinah.

"Don' mek no diffunce what de inst'ument is," Mandy
replied, "hit's de 'sult, hit's de 'sult."

When the news reached Stuart Mordaunt's ears he be-
came intensely interested. Anything that would convert
Jim, and make a model Christian of him would be provi-
dential on that plantation. It would save the overseers
many an hour's worry ; his horses, many a secret ride ;
and the other servants, many a broken head. So he
again went down to labor with Parker in the interest of
the sinner.

"Is he mou'nin' yit?" said Parker.

"No, not yet, but I think now is a good time to sow the
seeds in his mind."

"Oomph," said the old man, "reckon you bettah let
Jim alone twell dem sins o' his'n git him to tossin' an'
cryin' an' a mou'nin'. Den'll be time enough to strive

wid him.   I's allus willin' to do my pa't, Mas' Stuart, but
w'en hit comes to ol' time sinnahs lak Jim, I believe in
layin' off, an' lettin' de sperit do de strivin'.''

"But Parker," said his master, "you yourself know that
the Bible says that the spirit will not always strive."

"Well, la den, Mas', you don' spec' I gwine outdo de
sperit."

But Stuart Mordaunt was particularly anxious that Jim's
steps might be turned in the right direction.   He knew
just what a strong hold over their minds the Negroes'
own emotional religion had, and he felt that could he once
get Jim inside the pale of the church, and put him on
guard of his salvation, it would mean the loss of fewer of
his shoats and pullets.   So he approached the old preacher,
and said in a confidential tone,

"Now look here, Parker, I've got a fine lot of that good
old tobacco you like so up to the big house, and I'll tell
you what I'll do.   If you'll just try to work on Jim, and
get his feet in the right path, you can come up and take
all you want."

"Oom-oomph," said the old man, "dat sho' is mon-
st'ous fine terbaccer, Mas' Stua't."

"Yes, it is, and you shall have all you want of it."

"Well, I'll have a little wisit wid Jim, an' des' see how
much he 'fected, an' if dey any stroke to be put in fu' de
gospel ahmy, you des' count on me ez a mighty strong
wa'ior.   Dat boy been layin' heavy on my mind fu' lo,
dese many days."

As a result of this agreement, the old man went down
to Jim's cabin on a night when that interesting sinner was
suffering particularly from his rheumatic pains.

"Well, Jim," the preacher said, "how you come on?"

"Po'ly, po'ly," said Jim, "I des' plum' racked an' 'stracted f'om haid to foot."

"Uh, huh, hit do seem lak to me de Bible don' tell nuffin' else but de trufe."

"What de Bible been sayin' now?" asked Jim suspiciously.

"Des' what it been sayin' all de res' o' de time. 'Yo' sins will fin' you out.'"

Jim groaned and turned uneasily in his chair. The old man saw that he had made a point and pursued it.

"Don' you reckon now, Jim, ef you was a bettah man dat you wouldn' suffah so?"

"I do' know, I do' know nuffin' 'bout hit."

"Now des' look at me. I ben a-trompin' erlong in dis low groun' o' sorrer fu' mo' den seventy yeahs, an' I hain't got a ache ner a pain. Nevah had no rheumatics in my life, an' yere you is, a young man, in a mannah o' speakin', all twinged up wid rheumatics. Now what dat p'nt to? Hit mean de Lawd tek keer o' dem dat's his'n. Now Jim, you bettah come ovah on de Lawd's side, an' git erway f'om yo' ebil doin's."

Jim groaned again, and lifted his swollen leg with an effort just as Brother Parker said, "Let us pray."

The prayer itself was less effective than the request was just at that time, for Jim was so stiff that it made him fairly howl with pain to get down on his knees. The old man's supplication was loud, deep, and diplomatic, and when they arose from their knees there were tears in Jim's eyes, but whether from cramp or contrition it is not safe to say. But a day or two after, the visit bore fruit in the appearance of Jim at meeting where he sat on one of the very last benches, his shoulders hunched, and his head bowed, unmistakable signs of the convicted sinner.

The usual term of mourning passed, and Jim was converted, much to Mandy's joy, and Brother Parker's delight. The old man called early on his master after the meeting, and announced the success of his labors. Stuart Mordaunt himself was no less pleased than the preacher. He shook Parker warmly by the hand, patted him on the shoulder, and called him a "sly old fox." And then he took him to the cupboard, and gave him of his store of good tobacco, enough to last him for months. Something else, too, he must have given him, for the old man came away from the cupboard grinning broadly, and ostentatiously wiping his mouth with the back of his hand.

"Great work you've done, Parker, a great work."

"Yes, yes, Mas'," grinned the old man, "now ef Jim can des' stan' out his p'obation, hit'll be monstrous fine."

"His probation!" exclaimed the master.

"Oh, yes suh, yes suh, we has all de young convu'ts stan' a p'obation o' six months, fo' we teks 'em reg'lar inter de chu'ch. Now ef Jim will des' stan' strong in de faif——"

"Parker," said Mordaunt, "you're an old wretch, and I've got a mind to take every bit of that tobacco away from you. No. I'll tell you what I'll do."

He went back to the cupboard and got as much again as he had given Parker, and handed it to him, saying:

"I think it will be better for all concerned if Jim's probation only lasts two months. Get him into the fold, Parker, get him into the fold!" And he shoved the ancient exhorter out of the door.

It grieved Jim that he could not go 'possum hunting on Sundays any more, but shortly after he got religion, his rheumatism seemed to take a turn for the better and he felt that the result was worth the sacrifice. But as the pain decreased in his legs and arms, the longing for his old wicked pleasures became stronger and stronger upon him, though Mandy thought that he was living out the period of his probation in the most exemplary manner, and inwardly rejoiced.

It was two weeks before he was to be regularly admitted to church fellowship. His industrious spouse had decked him out in a bleached cotton shirt in which to attend divine service. In the morning Jim was there. The sermon which Brother Parker preached was powerful, but somehow it failed to reach this new convert. His gaze roved out of the window towards the dark line of the woods beyond, where the frost still glistened on the trees and where he knew the persimmons were hanging ripe. Jim was present at the afternoon service also, for it was a great day; and again, he was preoccupied. He started and clasped his hands together until the bones cracked, when a dog barked somewhere out on the hill. The sun was going down over the tops of the woodland trees, throwing the forest into gloom, as they came out of the log meeting-house. Jim paused and looked lovingly at the scene, and sighed as he turned his steps back towards the cabin.

That night Mandy went to church alone. Jim had disappeared. Nowhere around was his axe, and Spot, his dog, was gone. Mandy looked over towards the woods whose tops were feathered against the frosty sky, and away off, she heard a dog bark.

Brother Parker was feeling his way home from meeting late that night, when all of a sudden, he came upon a man creeping towards the quarters. The man had an axe and a dog, and over his shoulders hung a bag in which the outlines of a 'possum could be seen.

"Hi, oh, Brothah Jim, at it agin?"

Jim did not reply. "Well, des' heish up an' go 'long. We got to mek some 'lowances fu' you young convu'ts. W'en you gwine cook dat 'possum, Brothah Jim?"

"I do' know, Brothah Pahkah. He so po', I 'low I haveter keep him and fatten him fu' awhile."

"Uh, huh! well, so long, Jim."

"So long, Brothah Pahkah." Jim chuckled as he went away. "I 'low I fool dat ol' fox. Wanter come down an' eat up my one little 'possum, do he? huh, uh!"

So that very night Jim scraped his 'possum, and hung it out-of-doors, and the next day, brown as the forest whence it came, it lay on a great platter on Jim's table. It was a fat 'possum, too. Jim had just whetted his knife, and Mandy had just finished the blessing when the latch was lifted and Brother Parker stepped in.

"Hi, oh, Brothah Jim, I's des in time."

Jim sat with his mouth open. "Draw up a cheer, Brothah Pahkah," said Mandy. Her husband rose, and put his hand over the 'possum.

"Wha—wha'd you come hyeah fu'?" he asked.

"I thought I'd des' come in an' tek a bite wid you."

"Ain' gwine tek no bite wid me," said Jim.

"Heish," said Mandy, "wha' kin' o' way is dat to talk to de preachah?"

"Preachah or no preachah, you hyeah what I say," and he took the 'possum, and put it on the highest shelf.

" Wha's de mattah wid you, Jim? dat's one o' de 'quiah-ments o' de chu'ch."

The angry man turned to the preacher.

" Is it one o' de 'quiahments o' de chu'ch dat you eat hyeah ter-night?"

" Hit sholy am usual fu' de shepherd to sup wherevah he stop," said Parker, suavely.

" Ve'y well, ve'y well," said Jim, " I wants you to know dat I 'specs to stay out o' yo' chu'ch. I's got two weeks mo' p'obation. You tek hit back, an' gin hit to de nex' niggah you ketches wid a 'possum."

Mandy was horrified. The preacher looked longingly at the 'possum, and took up his hat to go.

There were two disappointed men on the plantation when he told his master the next day the outcome of Jim's probation.

DAT JIM

"You Old Scoundrel," Said a Well-known Voice

A SUPPER BY PROXY

THERE was an air of suppressed excitement about the whole plantation. The big old house stared gravely out as if it could tell great things if it would, and the cabins in the quarters looked prophetic. The very dogs were on the alert, and there was expectancy even in the eyes of the piccaninnies who rolled in the dust. Something was going to happen. There was no denying that. The wind whispered it to the trees and the trees nodded.

Then there was a clatter of horses' hoofs, the crack of a whip. The bays with the family carriage swept round the drive and halted at the front porch. Julius was on the box, resplendent in his holiday livery. This was the signal for a general awakening. The old house leered an irritating "I told you so." The quarters looked complacent. The dogs ran and barked, the piccaninnies laughed and shouted, the servants gathered on the lawn and, in the midst of it all, the master and mistress came down the steps and got into the carriage. Another crack of the whip, a shout from the servants, more antics from the piccaninnies, the scurrying of the dogs—and the vehicle rumbled out of sight behind a clump of maples. Immediately the big house resumed its natural appearance and the quarters settled back into whitewashed respectability.

Mr. and Mrs. Mordaunt were off for a week's visit. The boys were away at school, and here was the plantation left in charge of the negroes themselves, except for the presence of an overseer who did not live on the place.

The conditions seemed pregnant of many things, but a calm fell on the place as if every one had decided to be particularly upon his good behavior. The piccaninnies were subdued. The butlers in the big house bowed with wonderful deference to the maids as they passed them in the halls, and the maids called the butlers "mister" when they spoke to them. Only now and again from the fields could a song be heard. All this was ominous.

By the time that night came many things were changed. The hilarity of the little darkies had grown, and although the house servants still remained gravely quiet, on the return of the field hands the quarters became frankly joyous. From one cabin to another could be heard the sound of "Juba, Juba!" and the loud patting of hands and the shuffling of feet. Now and again some voice could be heard rising above the rest, improvising a verse of the song, as:

> "Mas' done gone to Philamundelphy, Juba, Juba.
> Lef' us bacon, lef' us co'n braid, Juba, Juba.
> Oh, Juba dis an' Juba dat, an' Juba skinned de yaller cat
> To mek his wife a Sunday hat, oh, Juba!"

Not long did the sounds continue to issue from isolated points. The people began drifting together, and when a goodly number had gathered at a large cabin, the inevitable thing happened. Some one brought out a banjo and a dance followed.

Meanwhile, from the vantage ground of the big house, the more favored servants looked disdainfully on, and at the same time consulted together. That they should do something to entertain themselves was only right and proper. No one of ordinary intelligence could think for a moment of letting this opportunity slip without taking advantage of it.   But a dance such as the quarters had ! Bah ! They could never think of it.   That rude, informal affair !   And these black aristocrats turned up their noses. No, theirs must be a grave and dignified affair, such as their master himself would have given, and they would send out invitations to some on the neighboring planta-tions.

It was Julius, the coachman, who, after winning around the head butler, Anderson, insisted that they ought to give a grand supper.   Julius would have gone on without the butler's consent had it not been that Anderson carried the keys.   So the matter was canvassed and settled.

The next business was the invitations, but no one could write.   Still, this was a slight matter ; for neatly folded envelopes were carried about to the different favored ones, containing—nothing, while at the same time the in-vitations were proffered by word of mouth.

"Hi, dah !" cried Jim to Julius, on the evening that the cards had been distributed ; "I ain't seed my inbitation yit."

"You needn't keep yo' eyes bucked looking fu' none, neithah," replied Julius.

"Uh, puttin' on airs, is you?"

"I don't caih to convuss wid you jest now," said Julius pompously.

Jim guffawed.   "Well, of all de sights I evah seed, a dahky coachman offen de box tryin' to look lak he on it! Go 'long, Julius, er you'll sholy kill me, man."

The coachman strode on with angry dignity.

It had been announced that the supper was to be a "ladies' an' gent'men's pahty," and so but few from the

quarters were asked.   The quarters were naturally angry
and a bit envious, for they were but human and not yet
intelligent enough to recognize the vast social gulf that
yawned between the blacks at the "big house" and the
blacks who were quartered in the cabins.

The night of the grand affair arrived, and the Mordaunt
mansion was as resplendent as it had ever been for one
of the master's festivities.   The drawing-rooms were gaily
festooned, and the long dining-room was a blaze of light
from the wax candles that shone on the glory of the Mor-
daunt plate.   Nothing but the best had satisfied Julius
and Anderson.   By nine o'clock the outside guests began
to arrive.   They were the dark aristocrats of the region.
It was a well-dressed assembly, too.   Plump brown arms
lay against the dainty folds of gleaming muslin, and
white-stocked, brass-buttoned black counterparts of their
masters strode up the walks.   There were Dudley Stone's
Gideon and Martha, Robert Curtis' Ike with Dely, and
there were Quinn, and Doshy, and, over them all, Aunt
Tempe to keep them straight.   Of these was the company
that sat down to Stuart Mordaunt's board.

After some rivalry, Anderson held the head of the table,
while Julius was appeased by being placed on the right
beside his favorite lady.   Aunt Tempe was opposite the
host where she could reprove any unseemly levity or
tendency to skylarking on the part of the young people.
No state dinner ever began with more dignity.   The con-
versation was nothing less than stately, and everybody
bowed to everybody else every time they thought about
it.   This condition of affairs obtained through the soup.
Somebody ventured a joke and there was even a light
laugh during the fish.   By the advent of the entree the

tongues of the assembly had loosened up, and their laughter had melted and flowed as freely as Stuart Mordaunt's wine.

"Well, I mus' say, Mistah An'erson, dis is sholy a mos' salub'ious occasion."

"Thank you, Mistah Cu'tis, thank you; it ah allus my endeavoh to mek my gues'es feel deyse'ves at home. Let me give you some mo' of dis wine. It's f'om de bes' dat's in my cellah."

"Seems lak I remembah de vintage," said Ike, sipping slowly and with the air of a connoisseur.

"Oh, yes, you drinked some o' dis on de 'casion of my darter's ma'ige to Mas'—to Mistah Daniels."

"I ricollec', yes, I ricollec'."

"Des lis'en at dem dahkies," said the voice of a listening field hand.

Gideon, as was his wont, was saying deeply serious things to Martha, and Quinn whispered something in Doshy's ear that made her giggle hysterically and cry: "Now, Mr. Quinn, ain't you scan'lous? You des seem lak you possessed dis evenin'."

In due time, however, the ladies withdrew, and the gentlemen were left over their cigars and cognac. It was then that one of the boys detailed to wait on the table came in and announced to the host that a tramp was without begging for something to eat. At the same instant the straggler's face appeared at the door, a poor, unkempt-looking white fellow with a very dirty face. Anderson cast a look over his shoulder at him and commanded pompously:

"Tek him to de kitchen an' give him all he wants."

The fellow went away very humbly.

22

In a few minutes Aunt Tempe opened the dining-room door and came in.

"An'erson," she cried in a whisper.

"Madam," said the butler rising in dignity, "excuse me—but ——"

"Hyeah, don't you come no foo'ishness wid me; I ain't no madam. I's tiahed playing fine lady. I done been out to de kitchen, an' I don' lak dat tramp's face an' fo'm."

"Well, madam," said Anderson urbanely, "we haven't asked you to ma'y him."

At this there was a burst of laughter from the table.

"Nemmine, nemmine, I tell you, I don' lak dat tramp's face an' fo'm, an' you'd bettah keep yo' eye skinned, er you'll be laughin' on de othah side o' yo' mouf."

The butler gently pushed the old lady out, but as the door closed behind her she was still saying, "I don' lak dat tramp's face an' fo'm."

Unused to playing fine lady so long, Aunt Tempe deserted her charges and went back to the kitchen, but the "straggler man" had gone. It is a good thing she did not go around the veranda, where the windows of the dining-room opened, or she would have been considerably disturbed to see the tramp peeping through the blinds —evidently at the Mordaunt plate that sparkled conspicuously on the table.

Anderson with his hand in his coat, quite after the manner of Stuart Mordaunt, made a brief speech in which he thanked his guests for the honor they had done him in coming to his humble home. "I know," he said, "I have done my po' bes'; but at some latah day I hopes to entertain you in a mannah dat de position an' character

of de gent'men hyeah assembled desuves. Let us now
jine de ladies."

His hand was on the door and all the gentlemen were
on their feet when suddenly the window was thrown up
and in stepped the straggler.

"W'y, w'y, how daih you, suh, invade my p'emises?"
asked Anderson, casting a withering glance at the in-
truder, who stood gazing around him.

"Leave de room dis minute!" cried Julius, anxious to
be in the fray. But the tramp's eyes were fastened on
Anderson. Finally he raised one finger and pointed at
him.

"You old scoundrel," he said in a well-known voice, as
he snatched off his beard and wig and threw aside his
disguising duster and stood before them.

"Mas' Stu'at!"

"You old scoundrel, you! I've caught you, have I?"

Anderson was speechless and transfixed, but the others
were not, and they had cleared that room before the
master's linen duster was well off. In a moment the
shuffling of feet ceased and the lights went out in the
parlor. The two stood there alone, facing each other

"Mas' Stu'at."

"Silence," said Mordaunt, raising his hand, and taking
a step towards the trembling culprit.

"Don' hit me now, Mas' Stu'at, don' hit me ontwell I's
kin' o' shuk off yo' pussonality. Ef you do, it'll be des'
de same ez thumpin' yo'se'f."

Mordaunt turned quickly and stood for a moment look-
ing through the window, but his shoulders shook.

"Well," he said, turning; "do you think you've at last
relieved yourself of my personality?"

"I don't know, I don't know. De gyahment sho' do fit monst'ous tight."

"Humph. You take my food, you take my wine, you take my cigars, and now even my personality isn't safe.

"Look here, what on earth do you mean by entertaining half the darkies in the county in my dining-room?"

Anderson scratched his head and thought. Then he said: "Well, look hyeah, Mas' Stu'at, dis hyeah wasn't rightly my suppah noways."

"Not your supper! Whose was it?"

"Yo'n."

"Mine?"

"Yes, suh."

"Why, what's the matter with you, Anderson? Next thing you'll be telling me that I planned it all, and invited all those servants."

"Lemme 'splain it, Mas', lemme 'splain it. Now I didn't give dat suppah as An'erson. I give it ez Mas' Stu'at Mordaunt; an' Quinn an' Ike an' Gidjon, dey didn't come fu' deyse'ves, dey come fu' Mas' Cu'tis, an' Mas' Dudley Stone. Don' you un'erstan', Mas' Stu'at? We wasn' we-all, we was you-all."

"That's very plain; and in other words, I gave a supper by proxy, and all my friends responded in the same manner?"

"Well, ef dat means what I said, dat's it."

"Your reasoning is extremely profound, Anderson. It does you great credit, but if I followed your plan I should give you the thrashing you deserve by proxy. That would just suit you. So instead of that I am going to feed you, for the next day or so, by that ingenious

method.   You go down and tell Jim that I want him up
here early to-morrow morning to eat your breakfast."

"Oh, Mas' Stu'at!   Whup me, whup me, but don't tell
dose dahkies in de quahtahs, an' don't sta've me!"   For
Anderson loved the good things of life.

"Go."

Anderson went, and Mordaunt gave himself up to
mirth.

The quarters got their laugh out of Anderson's dis-
comfiture.   Jim lived high for a day, but rumors from
the kitchen say that the butler did not really suffer on ac·
count of his supper by proxy.

THE FAITH CURE MAN

HOPE is tenacious. It goes on living and working when science has dealt it what should be its death-blow.

In the close room at the top of the old tenement house little Lucy lay wasting away with a relentless disease. The doctor had said at the beginning of the winter that she could not live. Now he said that he could do no more for her except to ease the few days that remained for the child.

But Martha Benson would not believe him. She was confident that doctors were not infallible. Anyhow, this one wasn't, for she saw life and health ahead for her little one.

Did not the preacher at the Mission Home say : " Ask, and ye shall receive " ? and had she not asked and asked again the life of her child, her last and only one, at the hands of him whom she worshiped ?

No, Lucy was not going to die. What she needed was country air and a place to run about in. She had been housed up too much ; these long Northern winters were too severe for her, and that was what made her so pinched and thin and weak. She must have air, and she should have it.

" Po' little lammie," she said to the child, " mammy's little gal boun' to git well. Mammy gwine sen' huh out in de country when the spring comes, whaih she kin roll in de grass an' pick flowers an' git good an' strong. Don' baby want to go to de country ? Don' baby want to see de sun shine?" And the child had looked up at her with wide, bright eyes, tossed her thin arms and moaned for reply

"Nemmine, we gwine fool dat doctah. Some day we'll th'ow all his nassy medicine 'way, an' he come in an' say : 'Whaih's all my medicine?' Den we answeh up sma't like : 'We done th'owed it out. We don' need no nassy medicine.' Den he look 'roun' an' say : 'Who dat I see runnin' roun' de flo' hyeah, a-lookin' so fat?' an' you up an' say : 'Hit's me, dat's who 'tis, mistah doctor man!' Den he go out an' slam de do' behin' him. Ain' dat fine?"

But the child had closed her eyes, too weak even to listen. So her mother kissed her little thin forehead and tiptoed out, sending in a child from across the hall to take care of Lucy while she was at work, for sick as the little one was she could not stay at home and nurse her.

Hope grasps at a straw, and it was quite in keeping with the condition of Martha's mind that she should open her ears and her heart when they told her of the wonderful works of the faith-cure man. People had gone to him on crutches, and he had touched or rubbed them and they had come away whole. He had gone to the homes of the bed-ridden, and they had risen up to bless him. It was so easy for her to believe it all. The only religion she had never known, the wild, emotional religion of most of her race, put her credulity to stronger tests than that. Her only question was, would such a man come to her humble room. But she put away even this thought. He must come. She would make him. Already she saw Lucy strong, and running about like a mouse, the joy of her heart and the light of her eyes.

As soon as she could get time she went humbly to see the faith doctor, and laid her case before him, hoping, fearing, trembling.

Yes, he would come.   Her heart leaped for joy.

" There is no place," said the faith curist, " too humble for the messenger of heaven to enter.   I am following One who went among the humblest and the lowliest, and was not ashamed to be found among publicans and sinners. I will come to your child, madam, and put her again under the law.   The law of life is health, and no one who will accept the law need be sick.   I am not a physician I do not claim to be.   I only claim to teach people how not to be sick.   My fee is five dollars, merely to defray my expenses, that's all.   You know the servant is worthy of his hire.   And in this little bottle here I have an elixir which has never been known to fail in any of the things claimed for it.   Since the world has got used to taking medicine we must make some concessions to its prejudices.   But this in reality is not a medicine at all.   It is only a symbol.   It is really liquefied prayer and faith."

Martha did not understand anything of what he was saying.   She did not try to ; she did not want to.   She only felt a blind trust in him that filled her heart with unspeakable gladness.

Tremulous with excitement, she doled out her poor dollars to him, seized the precious elixir and hurried away home to Lucy, to whom she was carrying life and strength. The little one made a weak attempt to smile at her mother, but the light flickered away and died into grayness on her face.

" Now mammy's little gal gwine to git well fu' sho'. Mammy done bring huh somep'n' good."   Awed and reverent, she tasted the wonderful elixir before giving it to the child. It tasted very like sweetened water to her, but she knew that it was not, and had no doubt of its virtues.

Lucy swallowed it as she swallowed everything her mother brought to her. Poor little one ! She had nothing to buoy her up or to fight science with.

In the course of an hour her mother gave her the medicine again, and persuaded herself that there was a perceptible brightening in her daughter's face.

Mrs. Mason, Caroline's mother, called across the hall : " How Lucy dis evenin', Mis' Benson ? "

" Oh, I think Lucy air right peart," Martha replied. " Come over an' look at huh."

Mrs. Mason came, and the mother told her about the new faith doctor and his wonderful powers.

" Why, Mis' Mason," she said, " 'pears like I could see de change in de child de minute she swallowed dat medicine."

Her neighbor listened in silence, but when she went back to her own room it was to shake her head and murmur : " Po' Marfy, she jes' ez blind ez a bat. She jes' go 'long, holdin' on to dat chile wid all huh might, an' I see death in Lucy's face now. Dey ain't no faif nur prayer, nur jack-leg doctors nuther gwine to save huh."

But Martha needed no pity then. She was happy in her self-delusion.

On the morrow the faith doctor came to see Lucy. She had not seemed so well that morning, even to her mother, who remained at home until the doctor arrived. He carried a conquering air, and a baggy umbrella, the latter of which he laid across the foot of the bed as he bent over the moaning child.

"Give me some brown paper," he commanded.

Martha hastened to obey, and the priestly practitioner dampened it in water and laid it on Lucy's head, all the time murmuring prayers—or were they incantations?—to himself. Then he placed pieces of the paper on the soles of the child's feet and on the palms of her hands, and bound them there.

When all this was done he knelt down and prayed aloud, ending with a peculiar version of the Lord's prayer, supposed to have mystic effect. Martha was greatly impressed, but through it all Lucy lay and moaned.

The faith curist rose to go. "Well, we can look to have her out in a few days. Remember, my good woman, much depends upon you. You must try to keep your mind in a state of belief. Are you saved?"

"Oh, yes, suh. I'm a puffessor," said Martha, and having completed his mission, the man of prayers went out, and Caroline again took Martha's place at Lucy's side.

In the next two days Martha saw, or thought she saw, a steady improvement in Lucy. According to instructions, the brown paper was moved every day, moistened, and put back.

Martha had so far spurred her faith that when she went out on Saturday morning she promised to bring Lucy something good for her Christmas dinner, and a pair of shoes against the time of her going out, and also a little doll. She brought them home that night. Caroline had grown tired and, lighting the lamp, had gone home.

"I done brung my little lady bird huh somep'n' nice," said Martha, "here's a lil' doll and de lil' shoes, honey. How's de baby feel?" Lucy did not answer.

"You sleep?" Martha went over to the bed. The little face was pinched and ashen. The hands were cold.

"Lucy! Lucy!" called the mother. "Lucy! Oh, Gawd! It ain't true! She ain't daid! My little one, my las' one!"

She rushed for the elixir and brought it to the bed. The thin dead face stared back at her, unresponsive.

She sank down beside the bed, moaning. "Daid, daid, oh, my Gawd, gi' me back my chile! Oh, don't I believe you enough? Oh, Lucy, Lucy, my little lamb! I got you yo' gif'. Oh, Lucy!"

The next day was set apart for the funeral. The Mission preacher read: "The Lord giveth and the Lord taketh away, blessed be the name of the Lord," and some one said "Amen!" But Martha could not echo it in her heart. Lucy was her last, her one treasured lamb.

THE WISDOM OF SILENCE

JEREMIAH ANDERSON was free. He had been free for ten years, and he was proud of it. He had been proud of it from the beginning, and that was the reason that he was one of the first to cast off the bonds of his old relations, and move from the plantation and take up land for himself. He was anxious to cut himself off from all that bound him to his former life. So strong was this feeling in him that he would not consent to stay on and work for his one-time owner even for a full wage.

To the proposition of the planter and the gibes of some of his more dependent fellows he answered, "No, suh, I's free, an' I sholy is able to tek keer o' myse'f. I done been fattenin' frogs fu' othah people's snakes too long now."

"But, Jerry," said Samuel Brabant, "I don't mean you any harm. The thing's done. You don't belong to me any more, but naturally, I take an interest in you, and want to do what I can to give you a start. It's more than the Northern government has done for you, although such wise men ought to know that you have had no training in caring for yourselves."

There was a slight sneer in the Southerner's voice. Jerry perceived it and thought it directed against him. Instantly his pride rose and his neck stiffened.

"Nemmine me," he answered, "nemmine me. I's free, an' w'en a man's free, he's free."

"All right, go your own way. You may have to come

back to me some time. If you have to come, come. I
don't blame you now. It must be a great thing to you,
this dream—this nightmare." Jerry looked at him.
" Oh, it isn't a nightmare now, but some day, maybe, it
will be, then come to me."

The master turned away from the newly made free-
man, and Jerry went forth into the world which was
henceforth to be his. He took with him his few belong-
ings ; these largely represented by his wife and four
lusty-eating children. Besides, he owned a little money,
which he had got working for others when his master's
task was done. Thus, burdened and equipped, he set
out to tempt Fortune.

He might do one of two things—farm land upon shares
for one of his short-handed neighbors, or buy a farm,
mortgage it, and pay for it as he could. As was natural
for Jerry, and not uncommendable, he chose at once the
latter course, bargained for his twenty acres—for land
was cheap then, bought his mule, built his cabin, and set
up his household goods.

Now, slavery may give a man the habit of work, but
it cannot imbue him with the natural thrift that long
years of self-dependence brings. There were times when
Jerry's freedom tugged too strongly at his easy incli-
nation, drawing him away to idle when he should have
toiled. What was the use of freedom, asked an inward
voice, if one might not rest when one would ? If he
might not stop midway the furrow to listen and laugh at
a droll story or tell one? If he might not go a-fishing
when all the forces of nature invited and the jay-bird
called from the tree and gave forth saucy banter like the
fiery, blue shrew that she was ?

There were times when his compunction held Jerry to his task, but more often he turned an end furrow and laid his misgivings snugly under it and was away to the woods or the creek. There was joy and a loaf for the present. What more could he ask?

The first year Fortune laughed at him, and her laugh is very different from her smile. She sent the swift rains to wash up the new planted seed, and the hungry birds to devour them. She sent the fierce sun to scorch the young crops, and the clinging weeds to hug the fresh greenness of his hope to death. She sent—cruelest jest of all—another baby to be fed, and so weakened Cindy Ann that for many days she could not work beside her husband in the fields.

Poverty began to teach the unlessoned delver in the soil the thrift which he needed; but he ended his first twelve months with barely enough to eat, and nothing paid on his land or his mule. Broken and discouraged, the words of his old master came to him. But he was proud with an obstinate pride and he shut his lips together so that he might not groan. He would not go to his master. Anything rather than that.

In that place sat certain beasts of prey, dealers, and lenders of money, who had their lairs somewhere within the boundaries of that wide and mysterious domain called The Law. They had their risks to run, but so must all beasts that eat flesh or drink blood. To them went Jerry, and they were kind to him. They gave him of their store. They gave him food and seed, but they were to own all that they gave him from what he raised, and they were to take their toll first from the new crops.

Now, the black had been warned against these same

beasts, for others had fallen a prey to them even in so
short a time as their emancipation measured, and they
saw themselves the re-manacled slaves of a hopeless and
ever-growing debt, but Jerry would not be warned. He
chewed the warnings like husks between his teeth, and
got no substance from them.

Then, Fortune, who deals in surprises, played him an-
other trick. She smiled upon him. His second year was
better than his first, and the brokers swore over his paid
up note. Cindy Ann was strong again and the oldest
boy was big enough to help with the work.

Samuel Brabant was displeased, not because he felt
any malice towards his former servant, but for the reason
that any man with the natural amount of human vanity
must feel himself aggrieved just as his cherished prophecy
is about to come true. Isaiah himself could not have
been above it. How much less, then, the uninspired Mr.
Brabant, who had his "I told you so," all ready. He had
been ready to help Jerry after giving him admonitions,
but here it was not needed. An unused "I told you so,"
however kindly, is an acid that turns the milk of human
kindness sour.

Jerry went on gaining in prosperity. The third year
treated him better than the second, and the fourth better
than the third. During the fifth he enlarged his farm and
his house and took pride in the fact that his oldest boy,
Matthew, was away at school. By the tenth year of his
freedom he was arrogantly out of debt. Then his pride
was too much for him. During all these years of his
struggle the words of his master had been as gall in his
mouth. Now he spat them out with a boast. He talked
much in the market-place, and where many people gath-

ered, he was much there, giving himself as a bright and shining example.

"Huh," he would chuckle to any listeners he could find, "Ol' Mas' Brabant, he say, 'Stay hyeah, stay hyeah, you do' know how to tek keer o' yo'se'f yit.' But I des' look at my two han's an' I say to myse'f, whut I been doin' wid dese all dese yeahs—tekin' keer o' myse'f an' him, too. I wo'k in de fiel', he set in de big house an' smoke. I wo'k in de fiel', his son go away to college an' come back a graduate. Das hit. Well, w'en freedom come, I des' bent an' boun' I ain' gwine do it no mo' an' I didn't. Now look at me. I sets down w'en I wants to. I does my own wo'kin' an' my own smokin'. I don't owe a cent, an' dis yeah my boy gwine graduate f'om de school. Dat's me, an' I ain' called on ol' Mas' yit."

Now, an example is always an odious thing, because, first of all, it is always insolent even when it is bad, and there were those who listened to Jerry who had not been so successful as he, some even who had stayed on the plantation and as yet did not even own the mule they ploughed with. The hearts of those were filled with rage and their mouths with envy. Some of the sting of the latter got into their re-telling of Jerry's talk and made it worse than it was.

Old Samuel Brabant laughed and said, "Well, Jerry's not dead yet, and although I don't wish him any harm, my prophecy might come true yet."

There were others who, hearing, did not laugh, or if they did, it was with a mere strained thinning of the lips that had no element of mirth in it. Temper and tolerance were short ten years after sixty-three.

The foolish farmer's boastings bore fruit, and one night when he and his family had gone to church he returned to find his house and barn in ashes, his mules burned and his crop ruined. It had been very quietly done and quickly. The glare against the sky had attracted few from the near-by town, and them too late to be of service.

Jerry camped that night across the road from what remained of his former dwelling. Cindy Ann and the children, worn out and worried, went to sleep in spite of themselves, but he sat there all night long, his chin between his knees, gazing at what had been his pride.

Well, the beasts lay in wait for him again, and when he came to them they showed their fangs in greeting. And the velvet was over their claws. He had escaped them before. He had impugned their skill in the hunt, and they were ravenous for him. Now he was fatter, too. He went away from them with hard terms, and a sickness at his heart. But he had not said "Yes" to the terms. He was going home to consider the almost hopeless conditions under which they would let him build again.

They were staying with a neighbor in town pending his negotiations and thither he went to ponder on his circumstances. Then it was that Cindy Ann came into the equation. She demanded to know what was to be done and how it was to be gone about.

"But Cindy Ann, honey, you do' know nuffin' 'bout bus'ness."

"'Tain't whut I knows, but whut I got a right to know," was her response.

"I do' see huccome you got any right to be a-pryin' into dese hyeah things."

23

" I's got de same right I had to wo'k an' struggle erlong an' he'p you get whut we's done los'."

Jerry winced and ended by telling her all.

" Dat ain't nuffin' but owdacious robbery," said Cindy Ann. " Dem people sees dat you got a little somep'n', an' dey ain't gwine stop ontwell dey's bu'nt an' stoled evah blessed cent f'om you. Je'miah, don't you have nuffin' mo' to do wid 'em."

" I got to, Cindy Ann."

" Whut fu' you got to ? "

" How I gwine buil' a cabin an' a ba'n an' buy a mule less'n I deal wid 'em ? "

" Dah's Mas' Sam Brabant. He'd he'p you out."

Jerry rose up, his eyes flashing fire. " Cindy Ann," he said, " you a fool, you ain't got no mo' pride den a guinea hen, an' you got a heap less sense. W'y, befo' I go to ol' Mas' Sam Brabant fu' a cent, I'd sta've out in de road."

" Huh ! " said Cindy Ann, shutting her mouth on her impatience.

One gets tired of thinking and saying how much more sense a woman has than a man when she comes in where his sense stops and his pride begins.

With the recklessness of despair Jerry slept late that next morning, but he might have awakened early without spoiling his wife's plans. She was up betimes, had gone on her mission and returned before her spouse awoke.

It was about ten o'clock when Brabant came to see him. Jerry grew sullen at once as his master approached, but his pride stiffened. This white man should see that misfortune could not weaken him.

"Well, Jerry," said his former master, "you would not come to me, eh, so I must come to you. You let a little remark of mine keep you from your best friend, and put you in the way of losing the labor of years."

Jerry made no answer.

"You've proved yourself able to work well, but Jerry," pausing, "you haven't yet shown that you're able to take care of yourself, you don't know how to keep your mouth shut."

The ex-slave tried to prove this a lie by negative pantomime.

"I'm going to lend you the money to start again."

"I won't ——"

"Yes, you will, if you don't, I'll lend it to Cindy Ann, and let her build in her own name. She's got more sense than you, and she knows how to keep still when things go well."

"Mas' Sam," cried Jerry, rising quickly, "don' len' dat money to Cindy Ann. W'y ef a ooman's got anything she nevah lets you hyeah de las' of it."

"Will you take it, then?"

"Yes, suh; yes, suh, an' thank 'e, Mas' Sam." There were sobs some place back in his throat. "An' nex' time ef I evah gets a sta't agin, I'll keep my mouf shet. Fac' is, I'll come to you, Mas' Sam, an' borry fu' de sake o' hidin'."

THE SCAPEGOAT

I

THE law is usually supposed to be a stern mistress, not to be lightly wooed, and yielding only to the most ardent pursuit. But even law, like love, sits more easily on some natures than on others.

This was the case with Mr. Robinson Asbury. Mr. Asbury had started life as a bootblack in the growing town of Cadgers. From this he had risen one step and become porter and messenger in a barber-shop. This rise fired his ambition, and he was not content until he had learned to use the shears and the razor and had a chair of his own. From this, in a man of Robinson's temperament, it was only a step to a shop of his own, and he placed it where it would do the most good.

Fully one-half of the population of Cadgers was composed of Negroes, and with their usual tendency to colonize, a tendency encouraged, and in fact compelled, by circumstances, they had gathered into one part of the town. Here in alleys, and streets as dirty and hardly wider, they thronged like ants.

It was in this place that Mr. Asbury set up his shop, and he won the hearts of his prospective customers by putting up the significant sign, " Equal Rights Barber-Shop." This legend was quite unnecessary, because there was only one race about, to patronize the place. But it was a delicate sop to the people's vanity, and it served its purpose.

Asbury came to be known as a clever fellow, and his business grew. The shop really became a sort of club, and, on Saturday nights especially, was the gathering-place of the men of the whole Negro quarter. He kept the illustrated and race journals there, and those who cared neither to talk nor listen to some one else might see pictured the doings of high society in very short skirts or read in the Negro papers how Miss Boston had entertained Miss Blueford to tea on such and such an afternoon. Also, he kept the policy returns, which was wise, if not moral.

It was his wisdom rather more than his morality that made the party managers after a while cast their glances towards him as a man who might be useful to their interests. It would be well to have a man—a shrewd, powerful man—down in that part of the town who could carry his people's vote in his vest pocket, and who at any time its delivery might be needed, could hand it over without hesitation. Asbury seemed that man, and they settled upon him. They gave him money, and they gave him power and patronage. He took it all silently and he carried out his bargain faithfully. His hands and his lips alike closed tightly when there was anything within them. It was not long before he found himself the big Negro of the district and, of necessity, of the town. The time came when, at a critical moment, the managers saw that they had not reckoned without their host in choosing this barber of the black district as the leader of his people.

Now, so much success must have satisfied any other man. But in many ways Mr. Asbury was unique. For a long time he himself had done very little shaving—

except of notes, to keep his hand in.   His time had been otherwise employed.   In the evening hours he had been wooing the coquettish Dame Law, and, wonderful to say, she had yielded easily to his advances.

It was against the advice of his friends that he asked for admission to the bar.   They felt that he could do more good in the place where he was.

"You see, Robinson," said old Judge Davis, "it's just like this: If you're not admitted, it'll hurt you with the people; if you are admitted, you'll move up-town to an office and get out of touch with them."

Asbury smiled an inscrutable smile.   Then he whispered something into the judge's ear that made the old man wrinkle from his neck up with appreciative smiles.

"Asbury," he said, "you are—you are—well, you ought to be white, that's all.   When we find a black man like you we send him to State's prison.   If you were white, you'd go to the Senate."

The Negro laughed confidently.

He was admitted to the bar soon after, whether by merit or by connivance is not to be told.

"Now he will move up-town," said the black community.   "Well, that's the way with a colored man when he gets a start."

But they did not know Asbury Robinson yet.   He was a man of surprises, and they were destined to disappointment.   He did not move up-town.   He built an office in a small open space next his shop, and there hung out his shingle.

"I will never desert the people who have done so much to elevate me," said Mr. Asbury.   "I will live among them and I will die among them."

This was a strong card for the barber-lawyer. The people seized upon the statement as expressing a nobility of an altogether unique brand.

They held a mass meeting and indorsed him. They made resolutions that extolled him, and the Negro band came around and serenaded him, playing various things in varied time.

All this was very sweet to Mr. Asbury, and the party managers chuckled with satisfaction and said, "That Asbury, that Asbury!"

Now there is a fable extant of a man who tried to please everybody, and his failure is a matter of record. Robinson Asbury was not more successful. But be it said that his ill success was due to no fault or shortcoming of his.

For a long time his growing power had been looked upon with disfavor by the colored law firm of Bingo & Latchett. Both Mr. Bingo and Mr. Latchett themselves aspired to be Negro leaders in Cadgers, and they were delivering Emancipation Day orations and riding at the head of processions when Mr. Asbury was blacking boots. Is it any wonder, then, that they viewed with alarm his sudden rise? They kept their counsel, however, and treated with him, for it was best. They allowed him his scope without open revolt until the day upon which he hung out his shingle. This was the last straw. They could stand no more. Asbury had stolen their other chances from them, and now he was poaching upon the last of their preserves. So Mr. Bingo and Mr. Latchett put their heads together to plan the downfall of their common enemy.

The plot was deep and embraced the formation of an

opposing faction made up of the best Negroes of the town.   It would have looked too much like what it was for the gentlemen to show themselves in the matter, and so they took into their confidence Mr. Isaac Morton, the principal of the colored school, and it was under his ostensible leadership that the new faction finally came into being.

Mr. Morton was really an innocent young man, and he had ideals which should never have been exposed to the air.   When the wily confederates came to him with their plan he believed that his worth had been recognized, and at last he was to be what Nature destined him for—a leader.

The better class of Negroes—by that is meant those who were particularly envious of Asbury's success— flocked to the new man's standard.   But whether the race be white or black, political virtue is always in a minority, so Asbury could afford to smile at the force arrayed against him.

The new faction met together and resolved.   They resolved, among other things, that Mr. Asbury was an enemy to his race and a menace to civilization.   They decided that he should be abolished ; but, as they couldn't get out an injunction against him, and as he had the whole undignified but still voting black belt behind him, he went serenely on his way.

"They're after you hot and heavy, Asbury," said one of his friends to him.

"Oh, yes," was the reply, "they're after me, but after a while I'll get so far away that they'll be running in front."

"It's all the best people, they say."

" Yes. Well, it's good to be one of the best people, but
. your vote only counts one just the same."

The time came, however, when Mr. Asbury's theory
was put to the test.   The Cadgerites celebrated the first
of January as Emancipation Day.   On this day there was
a large procession, with speech-making in the afternoon
and fireworks at night.   It was the custom to concede
the leadership of the colored people of the town to the
man who managed to lead the procession.   For two years
past this honor had fallen, of course, to Robinson Asbury,
and there had been no disposition on the part of anybody
to try conclusions with him.

Mr. Morton's faction changed all this.   When Asbury
went to work to solicit contributions for the celebration,
he suddenly became aware that he had a fight upon his
hands.   All the better-class Negroes were staying out of
it.   The next thing he knew was that plans were on foot
for a rival demonstration.

" Oh," he said to himself, " that's it, is it?   Well, if they
want a fight they can have it."

He had a talk with the party managers, and he had
another with Judge Davis.

" All I want is a little lift, judge," he said, " and I'll
make 'em think the sky has turned loose and is vomiting,
niggers."

The judge believed that he could do it.   So did the party
managers.   Asbury got his lift.   Emancipation Day came.

There were two parades.   At least, there was one parade
and the shadow of another.   Asbury's, however, was not
the shadow.   There was a great deal of substance about
it—substance made up of many people, many banners,
and numerous bands.   He did not have the best people.

Indeed, among his cohorts there were a good many of
the pronounced rag-tag and bobtail. But he had noise
and numbers. In such cases, nothing more is needed.
The success of Asbury's side of the affair did everything
to confirm his friends in their good opinion of him.

When he found himself defeated, Mr. Silas Bingo saw
that it would be policy to placate his rival's just anger
against him. He called upon him at his office the day
after the celebration.

"Well, Asbury," he said, "you beat us, didn't you?"

"It wasn't a question of beating," said the other calmly.
"It was only an inquiry as to who were the people—the
few or the many."

"Well, it was well done, and you've shown that you are
a manager. I confess that I haven't always thought that
you were doing the wisest thing in living down here and
catering to this class of people when you might, with your
ability, to be much more to the better class."

"What do they base their claims of being better on?"

"Oh, there ain't any use discussing that. We can't
get along without you, we see that. So I, for one, have
decided to work with you for harmony."

"Harmony. Yes, that's what we want."

"If I can do anything to help you at any time, why
you have only to command me."

"I am glad to find such a friend in you. Be sure, if I
ever need you, Bingo, I'll call on you."

"And I'll be ready to serve you."

Asbury smiled when his visitor was gone. He smiled,
and knitted his brow. "I wonder what Bingo's got up
his sleeve," he said. "He'll bear watching."

It may have been pride at his triumph, it may have

been gratitude at his helpers, but Asbury went into the ensuing campaign with reckless enthusiasm. He did the most daring things for the party's sake. Bingo, true to his promise, was ever at his side ready to serve him. Finally, association and immunity made danger less fearsome; the rival no longer appeared a menace.

With the generosity born of obstacles overcome, Asbury determined to forgive Bingo and give him a chance. He let him in on a deal, and from that time they worked amicably together until the election came and passed.

It was a close election and many things had had to be done, but there were men there ready and waiting to do them. They were successful, and then the first cry of the defeated party was, as usual, " Fraud ! Fraud ! " The cry was taken up by the jealous, the disgruntled, and the virtuous.

Some one remembered how two years ago the registration books had been stolen. It was known upon good authority that money had been freely used. Men held up their hands in horror at the suggestion that the Negro vote had been juggled with, as if that were a new thing. From their pulpits ministers denounced the machine and bade their hearers rise and throw off the yoke of a corrupt municipal government. One of those sudden fevers of reform had taken possession of the town and threatened to destroy the successful party.

They began to look around them. They must purify themselves. They must give the people some tangible evidence of their own yearnings after purity. They looked around them for a sacrifice to lay upon the altar of municipal reform. Their eyes fell upon Mr. Bingo. No, he was not big enough. His blood was too scant to wash away the political stains. Then they looked into each other's eyes and turned their gaze away to let it fall upon Mr. Asbury. They really hated to do it. But there must be a scapegoat. The god from the Machine commanded them to slay him.

Robinson Asbury was charged with many crimes— with all that he had committed and some that he had not. When Mr. Bingo saw what was afoot he threw himself heart and soul into the work of his old rival's enemies. He was of incalculable use to them.

Judge Davis refused to have anything to do with the matter. But in spite of his disapproval it went on. Asbury was indicted and tried. The evidence was all against him, and no one gave more damaging testimony than his friend, Mr. Bingo. The judge's charge was favorable to the defendant, but the current of popular opinion could not be entirely stemmed. The jury brought in a verdict of guilty.

"Before I am sentenced, judge, I have a statement to make to the court. It will take less than ten minutes."

"Go on, Robinson," said the judge kindly.

Asbury started, in a monotonous tone, a recital that brought the prosecuting attorney to his feet in a minute. The judge waved him down, and sat transfixed by a sort of fascinated horror as the convicted man went on. The before-mentioned attorney drew a knife and started for the prisoner's dock. With difficulty he was restrained. A dozen faces in the court-room were red and pale by turns.

"He ought to be killed," whispered Mr. Bingo audibly.

Robinson Asbury looked at him and smiled, and then he told a few things of him. He gave the ins and outs of some of the misdemeanors of which he stood accused. He showed who were the men behind the throne. And still, pale and transfixed, Judge Davis waited for his own sentence.

Never were ten minutes so well taken up. It was a tale of rottenness and corruption in high places told simply and with the stamp of truth upon it.

He did not mention the judge's name. But he had torn the mask from the face of every other man who had been concerned in his downfall. They had shorn him of his strength, but they had forgotten that he was yet able to bring the roof and pillars tumbling about their heads.

The judge's voice shook as he pronounced sentence upon his old ally—a year in State's prison.

Some people said it was too light, but the judge knew what it was to wait for the sentence of doom, and he was grateful and sympathetic.

When the sheriff led Asbury away the judge hastened to have a short talk with him.

"I'm sorry, Robinson," he said, "and I want to tell you that you were no more guilty than the rest of us. But why did you spare me?"

"Because I knew you were my friend," answered the convict.

"I tried to be, but you were the first man that I've ever known since I've been in politics who ever gave me any decent return for friendship."

"I reckon you're about right, judge."

In politics, party reform usually lies in making a scapegoat of some one who is only as criminal as the rest, but a little weaker. Asbury's friends and enemies had succeeded in making him bear the burden of all the party's crimes, but their reform was hardly a success, and their protestations of a change of heart were received with doubt.   Already there were those who began to pity the victim and to say that he had been hardly dealt with.

Mr. Bingo was not of these; but he found, strange to say, that his opposition to the idea went but a little way, and that even with Asbury out of his path he was a smaller man than he was before.   Fate was strong against him.   His poor, prosperous humanity could not enter the lists against a martyr.   Robinson Asbury was now a martyr.

II

A year is not a long time.   It was short enough to prevent people from forgetting Robinson, and yet long enough for their pity to grow strong as they remembered. Indeed, he was not gone a year.   Good behavior cut two months off the time of his sentence, and by the time people had come around to the notion that he was really the greatest and smartest man in Cadgers he was at home again.

He came back with no flourish of trumpets, but quietly, humbly.   He went back again into the heart of the black district.   His business had deteriorated during his absence, but he put new blood and new life into it.   He did not go to work in the shop himself, but, taking down the shingle that had swung idly before his office door during his imprisonment, he opened the little room as a news- and cigar-stand.

Here anxious, pitying custom came to him and he prospered again.   He was very quiet.   Up-town hardly knew that he was again in Cadgers, and it knew nothing whatever of his doings.

"I wonder why Asbury is so quiet," they said to one another. "It isn't like him to be quiet." And they felt vaguely uneasy about him.

So many people had begun to say, "Well, he was a mighty good fellow after all."

Mr. Bingo expressed the opinion that Asbury was quiet because he was crushed, but others expressed doubt as to this. There are calms and calms, some after and some before the storm. Which was this?

They waited a while, and, as no storm came, concluded that this must be the after-quiet. Bingo, reassured, volunteered to go and seek confirmation of this conclusion.

He went, and Asbury received him with an indifferent, not to say, impolite, demeanor.

"Well, we're glad to see you back, Asbury," said Bingo patronizingly. He had variously demonstrated his inability to lead during his rival's absence and was proud of it. "What are you going to do?"

"I'm going to work."

"That's right. I reckon you'll stay out of politics."

"What could I do even if I went in?"

"Nothing now, of course; but I didn't know ——"

He did not see the gleam in Asbury's half-shut eyes. He only marked his humility, and he went back swelling with the news.

"Completely crushed—all the run taken out of him," was his report.

The black district believed this, too, and a sullen, smouldering anger took possession of them. Here was a good man ruined. Some of the people whom he had helped in his former days—some of the rude, coarse people of the low quarter who were still sufficiently unenlightened to be grateful—talked among themselves and offered to get up a demonstration for him. But he denied them. No, he wanted nothing of the kind. It would only bring him into unfavorable notice. All he wanted was that they would always be his friends and would stick by him.

They would to the death.

There were again two factions in Cadgers. The schoolmaster could not forget how once on a time he had been made a tool of by Mr. Bingo. So he revolted against his rule and set himself up as the leader of an opposing clique. The fight had been long and strong, but had ended with odds slightly in Bingo's favor.

But Mr. Morton did not despair. As the first of January and Emancipation Day approached, he arrayed his hosts, and the fight for supremacy became fiercer than ever. The school-teacher brought the school-children in for chorus singing, secured an able orator, and the best essayist in town. With all this, he was formidable.

Mr. Bingo knew that he had the fight of his life on his hands, and he entered with fear as well as zest. He, too, found an orator, but he was not sure that he was as good as Morton's. There was no doubt but that his essayist was not. He secured a band, but still he felt unsatisfied. He had hardly done enough, and for the schoolmaster to beat him now meant his political destruction.

It was in this state of mind that he was surprised to receive a visit from Mr. Asbury.

"I reckon you're surprised to see me here," said Asbury, smiling.

"I am pleased, I know." Bingo was astute.

"Well, I just dropped in on business."

"To be sure, to be sure, Asbury. What can I do for you?"

"It's more what I can do for you that I came to talk about," was the reply.

"I don't believe I understand you."

"Well, it's plain enough. They say that the schoolteacher is giving you a pretty hard fight."

"Oh, not so hard."

"No man can be too sure of winning, though. Mr. Morton once did me a mean turn when he started the faction against me."

Bingo's heart gave a great leap, and then stopped for the fraction of a second.

"You were in it, of course," pursued Asbury, "but I can look over your part in it in order to get even with the man who started it."

It was true, then, thought Bingo gladly. He did not know. He wanted revenge for his wrongs and upon the wrong man. How well the schemer had covered his tracks! Asbury should have his revenge and Morton would be the sufferer.

"Of course, Asbury, you know what I did I did innocently."

"Oh, yes, in politics we are all lambs and the wolves are only to be found in the other party. We'll pass that, though. What I want to say is that I can help you to make your celebration an overwhelming success. I still have some influence down in my district."

24

" Certainly, and very justly, too. Why, I should be delighted with your aid. I could give you a prominent place in the procession."

"I don't want it ; I don't want to appear in this at all. All I want is revenge. You can have all the credit, but let me down my enemy."

Bingo was perfectly willing, and, with their heads close together, they had a long and close consultation. When Asbury was gone, Mr. Bingo lay back in his chair and laughed. "I'm a slick duck," he said.

From that hour Mr. Bingo's cause began to take on the appearance of something very like a boom. More bands were hired. The interior of the State was called upon and a more eloquent orator secured. The crowd hastened to array itself on the growing side.

With surprised eyes, the school-master beheld the wonder of it, but he kept to his own purpose with dogged insistence, even when he saw that he could not turn aside the overwhelming defeat that threatened him. But in spite of his obstinacy, his hours were dark and bitter. Asbury worked like a mole, all underground, but he was indefatigable. Two days before the celebration time everything was perfected for the biggest demonstration that Cadgers had ever known. All the next day and night he was busy among his allies.

On the morning of the great day, Mr. Bingo, wonderfully caparisoned, rode down to the hall where the parade was to form. He was early. No one had yet come. In an hour a score of men all told had collected. Another hour passed, and no more had come. Then there smote upon his ear the sound of music. They were coming at last. Bringing his sword to his shoulder, he rode forward

to the middle of the street. Ah, there they were. But—
but—could he believe his eyes? They were going in an-
other direction, and at their head rode—Morton! He
gnashed his teeth in fury. He had been led into a trap
and betrayed. The procession passing had been his—all
his. He heard them cheering, and then, oh! climax of
infidelity, he saw his own orator go past in a carriage,
bowing and smiling to the crowd.

There was no doubting who had done this thing. The
hand of Asbury was apparent in it. He must have known
the truth all along, thought Bingo. His allies left him
one by one for the other hall, and he rode home in a
humiliation deeper than he had ever known before.

Asbury did not appear at the celebration. He was at
his little news-stand all day.

In a day or two the defeated aspirant had further cause
to curse his false friend. He found that not only had the
people defected from him, but that the thing had been so
adroitly managed that he appeared to be in fault, and
three-fourths of those who knew him were angry at some
supposed grievance. His cup of bitterness was full when
his partner, a quietly ambitious man, suggested that they
dissolve their relations.

His ruin was complete.

The lawyer was not alone in seeing Asbury's hand in
his downfall. The party managers saw it too, and they
met together to discuss the dangerous factor which, while
it appeared to slumber, was so terribly awake. They de-
cided that he must be appeased, and they visited him.

He was still busy at his news-stand. They talked to
him adroitly, while he sorted papers and kept an impassive
face. When they were all done, he looked up for a mo-

ment and replied, "You know, gentlemen, as an ex-convict I am not in politics."

Some of them had the grace to flush.

"But you can use your influence," they said.

"I am not in politics," was his only reply.

And the spring elections were coming on. Well, they worked hard, and he showed no sign. He treated with neither one party nor the other. "Perhaps," thought the managers, "he is out of politics," and they grew more confident.

It was nearing eleven o'clock on the morning of election when a cloud no bigger than a man's hand appeared upon the horizon. It came from the direction of the black district. It grew, and the managers of the party in power looked at it, fascinated by an ominous dread. Finally it began to rain Negro voters, and as one man they voted against their former candidates. Their organization was perfect. They simply came, voted, and left, but they overwhelmed everything. Not one of the party that had damned Robinson Asbury was left in power save old Judge Davis. His majority was overwhelming.

The generalship that had engineered the thing was perfect. There were loud threats against the newsdealer. But no one bothered him except a reporter. The reporter called to see just how it was done. He found Asbury very busy sorting papers. To the newspaper man's questions he had only this reply, "I am not in politics, sir."

But Cadgers had learned its lesson.